COMPUTER SCIENCE, TECHNOLOGY AND APPLICATIONS

IMAGE PROCESSING

METHODS, APPLICATIONS AND CHALLENGES

COMPUTER SCIENCE, TECHNOLOGY AND APPLICATIONS

Additional books in this series can be found on Nova's website under the Series tab.

Additional e-books in this series can be found on Nova's website under the e-book tab.

COMPUTER SCIENCE, TECHNOLOGY AND APPLICATIONS

IMAGE PROCESSING

METHODS, APPLICATIONS AND CHALLENGES

VÍTOR HUGO CARVALHO
EDITOR

Nova Science Publishers, Inc.
New York

For permission to use material from this book please contact us:
Telephone 631-231-7269; Fax 631-231-8175
Web Site: http://www.novapublishers.com

Library of Congress Cataloging-in-Publication Data

Image processing : methods, applications, and challenges / [edited by] Vitor Hugo Carvalho.
p. cm.
Includes bibliographical references and index.
ISBN 978-1-62081-844-2 (hardcover)
1. Image processing. I. Carvalho, Vitor Hugo, 1979-
TA1637.I4374 2011
006.4'2--dc23
2012015281

Published by Nova Science Publishers, Inc. † New York

CONTENTS

PREFACE

ABOUT THE SUBJECT

The use of image processing is presenting nowadays an exponential increase in the development of new solutions to deal with challenges in industry and in the day-to-day life of Society.

The improvements of technology enable the recorrent use of image processing based applications with a market who as reached to mobile suppporting devices as smartphones and tablets.

Image Processing: Methods, Applications and Challenges is a collection of recent development studies in several fields of image processing.

With the objective of discussing the main issues, challenges, opportunities and trends related to image processing, the result is a compilation of studies available to the readers allowing them to achieve new technological developments, present practical solutions and state-of-the-art technologies, provide guidance for future research and to create a connection between research and application.

In the 11 chapters of this book there are covered several studies where are described methods, applications and challenges for health, textile industry, human emotions detection, satellite imagery, video surveillance, object detection, color models, illumination and digital signal processing.

ORGANIZATION OF THE BOOK

This book is a compilation of 11 highly valuable contributions to the area of image processing in their several fields of action. This 11 chapters are written by a group of 32 authors including internationally renowned and experienced researchers and specialits in the subjects presented. Contributions come from 3 continents and integrate academies and research institutes with a strong connection to industry representing a good state-of-the-art under the several areas of image processing acting.

Chapter 1 entitled "Image Processing: Characteristics and Applications in Textile Industry and Biomedicine" presents the main characteristics and functionalities of two systems based on image processing techniques applied to Textile Industry and Biomedicine. In Textile Industry image processing is used to determine yarn mass parameters as well as yarn production characteristics. A low cost solution based on a web-pc camera plus the optics of a low cost analogue microscope and a software tool based on IMAQ Vision from LabVIEW was designed. In Biomedicine image processing is used to develop a system capable of determining human blood types for emergency situations and so with a fast response. With this system it is possible to obtain a reliable result in less than 2 minutes, allowing the administration of the specific blood type of the individual in the first transfusion, as well as avoiding human errors witch several times can result in fatal consequences.

Chapter 2 entitled "Facial Expression Recognition Using Thermal Image Processing" describes a research to develop a robot that can perceive human feelings or mental states. The present investigation concerns the first stage of development wherein a robot acquires vision and the ability to detect human feeling or mental states. It is used pattern recognition through heuristic rules for facial expression recognition. In this method, the facial expressions are discriminable with good recognition accuracy when a person exhibits one of the intentional facial expressions of “angry”, “happy”, “neutral”, “sad”, and “surprise”.

Chapter 3 entitled "Applying Image Processing to In-Vitro Human Oocytes Characterization" presents an image processing tool developed to in-vitro human oocytes analysis required in fertilization processes to biological material classification. The application of the proposed tool allows a non-invasive method to define the quality of human oocytes before to be inseminated, enabling the possibility of selection the optimum one. Specific segmentation algorithms have been developed to specific biomedical images for identifying the cytoplasm area. The oocyte status (normal, medium and highly stressed state) has been defined in terms of a set of parameters extracted from the cytoplasm image. This status quantification allows advising the biomedical staff during oocyte selection, involving by the first time a useful metrics. Experimental results proof that 83% of cases analyzed match with the expert evaluation.

Chapter 4 entitled "Matching of Infrared and Visual Images using the Fourier-Mellin Transform" describes a frequency domain technique for matching infrared and visual images. Matching of images in different spectral bands is a difficult problem since the objects can appear very differently in both images. Classical spatial domain methods have difficulties in this problem due to the lack of common features between both images. Instead, the proposed technique uses a frequency domain matching method that relies on the common structure between the images. The method uses Fourier-Mellin transforms and Symmetric Phase-Only Matched Filtering to detect rotation, scaling and translation between images. This chapter presents the main principles of the method, gives implementation details and analyses its performance.

Chapter 5 entitled "Comparison of Four Fractal Dimensions and Two Lacunarities to Assess the Trabecular Bone Architecture of Proximal Femur" studies the differences between the values of different fractal dimensions (FD) and lacunarity (LAC) obtained on nine ROIs on the X-Ray images of proximal femur. It was designed an observational, transversal study on 100 conventional anteroposterior X-Ray from human femurs. The statistical analysis was performed with a repeated measures mixed-model factorial ANOVA. The calculation method of FD and LAC is critical so we must be careful in the description of the method and the comparison of different FD or LAC obtained by different methods.

Chapter 6 entitled "Image Processing for the Enhancement of Satellite Imagery" discusses image processing methods for increasing the potentialities of the satellite imagery provided by free Internet services, such as Google Maps, to the detection and survey of ancient remains, human modified landforms or landscape patterns. In particular, quite interesting results can be achieved by means of some tools freely available, developed originally for astrophysical researches. The use of the freely available satellite images is particularly suitable for the study of the remains of ancient landscapes. This archaeological survey is an important and challenging issue because there are continuously increasing worries and difficulties for the preservation of these ancient structures from the assault of urbanization and modern agricultural methods.

Chapter 7 entitled "Image Processing in the Analysis of Neuronal Dendritic Branching Patterns: Does Structure Follow Function Across Different Species?" describes the analysis of alpha retinal ganglion cells that are seen as preserving their function across species, to determine whether structure follows function, that is, whether similar structures can be observed. Two-dimensional images of the alpha retinal ganglion cells of three orders of mammals are investigated in order to determine the consistency of the dendritic branching pattern across eleven mammalian species. Using the linear two-dimensional Sholl method, it is presented a mathematical model, which includes the critical and maximal values of the number of intersections, and the abscissae of the inflection points of the branching points and terminal tips, with respect to the radius. Differences among these parameters for the eleven mammalian species were statistically significant. Therefore it is proposed a hypothesis that the morphology of the alpha retinal ganglion cells are not conserved in mammals, coming from different habitats and having a wide variety of behaviors, despite similar function.

Chapter 8 entitled "Color Models and Illumination Changes" refers that a color model representation allows characterizing in a quantitative manner, any defined color spectrum of visible light. To accomplish that, each model, or color space, is associated with a function that allows mapping the spectral power distribution of the visible electromagnetic radiation, in a space defined by a set of discrete values that quantify the color components composing the model. Some color spaces are sensitive to changes in lighting conditions. Others assure the preservation of certain chromatic features, remaining immune to these changes. Therefore, it becomes necessary to identify the strengths and weaknesses of each model in order to justify the adoption of color spaces in image processing and analysis techniques. This chapter will address the topic of digital imaging, main standards and formats, setting the mathematical model of the image acquisition sensor response, which enables assessment of the various color spaces, with the aim of determining their invariance to illumination changes.

Chapter 9 entitled "A Region-Based Algorithm for Automatic Bone Segmentation in Volumetric CT" presents an automated multistep approach for bone segmentation in volumetric CT datasets. It starts with a three-dimensional (3D) watershed operation on an image gradient magnitude. The outcome of the watershed algorithm is an over-partioning image of many 3D regions that can be merged, yielding a meaningful image partitioning. The bones contours were accurately defined according to the watershed regions outlines instead of considering the thresholding segmentation result. This new method was tested to segment the rib cage on 185 CT images, acquired at the São João Hospital of Porto (Portugal) and evaluated using the dice similarity coefficient as a statistical validation metric, leading to a coefficient mean score of 0.89. This could represent a step forward towards accurate and automatic quantitative analysis in clinical environments and decreasing time-consumption, user dependence and subjectivity.

Chapter 10 entitled "Proved Image Segmentation" it is addressd to the problem of automatic object detection in a digital image of arbitrary content. To formalize the segmentation it is used a proven model of Mumford-Shah, which enables to distinguish the segmented image from the images simply divided into pieces in some or another way. An iterative segment merging employed in Mumford–Shah model to obtain the optimal approximations of an image turns out insufficient. To overcome this challenge in addition to segment merging the operation of segment correction by means of reclassification of pixels is introduced. For pixel reclassification a formulae analogous to known expression for the criterion of segment merging are derived. A comparative analysis of the segmented images by the standard deviation is carried out. The improvement of optimization results is demonstrated and the computations are discussed.

The last contribution, Chapter 11 entitled "Automatic Visual Surveillance of Vehicles in Complex Scenarios" presents an automated visual surveillance system that would reduce the workload of the operators. In this work, it is proposed a vehicle detection method for traffic flow from the analysis of videos taken by cameras situated in high places on the road, such as bridges, thus making it possible to estimate important traffic parameters. The analysis of videos is based on image processing where it is proposed a methodology for different aspect like the background subtraction in changing environment, removing shadows of the vehicle and tracking the trajectories of different vehicles throughout the time. As a direct result the following information would be obtained: vehicle count, vehicle speed, vehicles travelling counter flow, stationary vehicles and those performing lane changes.

EXPECTATIONS

Over the 11 chapters of this book, the reader is faced with the discussions of the hot topic of image processing providing professionals, researchers and scholars with advanced research, developments, solutions and tecniques. It is expected to support a professional audience of engineers, academic audience of professors, researchers and students as well as the general public motivated and interesested in the topic. Moreover, the content of this book can also support courses of undergraduate and post-graduate associated to image processing.

ACKNOWLEDGMENTS

Editing a book requires a high number of hard but productive taks and steps in order to reach the audience goals. These tasks will not be possible without the help and support of several intervenients. As editor I would like to express my gratitute to these people who made this document possible, namely:

To all professionals at the Nova Science Publishers for all the availability and support during all the book editing process;

To all the authors for their relevant and fine contributions. It was a pleasure to compile such a group of recognized experts in the form of chapters. The process was highly greatfull, enriching and motivating;

To the reviewer for the availability and for the revision of this book;

Everyone that directly or non-directly have contributed in any manner to this work.

In: Image Processing
Editor: Vítor Hugo Carvalho

ISBN 978-1-62081-844-2

Chapter 1

IMAGE PROCESSING: CHARACTERISTICS AND APPLICATIONS IN TEXTILE INDUSTRY AND BIOMEDICINE

Vítor Carvalho[1,*], Filomena Soares[1], Nuno Gonçalves[1], Ana Ferraz[1], Rosa Vasconcelos[2] and Michael Belsley[3]

[1]Department of Industrial Electronics,
[2]Department of Textile Engineering,
[3]Department of Physics, Minho University, Guimarães, Portugal

ABSTRACT

This chapter presents the main characteristics and functionalities of two systems based on image processing techniques applied to Textile Industry and Biomedicine.

In Textile Industry we used image processing to determine yarn mass parameters as well as yarn production characteristics. A low cost solution based on a web-pc camera plus the optics of a low cost analogue microscope and a software tool based on IMAQ Vision from LabVIEW was designed. Several tests were performed and compared with other methodologies of yarn parameterization validating the proposed solution. With the results one can support that this can be an alternative solution to the traditional yarn testers, with several advantages (among others, low cost, weight, volume, easy maintenance and reduced hardware).

In Biomedicine we used image processing to develop a system capable of determining human blood types for emergency situations and so with a fast response. With this system it is possible to obtain a reliable result in less than 2 minutes, allowing the administration of the specific blood type of the individual in the first transfusion, as well as avoiding human errors witch several times can result in fatal consequences. As in the previous system, this solution is based on a web-pc camera plus and a software tool based on IMAQ Vision from LabVIEW, and so of low cost. Several tests were performed in order to validate the proposed methodology being obtained reliable results.

* E-mail address: vcarvalho@dei.uminho.pt.

INTRODUCTION

In Textile Industry, image processing is employed to characterize yarn diameter, hairiness, and mass as well as yarn production characteristics (fibers twist orientation, folded yarn twist step, folded yarn twist orientation and the existence of single, non-folded yarn, or multiple cables, folded yarn) [1-15]. The correct evaluation of yarns is of utmost importance for the textile industry as the quality of the final product relies directly on the yarn. Currently, there is commercial equipment capable of testing yarns; one of the most used is the Uster Tester 5. Despite their contribution to the yarn's characterization, these devices have some drawbacks, such as, high cost, large size and considerable weight in addition to a limited resolution and accuracy in determining mass parameters. Technological solutions based on Image Processing (IP), are characterized by high reliability and efficiency and can remove all the drawbacks identified in traditional solutions as well as introducing the determination of new parameters not yet determined by the traditional and commercial equipment (as example, the distinction between hairiness resulting from loop or protruding fibers and the yarn production characteristics). The acquisition system consists of a low cost CMOS camera coupled to a low cost analogue microscope in order to obtain the necessary optical amplification and reducing the camera resolution requirements. To analyze the acquired images an image processing application was developed using the IMAQ Vision software from LabVIEW from National Instruments.

In Biomedicine image processing is applied to develop a methodology to determine human blood types in emergency situations.

Determining the blood type of an individual is an essential procedure before administering a blood transfusion, avoiding injury and blood incompatibilities. Thus, the preceding blood test, even in case of medical emergency, is of upmost importance, allowing the correct administration of the blood type of the receiver in the first unit of blood transfusion. However, although two of the manual tests used in laboratory, the plate and the tube test, allow the analysis in a short time interval, which is suitable for emergency situations, they require travel to the lab and the intervention of a technician, thereby increasing the time spent and the possibility of human error. Given that human errors in the procedure of manual tests, in reading or interpreting the results, can lead to fatal consequences for patients, being one of the significant causes of fatal blood transfusions, it is important to automate the testing, the reading and the interpretation of results.

The developed system is based on the plate test for determining blood types and in custom developed software using the IMAQ Vision software from LabVIEW from National Instruments, using image processing techniques. The plate test consists of four different mixtures of one drop of blood and one drop of the specific reagent, being the result interpreted according to the occurrence or not of agglutination. The agglutination means that a reaction has occurred between the antibody and the cells, indicating the presence of the appropriate antigen. The combination of the occurrence of agglutination, or non-occurrence, determines the blood type of the individual. Thus, the developed software allows, through image processing techniques, to detect the existence of agglutination and consequently the blood type of an individual eliminating human error and in a short interval of time, to be used in emergency situations [10, 11, 16-23].

It is the author's believe that the proposed solutions based on image processing techniques enable a correct and complete yarn parameterization, that come across Textile Industry requirements, as well an accurate human blood type determination.

IMAGE PROCESSING AS A TOOL TO PARAMETERIZE YARN MASS PARAMETERS

This section presents the framework, the textile parameters theoretical configuration, the system development and the experimental results.

Framework

The correct and accurate evaluation of yarns is a subject of major importance to the Textile Industry, as the final fabric quality depends directly on the yarn quality. To undertake these yarn tests several companies have developed specific equipment. The Tester 5 from Uster is important for its relevant contribution to the development of quantitative yarn characterization. However, these yarn testers have a significant cost, require a considerable area for their installation and present limited resolution and precision in the evaluation of certain yarn parameters. As a result, many yarn producers do not have their own yarn testers and, instead, choose to subcontract dedicated testing laboratories for yarn quality determination. This process is time consuming and eliminates the possibility of acting in useful time during yarn production, reducing efficiency.

To overcome these drawbacks, new equipment, entitled YSQ (Yarn System Quality) [9] was developed. The YSQ measures yarn diameter, yarn hairiness and yarn irregularity based on optical and capacitive sensors. Moreover, it integrates an external module to obtain yarn production characteristics, based on image processing (IP). At present, in the Textile Industry there is no available commercial equipment or known prototypes to automatically obtain these characteristics. Instead, they are obtained manually by human ocular inspection or by using an analogue microscope, being the results susceptible to errors [24, 25].

The high precision levels of parameterization performed by the YSQ, together with its low cost and high portability make it a reliable and efficient solution for the Industry.

Furthermore, and after studying the image processing possibilities in the production characteristics module of the YSQ, we started considering to specify the traditional yarn mass parameters as technological solutions based on IP, as they are characterized by high reliability and efficiency and can present some advantages over the traditional methods (low cost, small size and weight, reduced hardware, reliability and possibility of high resolution).

IP (Image Processing) based applications have been used in the textile field since 1964 [3], although they have not yet been converted to viable quality control methods [6].

Due to its influence on the quality of textiles, yarn hairiness is considered to be one of the most significant parameters. In textile industry the equipment used to measure the hairiness are based on photoelectric methods, like the Shirley's apparatus and the Uster Tester 3 devices [7]. Several algorithms are currently under development to characterize the yarn hairiness with IP. The method proposed by [8], measures the real length of the protruding fibers from the yarn core, as well as, their number in order to quantify hairiness. In [2], it is introduced a new method to measure hairiness, based on the assumption that the hairs close and parallel to the yarn core would be a better indicator of hairiness, proposing then a new parameter: Hair Area Index. This concept measures the area covered by hairs and is divided by the area of the yarn core to obtain a dimensionless quantity. Nevertheless, it is still necessary to develop algorithms to detect and characterize loop fibers length and to clearly distinguish between protruding fibers and loop fibers when they are interlaced.

Another important parameter is the yarn diameter, since it is used to predict fabric structural parameters such as width, cover factor, porosity and fabric comfort [26]. The characterization of yarn diameter with IP can also be achieved with algorithms already applied to the extraction of yarn core [7, 8]. But, algorithms to measure the exact length of yarn irregularities (thin places, thick places and neps) [12] need to be developed. The characterization of yarn mass can be inferred from the yarn diameter, depending, among other parameters, on the yarn fiber density and porosity.

Besides the YSQ, this section presents a new solution to automatically characterize the mass parameters of yarn based on IP.

Textile Parameters Theoretical Considerations

This section describes the typical configuration of a yarn, the definition of faults, hairiness and the most important yarn production characteristics [9, 25, 26].

Yarn Configuration, Faults and Hairiness

The most important parameters used to specify yarn quality are linear density, structural features and fibre content. An example of yarn configuration is shown in Figure 1.

As Figure 1 suggests there is a direct relationship between the variation of yarn mass and the yarn diameter. Thus the calculation of the diameter can be obtained by the theoretical correlation d(mm) = 0.037sqrt(Tex) [26], where Tex is the mass of the yarn in one kilometer of length (g/km) – yarn linear mass. This relation allows the possibility of determining yarn irregularity based on yarn diameter measurements.

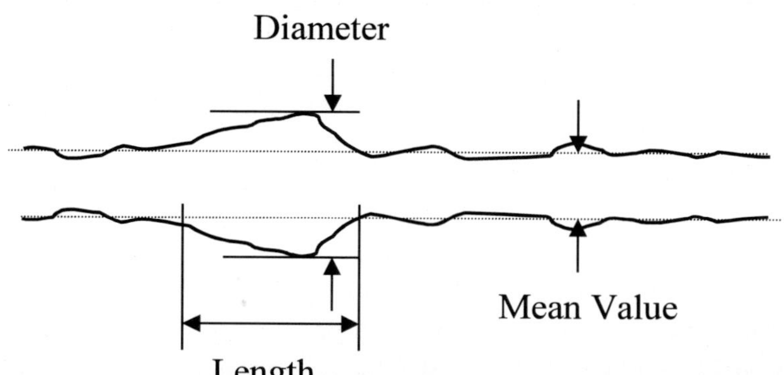

Figure 1. Example of yarn configuration.

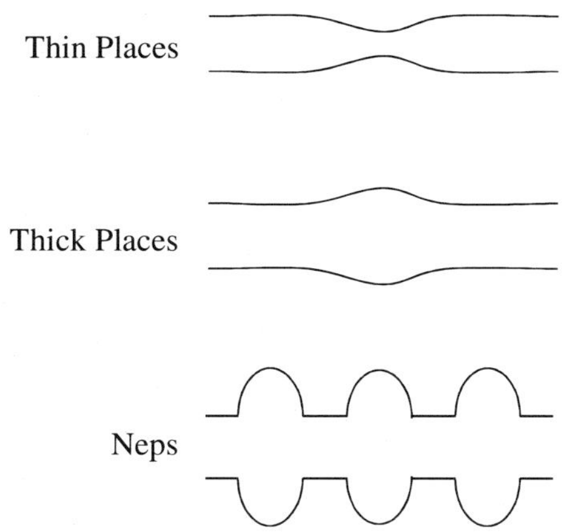

Figure 2. Types of yarn faults.

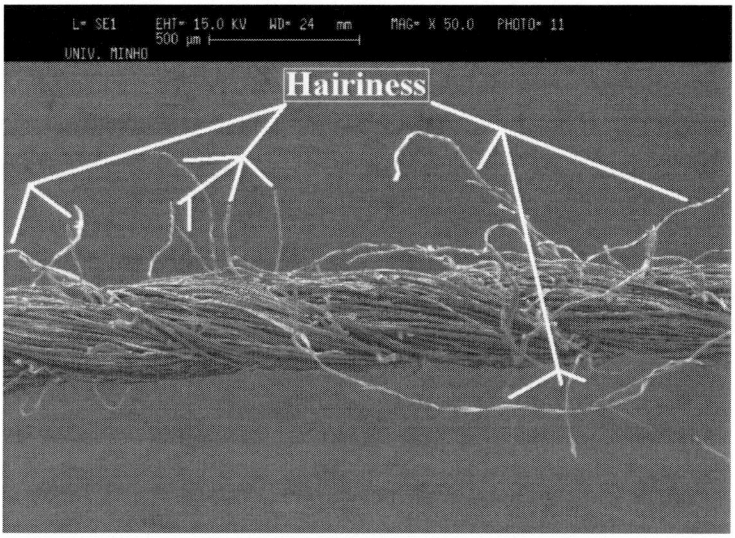

Figure 3. Identification of yarn hairiness in an electron microscope picture.

The number of yarn faults and yarn mass measurements enables a quality rating of the products tested. There are three kinds of yarn faults, classified as (Figure 2): thin places - a decrease in the mass during a short length (4 mm); thick places - an increase in the mass, usually less than 100 % of the sensitivity, and lasting more than 4 mm; neps - huge amount of yarn mass (equal or superior to 100 % of sensitivity) in a short length (typically from 1 mm to 4 mm).

Apart from faults, another important feature which greatly influences the appearance of fabrics is the level of yarn hairiness. Hairiness is the result of released fibres over the strand. Figure 3 presents an example of hairiness [9].

The hairiness coefficient (H) specifies the length of hairs in a meter of yarn. The measurements of yarn hairiness, mass and diameter, allow the determination of several statistical parameters which are relevant when characterizing yarn quality and, subsequently, the fabrics.

Yarn Production Characteristics

Four important production characteristics of commercial yarns are the fiber's twist orientation, the number of cables (folded yarns and non-folded yarns), the folded yarn twist step and the folded yarn twist orientation [9]. The two final production characteristics mentioned are only obtained when dealing with folded yarns.

Figure 4 identifies the four described production characteristics using as an example an electron microscope image of a 4.2 g/km cotton yarn. It is a folded yarn as two separate cables are clearly visible. The folded yarn twist step (d) is 0.3334 mm, with an orientation clockwise and a fiber twist orientation opposite (anti-clockwise) to the folded yarn direction.

This section describes experimental setup used in the image acquisition, as well as the yarn production characteristics software application, the diameter and imperfections software application, and the yarn hairiness determination software application.

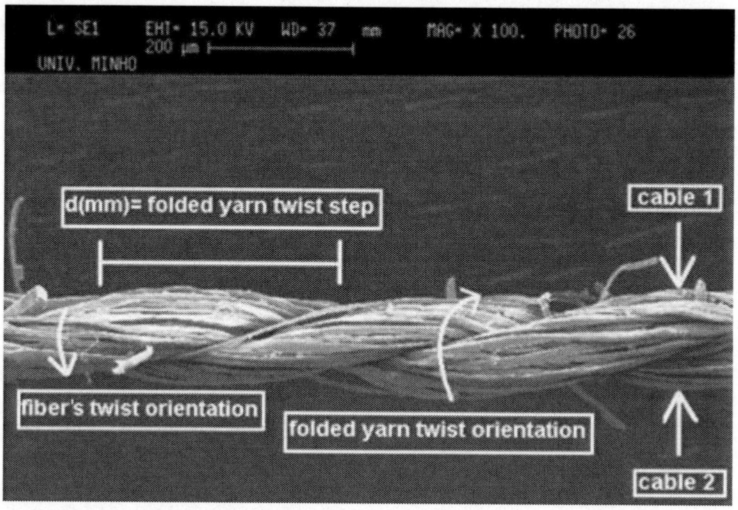

Figure 4. Identification of the yarn production characteristics in an electron microscope picture.

System Development

Experimental Setup – Acquisition Image Processing Systems

The experimental set-up for obtaining yam images consists of a low cost analogue microscope coupled to a common web CMOS camera. The microscope provides sufficient amplification and image detail, while there are no special requirements regarding the camera resolution. Figure 5 shows a flowchart of the designed system.

The analogue microscope used is the Biolux Al from Bresser [27], which has the following main characteristics:

- 2 oculars of 5X and 16X;
- 3 objectives of 4X, 10X and 40X;
- a Barlow lens of 2X;
- Led illumination.

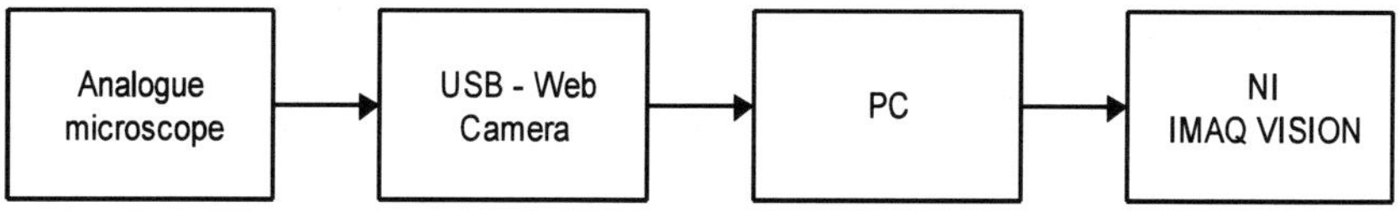

Figure 5. Designed system flowchart.

For the images described in this work, the 5X ocular lens was used, together with the 4X objective and the 2X Barlow lens, leading to an overall optical amplification of 40X (5x4x2). This amplification level was sufficient to obtain reliable results for yarns with a wide range of linear masses. However, if necessary, alternative magnifications can be used within the limits of the available set of lenses. The USB Web Camera employed is the Deluxe model from Hercules [28], which has the following characteristics:

- Photosensitive element: 1/4" CMOS sensor;
- Resolution: 640x480 pixels
- Video mode: VGA;
- Color format: 24 bit – true color.

The web camera was placed at the exit plane of the microscope ocular, capturing the analogue image produced by the microscope. With an optical amplification of 40X, a sensor resolution of 640x480 pixels is adequate to correctly evaluate the yarn production characteristics.

In order to obtain higher contrasts for the yarn geometry relief, the illuminated yarn surface must be as close as possible to a monochromatic light source. As the white led illumination available with the microscope emits a wide range of wavelengths, we decided to use an external yellow light source, which is somewhat closer to an ideal monochromatic light source. Figure 6 illustrate two different images acquired when using the white light source from the microscope and the external yellow light source respectively.

a)

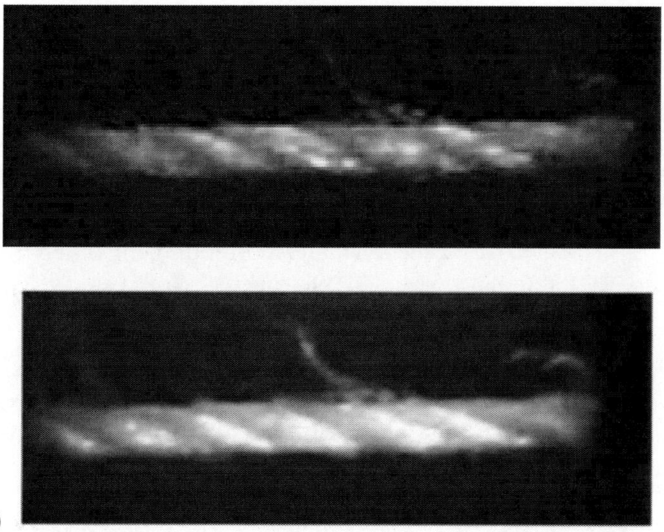

b)

Figure 6. Source images resulting from white (a) and yellow (b) illumination.

As shown in these images, with the yellow light source, the contrast between the yarn zones with higher relief is more accentuated. The regions which correspond to the most accentuated twist areas or yarn areas closer to the light source (Figure 1- 6 b)), are more clearly distinguished.

To analyze the acquired images an image processing application was developed using the IMAQ Vision software from LabVIEW from National Instruments.

Image Calibration

In order to calibrate the images, an image of an object with known dimensions was acquired (Figure 7).

In Figure 7 the real world distance between the lines is 1 mm, while, in the acquired image corresponds to 73 pixels.

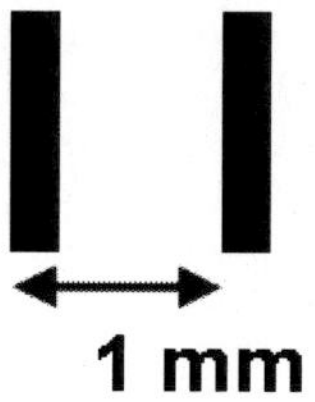

Figure 7. Image used for calibrating the system with real world measurements.

Yarn Production Characteristics Software Application

In this section we demonstrate the influence of the techniques employed, using two examples of the different yarns studied during the development of the system. The methodologies employed were validated through the common commercial range of 100% cotton linear mass yarns.

The raw images were processed with the following functions from the IMAQ Vision software in order to determine the production characteristics of a given yarn:

1. Contrasts adjust – expressed as a value between 1 and 89. The median value of 45 corresponds to a neutral setting, no contrast alteration, while higher values produce greater contrast. As it was intended to increase the contrast of the relief transition zones, the maximum value (89) was selected [10, 11].
2. Gamma Adjust – this specifies the value considered in Gamma Correction. Higher coefficients are associated with weaker intensity corrections. As it was intended to reduce as much as possible the intensity correction, in order to separate the relief transition zones, the highest value (10) was used [10,11].

Figure 9 presents the results obtained on the original image (Figure 8) after adjusting the contrast and gamma, to their highest values.

As a result of the steps 1 and 2, all pixels with intensities lower than those acquired in the transition zones have been effectively set to zero intensity.

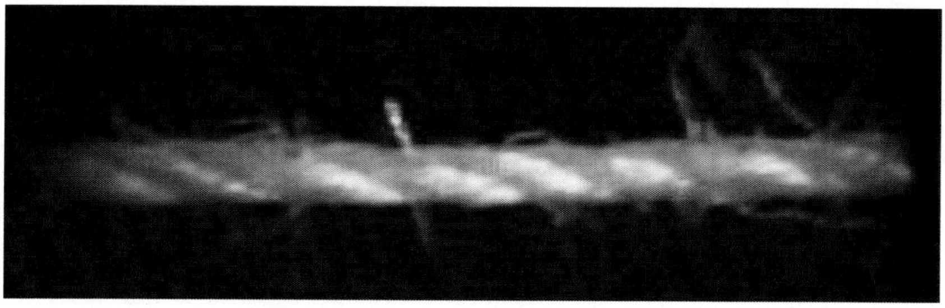

Figure 8. Original image as acquired by the web camera.

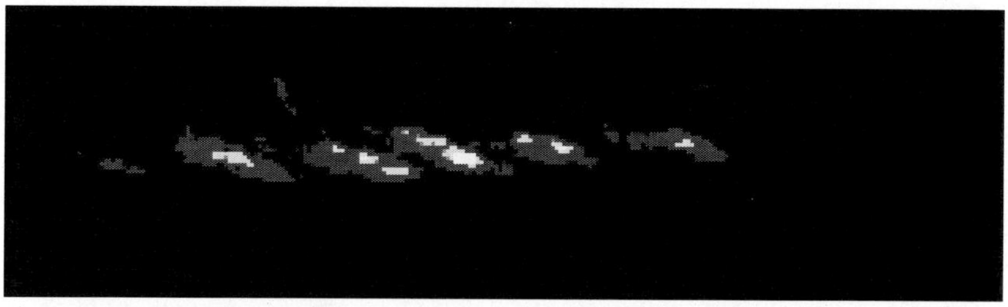

Figure 9. The resulting image after setting the contrast to 89 and the gamma adjust to 10.

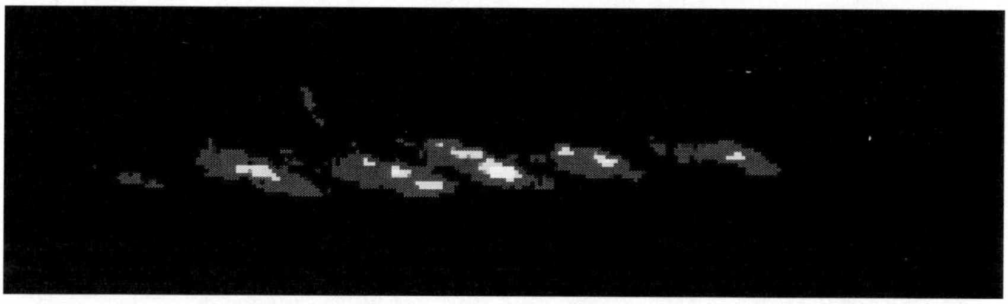

Figure 10. Image resulting from the application of the Removal of the Luminance Plane over the HSL to the image of Figure 9.

3. To simplify the binary image conversion process, it is desirable to homogenize the colour distributions in the image presented in Figure 9. This can be accomplished using the "Removal of the Luminance Plane over the HSL (Hue Saturation Luminance) Color Space" tool [10, 11].

Figure 10 presents the resulting image after applying the Removal of the Luminance Plane on the image in Figure 9.

This step converted the three different tonalities presented in Figure 9, namely, red, yellow and white, to dark gray, light gray and white, reducing significantly the color intensity spectrum of the original image.

4. Auto Threshold: Inter Variance – the Threshold function consists of segmenting an image into two regions, namely, a "particle" region and a background region, setting to "1" all the image pixels with a gray level equal to or above a given gray level threshold (threshold interval) and setting to "0" all the other pixels. This process is used to isolate certain areas in an image. In order to select the threshold interval

automatically, the Auto Threshold Interclass Variance tool was employed. This method determines an optimal threshold level by maximizing the between-class variation with respect to the threshold. The threshold value is the pixel value *k* (gray level chosen as the threshold) at which eq. 1 (variance) is maximized [10, 11].

$$\sigma_B{}^2(k) = \frac{\left[\sum_{i=0}^{N-1} ip(i) \times \sum_{i=0}^{k} p(i) - \sum_{i=0}^{k} ip(i)\right]^2}{\sum_{i=0}^{k} p(i)\left[1 - \sum_{i=0}^{k} p(i)\right]} \tag{1}$$

where, *N* is the number of gray levels in the image. The numbers *p(i)*, are the occurrence probability of a given gray level *i*, namely

$$p(i) = \frac{h(i)}{\sum_{i=0}^{N-1} h(i)} \quad . \tag{2}$$

Here, *h(i)*, represents the total number of pixels with a given gray level value *i*.

Figure 11 shows the resulting image after applying the Auto Inter Variance function to Figure 10. As expected, the application of the binary algorithm has isolated all the pixels with the relevant information (pixels different from black color, in this case).

Figure 11. Image resulting from the application of the Auto Threshold: Inter Variance, to the image of Figure 10.

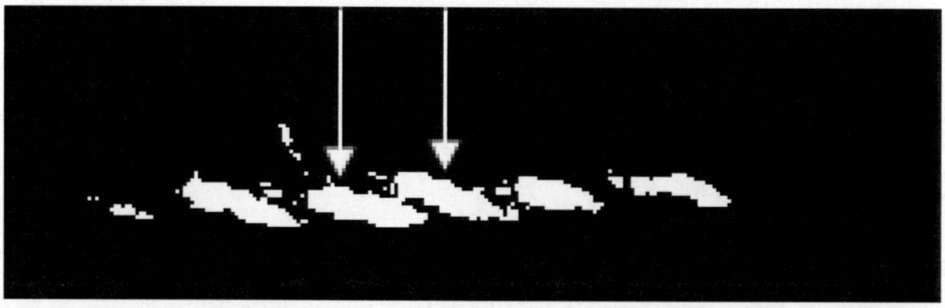

Figure 12. Image resulting from the application of the Hole Filling function to the image in Figure 11.

5. Hole Filling – this function fills the holes within continuous bright parts of the image in order to homogenize the binary images [10, 11].

The application of the Hole Filling function to Figure 11 is illustrated in Figure 12; three holes identified in Figure 11 by the white arrows have been filled.

6. Erosion – this function eliminates isolated pixels in the background and erodes the contour of particles according to a defined structuring element. This structuring element is a 2D binary mask, which defines the size and effect of the neighborhood on each pixel, controlling the effect of the binary morphological function on the shape and boundary of a particle. In this case we considered a 3x3 matrix containing values of 1. For a certain pixel P0, the structuring element is centered on P0. If the coefficient of the structuring element is equal to 1, the masked pixels are referred as Pi [10, 11]:

   a. If the value of one pixel Pi, is equal to 0, then P0 is set to 0, otherwise P0 is set to 1.
   b. If the logical AND of Pi is equal to 1, then P0 is set to 1, otherwise P0 is set to 0.

This function eliminates unwanted particles and avoids the possibility of object aggregation. Figure 13 presents the application of the Erosion function described above to the image of Figure 12.

As a result, the particles are now well separated. This is especially important for those particles that were particularly close to one another (identified with white arrows in Figure 12), which could easily been considered as one particle, rather than two. In addition, almost all the other irrelevant information has been also removed.

7. Convex Hull – this function *closes* particles in order to allow measurements even when the particle contour is discontinuous. It calculates a convex envelope around each particle, closing it [10, 11]. This function was used to allow use to carry out the necessary particle measurements.

As Figure 14 shows, the application of the Convex Hull function drastically reduces the discontinuity of the particles observed in Figure 13.

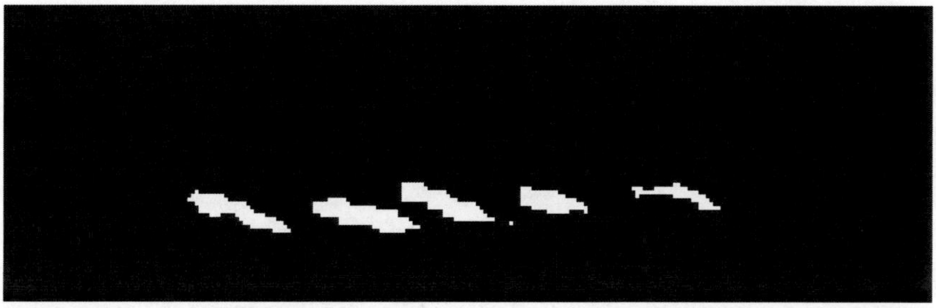

Figure 13. Image resulting from the application of the Erosion function to the image of Figure 12.

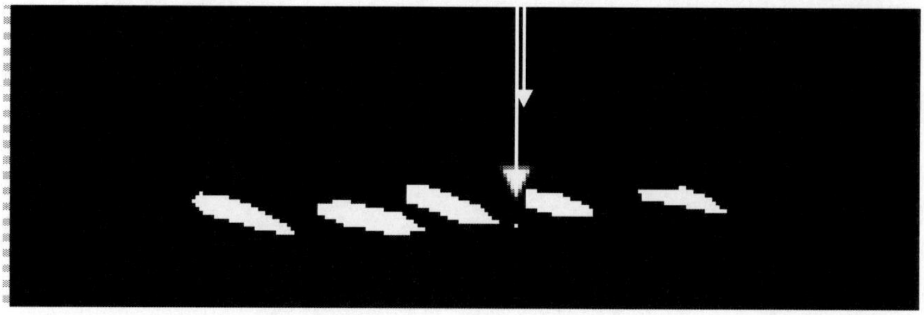

Figure 14. Image resulting from the application of the Convex Hull function to the image of Figure 13.

8. Small Objects Removal – This step is based on successive applications of the erosion tool followed by dilatation. This results in the elimination of the small particles and smoothing of the larger particle boundaries. Since erosion and dilatation are complementary transformations, for large particles, this operation does not significantly change the area or the shape as the borders removed by the erosion function are restored by the dilatation function [10, 11].

The result of a single application of this operation is shown in Figure 15. The small particles identified by the white arrow in Figure 12, have been removed in Figure 13, maintaining the other particles essentially unaltered. However, as this algorithm is for general use and, as in some cases the undesired small particles are slightly larger than the particles eliminated by a single iteration, a double iteration of this operation was used. In this example, the first particle on the right was eliminated (Figure 16). However, the loss of this particle is of little consequence as the number of particles remaining is enough to determine the desired parameters.

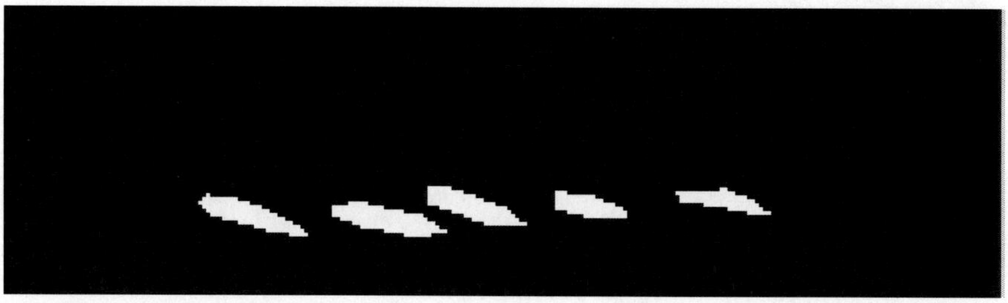

Figure 15. Image resulting from the first application of the Small Objects Removal function to the image of Figure 14.

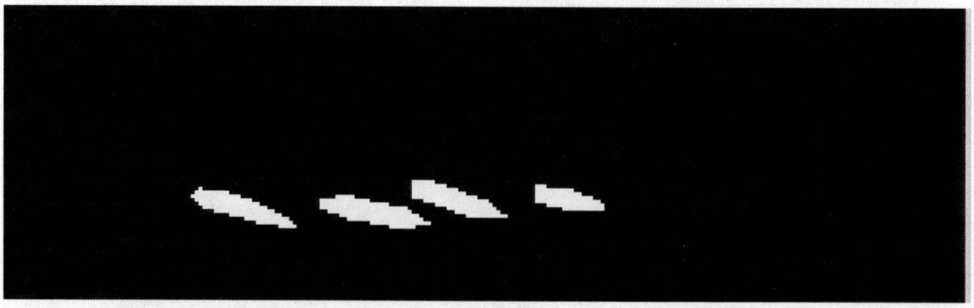

Figure 16. Image resulting from the second application of the Small Objects Removal function.

9. Particle Analysis - This function is used to perform several types of measurements over the particles of a binary image. Specifically in this study, the following parameters were employed [10, 11]:

   a. First horizontal pixel – the horizontal coordinate of the first particle pixel.
   b. Determination of Orientation: the angle (α) of the line that passes through the particle Centre of Mass corresponding to the lowest moment of inertia (eq. 3). The orientation angle is measured counter clockwise using the horizontal axis as a reference, over a range between 0° and 180° (190 ° is reported as a 10° angle).

$$\alpha(^{\circ}) = \frac{1}{2}\arctan\left(\frac{2\sum xy}{\sum yy - \sum xx}\right) \tag{3}$$

where, x and y are, respectively, the horizontal and vertical pixel coordinates of the line corresponding to the lowest moment of inertia.

   c. Area: area of the particle

Upon carrying out the above imaging processing procedures, it is possible to apply the following steps to determine the desired yarn production characteristics:

- Folded yarn twist step, which is the average of the horizontal pixel distance between particles: This parameter is only relevant when the yarn contains more than one cable (folded yarn), i.e. when at least two particles have been identified.
- Folded yarn twist orientation: This parameter is determined by the orientation angle for each particle:
  - If the orientation angle lies between 90° and 180°, then the twist orientation is anti-clockwise.
  - If the orientation angle lies between 0° and 90°, then the twist orientation is identified as being in the clockwise direction. Of course, the yarn must have at least two cables (folded yarn) in order to make it possible to determine the folded yarn twist orientation.
- Number of cables (folded or non-folded yarn):
  - If only one particle is identified then the yarn is identified as a single cable (non folded yarn).
  - If the number of particles is greater than one, then the yarn is identified as possessing multiple cables (folded yarn).
- Fibers twist orientation: two possible situations may occur:

- When the yarn is constituted by more than one cable (folded yarn), the fibers twist orientation is opposite to the folded yarn twist orientation. This is a universal situation in Textile Industry, done to avoid untwisting of the fibers over the yarns [3, 4].
- When considering a single cable yarn (non folded yarn) a new function is called.

In order to obtain the fibers twist orientation in non folded yarns, the following algorithm was used:

1. Removal of the intensity plane of the HIS (Hue, Saturation and Intensity) Color encoding scheme: In single cable yarns, a large region of the yarn should have a high intensity level [10, 11]. With the removal of the intensity plane, the intensity distribution over the yarn becomes more homogeneous.

Figure 17 presents the original yarn image and Figure 18 shows the result after the removal of the intensity plane which produces a much more uniform intensity distribution.

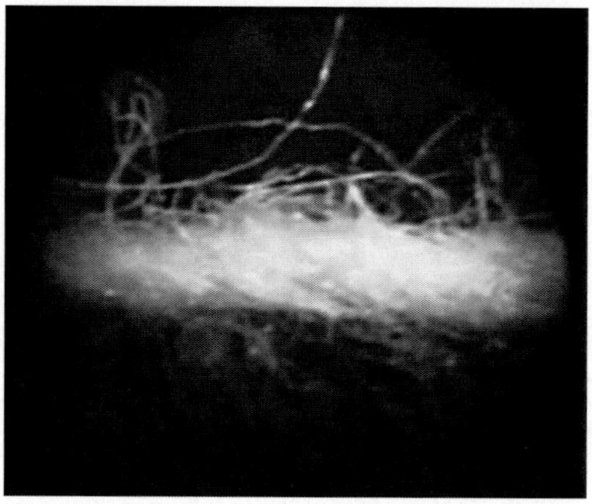

Figure 17. Image used for the development of the twist orientation for a single cable yarn.

Figure 18. Image resulting from the application of the intensity plane of the HIS color scheme.

2. Convolution – Highlight Details: A convolution is an algorithm that recalculates the value of a pixel based on its own value and the pixel values of its neighbors weighted by the coefficients of a convolution kernel. The convolution kernel defines how the associated filter alters the pixel values in a grayscale image. It is a 2D structure whose coefficients define how the filtered value at each pixel is computed. Considering several iterative tests, a 7x7 kernel containing 60 in the centre and -1 at all the other positions was used [10, 11]. Two iterations were performed in order to obtain a good definition of the high relief fibers (closer to the light source) which constitute the yarn.

Figure 19 presents the result of the convolution after the first iteration; in Figure 20 is the result after the second iteration. The image of figure is used 16 as a reference.

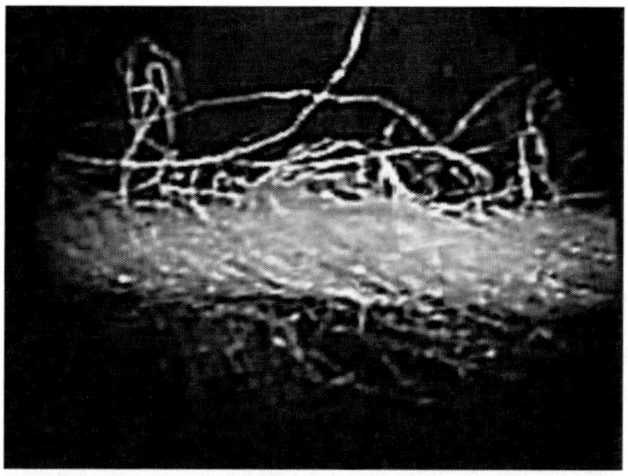

Figure 19. Image resulting from the application of the Convolution function to the image of Figure 18.

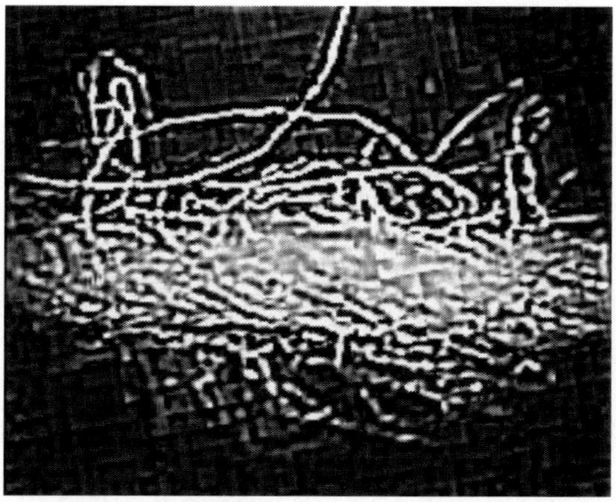

Figure 20. Image resulting from the second application of the Convolution function.

It was observed that only two iterations are needed to greatly increase the visibility of the exterior yarn fibers.

3. Auto Threshold-Moments: The threshold moments method is based on the assumption that the observed image is a blurred version of the theoretical binary

original. The blurring that is produced from the acquisition process, caused by electronic noise or a slight imperfection in the optics, is assumed not to alter significantly either the average or the variance of the pixels intensity distribution. This function recalculates a theoretical binary image. The kth moment m of an image is calculated by eq. 4 [10, 11].

$$m_k = \frac{1}{n}\sum_{i=0}^{i=N-1} i^k h(i) \tag{4}$$

where, n is the total number of pixels in the image.

The Auto Threshold - Moments were considered to isolate the white details obtained in the figure 18.

Figure 21. Image resulting from the application of the Auto Threshold – Moments function to the image of Figure 20.

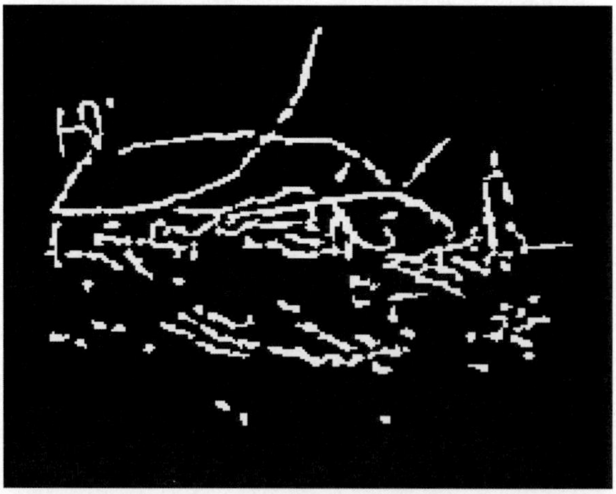

Figure 22. Image resulting from the application of the Small Objects Removal function to the image in Figure 21.

Figure 21 presents the results obtained after the application of the Auto Threshold – Moments function on the image of Figure 20, showing an excellent isolation of the image details.

4. Small Objects Removal: This option was used to remove all the small particles present in Figure 21[10, 11].

Figure 22 presents the results obtained upon applying the Small Objects Removal tool to the image of Figure 21.

5. Labeling: This function assigns a different gray level value to each particle in the image. The result is not a binary image, but a labeled image which uses a number of gray level values equal to the number of particles in the image, plus the gray level zero assigned to the background area. This function identifies particles using either connectivity-4 or connectivity-8 criteria. The connectivity criteria define the neighborhood a given pixel. For connectivity-4, only adjacent pixels in the horizontal and vertical directions are considered neighbors, for connectivity-8, all adjacent pixels are considered neighbors. For the cases studied, connectivity-4 produced better results [10, 11]. This reduces the influence of the neighborhood pixels and subsequently produces a more differentiated gray level labeling of the particles corresponding to fibers which protrude from the yarn core.

Figure 23 presents the results of the Labeling function used on the image of Figure 22. As observed, the binary image has been separated into several objects, identified by different colors and where the protruding particles are displayed with a lower grey level.

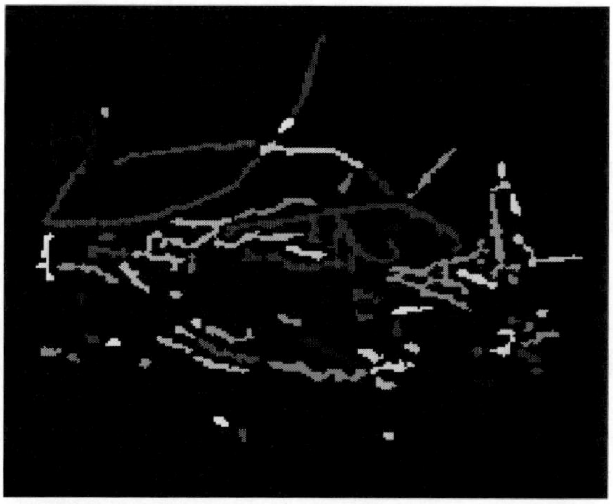

Figure 23. Image resulting from the application of the Labeling function to the image of Figure 22.

6. Exponential: This function decreases brightness and increases contrast in bright regions of an image, decreasing contrast in dark regions [10, 11]. Here, this step was important to eliminate fibers protruding from the yarn core.

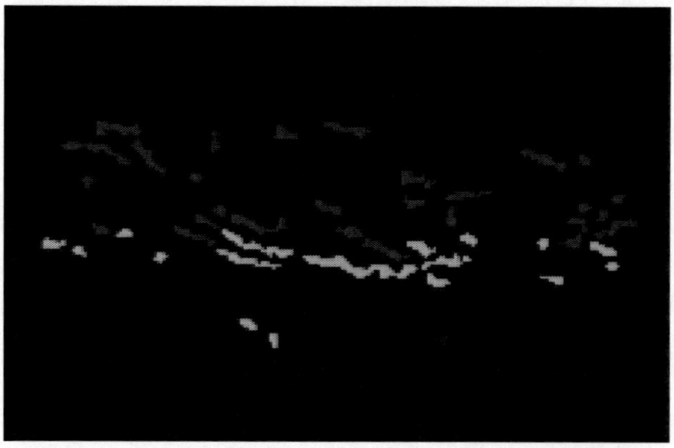

Figure 24. Image resulting from the application of the Exponential function to the image of Figure 23.

Figure 25. Image resulting from the application of the Convex Hull function to the image in Figure 24.

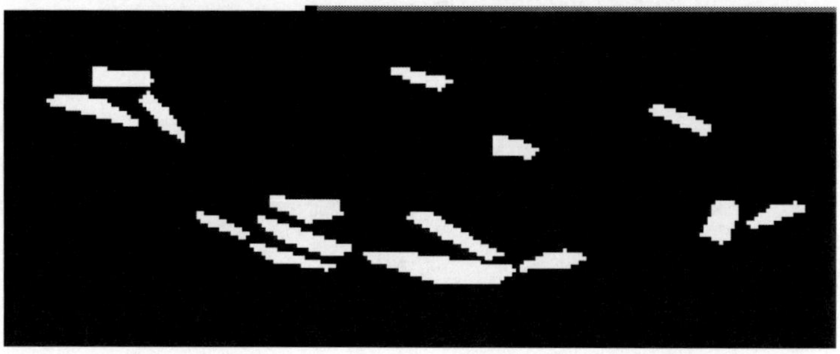

Figure 26. Image resulting from the application of the Particle Area Filter function to the image of Figure 1-25.

Figure 24 presents the result of applying the exponential function to Figure 23. Besides removing the protruding particles, the labeling color in the remaining particles has changed, due to the alterations in brightness.

7. Convex Hull – As previously, this function was used to permit the necessary particle measurements [10, 11].

After the application of the convex hull tool to the image of Figure 24, the image in Figure 25 was obtained. As intended, the level of discontinuity of each particle has been reduced.

Particle Filter: The goal of this function is to remove all the particles with reduced areas. Considering multiple case studies, it was concluded that for the optical amplification used, removing all particles with an area inferior to 34 pixels (threshold) allows proper results [10, 11].

Figure 26 presents the use of the particle area filter in the previous image.

8. Particle Analysis – Orientation: Measuring the orientation angle of each particle enables the determination of the twist orientation [10, 11]. The considered strategy calculates the average orientation of all particles in the image. Then, as in section B:

    a. If the average angle orientation lies between 90º and 180º, then the twist orientation is anti-clockwise.
    b. Conversely if the orientation angle within the interval from 0º to 90º, then the twist orientation is clockwise.

Diameter and Imperfections Software Application

This section describes the methodology used for measuring the diameter, for calculating of the hairiness coefficient and the detection of imperfections in the yarn, through image processing techniques.

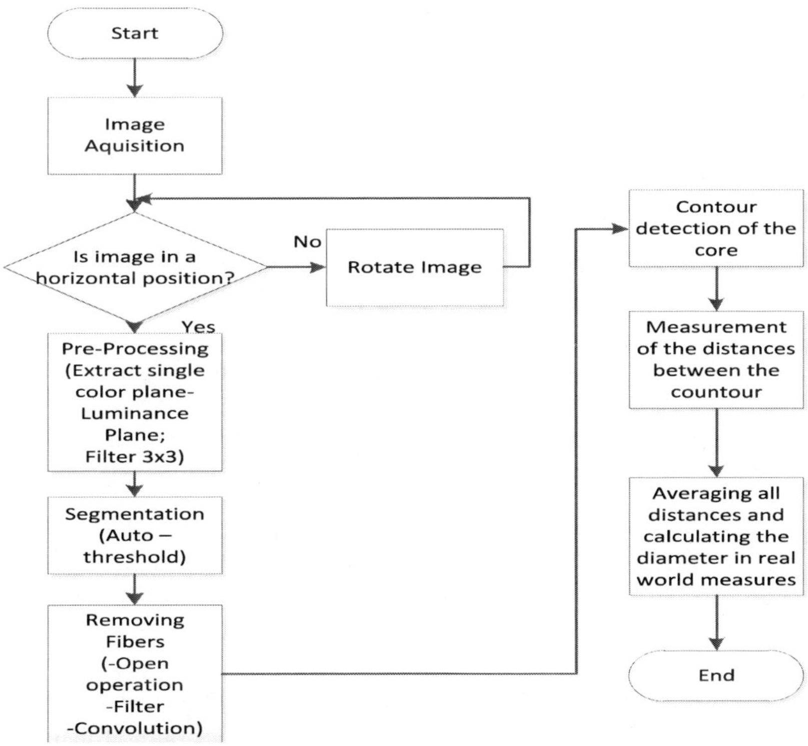

Figure 27. Diameter determination block diagram.

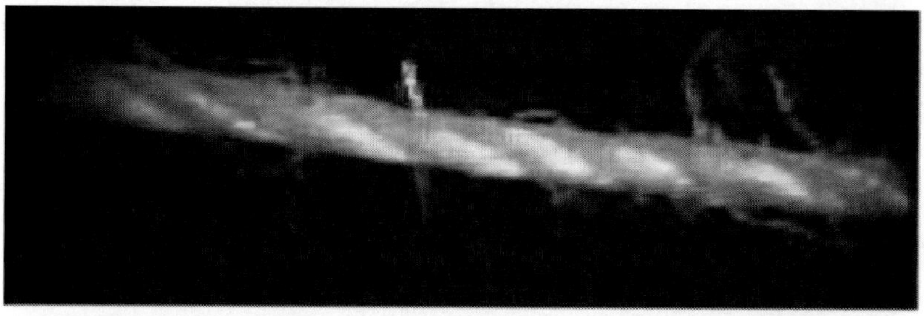

Figure 28.Original sample image acquired.

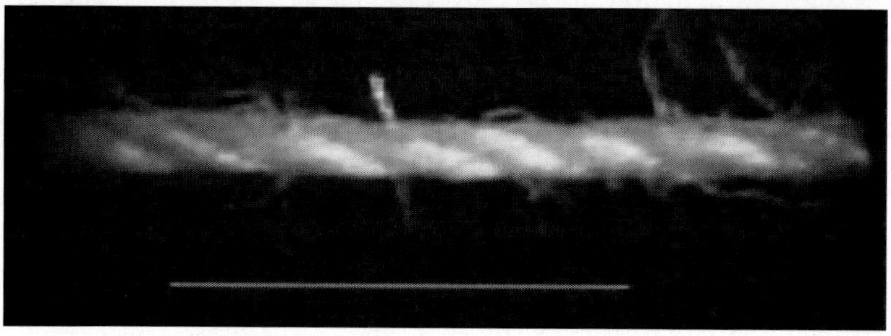

Figure 29. The resulting image after yarn rotating.

Figure 27 represents the block diagram of the algorithm used to determine the diameter by image processing techniques. The algorithm summarizes the application of various techniques of image processing that allows obtaining, as final result, the contours of the yarn core, excluding, all hairiness around the core. The diameter calculation is made through the detection of all the edges along a set of parallel searching lines. Once all edges are detected, the distance is calculated between the pairs of edges detected by all the search lines. The diameter is obtained by, the average of all the distances calculated. Once obtained the diameter, the yarn mass is easily acquired through the theoretical correlation between mass and diameter, presented previously. Figure 28 presents the image-based sample of the yarn captured by the image acquisition system. In the following, the sequence of functions used to obtain the yarn diameter is explained and their output is presented.

1. Function Rotate - If the yarn is not in the horizontal position, this function allows to rotate until the yarn is in the horizontal position [10, 11], as shown in Figure 29
2. Extract Single Color Plane, specify the luminance Plane over the HSL (Hue, Saturation and Luminance) - This function has the objective to homogenize the proximal colour patterns in order to simplify the binary image [10, 11] (Figure 30).
3. Filter nth order - The type of filter used was a zero order filter with a 3x3 matrix. With this type of filter it is possible to smooth the image and erode brighter objects, without changing the structure of the yarn [10, 11], Figure 31. This operation is highly relevant when the yarn has a large number of hairiness around the core.
4. Auto Threshold (cluster method) – This function is used to segment the image in two regions, a particle region and the background region. Threshold function converts the image to a binary image, with pixel values of 0 or 1. The clustering method is based on the following condition:

$$\frac{\mu_1+\mu_2}{2} = k \quad (5)$$

where μ_1 is the mean of all pixels values that lie between 0 and k, and μ_2 is the mean of all the pixel values between k+1 and 255. The option for look for the brighter objects was used to simplify the detection of the contours of the yarn in the following steps [10, 11]. This approach is possible because the yarn is mainly made up of brighter pixels. Figure 32 shows the result of the Auto Threshold function applied to Figure 31.

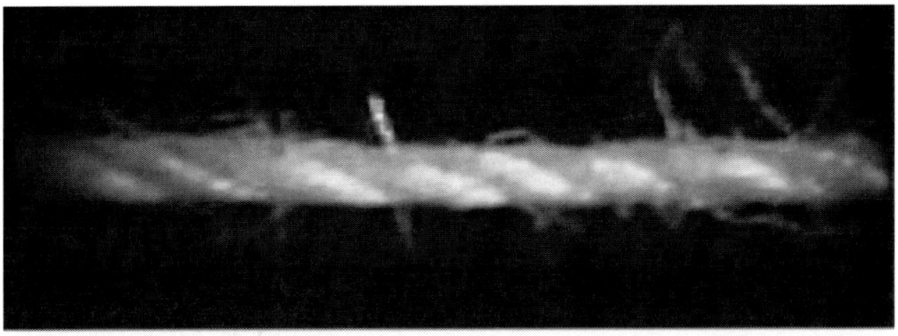

Figure 30. Image resulting after the removal of the luminance plane on the image of Figure 29.

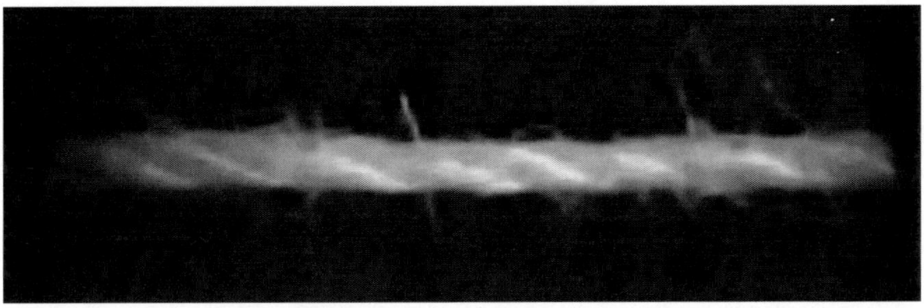

Figure 31. The resulting image from the application of the Filter to Figure 30.

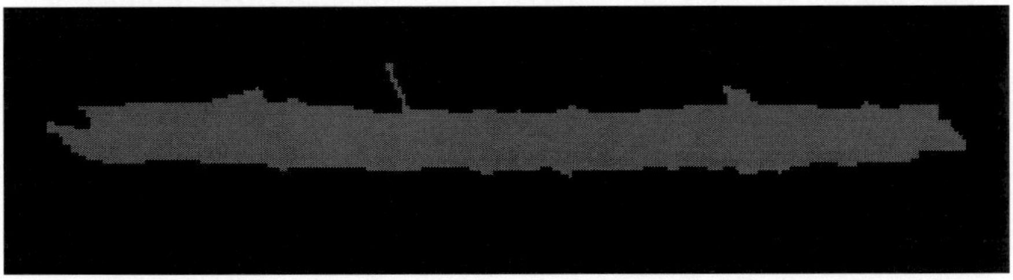

Figure 32. The resulting image from the application of the Auto threshold in Figure 31.

5. Remove particle – This function eliminates particles resistant to a specified number of 3 x 3 erosions. Five times was the number of erosion necessary in this function, to remove all small particles [10, 11], as presented in Figure 33.

6. Open - The open function consists of the operation of erosion followed by the dilation, it fills tiny holes and smoothes boundaries [10, 11] as shown in Figure 34. The value of the structuring element used was 1, using the following kernel [4, 5]:

$$\begin{bmatrix} 1 & 1 & 1 \\ 1 & 1 & 1 \\ 1 & 1 & 1 \end{bmatrix}$$

In comparison to all morphological operators, the open function showed minor changes to the yarn structure. This is an important factor to ensure greater accuracy in measuring the diameter.

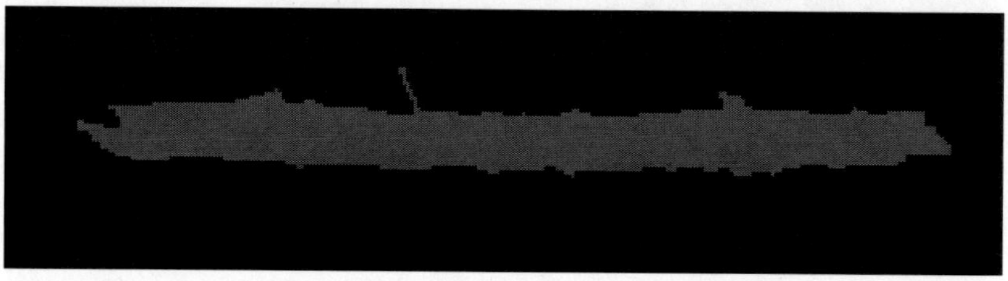

Figure 33. Image resulting after the application of the function remove particle to Figure 32.

Figure 34. Image resulting from the application of the open function to Figure 33.

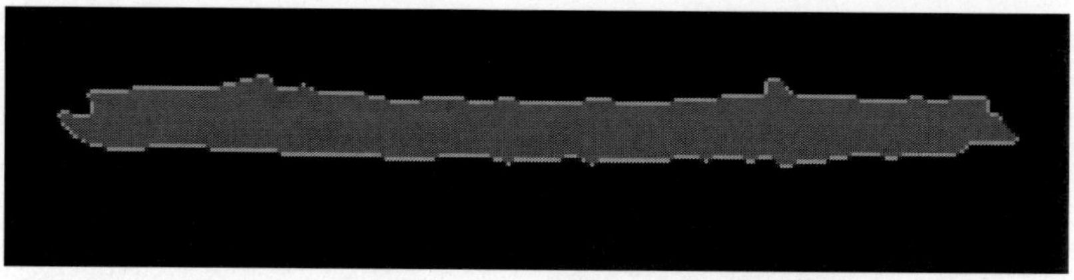

Figure 35. The resulting image after the application of the convolution function to Figure 34.

For example, when using the erosion or close function, they cause an increase or decrease in the yarn structure, which would influence the measurement of the diameter.

7. Convolute - This function allows recalculating the value of a pixel based on its own value as well as the pixel values of its neighbors weighted by the coefficients of a convolution kernel. The Laplacian convolution filter, a second-order derivate, was

used to extract the contour of objects and outline details, Figure 35, with the following kernel [10, 11]:

$$\begin{bmatrix} 0 & -1 & 0 \\ -1 & 5 & -1 \\ 0 & -1 & 0 \end{bmatrix}$$

8. Canny edge detection – This function uses a pixel value at any point along the pixel profile to define the edge strength at that point. To locate an edge point, several scans of the pixel profile are performed, pixel by pixel from the beginning to the end [10, 11], as shown in Figure 36.

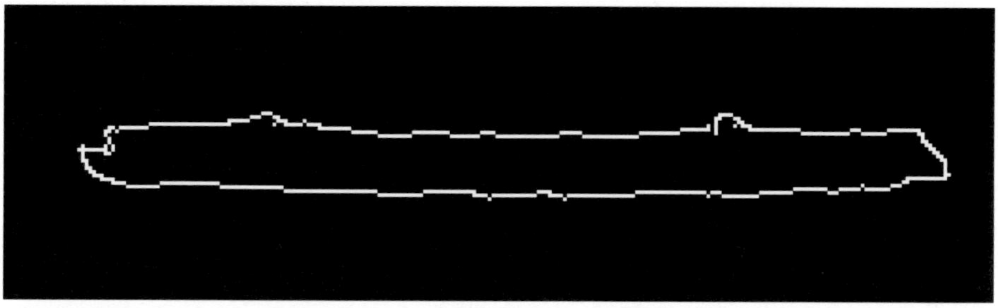

Figure 36. Image resulting from the application of the Canny edge detection.

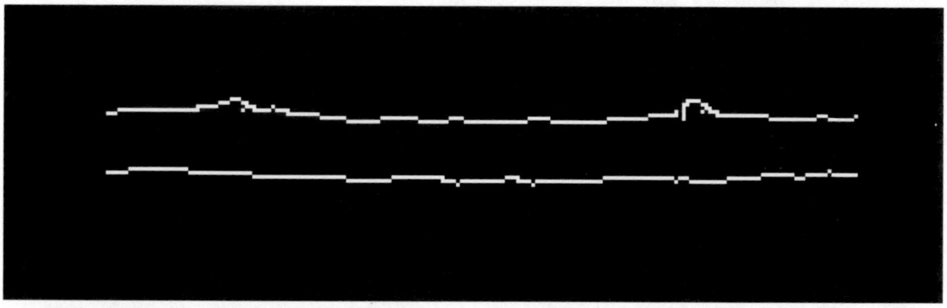

Figure 37. Image resulting from the application of a and logical between the rectangles mask and Figure 36.

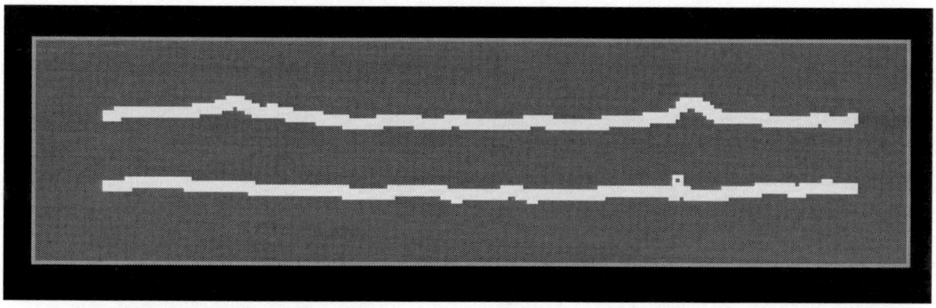

Figure 38. Final image to measure the diameter from the application the clamp vertical max function to Figure 37.

At this point it was essential eliminating the borders of the yarn, to reduce the error on measuring the distance between the edges of the yarn. For this, it was used the function *Particle analysis report*, that provides the coordinates of the center of mass of the object, which allow us to apply two rectangle mask based on these coordinates.

An *and* logical between the two rectangles masks and Figure 36 was performed resulting the image in Figure 37.

9. Clamp vertical max - This function allows finding all edges along a set of parallel searching lines, in a region of interest. The diameter is calculated by the average of the distance measured between the pair of edges detected by the searching lines. Figure 38 presents the final result.

Figure 39 presents the another image-based sample captured by the image acquisition system and Figure 40 the result after the application of the sequence of functions presented in Figure 38. With the yarn diameter and due to the correlation between the mass and the diameter, thick places, thin places and neps can be analyzed by comparing the distances measured along the yarn with the average diameter. Figure 41 shows the algorithm applied. After obtaining all measured distances in an array, it´s calculated the reference values for the thin places, thick places and neps. It's considered a thin place if the current value of the array is below 50% of the average diameter, as the thick places are considered if the current value is above 40% of the average diameter.

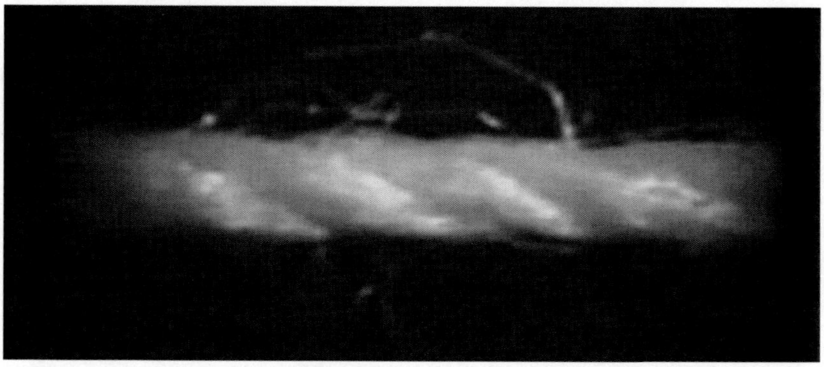

Figure 39. Original sample image acquired.

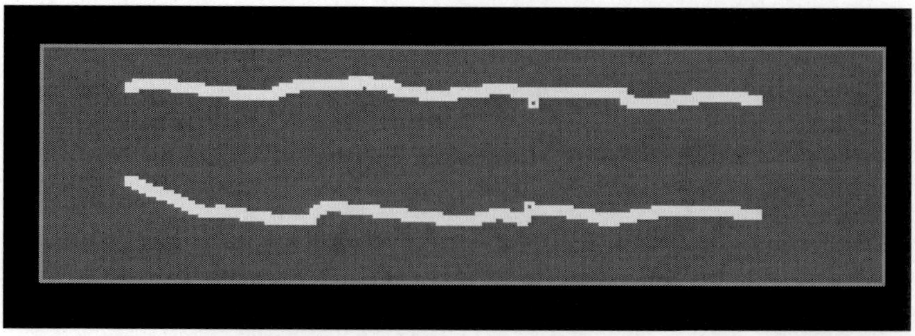

Figure 40. Image resultant from the application of the algorithm to Figure 39.

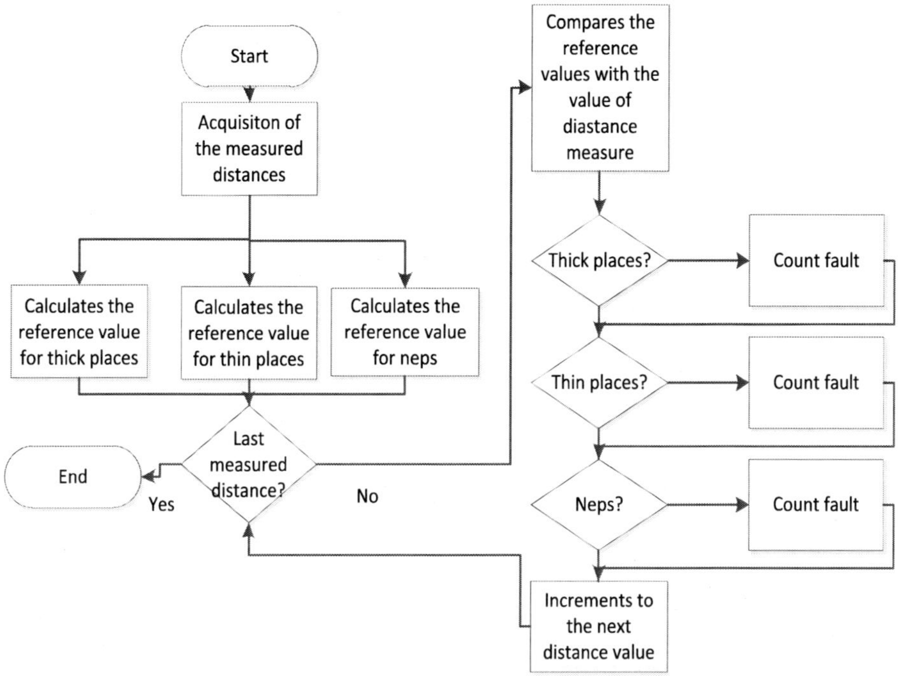

Figure 41. Algorithm used to detect yarn faults.

Finally the neps are contemplated for values above 100% of the average diameter. To avoid single values the current value it´s always compared to the previous value, and they have to match, otherwise it's not considered as a fault.

Yarn Hairiness Determination Software Application

In this study, spatial pre-processing techniques, as well as segmentation and spatial filtering techniques were used to isolate the yarn core and to highlight and quantify the protruding and loop fibers from the original image. In order to isolate the protruding and loop fibers from the yarn, logical operators were used between the image with the highlight fibers and the yarn core. Figure 42 presents the algorithm implemented.

Figure 43 shows the sample base yarn image where the image processing techniques were applied.

In the following the functions used to obtain yarn hairiness are explained and their output presented. The sample images were first converted to grayscale, Figure 44.

1. Function Rotate - If the yarn is not in the horizontal position, this function allows to rotate it until it is in the right position [10, 11], as shown in Figure 45.
2. Inverse – this function inverts the pixel intensities of an image to compute its negative [10, 11]. This operation allowed highlighting white and grey details over large areas of black pixels, Figure 46.
3. Equalize – This function redistributes the pixel values of an image to linearize the accumulated histogram [10, 11]. This function was used with the range between 200 to 230 in order to field the sample yarn with black pixels, Figure 47.

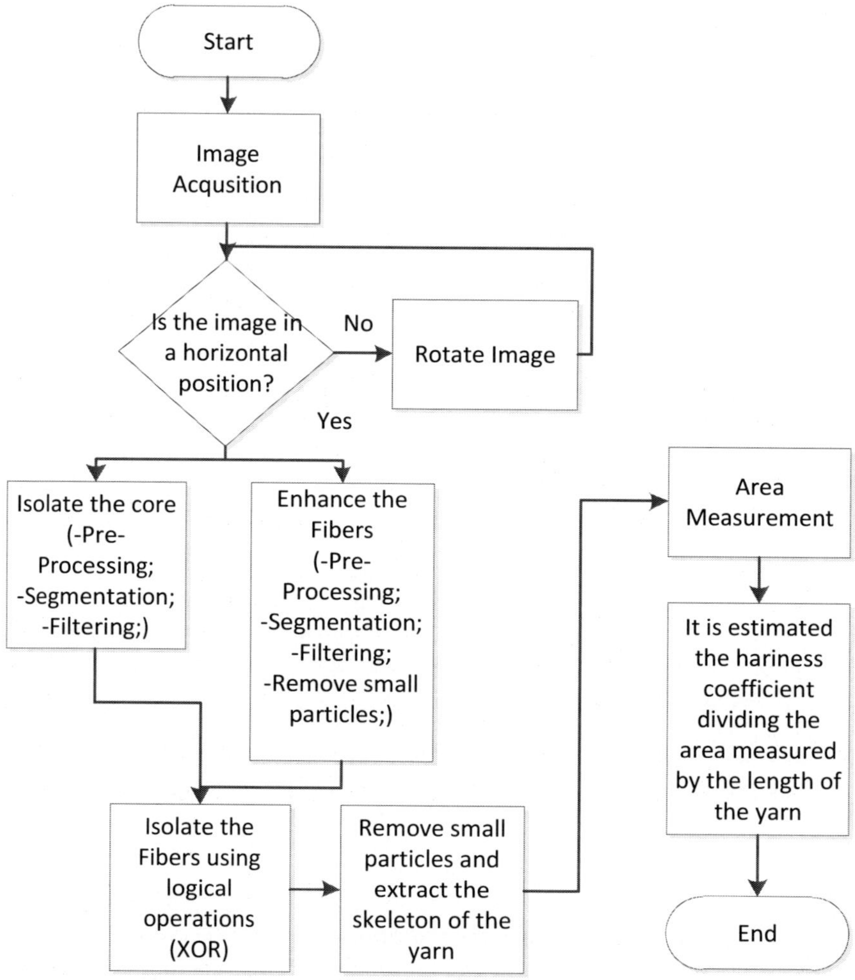

Figure 42. Algorithm used to measure the yarn hairiness index.

Figure 43. Original sample image acquired.

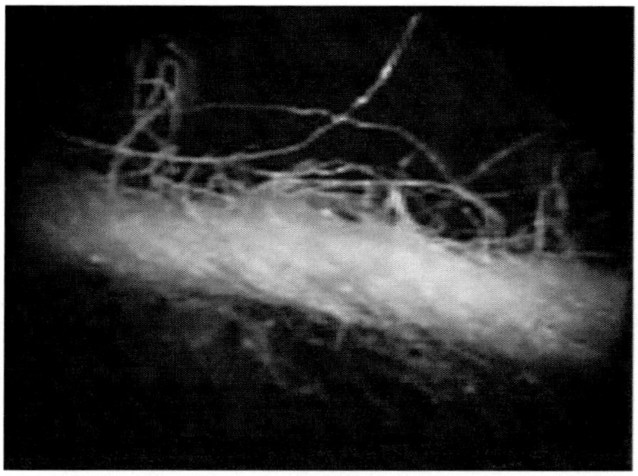

Figure 44. The resulting image in grayscale.

Figure 45. Image resultant after rotating.

Figure 46. Resultant image from the application of the inverse function in Figure 45.

Figure 47. Image resultant after the equalize function in Figure 46.

4. Auto Threshold - This function is used to segment the image in two regions, a particle region and a background region, Figure 48; limits between 0 and 1, as well as the option for look to the darkest objects were used.
5. Filter nth order - This function was used to apply a filter of nth order to eliminate the fibers, as presented in Figure 49. By trial and error, a kernel mask 7x7 with N=4 was used due to the good results obtained [10, 11].

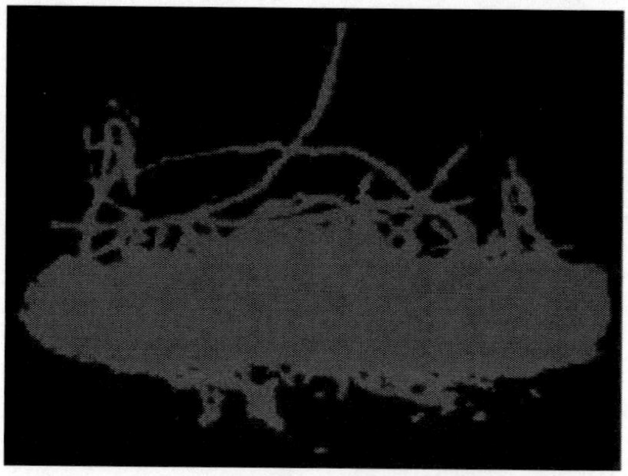

Figure 48. Image resultant from the application of the Auto threshold function in Figure 47.

Figure 49. Resultant image after the application of the filter in Figure 48.

Figure 50. Image resultant from the application of the remove particle function in Figure 49.

6. Remove particle – This function eliminates particles resistant to a specified number of 3 x 3 erosions. Five times was the number of erosion necessary in this function, to remove all small particles [10, 11], as presented in Figure 50

Algorithm to Measure the Hairiness Coefficient

This section describes the algorithm used to enhance the yarn, in particular to highlight the loop and protruding fibers, by removing the background and all unwanted particles.

In the following, the functions used to highlight the fibers are explained and the results presented. The first three functions described in the previous section were used with the same purpose.

1. Convolute - This function allows recalculating the value of a pixel based on its own value and the pixel values of its neighbours weighted by the coefficients of a convolution kernel. It was used a Laplace filter to detect points of discontinuity [10, 11] with the following kernel:

$$\begin{matrix} 0 & -1 & 0 \\ -1 & 5 & -1 \\ 0 & -1 & 0 \end{matrix}$$

Figure 51 shows the result of the convolution applied.

Figure 51. Resultant image after the application of the convolution function in Figure 47.

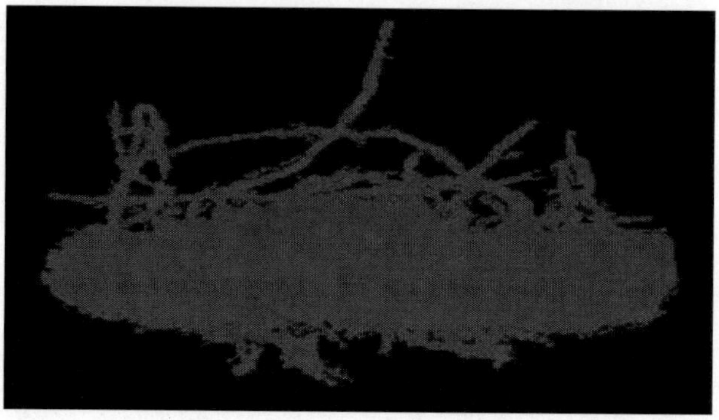

Figure 52. Image resultant from the application of threshold and small particles removal functions in Figure 51.

Figure 53. Resultant image after the logical operation and small objects removal function applied.

The final step involves the functions threshold and the removed particle, also described in the previous section, Figure 52.

2. The next step was to perform a logical exclusive or (XOR) between the Figure 50 and Figure 52 to isolate the fibers. A small objects removal was used to eliminate some remaining particles of the logical operation as shown in Figure 53.

In the following it is described the functions that allowed the measurement of the hairiness coefficient.

3. Skeleton - calculates the skeletons of the particles within an image or the lines delineating the zones of influence of the objects it applies a succession of thinning's until the width of each particle becomes equal to one pixel [10, 11]. The structuring element used was the skeleton L with the following kernel:

0	?	1
0	1	1
0	?	1

The resulting image is presented in Figure 54.

Once the fibers are isolated, the borders of the yarn must be eliminated to avoid its influence in the measurement of the hairiness. This was accomplished by using a two rectangles (200x15) mask with the filling value of 255 pixel and with the coordinates of the borders of the yarn, Figure 55.

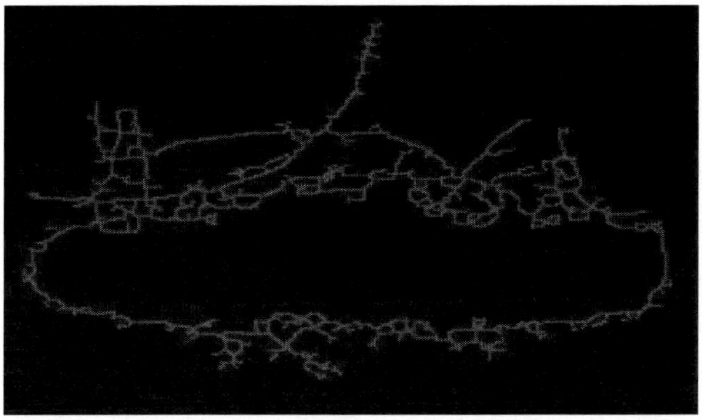

Figure 54. Image resultant from the application of the skeleton function in Figure 53.

Figure 55. Two rectangles mask used to eliminate the borders.

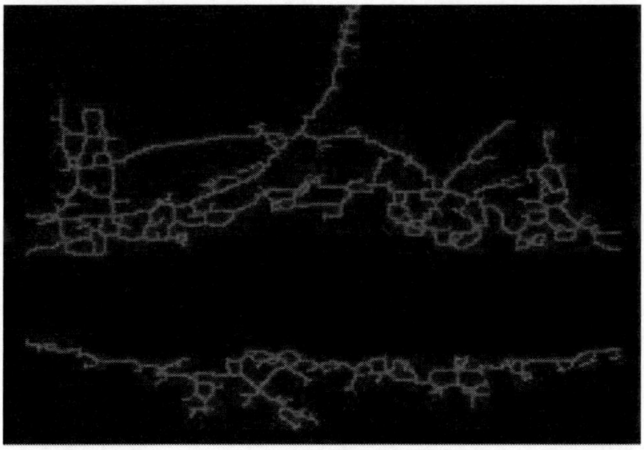

Figure 56. Resultant image from the logical operation between Figure 55 and Figure 54.

An *and* logical operation was performed in Figure 54 to eliminate the borders, Figure 56, and by the resource of the particle analysis report function, the area of hairiness is measured. Once the skeleton reduces the width of the fibers to one pixel, the measured area render the length of the fibers, expressed in pixel. The hairiness coefficient is calculated through the division of the measured area by the length of the yarn.

Experimental Results

This section presents experimental results to demonstrate the application of the determination of yarn production characteristics, diameter and hairiness algorithms showed in the previous sections.

Results Yarn Production Characteristics

This section presents the results obtained with the developed image processing techniques applied to four different cotton linear mass yarns, namely, 62 g/km (Figure 17), 55 g/km (Figure 57), 50 g/km (Figure 58) and 22 g/km (Figure 8).

For the 22 g/km yarn, the image processing application obtained the final image presented in Figure 16. The corresponding particle analysis data is presented in Table 1.

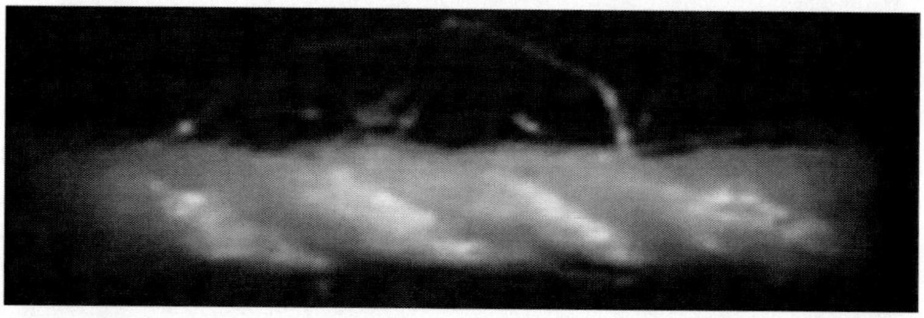

Figure 57. Initial image of the 55 g/km yarn.

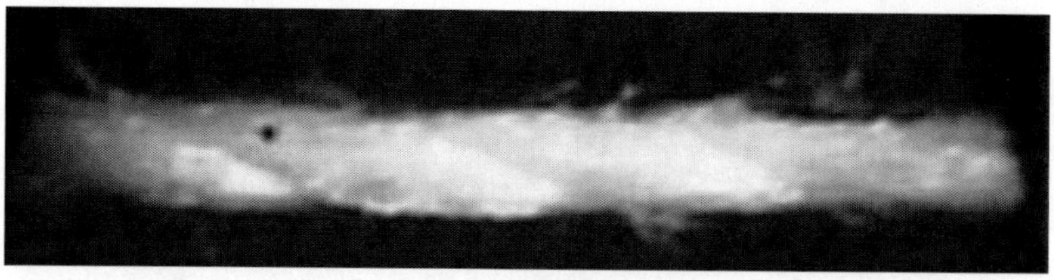

Figure 58. Initial image of the 50 g/km yarn.

Table 1. Results obtained for the 22 g/km yarn

Particles	First Horizontal Pixel	Orientation (°)	Area (pixels)
1	52	162.9	128
2	88	168.8	145
3	108	161.6	126
4	140	168.0	83

The average distance between particles together with its standard deviation is 29.3± 8.3 pixels.

Considering the data obtained in Table 1, the following yarn production characteristics were determined:

- Fibers twist orientation: clockwise;
- Folded yarn twist orientation: anti-clockwise;
- Number of cables: more than 1 cable (folded yarn);
- Folded yarn twist step: 0.4±0.1 mm.

Figure 59 shows the final 50 g/km yarn image after image processing while Table 2 displays the particle analysis data obtained.

The distance between the particles is 56.00 pixels. Considering the data obtained in Table 2, the following yarn production characteristics were determined:

- Fibers twist orientation: clockwise;
- Folded yarn twist orientation: anti-clockwise;
- Number of cables: more than 1 cable (folded yarn);
- Folded yarn twist step: 0.77 mm.

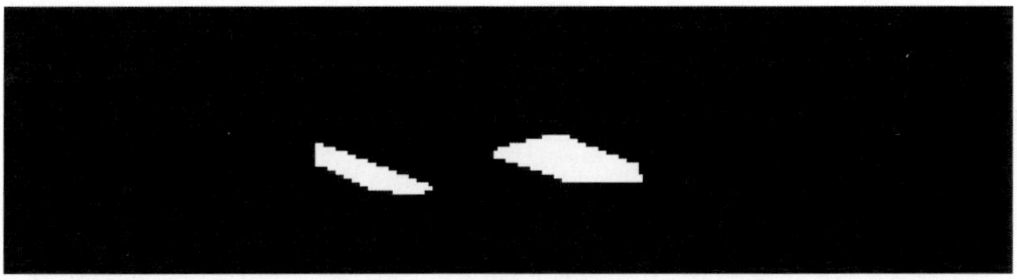

Figure 59. Image resulting from the developed application in the 50 g/km yarn.

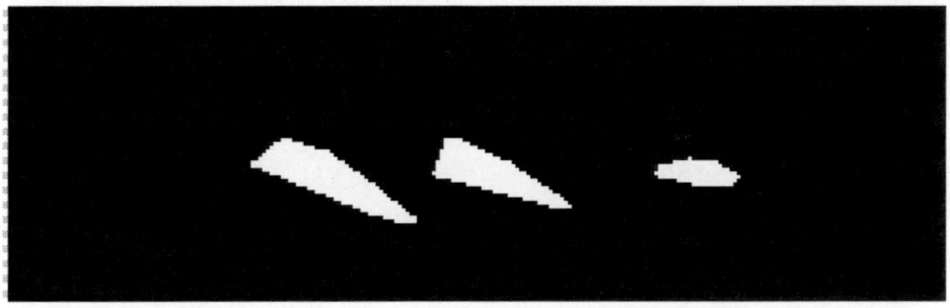

Figure 60. Image resulting from the application developed in the 55 g/km yarn.

Table 2. Results obtained for the 50 g/km yarn

Particles	First Horizontal Pixel	Orientation (°)	Area (pixels)
1	78	160.0	156
2	134	169.4	276

Table 3. Results obtained for the 55 g/km yarn

Particles	First Horizontal Pixel	Orientation (°)	Area (pixels)
1	73	154.5	377
2	116	158.0	292
3	181	174.6	120

Figure 61. Image resulting from the application developed in the 62 g/km yarn.

Table 4. Results obtained for the 62 g/km yarn

Particles	First Horizontal Pixel	Orientation (°)	Area (pixels)
1	132	176.6	5527

For the 55 g/km yarn, the final image obtained after image processing is presented in Figure 60, while the corresponding particle analysis data is presented in Table 3.

In this case the distance between particles is 54.±15 pixels. Considering the data obtained in table III, the following yarn production characteristics were determined:

- Fibers twist orientation: clockwise;
- Folded yarn twist orientation: anti-clockwise;
- Number of cables: more than 1 cable (folded yarn);
- Folded yarn twist step: 0.7+0.2 mm.

For the 62 g/km yarn, the final image obtained after image processing is shown in Figure 61 and the resulting particle analysis data is listed in Table 4.

As just one particle was detected, this is a single yarn cable and the function of twist orientation described previously in the previous section was activate. A particle orientation angle of 136° was obtained (Figure 61) and the following yarn production characteristics were determined:

- Fibers twist orientation: anti-clockwise;
- Folded yarn twist orientation: not available;
- Number of cables: 1 cable (non folded yarn);
- Folded yarn twist step: not available.

Afterwards, to show that the obtained image processing results are valid and reliable, they were compared with the parameters deduced from detailed electronic microscope pictures (amplification factor of 40X), for yarns of 50, 55 and 62 g/km, represented in Figure 62 to Figure 64, respectively. Observing Figure 62 and Figure 63 for 50 g/km and 55 g/km yarns, it is verified that these yarns are formed by more than one cable (folded yarns), with a folded yarn twist orientation, anti-clockwise and a fibers twist orientation in the clockwise direction. Considering, Figure 64 (62 g/km), it is verified that this yarn is constituted by a single cable (non folded yarn), with a fibers twist orientation in anti-clockwise direction.

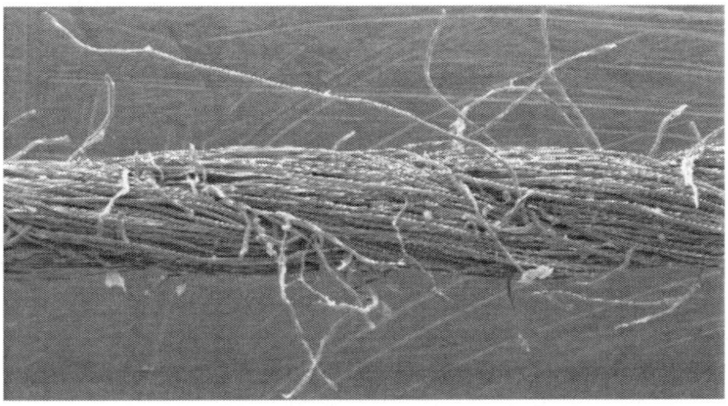

Figure 62. Electron microscope picture of the 50 g/km yarn.

Figure 63. Electron microscope picture of the 55 g/km yarn.

Figure 64. Electron microscope picture of the 62 g/km yarn.

Moreover, a folded yarn twist step between 0.74mm and 0.82mm has been measured over the image, for the 50 g/km, and between 0.64mm and 0.78mm, for the 55 g/km yarn. These results, obtained from the electron microscope images, are in agreement with the results obtained with the developed image processing tool.

This section presents the results obtained with the proposed method for the characterization of the yarn in terms of diameter and hairiness using image processing techniques. It is also performed a comparison between the experimental results of diameter, and the theoretical values of diameter, for different linear masses. Moreover, it is presented a comparison of the hairiness coefficient to the results of the analysis performed using the commercial equipment Uster Tester 3.

Results Obtained in Diameter Determination

The algorithm described in the previous section was applied to four sample images with different linear masses (22 g/km, 50 g/km, 55 g/km and 62 g/km) (Figure 65).

Figure 66 presents the images obtained after the application of the image processing techniques to quantify yarn diameter.

Table 5 presents the results in pixels (diameter in pixel – dp) and in real world units (mm) after conversion (diameter experimental – de). It also provides, for a better insight and precision of the algorithm, the values calculated by the theoretical relationship (d(mm)=0.060*sqrt(Tex)) between the yarn mass and the diameter (theoretical diameter - dt) for the respective linear masses.

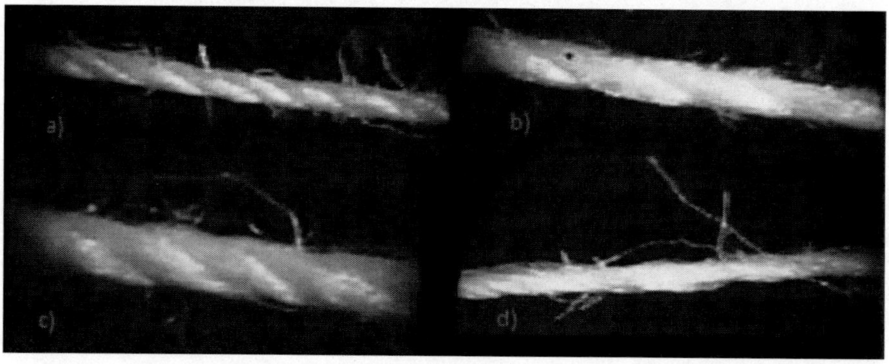

Figure 65. Acquired images a) 22 g/km yarn, b) 50 g/km yarn, c) 55 g/km yarn, c) 16.40 g/km yarn.

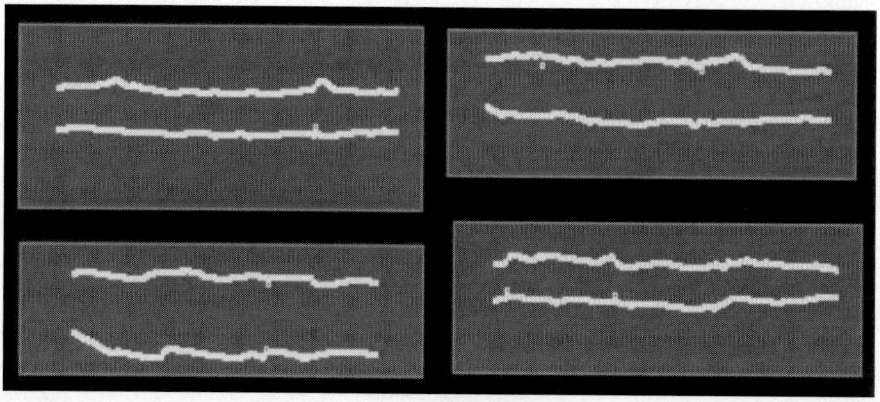

Figure 66. Application of the techniques of image processing to quantify yarn diameter to the images of Figure 65.

Table 5. Results of the diameter determination

Sample Number	Linear Mass (g/km)	dp (pixels)	dt (mm)	de (mm)	Standard Deviation (mm)
1	22	19.65	0.2814	0.2690	0.0086
2	50	26.11	0.4242	0.3576	0.0471
3	55	32.78	0.4449	0.4490	0.0028
4	16.40	17.71	0.2429	0.2426	0.0002

Results Obtained in the Analysis of the Imperfections of the Yarn

This study was performed through the theoretical correlation between mass and diameter, allowing determining thin places, thick places and neps when comparing the distances detected between the edges, to their average value, allowing identifying yarn imperfections.

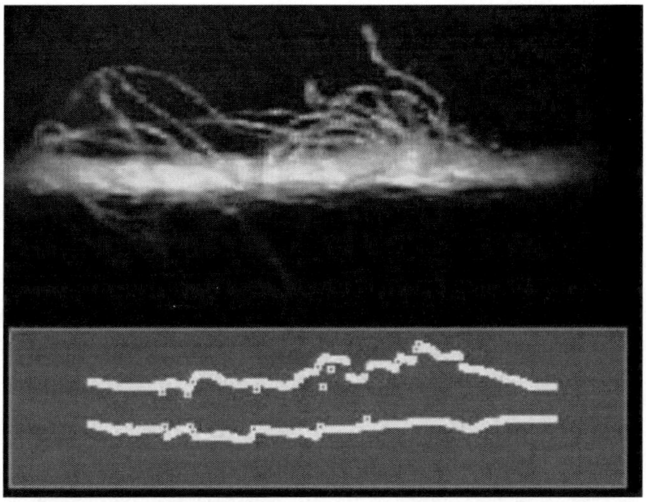

Figure 67. Example of yarn with imperfection.

Table 6. Yarn faults

Sample Number	Thick places	Thin places	Neps
1	0	0	0
2	0	0	0
3	2	0	0
4	0	0	0
5	0	0	0
6	2	1	0
7	4	1	0
8	0	0	0
9	0	0	0
10	2	0	0

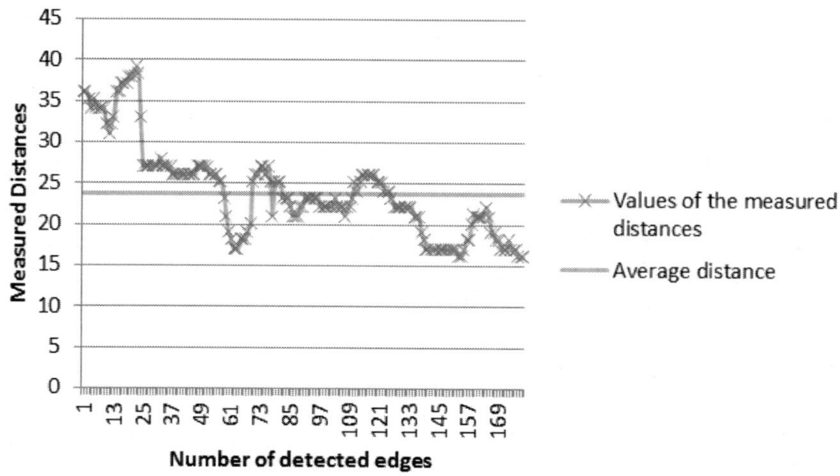

Figure 68. Distances measured over a point on the yarn.

A yarn with linear mass of 19.68 g/km was considered (Figure 67).

Table 6 shows the results of the yarn faults of the 19.68 g/km yarn along the 10 different points.

As it can be observed from Table 6 sample 7 has the higher number of thick places, only in two samples were detected thin places and none neps were detected.

In Figure 68 it can be observed the measured distances over the yarn with linear mass of 19.68 g/km, which corresponds to the sample number 3 of Table 7. By comparing the values with the average distance, clearly notices at least two thick places (distances values between 30 to 40 pixels).

Results Obtained in the Hairiness Determination

It was conducted a comparative test between the proposed approach and the analysis of commercial equipment Uster Tester 3. Five yarns with different linear masses (16.4 g/km to 98g/km) were analyzed, Figure 69.

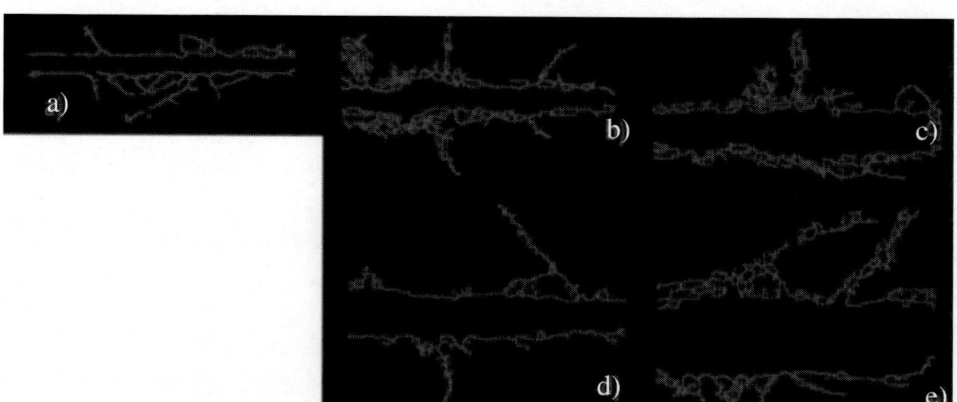

Figure 69. Results obtained for a)16.4 g/km yarn, b)19.68 g/km yarn, c)29.5 g/km yarn, d)36.9 g/km yarn, e)98 g/km yarn.

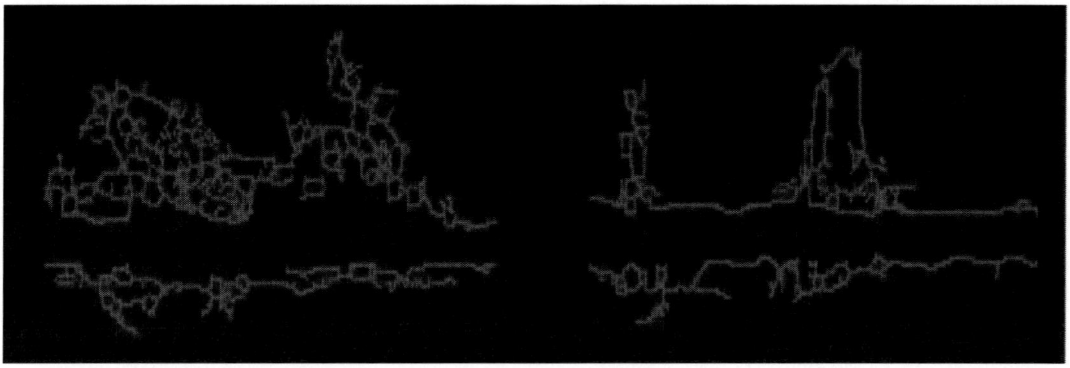

Figure 70. Example of two different points of the same yarn (19.68 g/km).

Table 7. Comparison between the average experimental values and the values of Tester 3

Sample Number	Linear Mass (g/km)	Vu	Average ve	Relative Error (%)
1	16.4	4.69	4.31	8.8
2	19.68	7.08	6.69	5.8
3	29.5	4.58	6.64	31.0
4	36.9	4.37	4.56	4.2
5	98	7.18	7.15	0.4
			Average Error:	10.04%

In the proposed system, images were acquired at ten different positions of the same yarn sample, Figure 70. This procedure was performed for the five yarns. It was calculated the average values obtained by the new methodology to ones acquired by the commercial equipment.

Table 7 presents the results obtained with the Uster Tester 3 (vu), the average experimental values for different positions of the same yarn obtained by the proposed methodology (ve) and its relative error |((vu-ve/ve)| * 100%). The coefficient of hairiness (v) is given by the ratio between the hairiness lengths and the length of yarn analyzed.

As it can be observed in Table 7 the calculation of the hairiness coefficient from the proposed method is very close to the ones obtained with the commercial equipment validating the approach. A small average error of 10.04% was obtained.

IMAGE PROCESSING AS A TOOL TO CHARACTERIZE HUMAN BLOOD *SAMPLES*

This section presents the framework, the image processing techniques, the database configuration, the system developed, the statistical analysis and the experimental results of an image processing tool to characterize human blood samples.

Framework

Determining the blood type of an individual is an essential procedure before administering a blood transfusion, avoiding damage and blood incompatibilities. Thus, the preceding blood test, even in case of medical emergency, is of upmost importance, allowing the administration of the blood type of the receiver in the first unit of blood transfusion. However, although two of the manual tests used in laboratory, the plate test and tube test, allow the analysis in a short time interval, which is suitable for emergency situations, they require travel to the lab and the intervention of a technician, thereby increasing the time spent and the possibility of human error. Given that human errors in the procedure of manual tests, in reading or interpreting the results, can lead to fatal consequences for patients, being one of the significant causes of fatal blood transfusions is extremely important to automate the testing, the reading and the interpretation of results [29-38].

In this sense, various systems were developed, Technicon Auto Analyzer [39-41], Technicon Auto Analyzer II [42, 43], Groupamatic [40, 44], Auto-Grouper [40] Olympus PK 7200 [40, 45-48] Immucor Galileo [49-53], Ortho AutoVue ® Innova System [54], Tango ® Automated Blood Bank [55] and Techno TwinStation [56].

But, none of the systems currently available allow obtaining results on useful time so they can be used in emergency situations [54]. This paper presents an innovative system to automatically perform tests to determine blood type, eliminating human error and in a short interval of time, so they can be used in emergency situations.

This system is based on the plate test for determining blood types and in software developed, using image processing techniques. The plate test consist of the mixture of one drop of blood, and one drop of each reagent, anti-A and anti-B, anti-AB and anti-D, being the result interpreted according to the occurrence or not of agglutination. The agglutination means that a reaction has occurred between the antibody and the cells indicating the presence of the appropriate antigen.

The combination of the occurrence of agglutination, or non-occurrence, determines the blood type of the individual [23]. Thus, the developed software allows, through image techniques, to detect the occurrence of agglutination and consequently the blood type of an individual.

Image Processing Techniques

The result of the plate test is captured by a CCD camera (Sony Cyber-shot DSC-S750) consisting of a color image composed of four samples of blood and reagent.

This image is processed by image processing techniques developed with the IMAQ Vision software from National Instruments [10]. However, since the original image also needs to be used again at a later stage of processing, it must remain available and unchanged. The following sequences of image processing techniques are used:

1. Image Buffer: Add Copy: This feature allows saving a copy of the original color image captured by the CCD camera after performing the test procedure for determining the blood type. It is the first function to be used as it is necessary to keep the original image intact, i.e. before undergoing transformations carried out by other

image processing functions. The image is stored in Buffer # 1 and is available for later use [10, 11]. The result of applying

This function is shown in Figure 71, for the four reagents, anti-A and anti-B, anti-AB and anti-D.

2. Color Plane Extraction: RGB Green Plane: This function is used to extracting green plans in a RGB image, allowing transforming the original color image composed of 32 bit in a grayscale image of 8 bit. This step is essential in order to use functions like threshold that can only be applied to binary images or images with 8 bit, 16 bit or float [10, 11]. The image obtained by applying this function to the image of Figure 72 is shown in Figure 71.

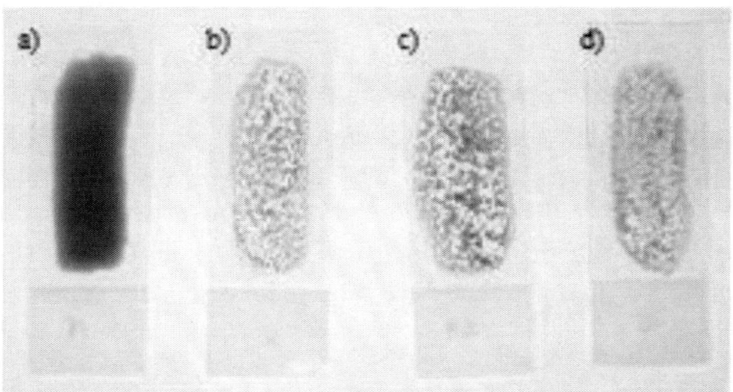

Figure 71. Original image captured by the CCD camera (a) Reagent Anti-A (b) Reagent anti-B (c) Reagent anti-AB (d) Reagent anti-D.

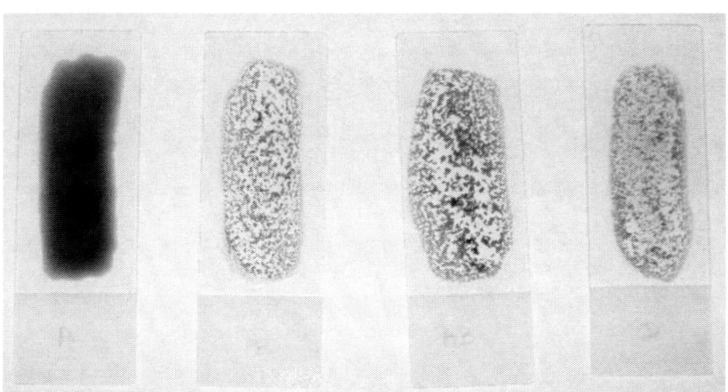

Figure 72. Image obtained by applying Color Plane Extraction: RGB Green Plan function in the original image of Figure 71.

3. Auto Threshold: Clustering: This function applies a threshold based on a statistical technique called clustering and it is used to separate the blood samples and reagent into two regions, designated "particle region" and "background region". This process is accomplished by changing all pixels that lie between the range of values

established (designated threshold range) changing all other image pixels to 0 [10, 11]. Thus, to isolate the particles of interest and convert the gray scale image (pixel values between 0 and 255) into a binary image (pixel values of 1 and 0). This function is an automatic threshold, as it is not necessary to specify the minimum and maximum light intensity. To draw the threshold, it is used the image histogram [10, 11]. The image obtained with the application of this function is shown in Figure 73.

Now that the particles of interest are separated from the background of the image, it is necessary to isolate the four particle image and eliminate any unwanted particles. So, there were used the following three functions, Local Threshold: Niblack, Advanced Morphology: Fill holes and Advanced Morphology: Remove small objects.

4. Local threshold: Niblack: In this function the threshold value for each pixel is calculated based on statistics from adjacent pixels. It uses a kernel, by default, of 32 width and 32 height, with a deviation factor which by default is 0.20 [10, 11]. This function is extremely important to isolate the particles to be analyzed. The result of applying this function on the image of Figure 73 can be seen in Figure 74.
5. Advanced Morphology: Fill holes: This function fills all the holes that are present inside the particles with a pixel of value 1. The binary image resulting from the application of this function contains particles intact, without holes, corresponding to samples of blood and reagent [10, 11]. The result of applying this function is presented in Figure 75.

Figure 73. Image obtained by applying the Auto Threshold: Clustering in the image of Figure 72.

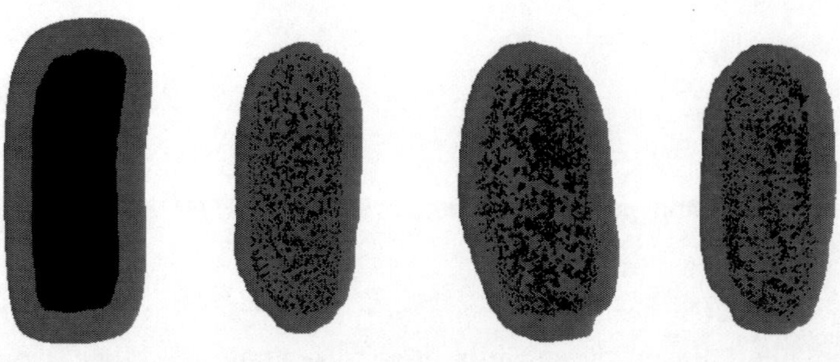

Figure 74. Image obtained by applying the Local Threshold: Niblack function under the image of Figure 73.

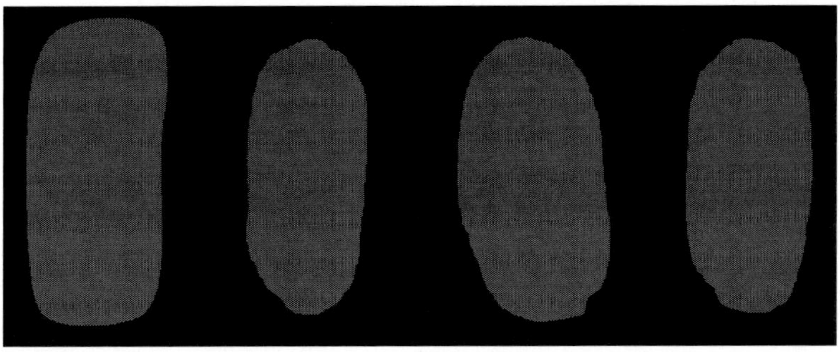

Figure 75. Image resulting from the application of Advanced Function Morphology: Fill holes function in the image of Figure 74.

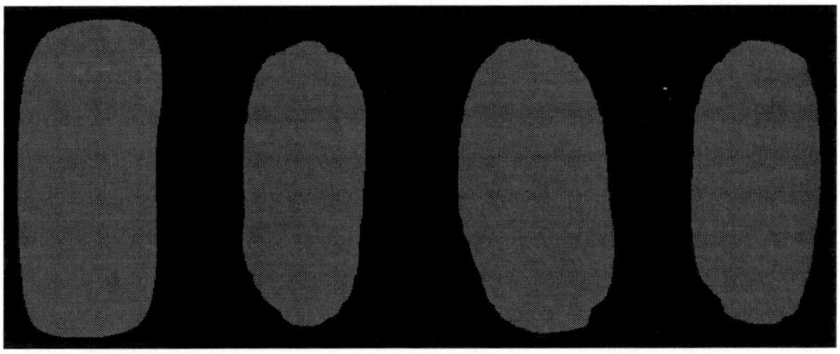

Figure 76. Image resulting from the application of Advanced Function Morphology: Remove small objects in the image of Figure 75.

6. Advanced Morphology: Remove small objects: This function uses a low pass filter to remove small particles and the possible noise in the binary image resulting from the previous function. The particles are removed according to their widths, as defined by a specific parameter, filter size. Thus, for a given filter size N, the low pass filter removes the particles whose widths are less than or equal to (N-1) pixels. These particles disappear after (N-1) / 2 erosions [10, 11]. The function removes particles that are not relevant to the analysis, leaving the rest of the particles (larger particles) untouchable. The particles that are removed from the step of erosion particles are assumed to be noise. It is mainly used to remove particles that may interfere with the analysis of the image, like little drops of blood or reagent at the background of the image [10, 11]. The result of this function is presented in Figure 76.

In this case, as there are only very small particles in Figure 75, which are difficult to see at naked eye, the application of this function is not noticeable in Figure 76.

However, when there are small drops of liquid (blood or reagent) present in the image, it becomes crucial to use this function to remove the unwanted particles.

The functions presented at this stage are essential for the automation of the process of determining the blood type.

1. Particle Analysis: A particle is a continuous group of nonzero values in an image. The particles can be characterized by measures related to their attributes such as

location of particles, area, and shape, among others. Therefore, this step is used to analyze the properties of particles in the image, considered as four particles corresponding to each of the mixtures of blood and reagent. These particles can be analyzed using various properties, being the center of mass highly important in this work. The result of this function is a table that contains all the selected properties and their values for each of the particles. The values of the center of mass X (coordinate X of the center of mass) and the center of mass Y (coordinate Y of the center of mass) for each particle are shown in Table 8.

Table 8. Results of Application of Particle Analysis Function on image of Figure 75

Particle	Center of Mass X	Center of Mass Y
1	338,48	537,65
2	1163,82	557,58
3	735,68	545,93
4	1570,67	545,81

2. Image Buffer: Retrieve Buffer # 1: This function retrieves a copy of the original color image stored in Buffer # 1, so it can be used in the next function. The original image consists of four samples of blood and reagents that will be processed and analyzed to detect the occurrence of agglutination [10, 11].The original image, as previously referred, is shown in Figure 71.
3. Color Plane Extraction: HSL Luminance Plane: This function is used to extract the planes of a color image light obtained with the previous function [10, 11] and allows transforming the original image constituted of 32 bit in a grayscale image constituted of 8 bit. Thus, it makes possible the use of the Quantify function that can only be applied to images of binary type, or images with 8-bit and 16 bit float, or grayscale images. The image obtained by applying this function to the image of Figure 71 is shown in Figure 77.
4. Set Coordinate System: This function defines a coordinate system based on the stage of particle analysis. The function of particle analysis obtains the coordinates (center of mass X and center of mass Y) needed to calculate the center of mass used in this function. This function is essential because it is based on the coordinate system, which is selected to analyze the region, depending on the center of mass calculated in the step of particle analysis. Thus, the selection process in the region of interest analysis is automatic and depends on the center of mass of each particle. This step is repeated for each of the particles to be analyzed. In this case it will be repeated four times, one for each sample of blood and reagent [29-31]. The image obtained by applying this function to each particle image is shown in Figure 78.
5. Quantify: This function can measure the intensity of pixels in the region of interest selected. This step uses the options, Reposition Region of Interest and Reference Coordinate System. The first option, Reposition Region of Interest, dynamically restores the region of interest based on the coordinate system previously defined. The second option, Reference Coordinate System, allows to select the coordinate system associated to the region of interest. The analysis of each sample is automatically

performed. The result of this function is a table that contains the area (percentage of surface examined for the full image), the mean (average value of pixels), standard deviation (standard deviation of pixels), the minimum and maximum value of pixels intensity. Using this feature, it allows identifying the occurrence of agglutination in the blood sample and reagent based on the value of standard deviation. As in the previous function, this step is repeated for each of the particles to be analyzed [10, 11]. The image obtained by applying this function is shown in Figure 79 and the resulting table is shown in Table 9.

The value of standard deviation is essential to detect the occurrence of agglutination. In samples where no agglutination occurs, the values of standard deviation do not exceed 16, taken normally, values between 0 and 10. Moreover, samples where agglutination occurs show standard deviation values greater than or equal to 16, showing even high standard deviation values between 20 and 70.

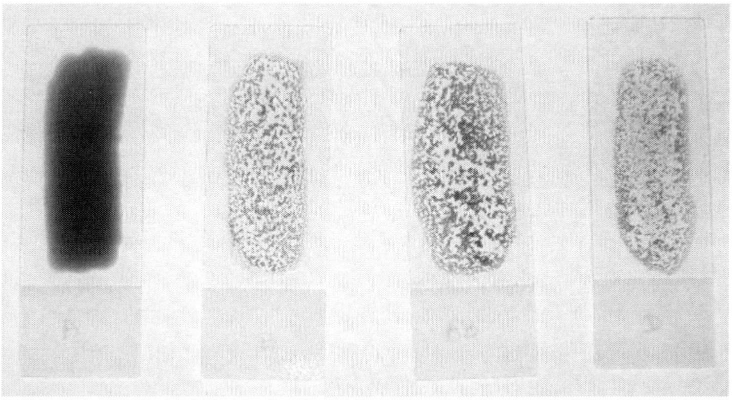

Figure 77. Image obtained by applying the Color Plane Extraction: HSL Luminance Plane function to the original image of Figure 71.

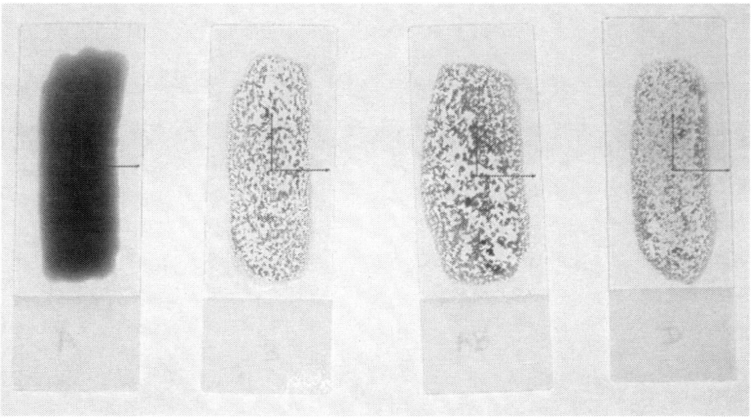

Figure 78. Image resulting of the application of Set Coordinate System functions to each of the particles in the image.

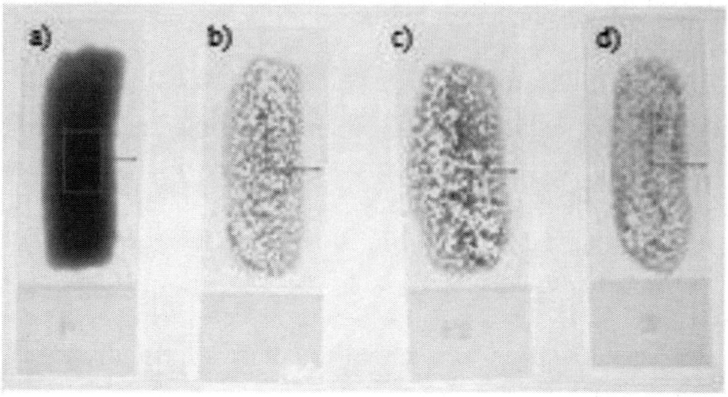

Figure 79. Image resulting from the application of the Quantify function.

Table 9. Results of Application of the Quantify Function in Figure 78

Fig.	Area	Mean Value	Standard Deviation	Minimal Value	Maximal Value
79 (a)	0.5	57.6	5.2	43.0	83.0
79 (b)	0.4	193.5	43.7	63.0	250.0
79 (c)	0.5	176.9	53.4	46.0	248.0
79 (d)	0.4	182.9	25.5	61.0	234.0

Thus, it was established as a threshold value for classification, a standard deviation of 16; samples with a standard deviation value below 16 are classified as samples with no agglutination and samples with a standard deviation value greater than or equal to 16 are classified as samples in which agglutination occurred. Having verified the occurrence of agglutination in anti-B reagent, anti-AB and anti-D, it is confirmed the presence of B antigens and Rh antigens in the blood sample analyzed. Thus, it can be concluded that the blood type in question is B Positive. Another example of the application of the methodology described is presented in Figure 80, where agglutination occurred in samples a), c) and d); in sample b), there was no agglutination. Through the standard deviation values of Table 10, this is also confirmed as samples a), c), d), present values of standard deviation of 57.8, 62.1 and 49.5 respectively (all above 16), sample b), obtained 3.4 (below 16).

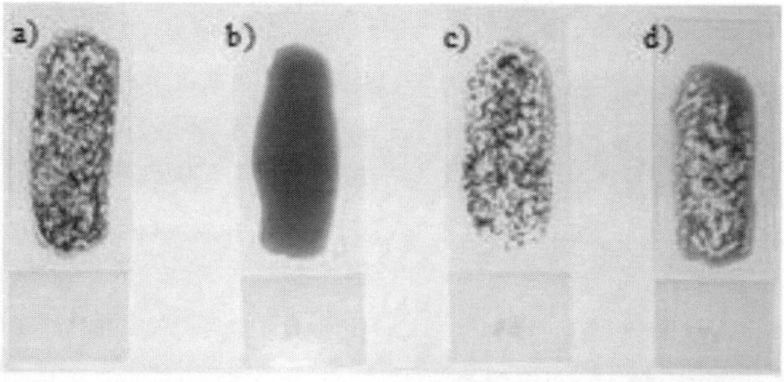

Figure 80. The original image of A Positive (a) Reagent Anti-A (b) Reagent anti-B (c) Reagent anti-AB (d) Reagent anti-D.

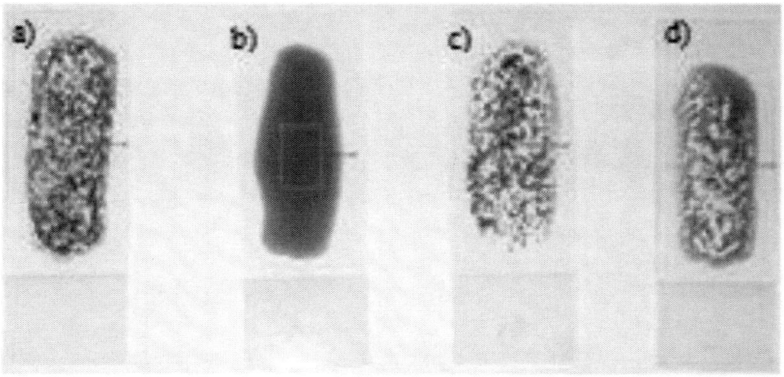

Figure 81. Image resulting from application of image processing techniques presented to the image of Figure 80.

Table 10. Results of Application of Quantify Function on image of Figure 81

Fig.	Area	Mean Value	Standard Deviation	Minimal Value	Maximal Value
81 (a)	0.5	144.3	57.8	20.0	238.0
81 (b)	0.5	83.4	3.4	64.0	95.0
81 (c)	0.4	147.4	62.1	32.0	240.0
81 (d)	0.4	139.3	49.5	34.0	222.0

Having verified the occurrence of agglutination in anti-A reagent, anti-AB and anti-D, it is confirmed the presence of A antigens and Rh antigens in the blood sample analyzed. Thus, it can be concluded that the blood type in question is A Positive.

Database

To store the information from the analysis of detection of agglutination performed through the techniques of image processing and the result of the classification algorithm developed to determine blood type, it was designed and implemented a database. This section presents the table of the database developed with Microsoft Office Access 2007, where information will be stored, Figure 82.

This table, Figure 82, stores the image captured and used in image processing (each image contains four samples of blood and reagents), the standard deviation calculated in each sample image, the occurrence or not of agglutination and the blood type.

System Developed

This section presents on one hand the software developed taking into consideration the studies performed in the previous sections and on the other hand the first prototype of the acquisition hardware designed.

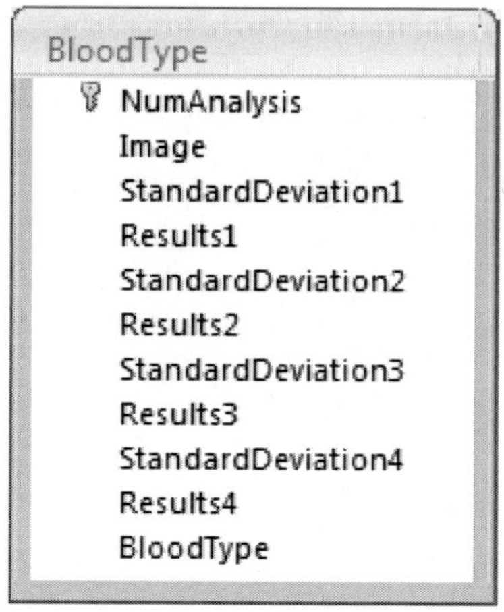

Figure 82. Base table where the information is entered.

Software Developed

The software was developed in LabIEW from National Instruments [10, 11].The front panel is shown in Figure 83.

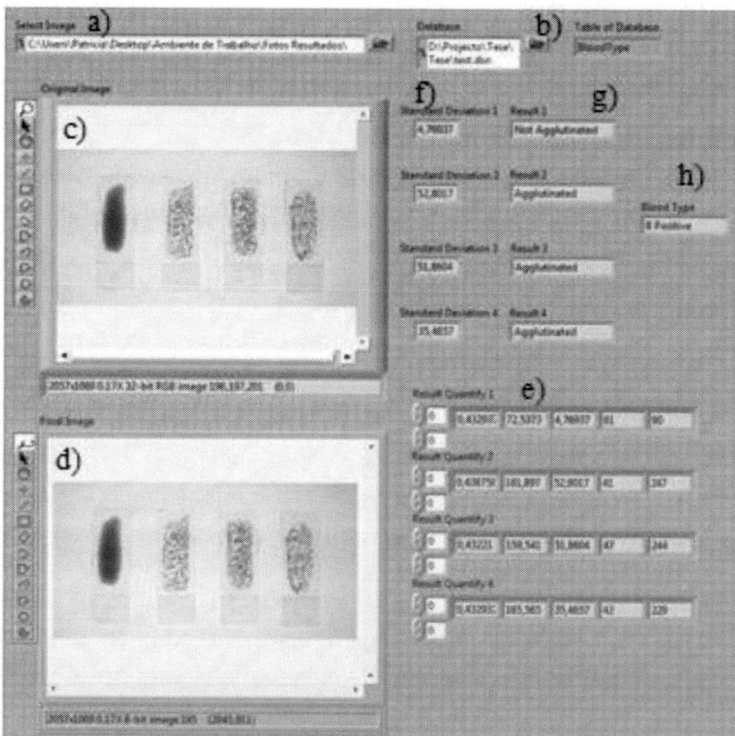

Figure 83. Developed Software. (a) Selection of the image (b) Selection of File Database.dsn and entering the name of the table of database (c) Original Image (d) Final image obtained with the image processing techniques (e) Results of the Quantify function (f) Values of standard deviation of each sample (g) Results based on the standard deviation of each sample (h) Result of the classification algorithm.

This software allows to select the image to be used, Figure 83(a), the database to establish a connection and the table from the database where information is added to the analysis, Figure 83(b), it displays the original image that is being used, Figure 83(c) as well as the final image obtained with the image processing techniques, Figure 83(d), it shows the results of the Quantify function, Figure 83(e), the results of the standard deviation, Figure 83(f), the results based on standard deviation values calculated Figure 83(g), and, finally, the result in terms of blood type, Figure 83(h).

Hardware Developed

The first prototype of the developed system, which automatically determines the blood type of an individual, using as reference the plate test [28], is shown in Figure 84.

The system requires that the blood samples and the reagents are manually placed, in plates, by the user. It is placed on the first plate the reagent anti-A, on the second plate the reagent anti-B, on the third plate the reagent anti-AB and on the fourth plate the reagent anti-D. Thereafter, the system moves the plates for the mixing area, where the blood and the reagents in each plate, are mixed. This mixture is performed with a DC motor and without contamination between the four samples. Upon completion of the mixing, blades are moved to the image capture area, where a motor drives the webcam Glossy, 5 Mega pixels, along the samples, capturing an image from each of the plates.

These images are stored for later analysis. The system is controlled by the microcontroller Arduino. Some of its characteristics are 14 digital I/O, 6 analog inputs. 16KB of flash memory, 512 bytes of SRAM, 512 bytes of EEPROM and a clock speed of 16 MHz.

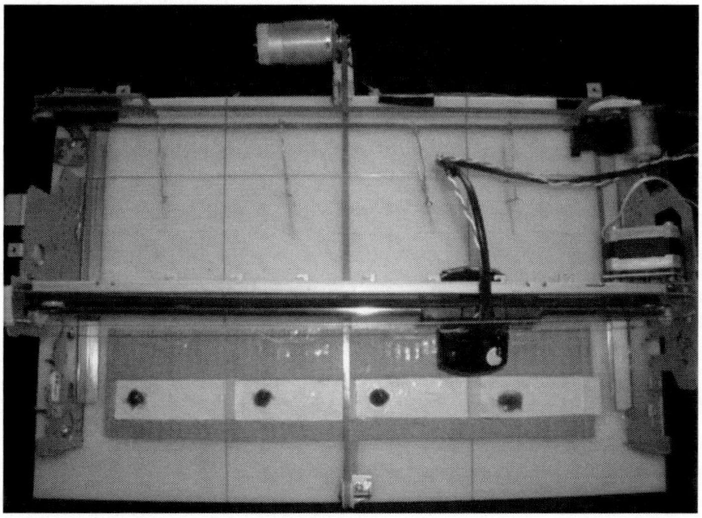

Figure 84. System Developed – first prototype.

Statistical Analysis

This section presents the statistical analysis used to prove that the boundary between the occurrence of agglutination and non-agglutination is reliable.

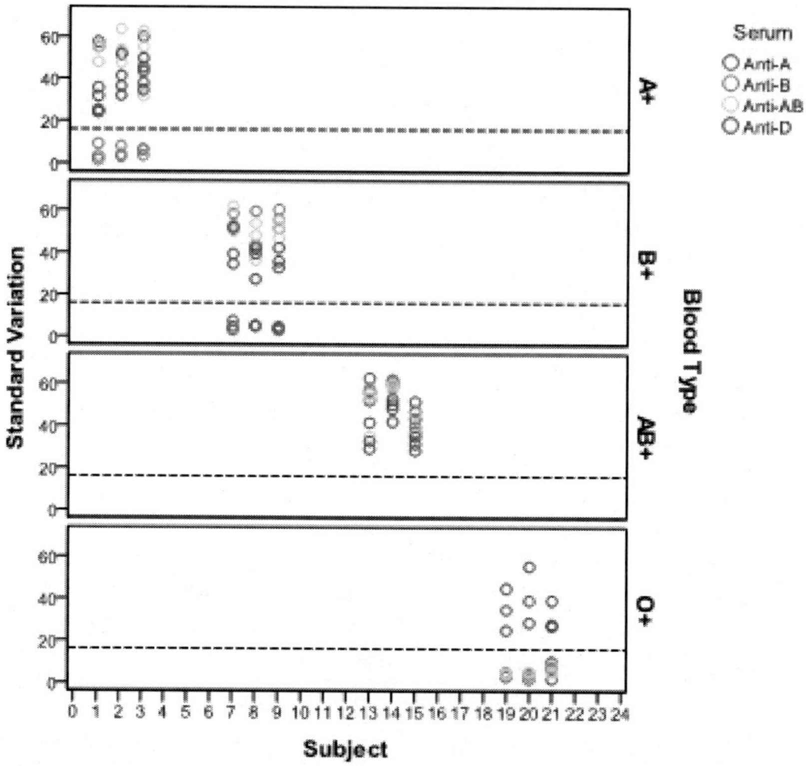

Figure 85. Standard deviation values obtained by the image processing techniques, for all individuals Rh Positive (D Positive).

Namely, there are no values of agglutinated samples below the limit (16) and there are no values upper the limit (16) for samples that are not agglutinated.

This statistical analysis allows determining the reliability of the methodology used as well as the limit set on the basis of the statistical tests.

To this end, tests were performed on determining blood type of 24 individuals, using the software developed in this work. For each individual, the procedure for determining the blood type was repeated three times in order to verify whether the results were similar. There were obtained a total of 288 results for analysis.

It is noteworthy that the blood type of the tested individuals was previously determined by the technique of determining the blood type currently used in laboratories, Cards-ID [23] in order to verify the validity of the technique developed in this work.

The results of statistical analysis were obtained using SPSS software (Version 17.0) [57], being the standard deviation value used to analyze the reliability of the technique. The statistical analysis was based on descriptive data analysis. The study of the variability for each blood type results is shown in Figure 85 and Figure 86.

The study of variability was performed, initially for individuals Rh positive and at a second stage, for individuals Rh Negative. The dashed line represents the limit of standard deviation, 16, set out to determine the occurrence or non-occurrence of agglutination. For all samples, there were no standard deviation values that could lead to wrong decisions. For example, in case of blood type A+ (A Positive), agglutination was not observed for the reagent anti-B in all tests (Figure 85, green).

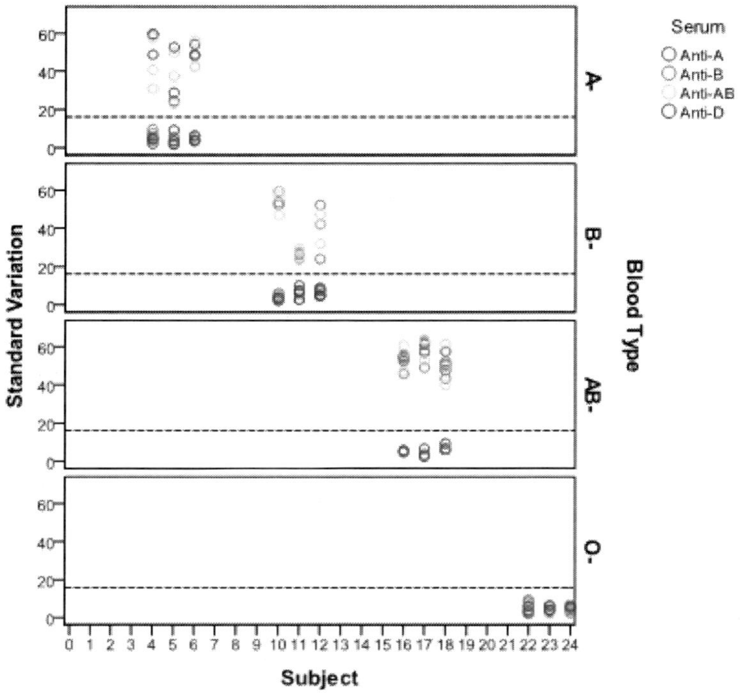

Figure 86. Standard deviation values obtained by the image processing techniques, for all individuals Rh Negative (D Negative).

For this case, all standard deviation values obtained are below the threshold. For the case of blood type O-(O Negative), agglutination does not occur in all reagents and in all tests, all standard deviation values obtained are below 16 (Figure 86). On the other hand, for blood type AB+ (AB Positive), all values are higher than 16 (Figure 85).

For each test the agglutination was detected always getting standard deviation values higher than or equal to 16. The same was true for the absence of agglutination, obtaining values of standard deviation always below 16.

CONCLUSION

Textile Industry Application

Regarding the results obtained for each of the parameterization performed (yarn production characteristics, yarn diameter and imperfections and yarn hairiness determination) it can be concluded that its reliability allows to take into consideration the option of use an image processing system instead of a traditional system based on capacitive and optical sensors. Apart from other benefits, its low cost, portability and reduced maintenance give proper indicators in order to justify its adoption to offline yarn analysis systems. Moreover, and with the prospect of continuing this project, among other developments, it is suggested improving the methods to detect and distinguish between the loop and protruding fibers supported by artificial intelligence algorithms. As for the methodologies developed there is still the possibility to test them in different types of yarns, such as fancy yarns.

Biomedicine Application

The methodology used in this work (previously validated by conventional methods) is capable to determinate blood types safely and in a short time (approximately 2 minutes) allowing it to be used in emergency situations. As demonstrated, the techniques applied are able to detect the agglutination (using a standard deviation value of 16 as threshold), and consequently blood types. The equipment developed is able to determine blood types using the plate test and to automatically perform the analysis, with exception to the introducing of blood and reagents that at this stage of development is performed manually. For future work, it is intended to evolve the system, reducing its size, automate all the processes and incorporate GSM technology, among other features.

REFERENCES

[1] M. Kuzanski and L. Jackowska-Strumillo,Yarn Hairiness Determination – The algorithms of computer measurement methods. MEMSTECH'2007, May 23-26, Lviv-Polyana, Ukraine, p.154-157.

[2] M. Kuzanski, Measurement Methods for Yarn Hairiness Analysis – the idea and construction of research standing. MEMSTECH'2006, May 24-27, Lviv-Polyana, Ukraine, p.87-90.

[3] Shiloh, M., A computer for the evaluation of the crimp diameter of textile fibers. *Textile Research Journal*, 1964, 34(5): p. 430-434.

[4] S. Jaganathan, Characterization Methods and Physical Properties of Novelty Yarn. MSc Thesis, North Carolina State University, Raleigh, 2005.

[5] Anirban Guha, C. Amarenath, S. Pateria and R, Measurement of yarn hairiness by digital image processing. *The journal of the Textile Institute*, Vol. 101, Issue 3, March 2010, pp. 214-222.

[6] http://www.indiantextilejournal.com/articles/FAdetails.asp?id=552 (access in March 2011).

[7] M. Kuzanski, The Algorithms of the Yarn Shape Detection and Calculation of the Protruding Fibres Length. MEMSTECH'2008, May 21-24, Lviv-Polyana, Ukraine, p.98-100.

[8] W. Jian and Y. Li, Evaluation of Yarn Regularity Using Computer Vision. *9th International Conference on Pattern Recognition*, Vol. 2, November 14-17, p.854-856.

[9] V. Carvalho, Automatic Yarn Characterization System. PhD Thesis, Minho University, Braga, 2008.

[10] IMAQ, IMAQ Vision Concepts Manual. *National Instruments*, Austin, 2004.

[11] C. Relf, Image Acquisition and Processing with LabVIEW. CRC, Boca Raton, 2003.

[12] N. Gonçalves, V. Carvalho, F. Soares, Rosa Vasconcelos and Michael Belsley, Yarn mass parameters determination using Image Processing techniques. CMNE 2011, Coimbra, Portugal, 11-17 June.

[13] V. Carvalho , F. Soares, Rosa Vasconcelos, Michael Belsley and N. Gonçalves, Yarn hairiness determination using Image Processing techniques. ETFA 2011, Toulouse, France, 21-27 August 2011.

[14] V. Carvalho, M. Belsley, R. Vasconcelos and F. O. Soares, Determination of Yarn Production Characteristics Using Image Processing. (*International Journal of Imaging Systems and Technology*, Vol. 20, November 2010, pp. 391-399).
[15] N. Gonçalves, Parametrização de Fio Têxtil Baseada em Técnicas de Processamento de Imagem. Msc. Thesis, Minho University, Braga 2010 (in portuguese)
[16] Ferraz, V. Carvalho, F.Soares and C.P. Leão, Characterization of Blood Samples Using Image Processing Techniques. Sensors and Actuators A, published online in 25th, February 2011, doi: 10.1016/j.sna.2011.02.022.
[17] Ferraz , V. Carvalho and P. Brandão, Automatic Determination of Human Blood Types using Image Processing Techniques. BIODEVICES 2010, 20-23 January 2010, Valencia, Spain).
[18] Ferraz, V. Carvalho and F. Soares, Development of Human Blood Type Detection Automatic System. EUROSENSORS 2010, 5-8 September, 2010, Linz, Austria.
[19] Ferraz, V. Moreira, D. Silva, V. Carvalho and F. Soares, Automatic system for blood type classification using image processing techniques. *BIODEVICES* 2011, Rome, Italy, 26-29 January, 2011.
[20] Ferraz V. Moreira, V. Carvalho and F. Soares, Automatic system of human blood types determination. 1° Encontro Nacional de Bioengenharia, Lisbon, Portugal IST, 1-4 March 2011.
[21] M. R. Brown, P. Crim., Organizing the antibody identification process. *Clin. Lab. Sci.*, vol. 20, 2007, pp. 122–126.
[22] A. Myhre and D. McRuer, Human error – a significant cause of transfusion mortality. *Transfusion*, vol. 40, Jul. 2000, pp. 879–885.
[23] Datasheet of Diamed-ID Micro Typing System, Card-ID. Diaclon ABO\Rh for patients. Cressier, 2008.
[24] R. Furter, Evenness Testing in Yarn Production: part I, The Textile Institute and Zellweger Uster AG, Manchester: 1982.
[25] M. Castro and M. Araújo, Manual de Engenharia Têxtil - Vol. II, Gulbenkian, Lisbon, 1986.
[26] Goswami, J. Martindale and F. Scardino, Textile Yarns: Technology, Structure and Applications, 2nd Edition, John Wiley and Sons, New York, 1977.
[27] http://www.bresseroptics.co.uk (access in March 2011).
[28] http://www.hercules.com (access in March 2011).
[29] M. R. Brown and P. Crim. Organizing the antibody identification process. *Clin. Lab. Sci.,* vol. 20, 2007, pp. 122–126.
[30] A. Myhre and D. McRuer, Human error – a significant cause of transfusion mortality. *Transfusion*, vol. 40, Jul. 2000, pp. 879–885.
[31] J. Petaja, S. Andersson and M. Syrjala, A simple automatized audit system for following and managing practices of platelet and plasma transfusions in a neonatal intensive care unit. *Transfus Med.*, vol. 14, 2004, pp. 281–288.
[32] M. Delamaire, Automation of the immunohematology laboratory. *Transfus Clin. Biol.*, vol. 12, 2005, pp. 163–168.
[33] A. Henneman, G. S. Avrunin, L. A. Clarke, L. J. Osterweil, C. Jr. Andrzejewski, K. Merrigan, R. Cobleigh, K. Frederick, E. Katz-Bassett and P. L. Henneman, Increasing patient safety and efficiency in transfusion therapy using formal process definitions. *Transfus Med. Rev.,* vol. 21, 2007, pp. 49–57.

[34] A. Wagar, L. Tamashiro, B. Yasin, L. Hilborne and D. A. Bruckner, Patient safety in the clinical laboratory: a longitudinal analysis of specimen identification errors. *Arch. Pathol. Lab. Med.*, vol. 130, 2006, pp. 1662–1668.

[35] L. Turner, A. C. Casbard and M. F. Murphy, Barcode technology: its role in increasing the safety of blood transfusion. *Transfusion*, vol. 43, 2003, pp. 1200–1209.

[36] J. L. Callum, H. S. Kaplan, L. L. Merkley, P. H. Pinkerton, B. R. Fastman, R. A. Romans, A. S. Coovadia and M. D. Reis, Reporting of near-miss events for transfusion medicine: improving transfusion safety. *Transfusion*, vol. 41, 2001, pp. 1204–1211.

[37] M. M. Mueller and E. Seifried, Blood transfusion in Europe: basic principles for initial and continuous training in transfusion medicine: an approach to an European harmonization. *Transfus Clin. Biol.*, vol. 13, 2006, pp. 282–285.

[38] Stainsby, H. Jones, D. Asher, C. Atterbury, A. Boncinelli, L. Brant, C. E. Chapman, K. Davison, R. Gerrard, A. Gray, S. Knowles, E. M. Love, C. Milkins, D. B. McClelland, D. R. Norfolk, K. Soldan, C. Taylor, J. Revill, L. M. Williamson and H. Cohen. for the SHOT Steering Group, Serious hazards of transfusion: a decade of hemovigilance in the UK. *Transfus Med. Rev.*, vol. 20, 2006, pp. 273–282.

[39] "Blood Policy and technology", Congress, Office of Technology Assessment, Washington, DC: U.S. January 1985. Available: FAS http://www.fas.org/ota/reports/8505.pdf.

[40] P. Sturgeon, Automation: its introduction to the field of blood group serology. *Immunohematology Journal of Blood Group Serology and Education*, vol. 17, no. 4, 2001.

[41] W. A. Coakly, Handbook of Automated Analysis. Mercel Dekker, 1981 pp. 61.

[42] W. Ewing, Analytical Instrumentation Handbook. 2nd ed., Ed. New York: Marcel Dekker, pp.152.

[43] AutoAnalyzerhttp://weather.nmsu.edu/Teaching_Material/soil698/Student_Material/Autoanalyzer/Autodiag.html (accessed in July 2010).

[44] M. Garretta, J. Gener, A. Muller, C. Matte and J. Moullec, The Groupamatic System for Routine Immunohematology. Transfusion, vol. 15, Sep.-Oct. 1975, pp. 422-431.

[45] Zaccarelli, G. Monti, J. Malaguti, D. Marchesini, F. Figliola, G. Cagliari, C. basile and P. Zucchelli, Esperienza di automazione nella determinazione dei gruppi sanguigni. La Transfusione del Sangue, vol. 45, no. 1, gennaio – febbraio 2000.

[46] Olympus http://www.olympus-global.com/en/magazine/techzone/vol67_ e/page5.cfm (accessed in July 2010).

[47] Fuji http://www.mastgrp.com/Fuji/IFU/TPPAauto.pdf (accessed in July 2010).

[48] Olympus, Formulated for use in Automated System Olympus® PK® Systems, December 2007.

[49] Immucorhttp://immucor.com/site/aum_company_profile.jsp (accessed in July 2010).

[50] Wittmann, J. Frank, W. Schram and M. Spannagl., Automation and Data Processing with the Immucor Galileo® System in a University Blood Bank. *Transfusion Medicine Hemotherapy*. vol. 34, pp. 347-352. Available: Kargerwww.karger.com/tmh (2007).

[51] Briefingresearchhttp://www.briefingresearch.com/GeneralContent/Investor/Active/ArticlePopup/ArticlePopup.aspx?SiteName=InvestorPopUpandArticleId=NS20070619155112AheadOfTheCurve (accessed in July 2010).

[52] Stanford http://securities.stanford.edu/1035/BLUD05_01/200622_r01c_0502276.pdf (accessed in July 2010).

[53] Biologichttp://www.fda.gov/downloads/BiologicsBloodVaccines/BloodBloodProducts/ApprovedProducts/LicensedProductsBLAs/BloodDonorScreening/BloodGroupingReagent/ucm080763.pdf (accessed in July 2010).

[54] Dada, D. Beck and G. Schmitz., Automation and Data Processing in Blood Banking Using the Ortho AutoVue® Innova System. *Transfusion Medicine Hemotherapy*, vol. 34, pp. 341–346. Available: Kargerwww.karger.com/tmh, (2007).

[55] S. Y. Shin, K. C. Kwon, S. H. koo, J. W. Park, C. S. Ko, J. H. Song, and J. Y. Sung, Evaluation of two automated instruments for pre-transfusion testing: AutoVueInnova and Techno TwinStation, *Korean J. Lab. Med.*, vol. 3, Jun. 2008, pp. 214-220.

[56] Dada, D. Beck and G. Schmitz. (2007), Automation and Data Processing in Blood Banking Using the Ortho AutoVue® Innova System. Transfusion Medicine Hemotherapy, vol. 34, pp. 341–346. Available: Kargerwww.karger.com/tmh.

[57] SPSS 17.0, SPSS http://www.spss.com/ (accessed in July 2010).

In: Image Processing
Editor: Vítor Hugo Carvalho
ISBN 978-1-62081-844-2

Chapter 2

FACIAL EXPRESSION RECOGNITION USING THERMAL IMAGE PROCESSING

Yasunari Yoshitomi*[*]*, Masayoshi Tabuse and Taro Asada
Division of Environmental Sciences, Graduate School of Life and Environmental Sciences, Kyoto Prefectural University, Shimogamo, Sakyo-ku, Kyoto, Japan

ABSTRACT

The goal of our research is to develop a robot that can perceive human feelings or mental states. The present investigation concerns the first stage of development wherein a robot acquires vision and the ability to detect human feeling or mental states. Although the mechanism for recognizing facial expressions of human feelings has received considerable attention in computer vision research, it currently falls far short of human capability. This is due to the decreased accuracy of facial expression recognition, which is influenced by the inevitable change of gray levels due to nuances of shade, reflection, and local darkness. To avoid this problem and to develop a robust method for facial expression recognition applicable under widely varied lighting conditions, we use an image registered by infrared rays (IR) to describe the thermal distribution of the face. Although a human cannot detect IR, it is possible for a robot to process the information around it using thermal images created by IR.

The timing of recognizing facial expressions is also important for a robot because the processing can be time-consuming. We adopted an utterance as the key of expressing human feelings because humans tend to say something when expressing their feelings.

In this chapter, we introduce our method for facial expression recognition of a speaker. For facial expression recognition, we pick three images: (i) just before speaking, in speaking (ii) the first and (iii) the last vowels of an utterance. The face direction is estimated to select front-view faces as the targets of facial expression recognition using thermal image processing. A two-dimensional discrete cosine transformation is performed for transforming grayscale values on each block in focused face parts of an image into their frequency components, which are used for generating feature vectors. We use pattern recognition through our heuristic rules for facial expression recognition.

[*] E-mail address: yoshitomi@kpu.ac.jp

In this method, the facial expressions are discriminable with good recognition accuracy when a person exhibits one of the intentional facial expressions of "angry", "happy", "neutral", "sad", and "surprise".

INTRODUCTION

To better integrate robots into our society, a robot should be able to interact in a friendly manner with humans. The goal of our research is to develop a robot that can perceive human feelings and mental states. For example, a robot could encourage a human who looks sad, advise a person to stop working and rest for a while when he or she looks tired, or take care of an elderly person.

The present investigation concerns the first stage of development of a robot that has the ability to detect human feeling or inner mental states visually. Although the mechanism for recognizing facial expressions has received considerable attention in the field of computer vision research [1]–[6], its present stage still falls far short of human capability, especially from the viewpoint of robustness under widely varying lighting conditions. One of the reasons is that nuances of shade, reflection, and local darkness influence the accuracy of facial expression recognition through the inevitable change of gray levels.

To develop a robust method for accurate facial expression recognition applicable under widely varied lighting conditions, we do not use a visible ray (VR) image. Instead, we use an image produced by infrared rays (IR) to describe the thermal distribution of the face [7]–[17]. Although a human cannot detect IR, it is possible for a robot to process the information around it using the thermal images created by IR. Therefore, as a new mode of robot vision, thermal image processing is a practical method that is viable under natural conditions.

The timing of recognizing facial expressions is also important for a robot because the processing can be time-consuming. We adopted an utterance as the key to expressing human feelings or mental states because humans tend to say something when expressing their feelings [11]–[17].

In this chapter, we introduce our method for the facial expression recognition of a speaker. For facial expression recognition, we select three images: (i) just before speaking; speaking (ii) the first and (iii) the last vowels in an utterance. A frame of the front-view face in a dynamic image is selected by estimating the face direction [16]. A two-dimensional discrete cosine transformation (2D-DCT) is performed to transform the grayscale values of each block in the face portion of an image into their frequency components, which are used to generate feature vectors. With our method, facial expressions are discriminable with good recognition accuracy when a person exhibits one of the intentional facial expressions of "angry", "happy", "neutral", "sad", and "surprised".

IMAGE ACQUISITION

The principle behind thermal image generation is the Stefan-Boltzmann law, which is expressed as $W = \varepsilon\sigma T^4$, where ε is emissivity, σ is the Stefan-Boltzmann constant ($=5.6705 \times 10^{-12}$ W/cm^{2}K^4), and T is the temperature (K). For human skin, ε is estimated as 0.98 to 0.99 [18], [19]. In this study, however, the approximate value of 1 was used as ε for human skin. Since the value of ε for almost all substances is lower than that for human skin [18], the human face region is easily extracted from an image using the value of 1 for ε when a range of skin temperatures is selected to produce a thermal image [7]–[17], [20]. Figure 1 shows examples of male face images obtained using VR and IR. We can obtain a thermal image expressing the face without light, even at night. In principle, the temperature measurement by IR does not depend on skin color [19], darkness, or lighting condition, and so the face region and its characteristics are easily extracted from a thermal image.

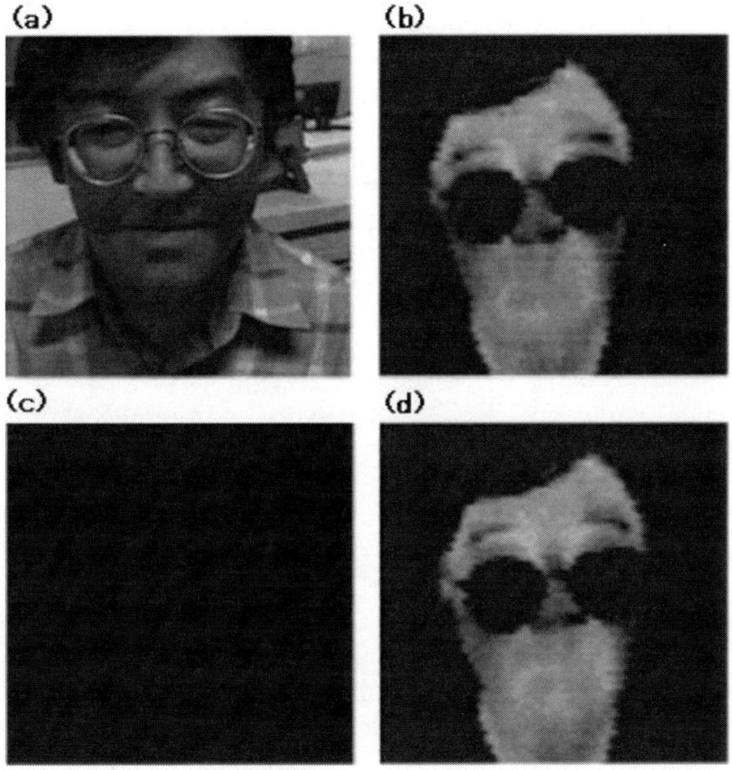

Figure 1. Examples of a face image at night: (a) VR with lighting, (b) IR with lighting, (c) VR without lighting, (d) IR without lighting [9].

PROPOSED METHOD

In this study, as a pre-processing module, we add a judgment function [20] of a front-view face to our reported method [14] for facial expression recognition [16].

Figure 2 illustrates the flow chart of our method. We have two modules in our system. The first is a module for speech recognition and dynamic image analysis, and the second is a module for learning and recognition. We embed the module for front-view face judgment in the module for learning and recognition. The procedure including the proposed pre-processing module for front-view face judgment [16] is explained in the following.

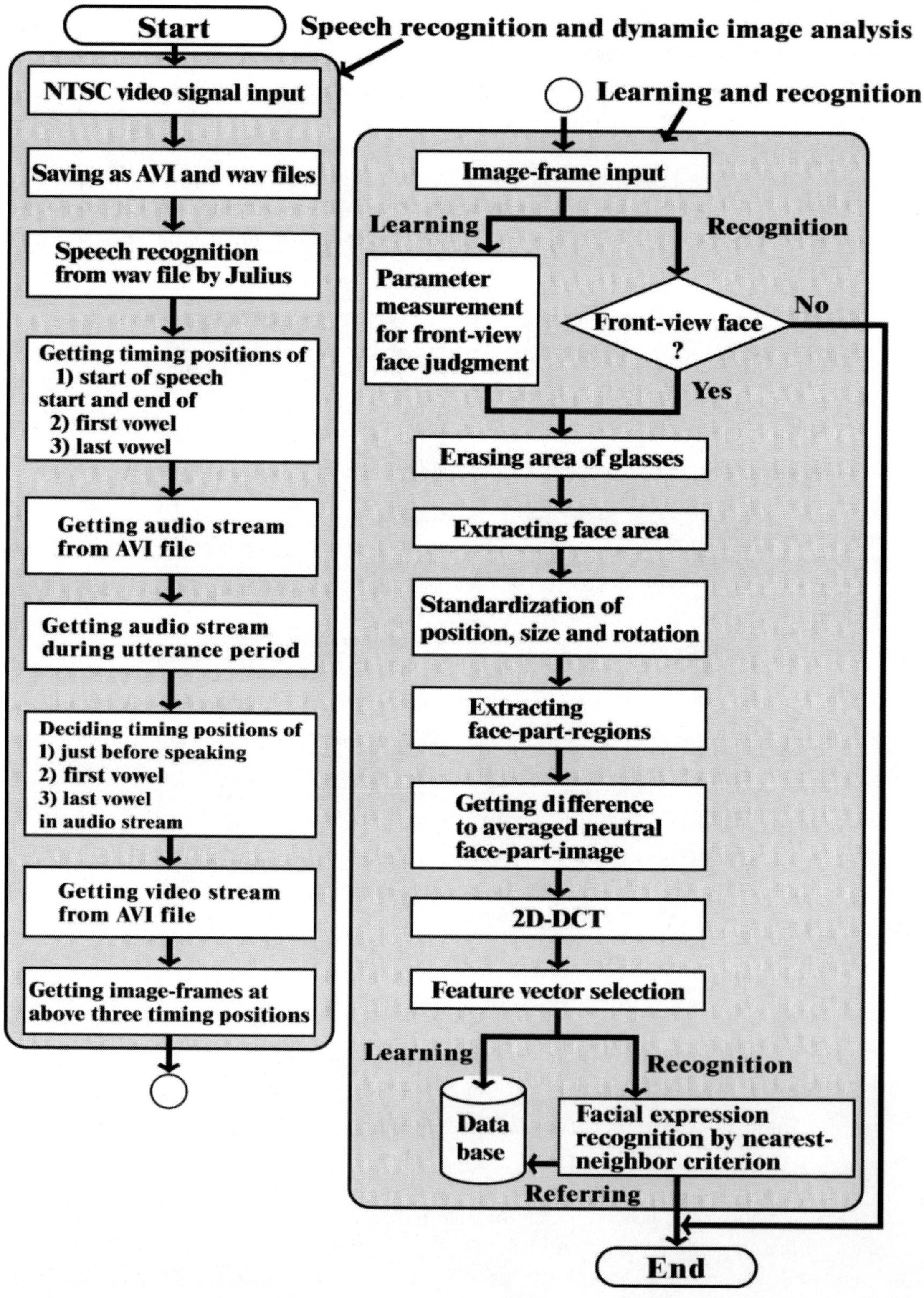

Figure 2. Flow chart of our method [16].

Front-view Face Judgment

We first define the face rotation around the *X*, *Y*, and *Z* axes, as demonstrated in Figure 3. The training data is calculated from the images of a front-view face. After normalizing the horizontal Feret's diameter of the segmented face image, the centerline of the face region is drawn as the first standard line. Each pixel point in the centerline has the same number of pixels on both the left and the right sides of the point. Then, a straight line as the second standard line is drawn from the upper to the lower edge points of the centerline. The two standard lines are used to estimate the deviation from the front-view face. To evaluate the face direction, we use four feature parameters (*nod*, *up*, *rotate*, *lean*), explained below.

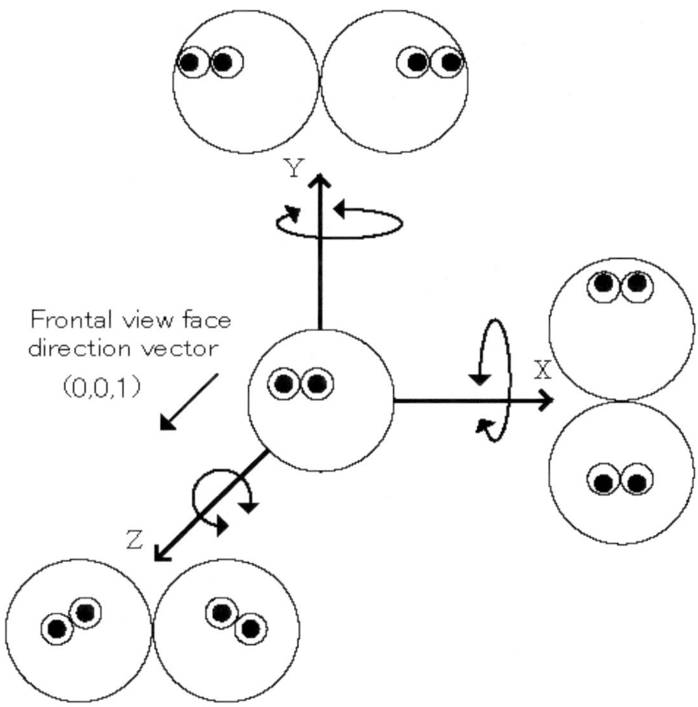

Figure 3. The three-dimensional coordinate system [16].

Parameter Nod

The feature parameter *nod* is obtained from the value of the vertical Feret's diameter divided by the value of the horizontal Feret's diameter on the segmented face image. This parameter is used to evaluate the downward rotation around the X axis (Figure 4).

Here, to reduce the influence of the hair style and the throat region on the segmented face image as much as possible, the area having horizontal pixels less than an experimentally decided threshold is ignored in the measurement of the vertical Feret's diameter on the segmented face image, and the area having vertical pixels less than another experimentally decided threshold is also ignored in the measurement of the horizontal Feret's diameter on the segmented face image (Figure 4). When a subject looks downward, the feature parameter *nod* tends to be smaller than that of the front-view face of the subject.

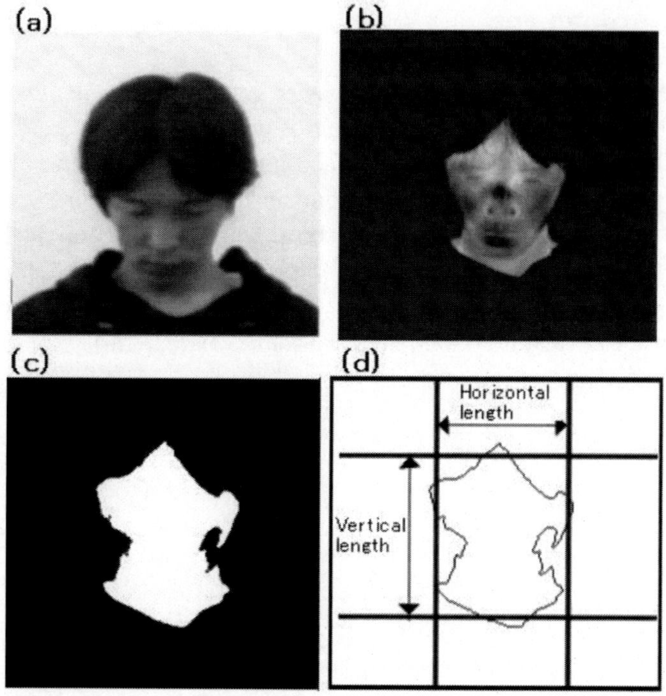

Figure 4. Downward rotation: (a) visible image, (b) thermal image, (c) binary image, (d) schematic diagram for the parameter *nod* [16].

Parameter up

The feature parameter *up* is the area ratio of the region having a gray level of "0" in the rectangle defined by the straight lines determined by the measurements of the horizontal and vertical Feret's diameters to the rectangular area on the segmented face image. This parameter is used to evaluate the upward rotation around the X axis (Figure 5).

When a subject looks upward, the feature parameter *up* tends to be smaller than that of the front-view face of the subject.

Parameter Rotate

The feature parameter *rotate* is the area of the region surrounded by the first and the second standard lines, which are explained in the first paragraph in sub-section entitled "Front-view Face Judgment". This parameter is used to evaluate the rotation around the Y axis (Figure 6).

Here, to reduce the influence of the hair style and the throat region on the segmented face image as much as possible, the top and bottom of both the first and second standard lines are set inside the face region by each constant pixel, which is also decided experimentally (Figure 6).

The feature parameter *rotate* tends to increase when the rotation from the front-view face around the Y axis increases.

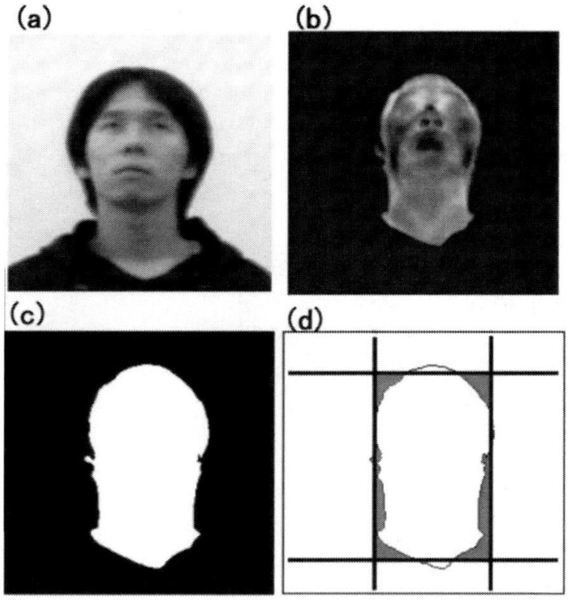

Figure 5. Upward rotation: (a) visible image, (b) thermal image, (c) binary image, (d) schematic diagram for the parameter *up* [21].

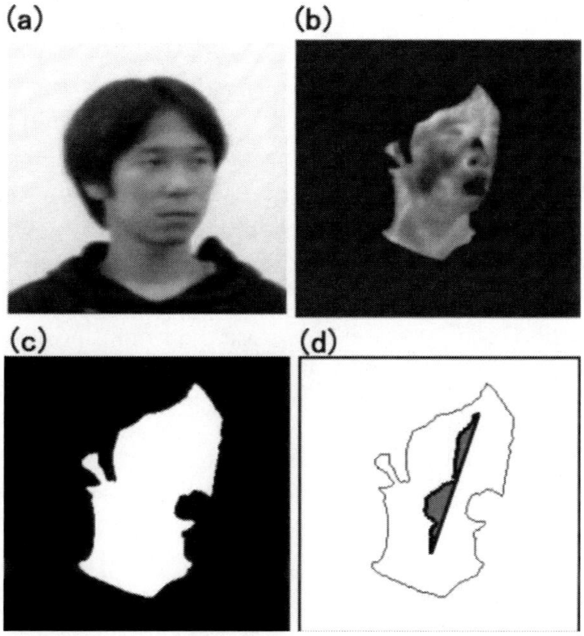

Figure 6. Face rotation around the *Y* axis: (a) visible image, (b) thermal image, (c) binary image, (d) schematic diagram for the parameter *rotate* [21].

Parameter Lean

The feature parameter *lean*, which is the angle between the second standard straight line and the horizontal line, is used to estimate the rotation around the Z axis (Figure 7). The value of *lean* is never greater than 90 degrees. The rotation is estimated to be small when the deviation of the value of *lean* from 90 degrees is small.

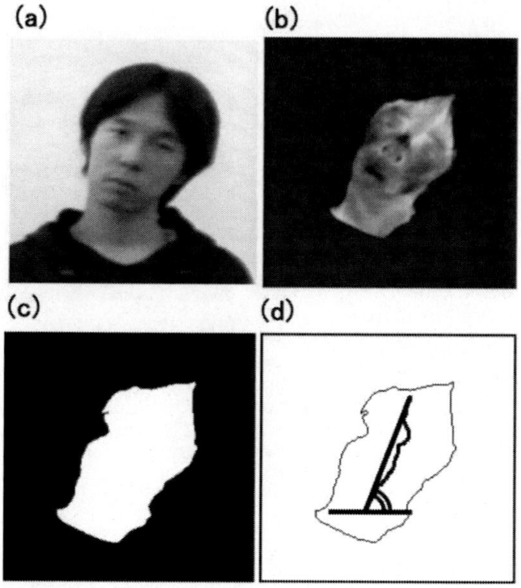

Figure 7. Face rotation around the Z axis: (a) visible image, (b) thermal image, (c) binary image, (d) schematic diagram for the parameter *lean* [21].

Speech Recognition and Dynamic Image Analysis

We use a speech recognition system named Julius [22] to obtain the timing positions at the start of speech, and the first and the last vowels in a WAV file [14]. Figure 8 shows an example of the waveform of the Japanese name "Taro"; the timing position at the start of speech and the timing ranges of the first vowel (/a/) and the last vowel (/o/) are decided by Julius. Using the timing position of the start of speech and the timing ranges of the first and last vowels obtained from the WAV file, three image frames are extracted from an AVI file. For the timing position just before speaking, we use the timing position of 84 ms before the start of speech, as determined in our previously reported study [13].

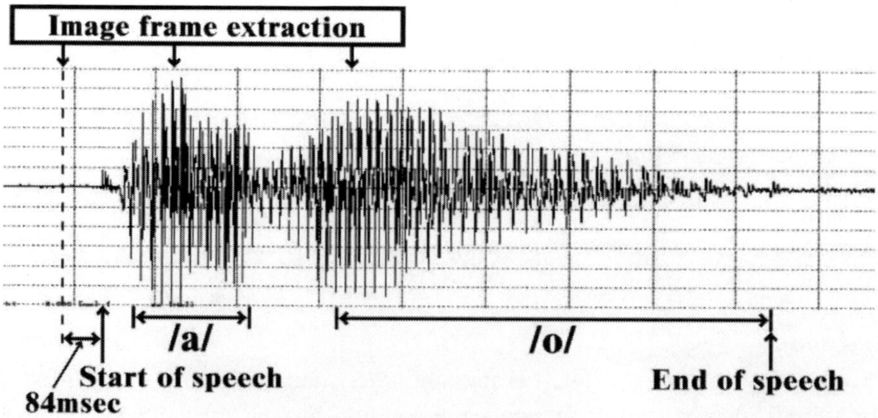

Figure 8. Speech waveform of "Taro" and timing positions for image frame extraction [14].

For the timing position of the first vowel, we use the position where the absolute value of the amplitude of the waveform is the maximum while speaking the vowel.

For the timing position of the last vowel, we apply the same procedure used for the first vowel.

Learning and Recognition

For the static images obtained from the extracted image frames, the process of erasing the area of the glasses, extracting the face area, and standardizing the position, size, and rotation of the face are performed according to the method described in our previously reported studies [12], [13].

The important parts of the process are as follows.

Face-Part Extraction from Thermal Face Image

A. Extraction of Skin Region

For extracting the skin region in an original thermal image (Figure 9 (a)), a maximum-selection filter for pixel size 5×5 is applied to reduce the influence of hair on facial expression recognition to the utmost, followed by segmentation to obtain a binary image (Figure 9 (b)).

Because some subjects wear glasses that have a corresponding gray level of "0" after the segmentation, the gray levels of pixels corresponding to glasses are changed to "1" by our proposed method to make the facial expression recognition as precise as possible [13].

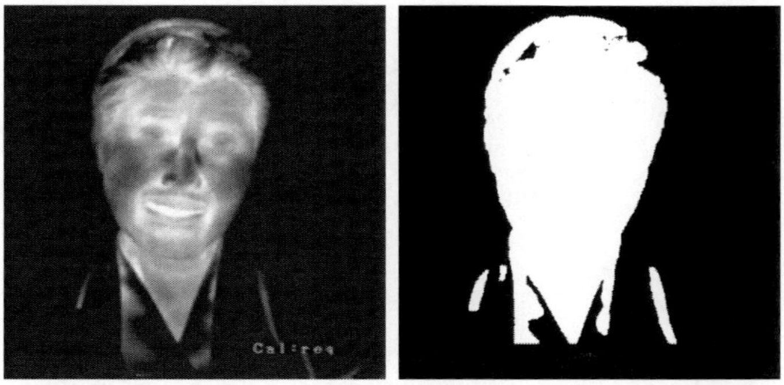

(a) (b)

Figure 9. (a) The input image of the skin region, and (b) the binary image extracted by segmentation [12].

B. Erasing Small Isolated Areas and Extraction of Potential Face Region

After erasing small isolated areas on potential skin regions, the horizontal Feret's diameter is measured for the potential face region. To diminish the influence of hair and neck regions on the position of the center of gravity of the face region, areas from the top and bottom of the potential face region to areas having c times the width to the horizontal Feret's diameter are deleted line by line in the vertical direction, resulting in a potential face region and its face image (Figure 10).

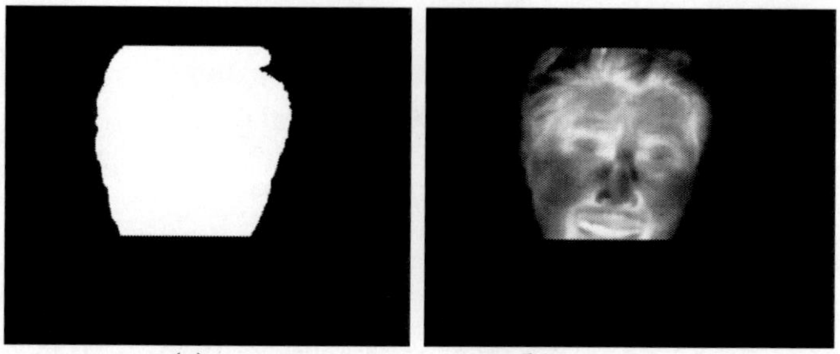

(a) (b)

Figure 10. (a) The face region, and (b) the face after deleting the hair and neck regions [12].

Based on the images for the training data, the value of c is experimentally decided and its typical value is 2/3.

C. Standardization of Rotation, Location, and Size on Potential Face Region

The rotation of the face influences the accuracy of facial expression recognition. Accordingly, the face rotation is standardized using the potential face region as follows.

As shown in Figure 11 (a), each pixel having the same number of pixels on the left and right sides from its position on the horizontal line is selected, and then measurement of angle θ of the lean of the selected pixels is given by the linear regression model (Figure 11 (b)).

When the angle θ is 90 degrees, the face is judged as having a standard lean.

Then, the deviation from 90 degrees is used as the rotation angle for standardizing the lean of the face on both the face region and the input image. Using the horizontal Feret's diameter and the coordinate of the center of gravity of the face region after standardizing the lean of the face region, the input image is moved to the standard position, followed by transferring the size of the face to the standard front-view face (Figure 12).

In our method, template matching with the Sequential Similarity Detection Algorithm and a one-dimensional template $a[j]$, where j denotes a coordinate of the vertical direction, are used for more accurate standardization of the position of the face on an image.

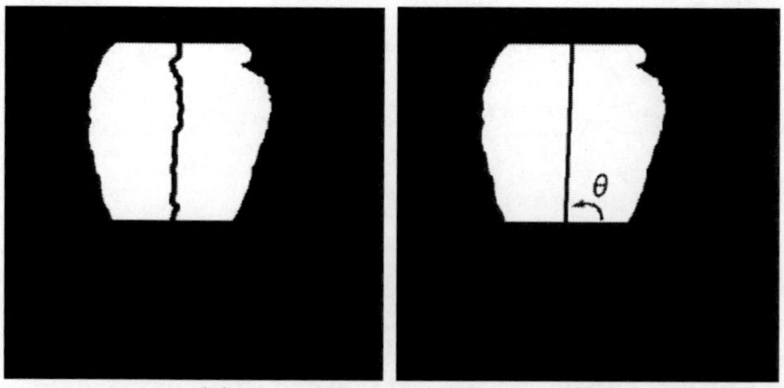

(a) (b)

Figure 11. (a) The middle point coordinates in the horizontal direction, and (b) the calculation of angle θ from the linear regression model [12].

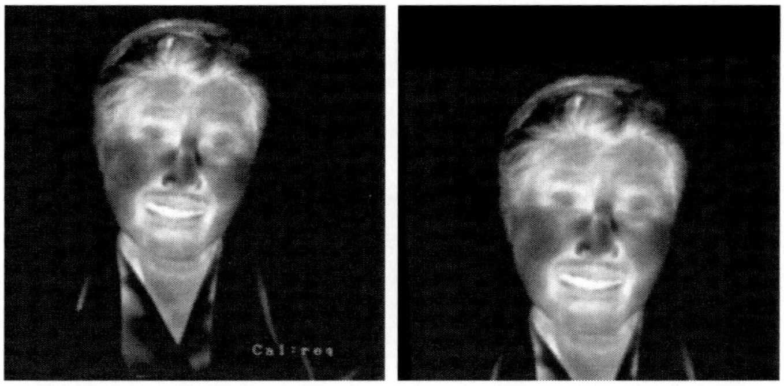

(a) (b)

Figure 12. (a) The input image, and (b) the image after compensation of size, position and rotation [12].

The residual error $s[k]$ defined by eq. (1) is calculated with a shift value $k\,(0 \le k \le 50)$ in pixel units.

$$s[k] = \sum_j (s[j][k] - a[j])^2, \qquad (1)$$

where j denotes a coordinate of the vertical direction, and $s[j][k]$ denotes the sum of the gray levels at each pixel in the horizontal direction of the object image shifted in the vertical direction by k. The optimum shift value is decided by eq. (2).

$$k_m = \arg\min_k s[k] \qquad (2)$$

The image is transformed by k_m in the vertical direction. In order to make the three one-dimensional templates, we use three averaged images expressing the facial expressions of "neutral" at (i) just before speaking, and speaking (ii) the first vowel and (iii) the last vowel in an utterance. Figure 13 shows an image after shifting by k_m in the vertical direction.

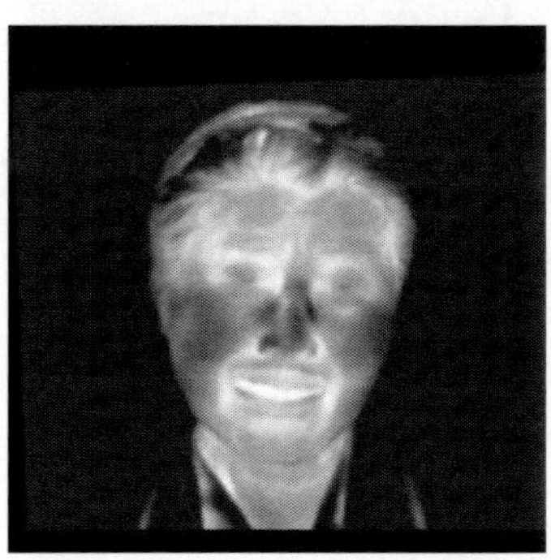

Figure 13. Thermal image after compensation in the vertical direction with template matching [12].

D. Extraction of Face-Part Region

The face region is extracted from the thermal image obtained by pre-processing (described up to the sub-section entitled "Standardization of Rotation, Location, and Size on Potential Face Region" in the section entitled "Proposed Method"). According to a psychological investigation on facial expression analysis [23] and our research on facial expression recognition using thermal image processing [11], six face-part areas for facial expression recognition, as shown in Figure 14 (a), were experimentally decided using the thermal face image obtained by the pre-processing (described up to the sub-section entitled "Standardization of Rotation, Location, and Size on Potential Face Region" in the section entitled "Proposed Method").

The thermal face image was captured for generating the training data just before speaking. Figure 14 (b) shows the extracted image of the face-part areas.

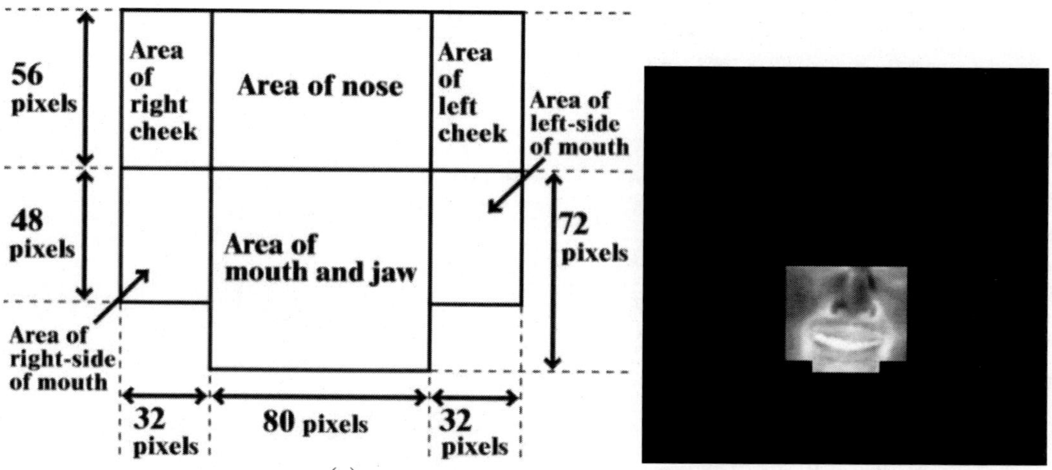

(a) (b)

Figure 14. (a) Blocks for extracting face-part areas, and (b) thermal image after face-part extraction [12].

Measurement of Feature Parameters for Facial Expression

A. Preparation for Making the Feature Vector

For detecting a change of facial expression, we generate difference images between the averaged neutral face image and the target face image in the extracted face areas, followed by a 2D-DCT performed for each domain having 8×8 pixels. The high-frequency components in the 2D-DCT coefficients tend to express a minute change in the data, resulting in the presence of noise.

Therefore, we select 15 low-frequency components in the 2D-DCT coefficients, except for a direct current component, as feature parameters for expressing facial expression (Figure 15).

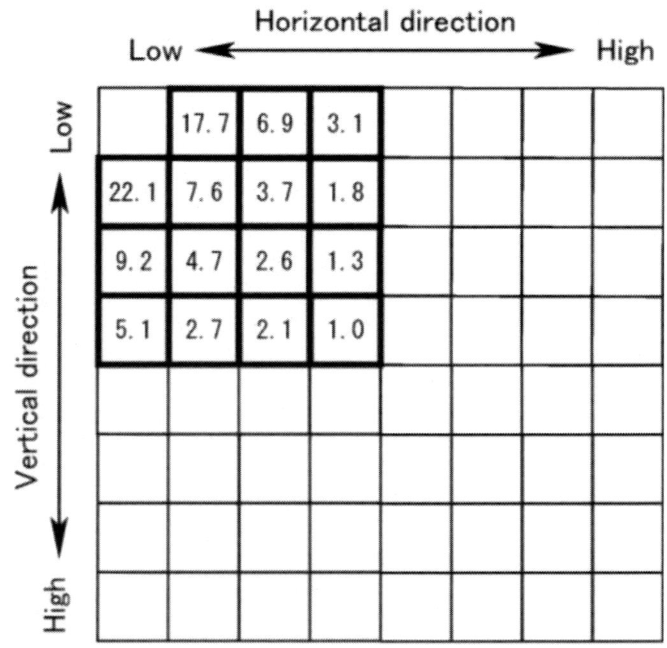

Figure 15. Special frequency bands used for the analysis.

B. Facial Expression Recognition Using the Feature Vector

The feature vector is generated from the 2D-DCT coefficients according to a heuristic rule. In this sub-section, the process for making the feature vector is explained step by step.

As described in the sub-section entitled "Preparation for Making the Feature Vector", we obtain 15 feature parameters for each block having 8×8 pixels. The number of blocks is not equal for all face-parts, as can be seen in Figure 14 (a). Each face-part area of the left and right cheeks has 28 blocks, and each face-part area of the left and right sides of the mouth has 24 blocks, the face-part area of the nose has 70 blocks, and the face-part area of the mouth and jaw has 90 blocks.

Because we do not know the combination of the place in a face and the frequency component in 2D-DCT coefficients to successfully recognize a facial expression, we adopt the strategy described below.

To gather useful information from the difference images between the averaged neutral face image and the target face image in the extracted face areas, we attain the absolute value of 2D-DCT coefficients obtained by the method described in the sub-section entitled "Preparation for Making the Feature Vector", then we obtain the mean of the absolute value for each 2D-DCT coefficient component in each face-part area (Figure 16). The number of 2D-DCT coefficient components is 15, as described in the sub-section entitled "Preparation for Making the Feature Vector", and the number of face parts is 6. Therefore, we obtain 90 values, each of which is hereinafter referred to as the DCT Feature Parameter, as candidates for the elements of the feature vector.

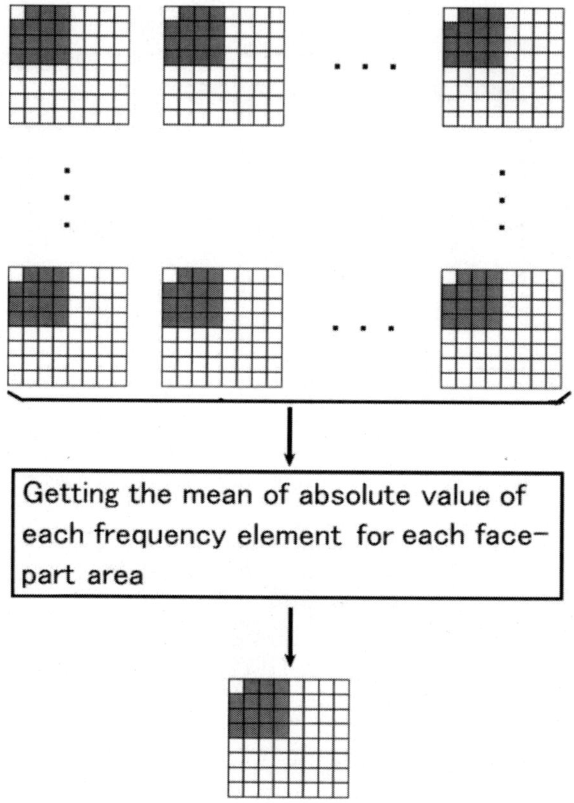

Figure 16. Schematic diagram of the DCT Feature Parameter calculation in the face-part area.

Next, we select several elements of the feature vector from the 90 DCT Feature Parameters obtained with the training data using the heuristic rules [12], [13] described below.

***Rule 1*:**

For each DCT Feature Parameter, each value corresponding to a facial expression class is set on a number line. Each average for a pair of facial expression classes is obtained as a half value of the sum of two means for the facial expression classes, which are bounded on the line. The line is divided into n_c regions by the $(n_c - 1)$ averages obtained for the $(n_c - 1)$ pairs of facial expression classes, where n_c expresses the number of classes for facial expressions. Each region hereinafter is referred to as a Divided Region.

***Rule 2*:**

For each DCT Feature Parameter, all data obtained for all facial expression classes are put on the number line.

***Rule 3*:**

For each facial expression class of each DCT Feature Parameter, the Divided Region, for which the frequency of the data put on the number line has the maximum value among that of all Divided Regions, is searched.

***Rule 4*:**

Only the DCT Feature Parameters, for which the Divided Region obtained for the facial expression of "neutral" by Rule 3 corresponds to the region having the smallest value of DCT Feature Parameters among all regions, survive.

***Rule 5*:**

Among the DCT Feature Parameters selected by Rule 4, only those having two or more facial expression classes with a maximum frequency of P% or over in their corresponding Divided Regions survive.

***Rule 6*:**

Among the DCT Feature Parameters nominated by Rule 5, when three or more kinds of Divided Regions, for which the frequency of the data for the facial expression class has the maximum value among all Divided Regions, are obtained for n_c facial expression classes, the DCT Feature Parameters are decided as elements of the feature vector.

Rule 4 is adopted because the DCT Feature Parameters are calculated from the difference images between the averaged neutral face image and the target face image. In Rule 5, P is experimentally decided.

We created the above rules by trial and error of several training data. We explain an example using Figures 17 and 18, assuming that the number of facial expression classes involves "angry," "happy," "neutral," "sad," and "surprised." The mean of the feature parameter obtained for the facial expression of "neutral" is the smallest value among those of the five facial expression classes (Figure 17). Therefore, this feature parameter satisfies Rule 4. In addition, when assuming $P = 70$ in Rule 5, two classes of facial expressions have frequencies above 70% (Figure 18). Therefore, this feature parameter also satisfies Rule 5. In the case of this feature parameter, five kinds of facial expression classes have the highest frequencies on four kinds of Divided Regions. Therefore, this feature parameter also satisfies Rule 6. Finally, because this feature parameter obtained for a face-part area and a frequency component satisfied all of the rules described above, it is adopted as a component of the feature vector.

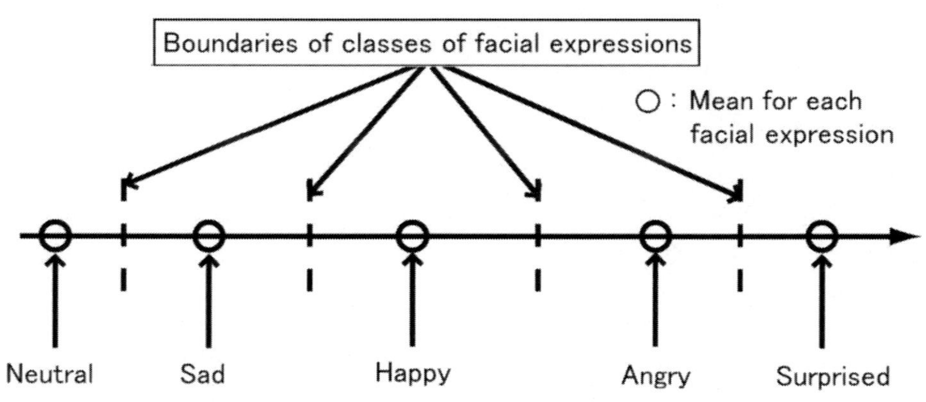

Figure 17. Number line having domains distributed for each class.

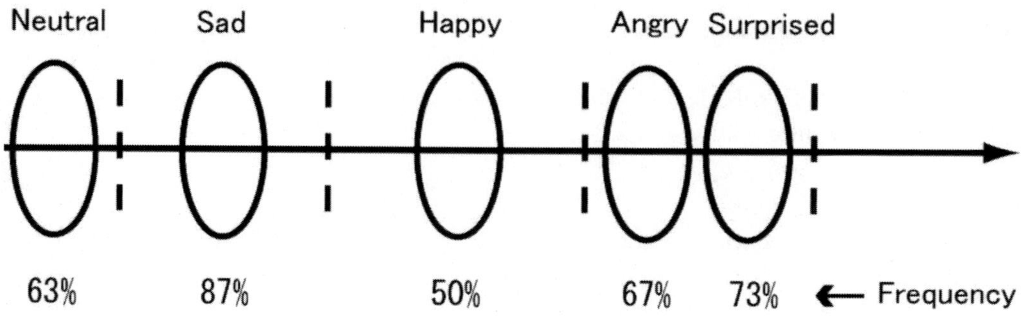

Figure 18. Distribution of domains having the highest frequency for each class on the number line.

The facial expression of the test image is recognized by the nearest-neighbor criterion in the feature vector space obtained with principal component analysis for the training data just before speaking and just speaking the phonemes of the first and the last vowels.

EXPERIMENTS

Conditions

Experiment 1

The thermal image produced by the thermal video system (Nippon Avionics TVS-700) and the sound captured from an Electret condenser microphone (Sony ECM-23F5), amplified by a mixer (Audio-Technica AT-PMX5P), were transformed into a digital signal by an A/D converter (Thomson Canopus ADVC-300) and input into a computer (Dell Optiplex 760, CPU: Intel Core 2 Duo E7400 2.80 GHz, main memory: 2.0 GB, and OS: Windows XP (Microsoft)) with an IEEE1394 interface board (I·O Data Device 1394-PCI3/DV6). We used Visual C++ 6.0 (Microsoft) as the programming language. To generate a thermal image, we applied the condition that the thermal image had 256 gray levels for the range 5 to 12.9 K. Accordingly, one gray level corresponded to 1.95×10^{-2} to 5.04×10^{-2} K. The temperature range for generating a thermal image was decided for each subject in order to easily extract the face area on the image. We saved the visual and audio information in the computer as a Type 2 DV-AVI file, in which a frame had a spatial resolution of 720×480 pixels and 8-bit gray levels, and the sound was saved in a stereo PCM format of 48 kHz and 16-bit levels.

Six subjects exhibited in alphabetic order each of the intentional facial expressions of "angry," "happy," "neutral," "sad," and "surprised," while speaking the semantically neutral utterance "Taro". Figure 19 shows examples of the thermal image of each subject. Subjects A and B were males with glasses. Subjects C and D were females without glasses. Subject E was a male without glasses. Subject F was a male with a cap. Figure 20 shows examples of images of Subject A.

In the experiment, all subjects kept intentionally front-view faces in the AVI files saved as the training data, and they freely changed their face direction in the AVI files saved as the test data.

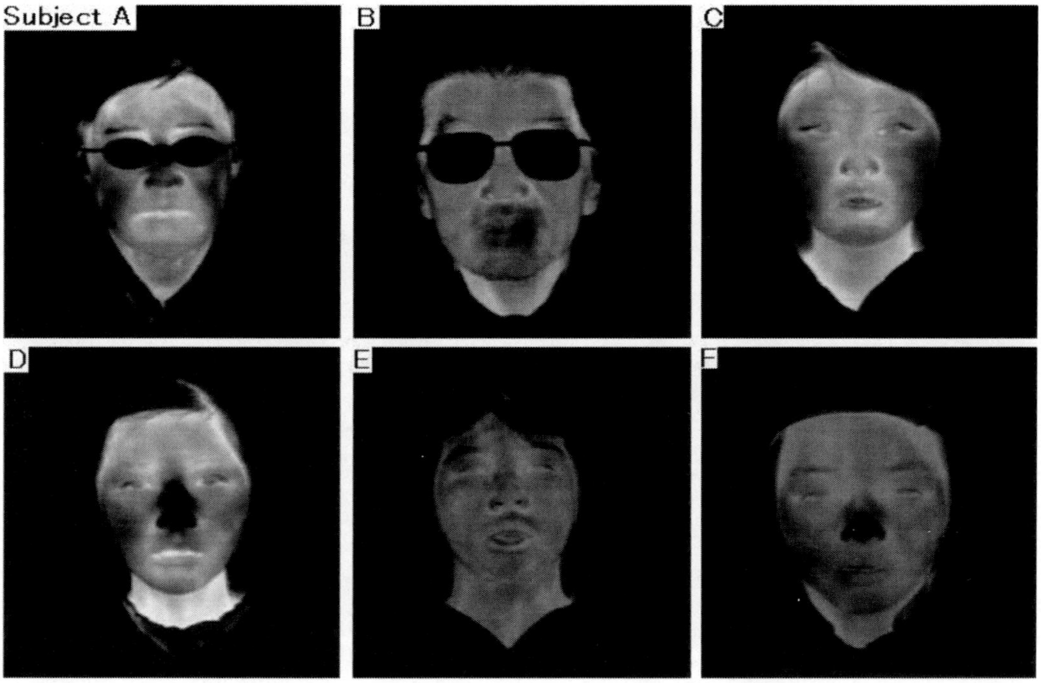

Figure 19. Examples of thermal images having a neutral facial expression just before speaking [16].

We obtained the feature parameter ranges for judging the front-view face using the training data and the proposed method mentioned in the sub-section entitled "Front-view Face Judgment". The range was calculated as $a_i - \sigma_i < x_i < a_i + \sigma_i$ for the *nod*, *up*, and *rotate* parameters of Subject A, and $a_i - 2\sigma_i < x_i < a_i + 2\sigma_i$ for the *lean* parameter of Subject A and all feature parameters of other subjects, where x_1, x_2, x_3, x_4 were *nod*, *up*, *rotate*, and *lean*, and a_1, a_2, a_3, a_4 were their mean values and $\sigma_1, \sigma_2, \sigma_3, \sigma_4$ were their standard deviation values, respectively.

In the case of Subject A, the difference of *nod*, *up*, and *rotate* between the front-view and the non-front-view faces was relatively small, and so the feature parameter ranges for judging the front-view face were set to be narrower than those of the other subjects.

We assembled twenty samples as training data and ten or less samples as test data, in which all facial expressions of all subjects were judged as front-view faces by the proposed method.

The number of samples of test data was decided as a result of the front-view face judgment. From one sample, we obtained three images at the timing positions of just before speaking and just speaking the phonemes of the first and the last vowels. We had the training data of only /a/ for the first vowel and only /o/ for the last vowel.

If Julius misrecognized the vowel of the test sample, the corresponding image was not used for facial expression recognition.

We had four cases of misrecognition for vowel(s); (1) no misrecognition for the first and the last vowels, (2) misrecognition only for the first vowel, (3) misrecognition only for the last vowel, (4) misrecognition for both the first and the last vowels. We prepared feature vectors of the training data for each of the four cases.

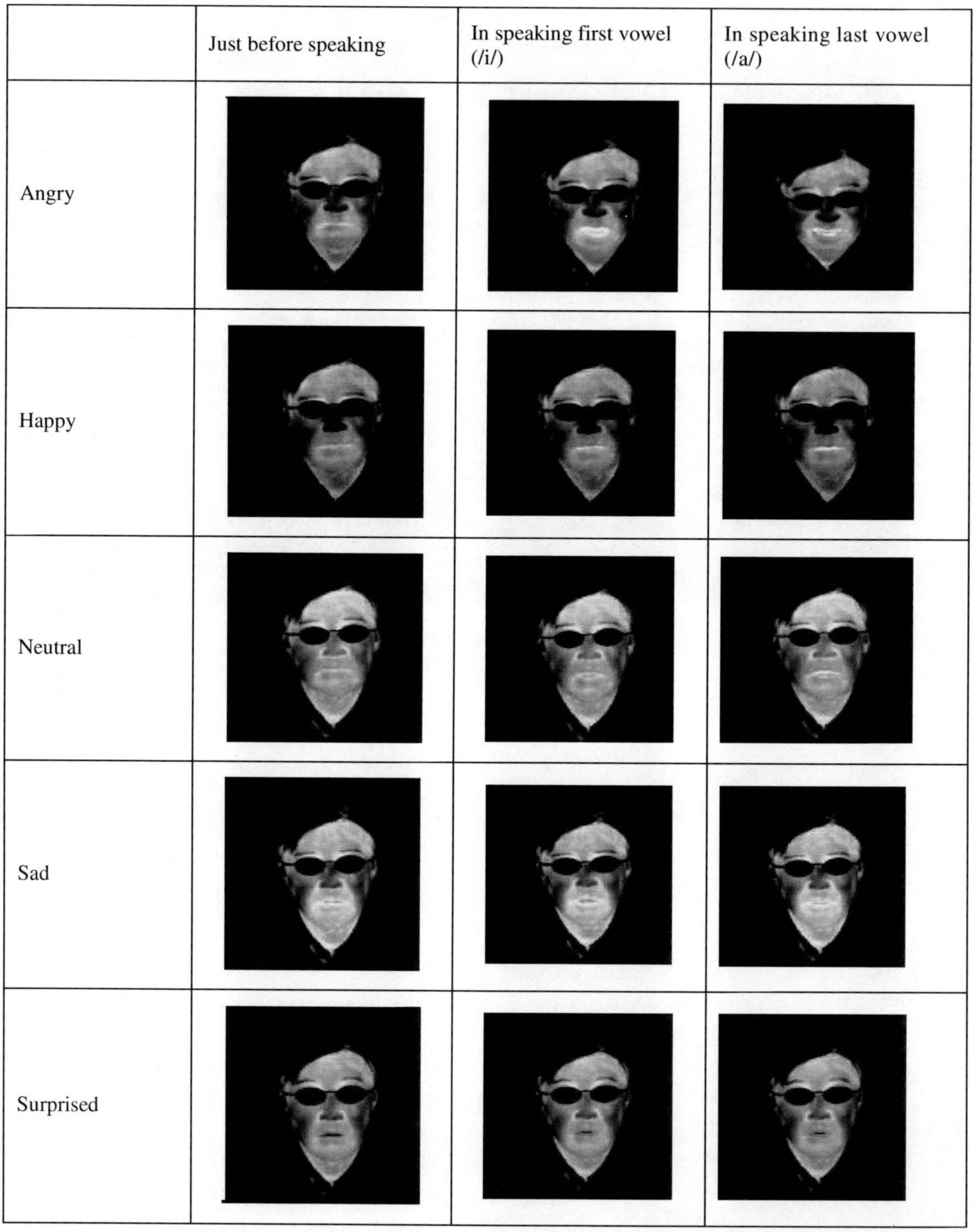

Figure 20. Examples of thermal images of Subject A having each facial expression in speaking "Taro"[16].

Experiment 2

The thermal image produced by the thermal video system (Nippon Avionics TVS-700) and the sound captured from an Electret condenser microphone (Sony ECM-23F5), amplified by a mixer (Audio-Technica AT-PMX5P), were transformed into a digital signal by an A/D converter (Thomson Canopus ADVC-300) and input into a computer (DELL Optiplex GX620, CPU: Pentium IV 3.4 GHz, main memory: 2.0 GB, and OS: Windows XP (Microsoft)) with an IEEE1394 interface board (I·O Data Device 1394-PCI3/DV6). We used Visual C++ 6.0 (Microsoft) as the programming language. To generate a thermal image, we applied the condition that the thermal image had 256 gray levels for the detected temperature range. This range was decided independently for each subject in order to best extract the face area. We saved the visual and audio information in the computer as a Type 2 DV-AVI file, in which a frame had a spatial resolution of 720 × 480 pixels and 8-bit gray levels, and the sound was saved in a stereo PCM format of 48 kHz and 16-bit levels.

All subjects exhibited in alphabetic order each of the intentional facial expressions of "angry," "happy," "neutral," "sad," and "surprised," while speaking the semantically neutral utterance of each of the 25 Japanese first names listed in Table 1. Figure 21 shows examples of thermal images of each subject. There were three subjects in this experiment. Subject A was a male with glasses, Subject C was a female without glasses, and Subject G was a male without glasses.

Subject G was a new subject. Figures 22 to 24 show examples of images of each subject.

Table 1. Japanese first names used in the experiment [17]

		First vowel				
		a	i	u	e	o
Last vowel	a	ayaka	shinnya	tsubasa	keita	tomoya
	i	kazuki	hikari	yuki	megumi	koji
	u	takeru	shigeru	fuyu	megu	noboru
	e	kaede	misae	yusuke	keisuke	kozue
	o	taro	hiroko	yuto	keiko	tomoko

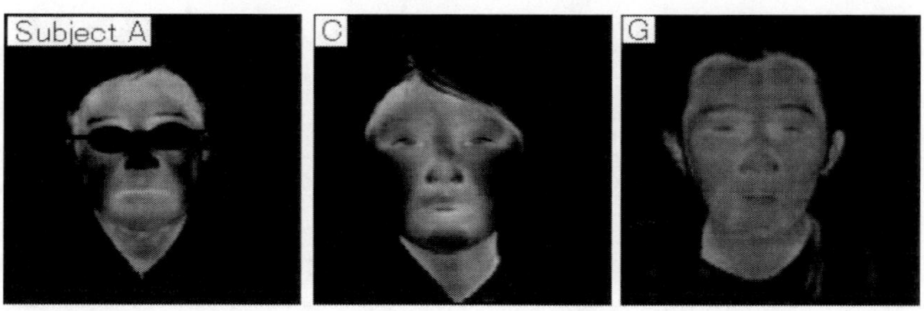

Figure 21. Examples of thermal images having a neutral facial expression just before speaking "Ayaka" [17].

In the experiment, all subjects kept intentionally front-view faces in the AVI files saved as both the training and test data.

Accordingly, the pre-processing module for judging the front-view face [16] was not used in the experiment. We assembled 20 samples as training data and 10 samples as test data. From one sample, we obtained three images at the timing positions of just before speaking and just speaking the phonemes of the first and last vowels. We obtained training data for all combinations of the vowel type of the first and last vowels.

	Just before speaking	In speaking first vowel (/i/)	In speaking last vowel (/a/)
Angry		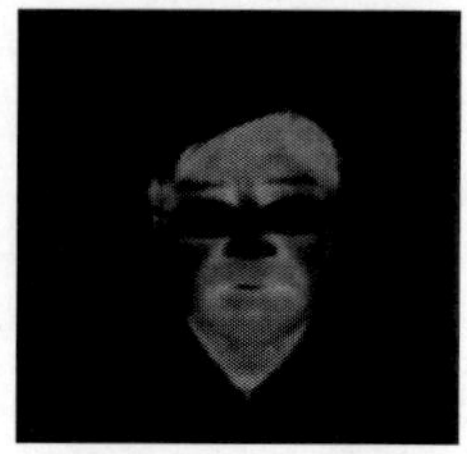	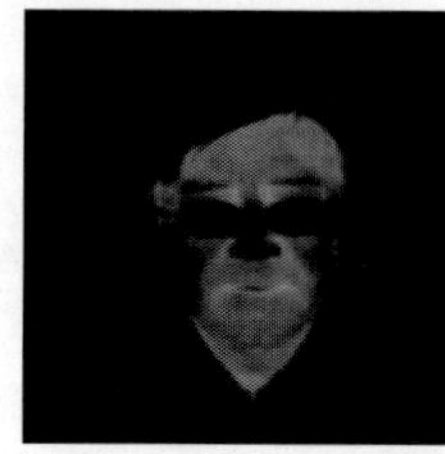
Happy	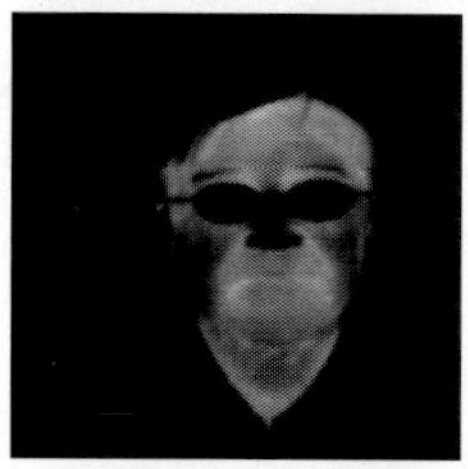	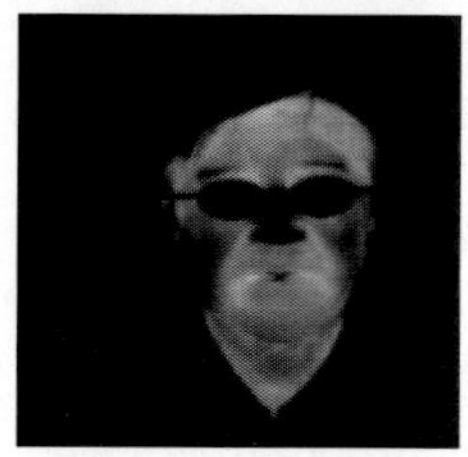	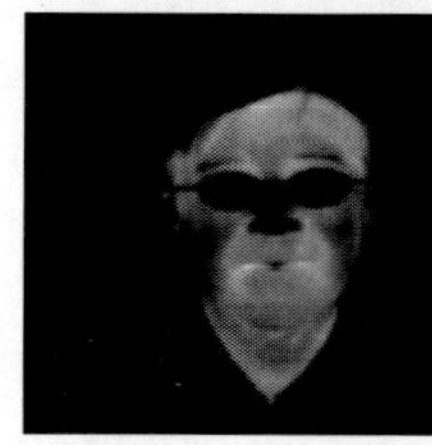
Neutral	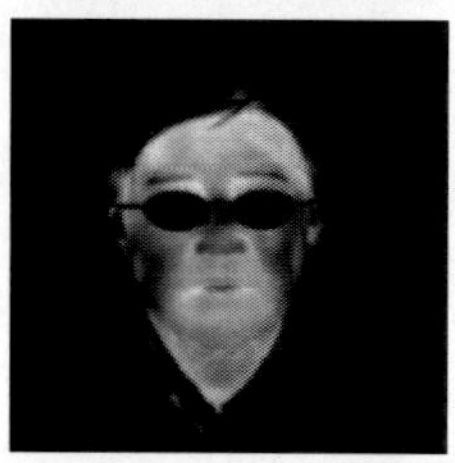	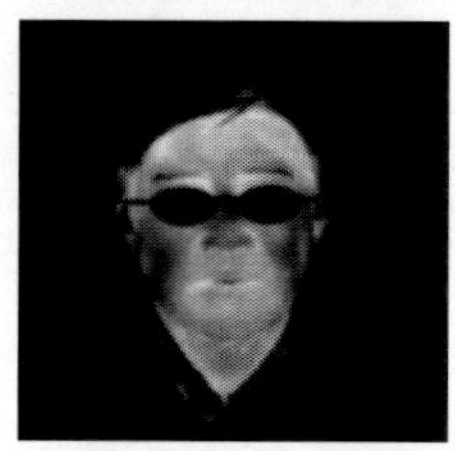	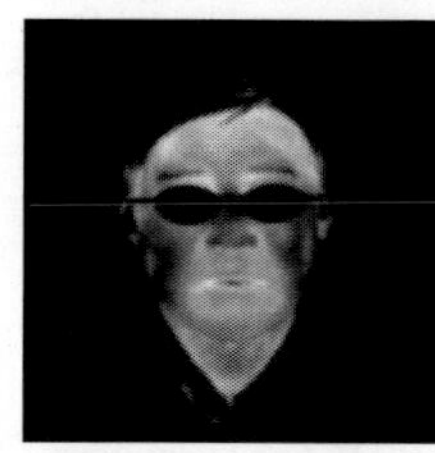
Sad	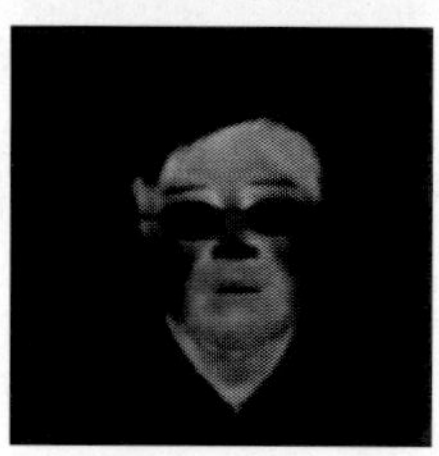	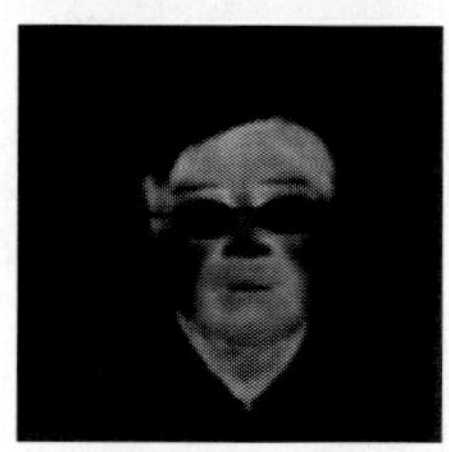	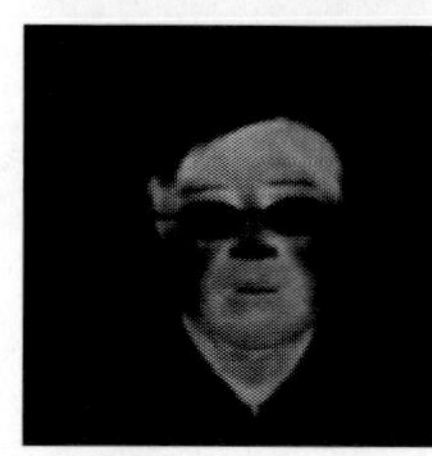
Surprised	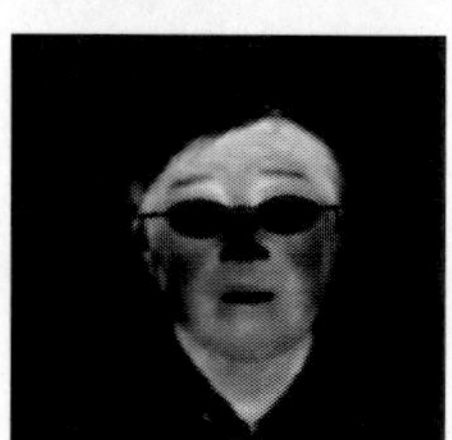	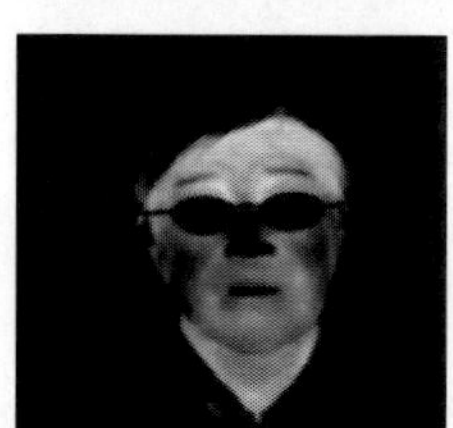	

Figure 22. Examples of thermal images of Subject A having each facial expression in speaking "Shinnya" [24].

	Just before speaking	In speaking first vowel (/i/)	In speaking last vowel (/a/)
Angry	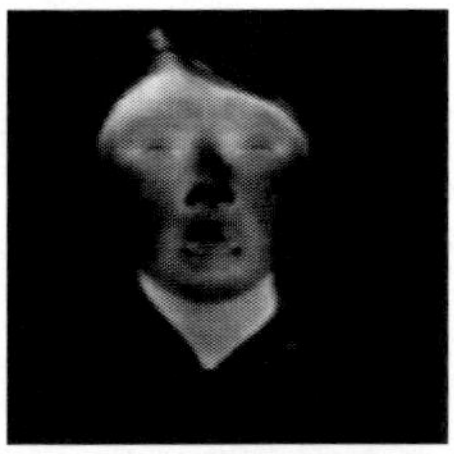	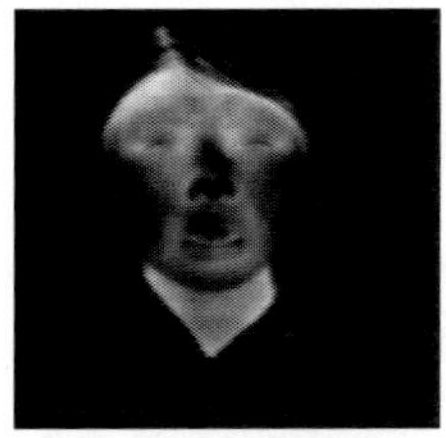	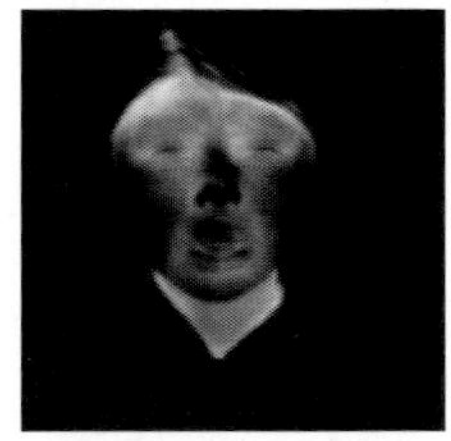
Happy	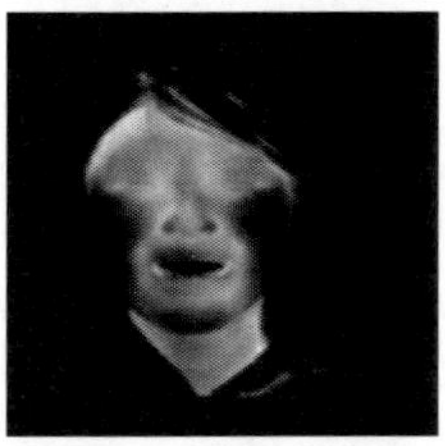	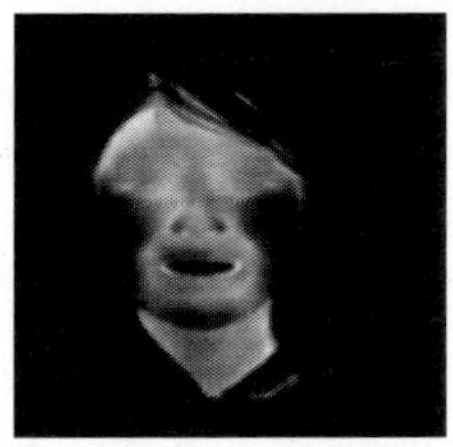	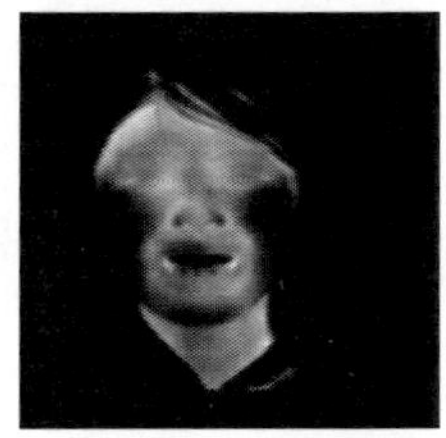
Neutral	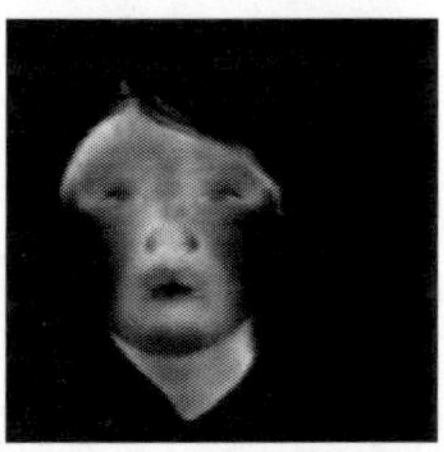	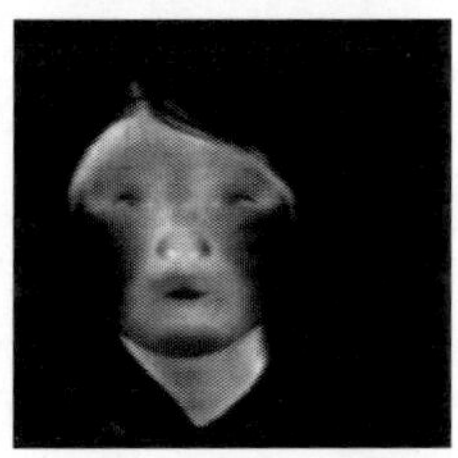	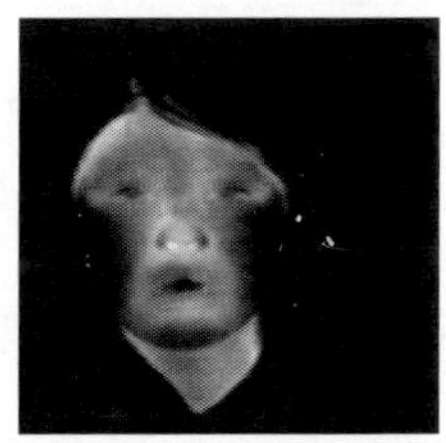
Sad	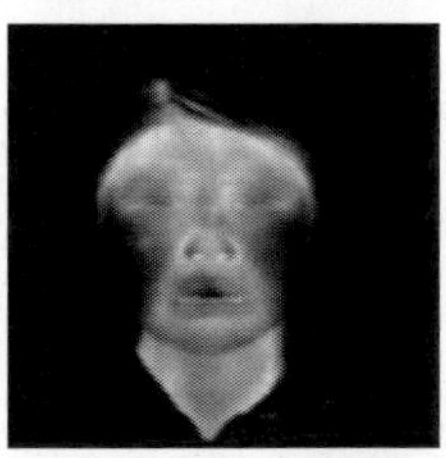	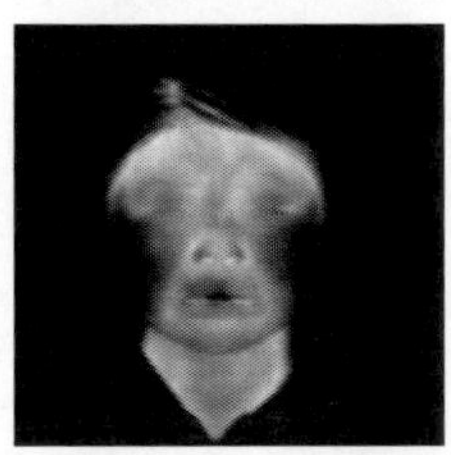	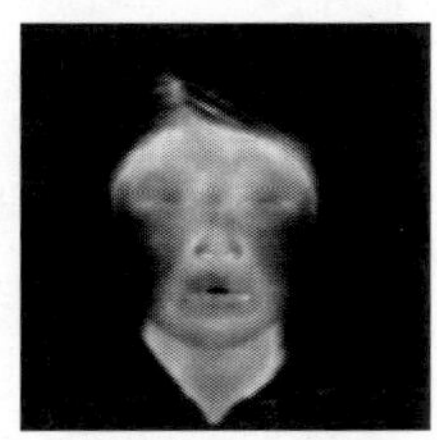
Surprised	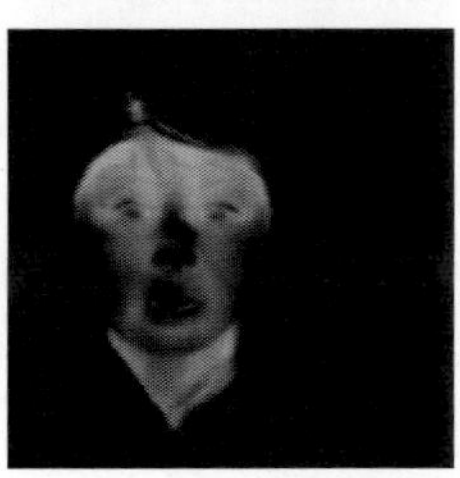	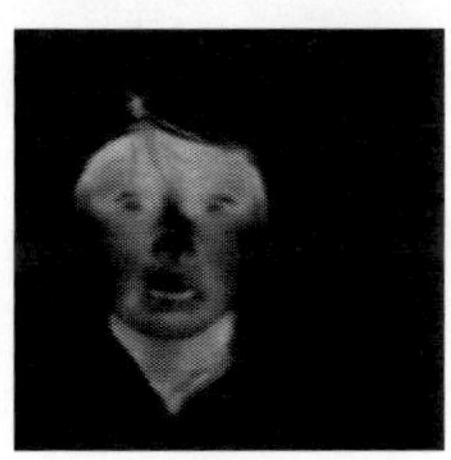	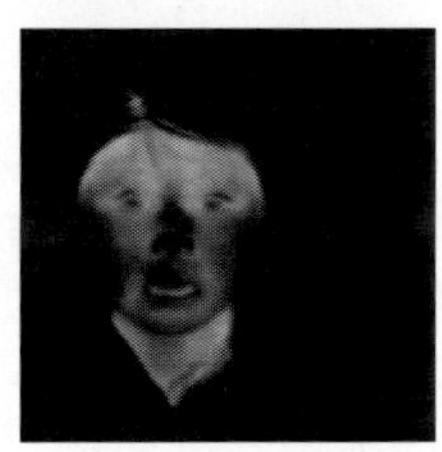

Figure 23. Examples of thermal images of Subject C having each facial expression in speaking "Shinnya" [24].

	Just before speaking	In speaking first vowel (/i/)	In speaking last vowel (/a/)
Angry	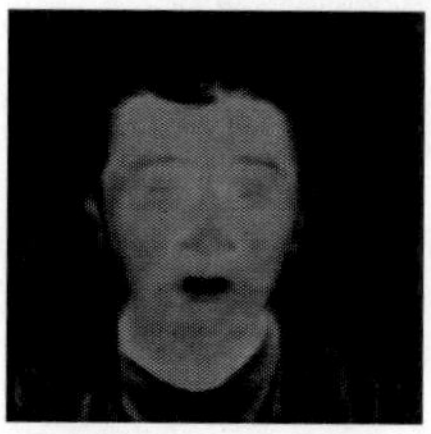	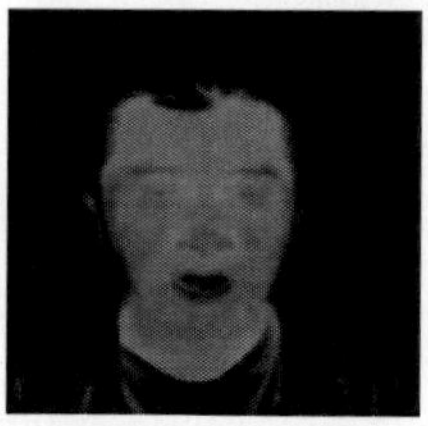	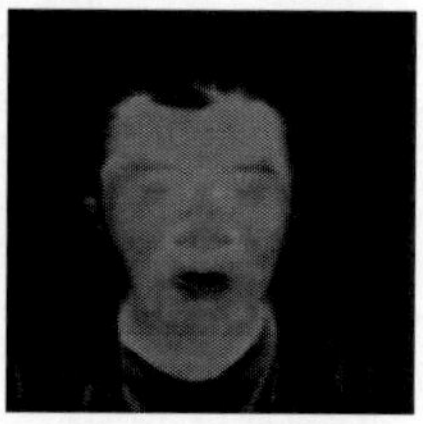
Happy	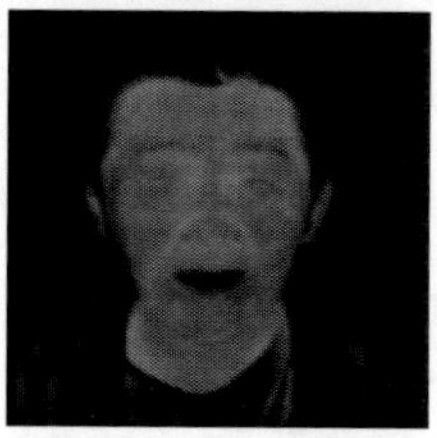	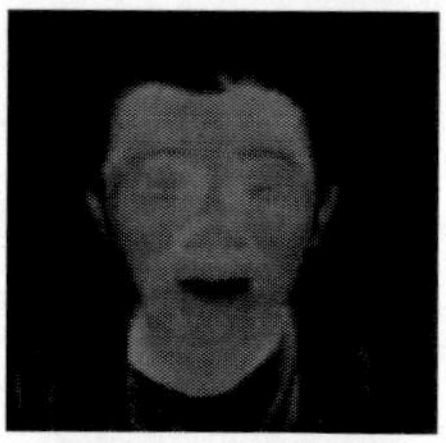	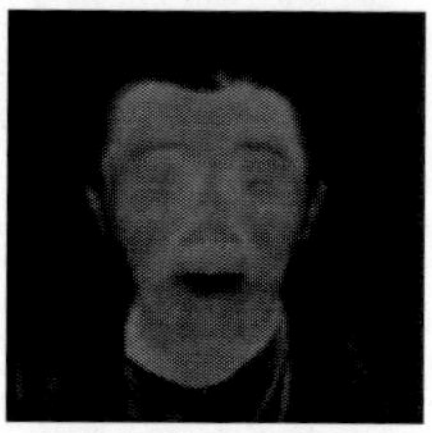
Neutral	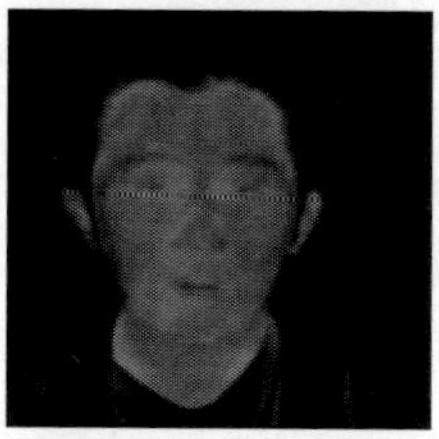	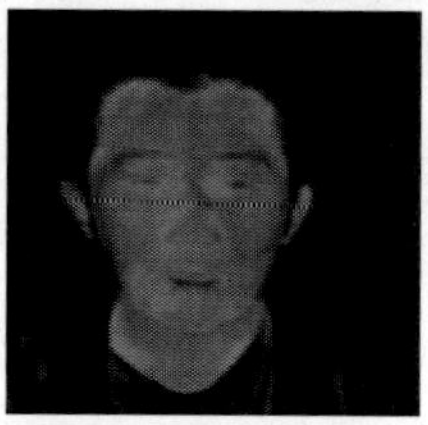	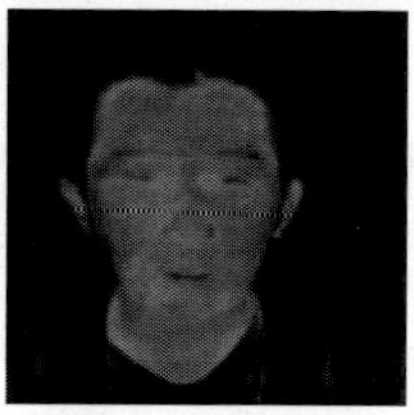
Sad	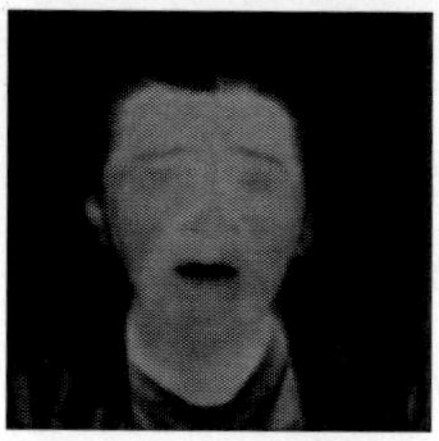	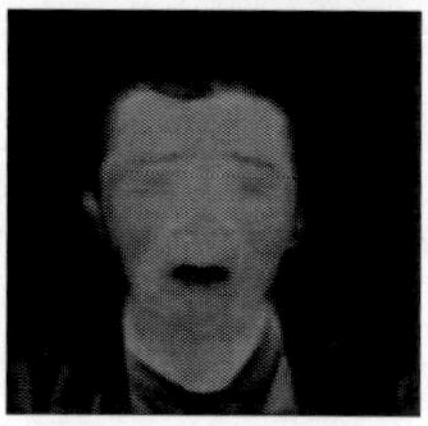	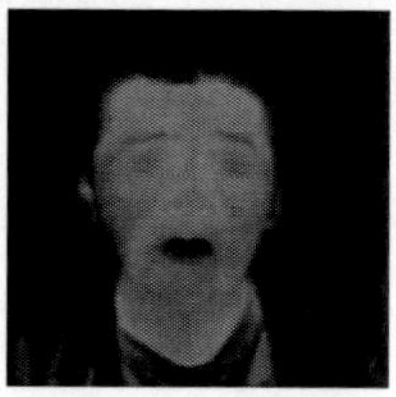
Surprised	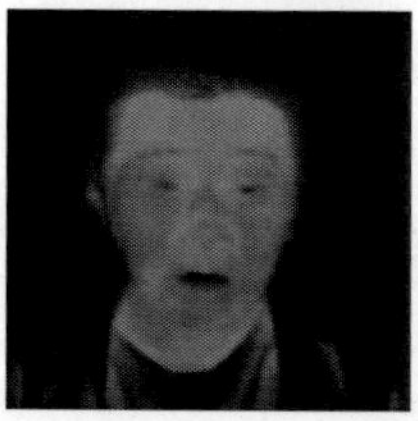	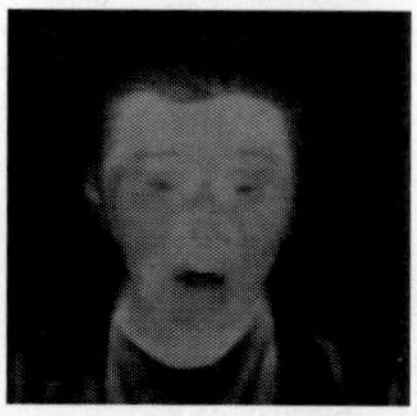	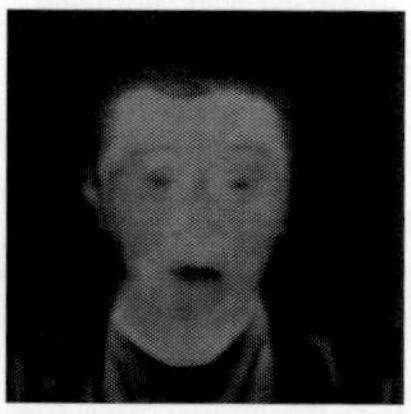

Figure 24. Examples of thermal images of Subject G having each facial expression in speaking "Shinnya" [24].

Results and Discussion

Experiment 1

In this experiment, six subjects spoke the word "Taro." The mean value of the front-view face judgment accuracy for all subjects was 99.5%. The mean value of the speech recognition accuracy of vowels decided by Julius for all subjects was 88.2% for the first vowel (/a/) and 88.3% for the last vowel (/o/). Table 2 shows the facial expression recognition accuracy for all subjects.

The mean recognition accuracy was 84.0%. The mean recognition accuracy for each subject was 82% for Subject A, 78% for Subject B, 84% for Subject C, 82% for Subject D, 84% for Subject E, and 94% for Subject F.

Table 2. Facial recognition accuracy for all subjects [16]

		Input facial expression				
		Angry	Happy	Neutral	Sad	Surprised
Output	Angry	**93.3**	0.0	0.0	13.9	6.7
	Happy	1.7	**90.0**	0.0	0.0	1.7
	Neutral	0.0	0.0	**80.0**	3.3	1.7
	Sad	5.0	3.3	5.0	**71.7**	6.7
	Surprised	0.0	6.7	15.0	11.1	**85.0**

Experiment 2

In this experiment, three subjects spoke 25 Japanese first names. The accuracy of Subject A was 87.4% for the first vowel and 80.4% for the last vowel. That of Subject C was 84.7% for the first vowel and 70.8% for the last vowel. The speech recognition accuracy of Subject G as a mean value over all five emotions was 94.1% for the first vowel and 87.0% for the last vowel. The speech recognition accuracy for the first vowel and the last vowel as a mean value over all five emotions was 84.1% for all subjects. Table 3 shows the speech recognition accuracy for the first and last vowels of Subject G. In Table 3, the recognition accuracy means the ratio in percentage of the cases where both the first and last vowels were correctly recognized.

Table 4 shows the facial expression recognition accuracy as mean values over all combinations of first and last vowels. The mean recognition accuracy of the facial expressions of all subjects was 79.8%. The mean recognition accuracy of the facial expressions was 74.1% for Subject A, 79.7% for Subject C, and 85.5% for Subject G. Tables 5 to 7 show all the values of the recognition accuracy of the facial expressions of each subject.

We investigated the case of perfect recognition of both the first and the last vowels [24]. In this case, the mean recognition accuracy of the facial expressions of all subjects was 87.0%, and the mean recognition accuracy of the facial expressions was 82.5% for Subject A, 88.7% for Subject C, and 89.7% for Subject G [24]. Accordingly, future improvement in the recognition of the first and the last vowels might lead to improvement of the mean value of facial expression recognition by 7.2 % at most [24]. As a continuation of our work, we will apply our method for facial expression recognition using other subjects.

Table 3. Accuracy (%) of speech recognition of Subject G [17]

First-last vowel	Angry	Happy	Neutral	Sad	Surprised	Mean
a-a	50	100	100	80	0	66.0
a-i	100	100	100	90	80	94.0
a-u	90	0	100	100	70	72.0
a-e	80	100	100	90	100	94.0
a-o	80	60	100	90	80	82.0
i-a	100	100	100	100	100	100.0
i-i	100	80	100	100	60	88.0
i-u	100	80	100	100	90	94.0
i-e	30	100	70	40	0	48.0
i-o	100	100	30	20	100	70.0
u-a	80	70	40	70	60	64.0
u-i	100	90	20	10	100	64.0
u-u	90	100	70	70	100	86.0
u-e	100	100	100	100	100	100.0
u-o	100	100	70	100	100	94.0
e-a	50	100	80	100	10	68.0
e-i	100	100	100	100	100	100.0
e-u	30	40	100	100	90	72.0
e-e	50	80	100	90	90	82.0
e-o	100	100	60	100	90	90.0
o-a	80	80	100	100	60	84.0
o-i	100	100	100	100	100	100.0
o-u	100	100	100	100	100	100.0
o-e	100	100	100	100	70	94.0
o-o	40	100	10	40	60	50.0
Mean	82.0	87.2	82.0	83.6	76.4	82.2

Table 4. Accuracy (%) of facial expression recognition [17]

Subject A		Input facial expression				
		Angry	Happy	Neutral	Sad	Surprised
Output	Angry	**64.1**	5.2	5.2	6.7	9.2
	Happy	10.8	**77.2**	0.8	7.3	13.4
	Neutral	0.0	4.0	**83.6**	0.0	0.0
	Sad	7.2	7.6	2.0	**78.0**	9.7
	Surprised	17.9	6.0	8.4	8.0	**67.7**
Subject C		Input facial expression				
		Angry	Happy	Neutral	Sad	Surprised
Output	Angry	**78.8**	4.4	7.2	5.2	0.8
	Happy	2.4	**77.1**	3.6	2.4	0.0
	Neutral	10.8	2.0	**71.9**	3.2	2.0
	Sad	2.8	11.3	12.9	**78.8**	5.2
	Surprised	5.2	5.2	4.4	10.4	**92.0**

Subject G		Input facial expression				
		Angry	Happy	Neutral	Sad	Surprised
Output	Angry	**90.4**	0.4	0.0	6.0	2.4
	Happy	3.6	**94.8**	9.6	4.8	7.2
	Neutral	0.0	0.0	**87.2**	0.0	0.0
	Sad	0.4	2.8	0.4	**78.8**	14.0
	Surprised	5.6	2.0	2.8	10.	**76.4**

Table 5. Accuracy (%) of facial expression recognition of Subject A [17]

First-last vowel	Angry	Happy	Neutral	Sad	Surprised	Mean
a-a	10	70	10	90	90	54.0
a-i	50	50	100	40	44	56.9
a-u	80	90	100	89	90	89.8
a-e	22	100	100	78	80	76.0
a-o	30	100	100	60	50	68.0
i-a	100	30	90	70	80	74.0
i-i	40	80	100	90	10	64.0
i-u	70	100	100	100	100	94.0
i-e	90	100	90	90	78	89.6
i-o	60	100	100	90	80	86.0
u-a	60	0	70	90	50	54.0
u-i	0	90	90	40	70	58.0
u-u	100	40	40	90	70	68.0
u-e	100	100	100	83	100	96.7
u-o	80	40	100	80	90	78.0
e-a	90	90	90	90	90	90.0
e-i	90	90	100	90	0	74.0
e-u	10	80	100	90	20	60.0
e-e	100	100	10	100	70	76.0
e-o	90	100	100	100	80	94.0
o-a	50	90	100	70	90	80.0
o-i	50	60	100	10	50	54.0
o-u	50	80	100	80	80	78.0
o-e	80	90	0	100	60	66.0
o-o	100	60	100	40	70	74.0
Mean	64.1	77.2	83.6	78.0	67.7	74.1

Table 6. Accuracy (%) of facial expression recognition of Subject C [17]

First-last vowel	Angry	Happy	Neutral	Sad	Surprised	Mean
a-a	100	67	30	40	80	63.3
a-i	80	50	100	30	60	64.0
a-u	70	100	80	70	100	84.0
a-e	60	70	10	60	60	52.0
a-o	100	50	78	60	100	77.6
i-a	80	100	100	100	90	94.0
i-i	80	100	100	60	90	86.0
i-u	40	70	90	60	60	64.0
i-e	70	40	70	30	100	62.0
i-o	60	80	90	80	90	80.0
u-a	80	100	90	90	90	90.0
u-i	90	10	50	90	100	68.0
u-u	60	90	90	100	100	88.0
u-e	80	100	100	80	100	92.0
u-o	90	10	10	90	100	60.0
e-a	100	100	70	80	100	90.0
e-i	90	100	100	100	100	98.0
e-u	100	80	40	60	100	76.0
e-e	90	100	100	100	100	98.0
e-o	90	100	30	100	100	84.0
o-a	40	80	80	100	100	80.0
o-i	90	60	80	90	80	80.0
o-u	70	90	20	100	100	76.0
o-e	90	100	100	100	100	98.0
o-o	70	80	90	100	100	88.0
Mean	78.8	77.1	71.9	78.8	92.0	79.7

Table 7. Accuracy (%) of facial expression recognition of Subject G [17]

First-last vowel	Angry	Happy	Neutral	Sad	Surprised	Mean
a-a	90	100	100	100	0	78.0
a-i	100	100	70	100	90	92.0
a-u	90	100	100	100	100	98.0
a-e	100	100	100	100	100	100.0
a-o	100	100	100	70	70	88.0
i-a	60	80	100	50	100	78.0
i-i	100	100	70	100	100	94.0
i-u	100	100	100	100	40	88.0
i-e	100	100	90	90	100	96.0

First-last vowel	Angry	Happy	Neutral	Sad	Surprised	Mean
i-o	90	100	30	90	100	82.0
u-a	100	100	70	30	80	76.0
u-i	100	100	100	0	100	80.0
u-u	90	100	70	90	100	90.0
u-e	100	100	100	100	100	100.0
u-o	100	100	70	100	90	92.0
e-a	90	90	100	100	20	80.0
e-i	80	100	100	80	100	92.0
e-u	100	80	100	90	100	94.0
e-e	100	90	100	70	20	76.0
e-o	0	100	100	50	30	56.0
o-a	100	50	100	100	10	72.0
o-i	100	90	100	80	100	94.0
o-u	100	100	100	20	100	84.0
o-e	100	100	100	90	80	94.0
o-o	70	90	10	70	80	64.0
Mean	90.4	94.8	87.2	78.8	76.4	85.5

On-Line System and Efficient Updating Training Data

We briefly summarize our recent studies in this sub-section.

Based on our previously reported method [15], [16], we proposed an on-line system for recognizing the facial expression of a speaker using front-view face judgment, vowel judgment, and thermal image processing [25]. Using the proposed system, the facial expressions of a subject were discriminable with 76% accuracy for the facial expressions of "happy," "neutral," and "others" when they exhibited one of the intentional facial expressions of "angry," "happy," "neutral," "sad," and "surprised." We expect the proposed system to be applicable for recognizing facial expressions in daily conversations.

We also proposed a method for efficiently updating training data, such that the training data of only the facial expressions of "happy" and "neutral" were updated after an interval such as approximately three and a half years [26]. Using this proposed method, the facial expressions of two subjects were discriminable with 87.0% accuracy for the facial expressions of "happy," "neutral," and "others" when they exhibited one of the intentional facial expressions of "angry," "happy," "neutral," "sad," and "surprised."

CONCLUSION

We introduced our method for facial expression recognition of a speaker using thermal image processing and a speech recognition system. In this study, using the speech recognition system, thermal static images were saved at the timing positions of just before speaking, and just speaking the phonemes of the first and the last vowels.

Using our method, five kinds of facial expressions were discriminable with good recognition accuracy. We expect that the proposed method will be applicable for recognizing facial expressions in daily conversations.

ACKNOWLEDGMENTS

We would like to thank all the co-researchers who contributed to our papers (cited in the references). We would also like to thank all the subjects who cooperated with us in the experiments. This work was partially supported by KAKENHI (22300077).

REFERENCES

[1] Yuille AL, Cohen DS, and Hallinan PW, Feature extraction from faces using deformable templates. *Proceedings of IEEE Conference on Computer Vision and Pattern Recognition*, San Diego, California , USA, Jun 4-8, 1989, pp 104-109, (1989).

[2] Harashima H, Choi CS, and Takebe, T 3-D model-based synthesis of facial expressions and shape deformation (in Japanese). *Human Interface*, 4:157-166, (1989).

[3] Mase K, An application of optical flow – extraction of facial expression. *Proceedings of IAPR Workshop on Machine Vision and Application*, Kokubunji, Tokyo, Japan, Nov 28-30, 1990, pp 195-198, (1990).

[4] Mase K, Recognition of facial expression from optical flow. *Trans IEICE* E74(10): 3474-3483, (1991).

[5] Matsuno K, Lee C, and Tsuji S, Recognition of facial expressions using potential net and KL expansion (in Japanese). *Trans IEICE* J77-D-II(8):1591-1600, (1994).

[6] Kobayashi H and Hara F, Analysis of neural network recognition characteristics of 6 basic facial expressions. *Proceedings of 3rd IEEE International Workshop on Robot and Human Communication*, Nagoya, Japan, Jul 18-20, 1994, pp 222-227, (1994).

[7] Yoshitomi Y, Kimura S, Hira E, and Tomita S, Facial expression recognition using infrared rays image processing. *Proceedings of the Annual Convention IPS Japan*, Osaka, Japan, Sep 4-6, 1996, 2:339-340, (1996).

[8] Yoshitomi Y, Kimura S, Hira E, and Tomita S, Facial expression recognition using thermal image processing. *IPSJ SIG Notes*, CVIM103-3, Kyoto, Japan, Jan 23-24, 1997, pp 17-24, (1997).

[9] Yoshitomi Y, Miyawaki N, Tomita S, and Kimura S, Facial expression recognition using thermal image processing and neural network. *Proceedings of 6th IEEE International Workshop on Robot and Human Communication*, Sendai, Japan, Sep 29-Oct 1, 1997, pp 380-385, (1997).

[10] Sugimoto Y, Yoshitomi Y, and Tomita S, A method for detecting transitions of emotional states using a thermal face image based on a synthesis of facial expressions. *J. Robotics and Autonomous Systems* 31(3):147-160, (2000).

[11] Yoshitomi Y, Kim SIll, Kawano T, and Kitazoe T, Effect of sensor fusion for recognition of emotional states using voice, face image and thermal image of face. *Proceedings of 6th IEEE International Workshop on Robot and Human Interactive Communication*, Osaka, Japan, Sep 27-29, 2000, pp 178-183, (2000).

[12] Ikezoe F, Ko R, Tanijiri T, and Yoshitomi Y, Facial expression recognition for speaker using thermal image processing (in Japanese). *Trans Human Interface Society* 6(1):19-27, (2004).

[13] Nakano M, Ikezoe F, Tabuse M, and Yoshitomi Y, A study on the efficient facial expression using thermal face image in speaking and the influence of individual variations on its performance (in Japanese). *J IEEJ* 38(2):156-163, (2009).

[14] Koda Y, Yoshitomi Y, Nakano M, and Tabuse M, Facial expression recognition for a speaker of a phoneme of vowel using thermal image processing and a speech recognition system. *Proceedings of 18th IEEE International Symposium on Robot and Human Interactive Communication*, Toyama, Japan, Sep 29 - Oct 1, 2009, pp 955-960, (2009).

[15] Yoshitomi Y, Facial expression recognition for speaker using thermal image processing and speech recognition system. *Proceedings of 10th WSEAS International Conference on Applied Computer Science*, Appi Kogen, Iwate, Japan, Oct 4-6, 2010, pp 182-186, (2010).

[16] Fujimura T, Yoshitomi Y, Asada T, and Tabuse M, Facial expression recognition of a speaker using front-view face judgment, vowel judgment, and thermal image processing. *J. Artificial Life and Robotics,* 16(3): 411–417, (2011).

[17] Yoshitomi Y, Asada T, Shimada K, and Tabuse M, Facial expression recognition of a speaker using vowel judgment and thermal image processing. *J. Artificial Life and Robotics*, 16(3): 318–323, (2011).

[18] Kuno H (1994) Infrared rays engineering (in Japanese). Tokyo, IEICE, pp 22.

[19] Kuno H (1994) Infrared rays engineering (in Japanese). Tokyo, IEICE, pp 45.

[20] Yoshitomi Y, Tsuchiya A, and Tomita S, Face recognition using dynamic thermal image processing. *Proceedings of 7th IEEE International Workshop on Robot and Human Communication*, Takamatsu, Kagawa, Japan, Sep 30- Oct 2, 1998, pp 443-448, (1998).

[21] Yamazaki S, Kamakura H, Tanijiri T, and Yoshitomi Y, Three-dimensional CG expression of face rotation using Fuzzy algorithm and thermal face image (in Japanese). *Trans Human Interface Society* 6(3):321-331, (2004).

[22] http://julius.sourceforge.jp/.

[23] Ekman, P and Friesen, W V, Unmasking the face -A guide to recognizing emotions from facial expressions. Prentice-Hall, Inc., Eglewood Cliffs, New Jersey, (1975).

[24] Yoshitomi Y, Asada T, and Tabuse M, Vowel judgment for facial expression recognition of a speaker. Speech technologies. In Tech, India, pp 405-424, (2011).

[25] Asada T, Yoshitomi Y, Tabuse M, A system for facial expression recognition of a speaker using front-view face judgment, vowel judgment and thermal image processing. *Proceedings of 17th International Symposium on Artificial Life and Robotics*, Beppu, Oita, Japan, Jan 19-21, 2012, pp 204-209, (2012).

[26] Nakanishi Y, Yoshitomi Y, Asada T, Tabuse M, Robust facial expression recognition of a speaker using thermal image processing and updating of fundamental training-data. *Proceedings of 17th International Symposium on Artificial Life and Robotics*, Beppu, Oita, Japan, Jan 19-21, 2012, pp 210-215, (2012).

In: Image Processing
Editor: Vítor Hugo Carvalho

ISBN 978-1-62081-844-2

Chapter 3

APPLYING IMAGE PROCESSING TO *IN-VITRO* HUMAN OOCYTES CHARACTERIZATION

***Javier Aragón*[3]*, Antonio L. González*[2] *and Alberto Yúfera*[1,3,*]
[1]Seville Microelectronics Institute (IMSE),
Microelectronics National Center (CNM), Spain
[2]Mas Vida Medical Center, Seville, Spain
[3]Department of Electronic Technology, University of Seville, Spain

ABSTRACT

This book chapter presents an image processing tool developed to in-vitro human oocytes analysis required in fertilization processes to biological material classification. The application of the proposed tool allows a non-invasive method to define the quality of human oocytes before to be inseminated, enabling the possibility of selection the optimum one. Specific segmentation algorithms have been developed to particularbiomedical images for identifying the cytoplasm area. The oocyte status (normal, medium and highly stressed state) has been defined in terms of a set of parameters extracted from the cytoplasm image. This quantification allows advising the biomedical staff during oocyte selection, involving by the first time a useful metrics. Experimental results proof that 83% of cases analyzed match with the expert evaluation.

INTRODUCTION

The quality of gametes (spermatozoa and oocytes) and embryos at human in-vitro fertilization is fundamental for the success of this process. The viability analysis, as a consequence of the nature and sensitivity material in assisted human reproduction, must be made by non-invasive methods. During embryos development, there are a wide number of techniques to distinguish the embryo viability, as morphological characteristics (cleavage rate, fragmentation, multinucleation, cellular symmetry…) in time-lapse observations and/or metabolomic based- assays.

---

* E-mail address: yufera@imse-cnm.csic.es.

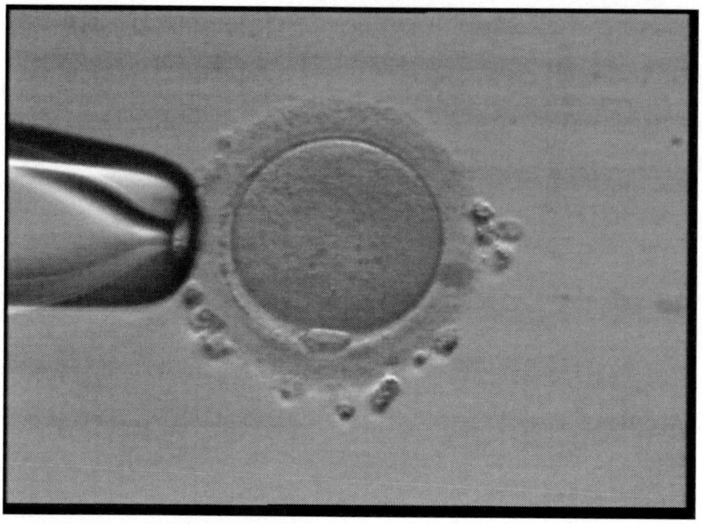

Figure 1. An oocyte image during in-vitro manipulation.

On the other hand, some of the spermatozoa characteristics have been defined as markers to increase the efficiency of such processes (motility, morphology, etc.), with the possibility of selection the viable spermatozoa throw of different techniques as mush conventional (swimp-up, density gradient…) as specific (inmuno-magnetic, hyaluronic binding-sperm, high magnification selection…). However, there is not a counterpart for oocytes in order to select the most competent to be fertilized. Experts in this area establish their decisions on the own experience and empirical observations, being most of them based on morphological appearance, such as cytoplasm granularity, size, and some of the bodies or inclusions present at the cell (polar body, vacuoles, organelles aggregation…). In this form, it is obtained a subjective oocyte selection criterion poor correlated with the success of the post-insemination process. Some actual approaches [1], are based on the definition of the refractive index of some oocyte areas, as marker of maturity, but without conclusive results for the oocyte selection method. Recently, some processing image techniques [2] have been proposed as a way to bypass the excitation problem, and to enable a non-invasive procedure for oocyte cytoplasm analysis. This work does not consider the search for inclusions and bodies, but it represents a starting point for quantifying the process of the oocytes classification in terms of its quality. The here proposed work describes a computer tool for processing images of oocytes useful during in-vitro fertilization process. The main objective of the analysis is to classify a human oocyte, as shown in Figure 1, in three main sets (normal, medium and highly stressed) defined by the bio-medical experts, creating a metrics for "measuring" the affinity to one of them. Also, bodies and inclusions should be detected for the whole structure oocyte description, but they are not the main objective of the here presented work. The image processing tool starts always from images taken by in-vitro process and performs a series of tasks that can be classified mainly in two: segmentation and clustering. Specific algorithms were developed to first detect the cytoplasm area, and second to define its texture. Final results are displayed visually and quantitatively, creating a new metric that can be employed by the bio-medical staff as decision advice, in the sense that a number it is associated to an oocyte state based on its texture, showing its maturity and stress degree. Experts can incorporate this tool during the diagnosis processes and correlate it with their empirical observations and the process end. A specific expert criterion [6] was considered for clustering process, but it can be customized in each lab, as a function of the empirical data received from different experts and also the corresponding lab optics. Once the tool is trained, it can be employed for automatic oocyte classification and traceability in assays at in-vitro processes. The proposed contents of the book chapter are the followings. First section gives a general overview and motivation of the work, identifying the image processing as a potential non-invasive technique for human oocytes processing to define its viability in fertilization processes. Image segmentation for cytoplasm area will be described in section "Segmentation". After that, sections "Texture Analysis" and "Clustering" are related with the cytoplasm texture analysis and its application to oocyte classification or clustering respectively. A brief description of the tool and its functionalities are shown in section "Tool Description". Results are described from images delivered for medical staff, showing a success tax of 83% of cases in which the tool evaluation match with the expert one. At the end, the Conclusions are given.

SEGMENTATION

The processing steps programmed over an oocyte image are defined on the basis that all the images will have a similar appearance, taken at the same light conditions, with the same optics and zoom. This fact defines the programming steps followed for the main algorithm employed. Before to describe them, a short view of one of these images is given.

An Oocyte Image

Several areas and bodies can be identified at an oocyte image as in Figure 1. Images were taken up with invertoscopy NIKON Eclipse TE2000-S, with 800x600 bit resolution, in bitmap format. It can be identified the next elements:

- The cytoplasm represents a high percent of the total area of the oocyte. It is circumvent by the plasmatic membrane.
- The pipettes for biomedical manipulation of samples.
- The pellucid zone is around the oocyte, acting as oocyte protection.
- The polar body, placed around the cytoplasm, between the zona pellucida and cytoplasm. Normally, there is only one, but it is possible to find two or fragmented.
- The plasmatic membrane, around the cytoplasm.
- Inclusions, sometime present, as vacuoles and liposomes, inside the cytoplasm area.

Main images processing tasks are focused on determine the granularity or texture type of the cytoplasm, so programming must solve two general problems. First, the cytoplasm area should be detected and measured by using a proposed segmentation method. Second, the defined area will be analyzed for texture characterization. In this section, segmentation will be done, while texture analysis and clustering are described in sections "Texture Analysis" and "Clustering".

Cytoplasm Detection

The microscopic images taken from oocytes during fertilization processes have a large quantity of elements. For texture analysis, some of them can be useful, but others must be eliminated. The main objective of segmentation is to select the cytoplasm area, in which texture analysis will be done. Relevant information will be extracted from this partial image, reducing the image size for an easy further processing. This process is based on the application of the Hough transform to look for a circle including the cytoplasm area. To highlight and add to this process, a four steps process is done. The Hough transform is an algorithm employed in pattern recognition to find some shapes, in our case, circles. It works in a statistical from, and it could be time and memory expensive. However, the present application has always oocytes of similar size and shape, so it can be limited the search algorithm to those with a given radius, or in an interval of this, optimizing the search process. In the space of all circles possible found, it must be selected one evolving the cytoplasm. This matching process is done highlighting the original image with a Sobel filter that makes more evident the plasmatic membrane. Common pixels to this and Hough circles are used as from to identify the best matching circle. Finally, we extract from the original image all the data enclosed on the selected circle. This process is illustrated at Figure 2.

Segmentation Algorithm: Cytoplasm Area Definition

Step 1: To apply the Hough transform over the original image.
Step 2: To highlight borders by using Sobel filter on the original image.
Step 3: To look for the best fitting circle at the given by the Hough transform including the cytoplasm.
Step 4: To substrate the result from the initial image.

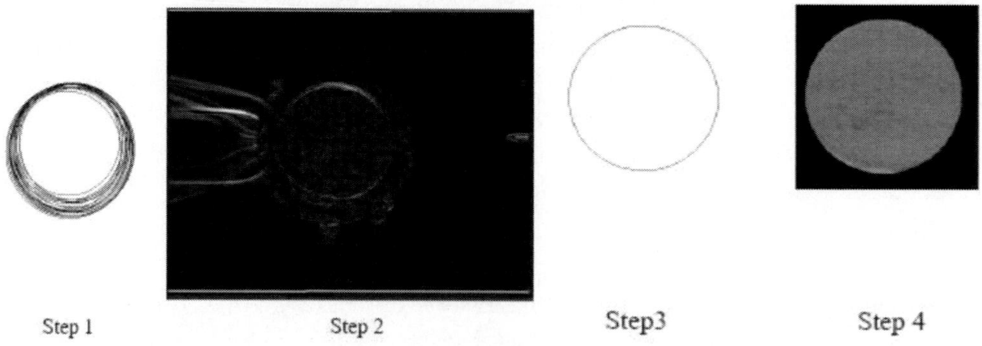

Figure 2. Segmentation algorithm: steps 1 to 4.

TEXTURE ANALYSIS

Biomedical experts believe that the stress state of an oocyte is directly related with the texture or granularity observed at the cytoplasm surface. This idea is established on the basis of relaxed oocytes have low internal metabolic activity, and this status is derived on low surface granularity at the cytoplasm surface.

This activity could be monitorized along the entire surface, so the full cytoplasm area could have potential interest on oocyte status definition.

Texture Concept

Textures are properties of external surfaces on bodies, and it is related with the sensitive effect performed over the human perception. It is a concept difficult to define and mathematically to formalize because it has a subjectivity component. From computer science point of view, texture is defined in terms of visual patterns, measurable in some form, in such a way that it is possible to find math equations to describe and compute them. To differentiate a set of textures, the proposal is to define a set of adequate descriptors. In [2] are defined a set from cytoplasm histogram information that we have, in part, adopted as starting point.

Functions and Parameters

A random variable is defined from the histogram information as random density function, is such a way that if x represent the grey level of the cytoplasm histogram, $x \in [0, L\text{-}1]$, the probability to find a pixel u with a given grey level x is,

$$p_u \approx \text{Prob}[\mu = x]$$

with $x = 0, \ldots, L\text{-}1$, and $p_u : \{0, \ldots, L-1\}$ at the interval [0,1]. The corresponding moments, associated to de p_u are:

$$m^i = \sum_{x=0}^{L-1} x^i . p_u(x) \qquad i = 1,2,\ldots$$

and the central moments,

$$\mu^i = \sum_{x=0}^{L-1} (x - m_1)^i . p_u(x) \qquad i = 1,2,\ldots$$

From they can be derived and defined a set of properties useful in texture identification.

Mean: It is the first moment, m_1. It gives a mean value of all the grey levels and shows a general overview of the image intensity. An image with high granularity contains many shadows that decrease the grey level mean.

Variance: It is the central moment $\mu_2(u)$, and gives a measure for the contrast between grey levels. High contrast is related with high granularity and shadow areas derived from.

Smoothness: It is defined as:

$$R = 1 - \frac{1}{1 + \mu_2(u)}$$

The R value is zero, when intensity is constant and one when μ_2 has large values (roughness areas). The region where the grey level is constant are classified as uniforms, and considered as low granularity regions.

Asymmetry: Represent the third moment $\mu_3(u)$, and it is a parameter to measure the symmetry of the histogram. Negative values correspond to histograms weighted to the left, while when it is positive are oriented to the right. It can be obtained information about the grey levels if they are focused to the darkness or to the lightness.

Homogeneity: It is defined as,

$$U = \sum_{x=0}^{L-1} p_u{}^2(x)$$

Being maximum for an image with all grey level equals. A homogeneous histogram tends to be uniformly distributed around all values, meaning the same light level in all image, and a low granularity.

Entropy: It is defined as,

$$E = -\sum_{x=0}^{L-1} p_u(x).\log_2 p_u(x)$$

It is zero when all pixels of image are constant. It is used to measure the invariance of an image. High entropy means large variation at grey level and a high granularity.

Texture Pre-Processing Filters

The histogram of two images with different levels of granularity can be or not different. For example, an image with a large dark zone can have a histogram similar to one with many and small black zones and, however, this second has probably a biggest granularity.

The direct application of statistics parameter definition from the original histogram can lead us to erroneous perception of texture. The proposed solution is this case relies on the use of some pre-filtering processes to normalize the histogram, in such a way that only images with similar textures will have similar histograms too.

Low-Pass (LP) and High-Pass (HP) two dimensional filters were employed in [2] to normalize the light conditions for oocyte images. One of the main drawbacks of this pre-processing method is the selection of the cuf-off frequency for the filters; because of the final result it is very sensitive to them.

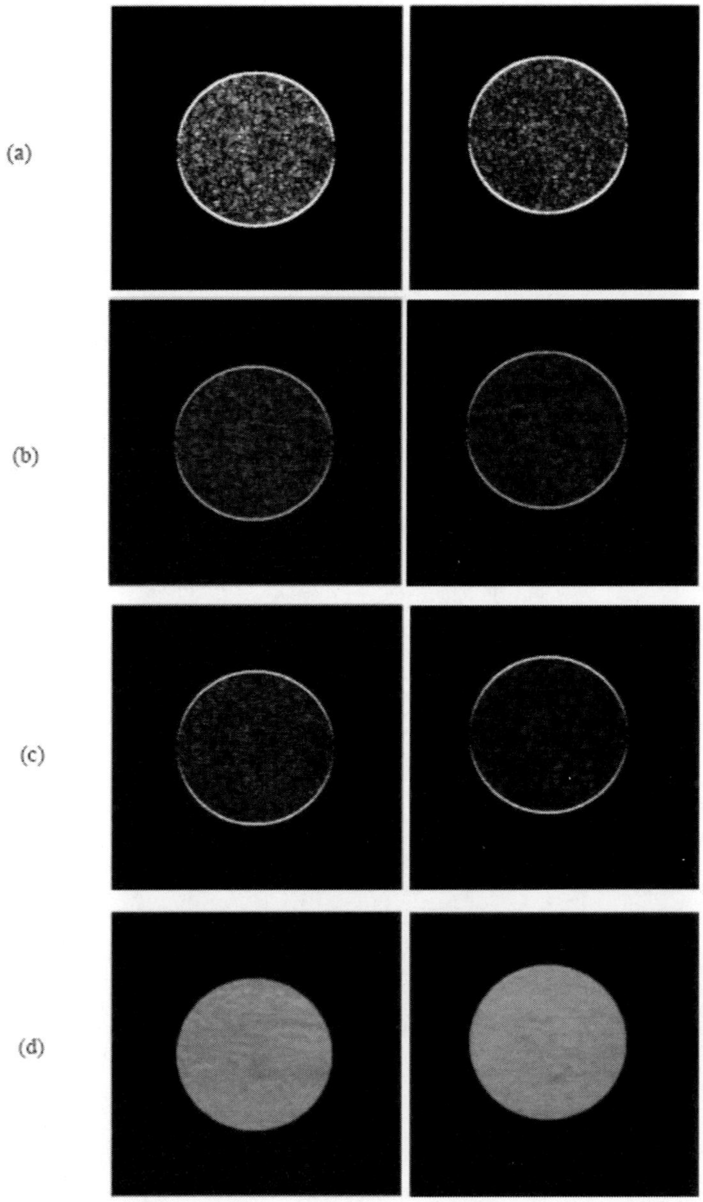

Figure 3. Texture pre-processing for stressed (left) and normal (right) oocytes based on application of Sobel Filters (SF) and Gaussian Filters (GF): (a) SF+SF. (b) SF+GF. (c) GF+SF and (d) GF+GF.

This work proposes an alternative filtering process based on highlight and smooth borders in the image. This is done by using a Sobel Filter (SF) and a Gaussian Filter (GF).

The HP filters enhance the borders and contours so Sobel filter is a good alternative. SF detects a border when strong changes in light conditions (grey levels) are produced. High granularity generates a lot of dark zones isolates and hence large changes in image contrast in this areas. SF identifies this change as a border. Also, a LPF try to smooth the image, as for example, the Gaussian Filter. When an image has a large granularity, it will be more difficult to smooth than if granularity is low. The combination of SF and GF will remarks the main borders corresponding to the more evident image irregularities. Finally, SF and GF simultaneous application by pairs will generate four different instances of the same image. Based on the histograms of these images, it will be applied the six functions of the section "Functions and parameters". In the next, are represented two examples, with the four pre-filtered images showing a cytoplasm with granularity high (stressed, on the left) and normal granularity (not stressed, on the right).

Image Parameters

The oocyte is a large cell and its metabolic activity can be irregular and non-homogeneous from the area point of view, so it is convenient to analized all the citoplasm area and to divide the area for this task. Follwing the advise of experts, the full cytoplasm area has been divided in four equal parts to be analyzed in terms of the texture parameters defined before. This means that for each oocyte, 24 parameters will characterize the four areas. Each quarter will be analyzed independently, and its texture quantifyed.

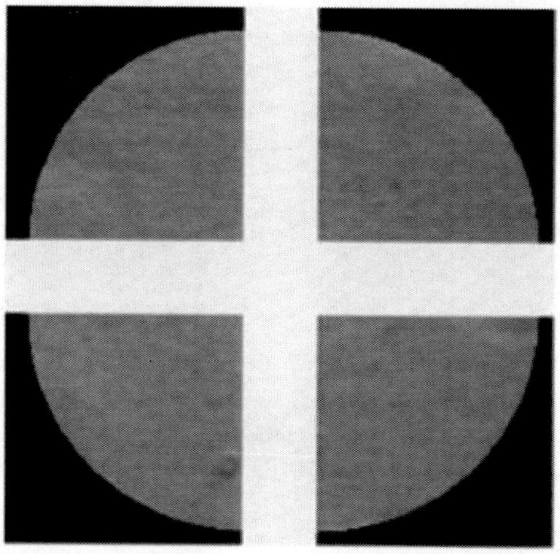

Figure 4. Cytoplasm area division in four zones for texture analysis.

CLUSTERING

Each oocyte is defined by 24 parameters, and now, they must be classified in one of the following sets: normal, medium and high stress degree. This process in usually called as clustering, or grouping the analyzed samples into three groups in terms of the texture parameters calculated.

Fuzzy Algorithm

Traditional techniques in clustering are oriented to group the data in such a way that each data belong to only one group. However, a texture could belong to more than one group or cluster because of contains characteristics of more than one cluster. So this work gives a more wide interpretation of texture. It has been selected a fuzzy algorithm (fuzzy c-mean, FCM) following the indications given at [2]. This algorithm it is based on the minimization of the following objective function,

$$F_m = \sum_{i=1}^{n} \sum_{c=1}^{C} \mu_{ic}{}^{m} . \left\| x_i - v_c \right\|^2 \quad (1)$$

Being m a fuzzy exponent, C the number of clusters represented by the vector v_c, x_i the data to be classified, and $\mu^m{}_{ic}$ is the fuzzy partition matrix.

Classification Process

Given an oocyte, to identify the stress group to which belong an iterative process is followed under the basis of there are desired three group or clusters. Iterations look for a group estimation in which data distance from centroids at each group is minimized. In our case, centroids are six dimension vectors defined by the before defined texture parameters.

Each texture is represented by means of a vector with 24 characteristics (components), in which it can be characterized N textures by means of an X matrix of N files and 24 columns. The final objective in FCM optimization is to divide this data set represented in c disjoint groups.

The use of the fuzzy partitioning matrix allows the calculus of the belonging degree for any of the $N.x_i$ cases, at the c sets, identifying every centre as v_c. The problem is then reduced to look for the pair (μ,V) that better classify the X data. The fuzzy matrix is given by:

$$\mu_{ci}(z) = \frac{1}{\sum_{j=1}^{c} \left(\frac{\left\| x - v_i \right\|^2}{\left\| x - v_j \right\|^2} \right)^{\frac{1}{m-1}}} \quad (2)$$

The following equation calculates the value of v_i as the weigted mean for all data in the cluster, being the weights the belonging functions.

$$v_i = \frac{\sum_{z} (\mu_{ci}(X))^m .x}{(\mu_{ci}(X))^m} \quad (3)$$

The coordinates of the centroids are then stored. In general, images from one set of oocytes to another are quite similar, so the stored centroids can be employed as initial value for FCM iterations.

This optimization process can be seen with and example. As initial values, we have a set of points in a file of the X matrix:

1	1.5
1	2
1	2.5
2	2
3	2
4	2
5	1.5
5	2
5	2.5

The objective is to divide this set of points in two groups with common characteristics. For that, it must be looked the centre of every group (centroids). The centroids are initialized randomly in a matrix C, for example:

1	2.5
5	1.25

This graphic represents the points with the centroids. The belonging degree to each centroid can be calculated with the help of the fuzzy matrix in (2). It is obtained the following result:

0.9662	0.0338
0.9662	0.0038
0.9665	0.0035
0.9000	0.1000
0.5290	0.4710
0.1471	0.8529
0.0038	0.9962
0.0338	0.9662
0.0887	0.9113

It can be seen that the five first values belong to centroid number 1 and the other four to centroid number 2. Next, the centroid values are update with (3), leading to matrix:

1.3641	2.0083
4.6756	1.9781

At the process end, the final centroids obtained are:

1.3560	2.0003
4.6576	1.9992

Graphically, it can be seen how evolves this process. Each iteration, the centroids are approaching to the centre of two disjoint data sets.

This process is repeated until optimization condition of objective function is satisfied.

Tool Description

The tool has been developed using C++ programming language. This option allows the development of fast programs, with low memory resources requirements, important in this application for processing large images. This is also an object oriented language, allowing a very low level control. An image library has been employed: OpenCV [7,8], with a large number of functions for vision processing and applications. The graphic user interface was implemented by Microsoft. Net Framework 3.0, by the set of APIs available, and documented, easy to employ.

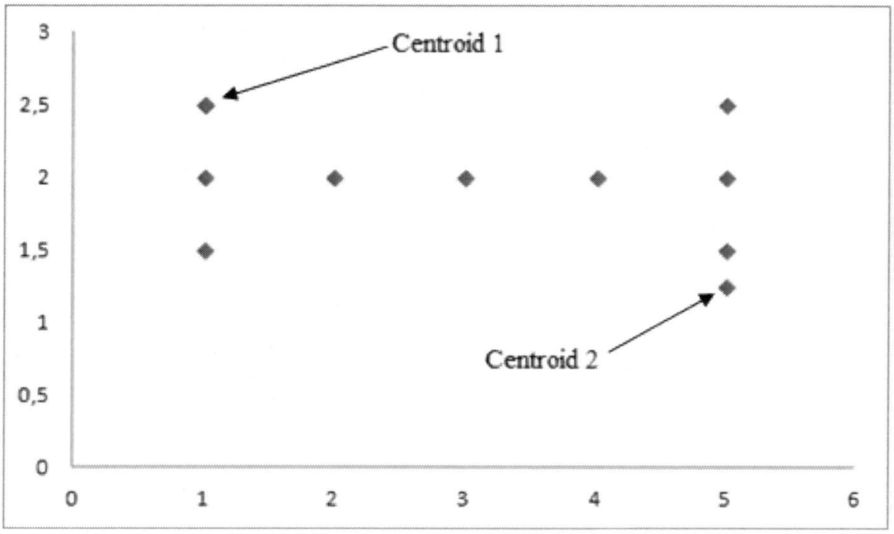

Figure 5. Initial position of the centroids in FCM optimization.

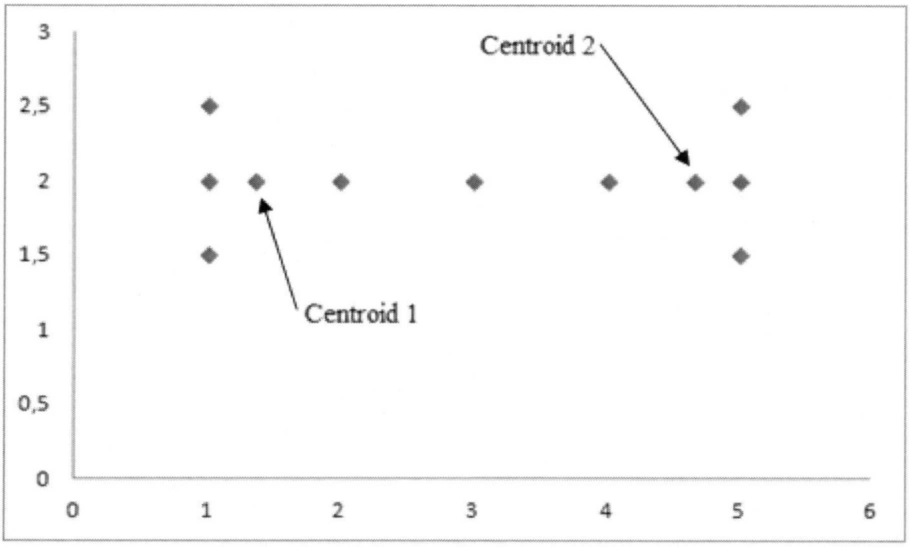

Figure 6. Final centroid positions after FCM optimization.

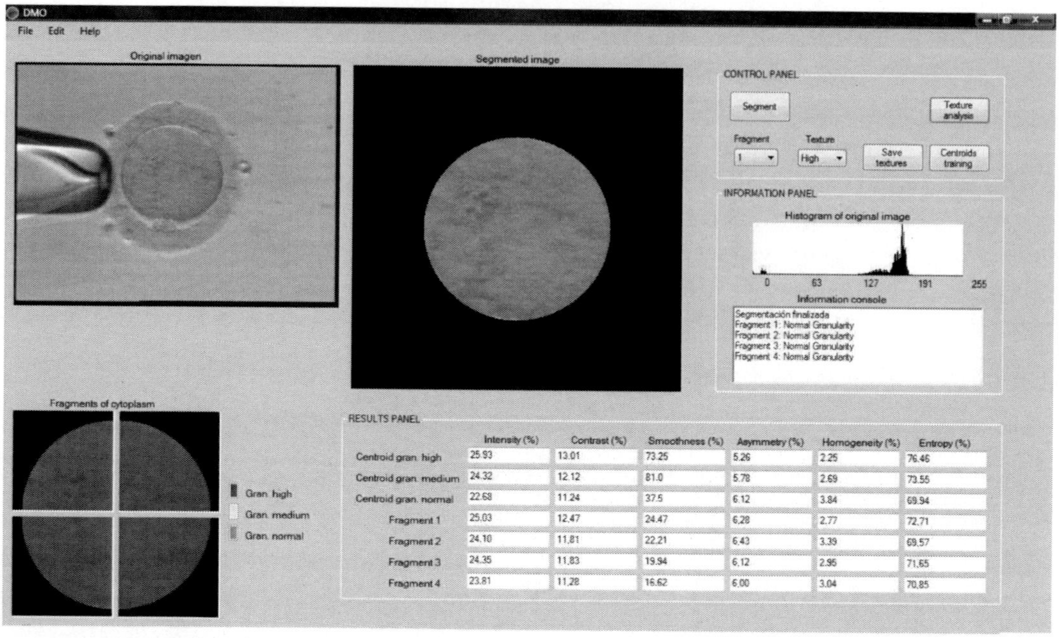

Figure 7. Front panel of the image processing tool. There are shown the initial oocyte image and segmented cytoplasm image. Texture results are classified into three groups: normal, medium and high (green, yellow and red colors), and the texture quantification is given for each cytoplasm quarter: intensity, contrast, smoothness, asymmetric, homogeneity and entropy parameters were selected and defined from cytoplasm histogram.

Basic actions performed by the presented tool can by identify from the main panel in Figure 5. Initial image is always displayed at the top left side, while the results from segmentation algorithm 1 and 2, at the top center. The buttons programmed actions are:

- Cytoplasm segmentation
- Texture analysis

Also, some interest information about the process is displayed, as for example, the histogram for the initial image. The texture result is shown at the bottom left. Green, yellow and red colors are selected for normal, medium and high stressed oocytes. Also, numerical data from clustering results are displayed: the centroid coordinates, and the actual texture parameter for the four quadrant cytoplasm is being analyzed.

RESULTS

Oocyte images were analyzed by the proposed tools. There were considered 52 images at segmentation and 15 for texture analysis. Images were delivered by the medical team [6].

In this set, 51 images of the cytoplasm were correctly isolated. The errors in this process are dues because of the Hough transform do not find a circle, involving the cytoplasm with the size range specified. This leads to and 98% of success.

The texture analysis was performed over 15 of the cytoplasm isolated. The resulting data (60 partial images) were clustered in three sets on the basis of the texture parameters, resulting for the three centroids whose results can be seen at the following figures (Figure 8 to 13).

Intensity: The stress increases the intensity.

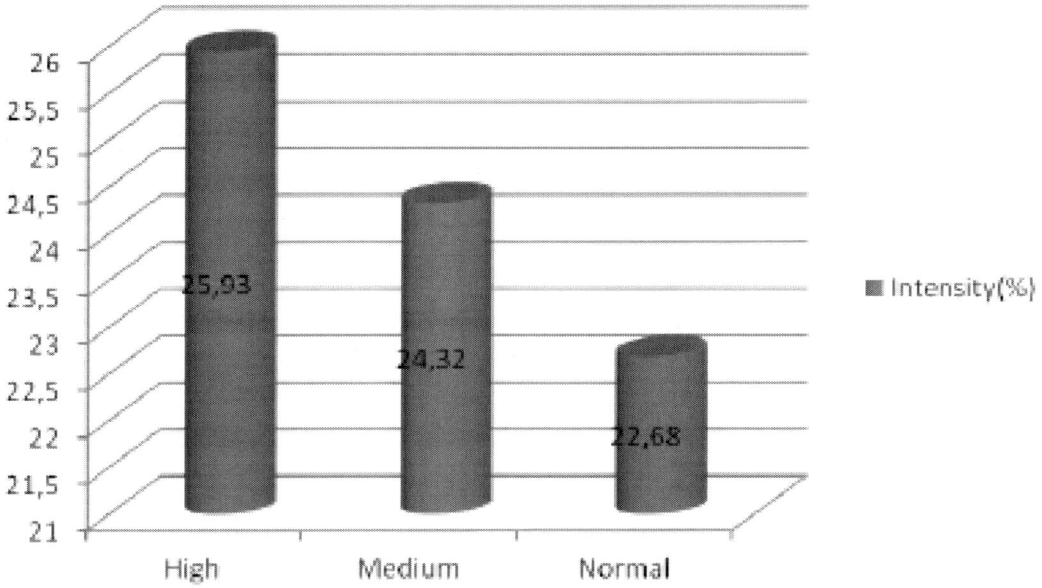

Figure 8. Intensity.

Contrast: The stress increases the contrast.

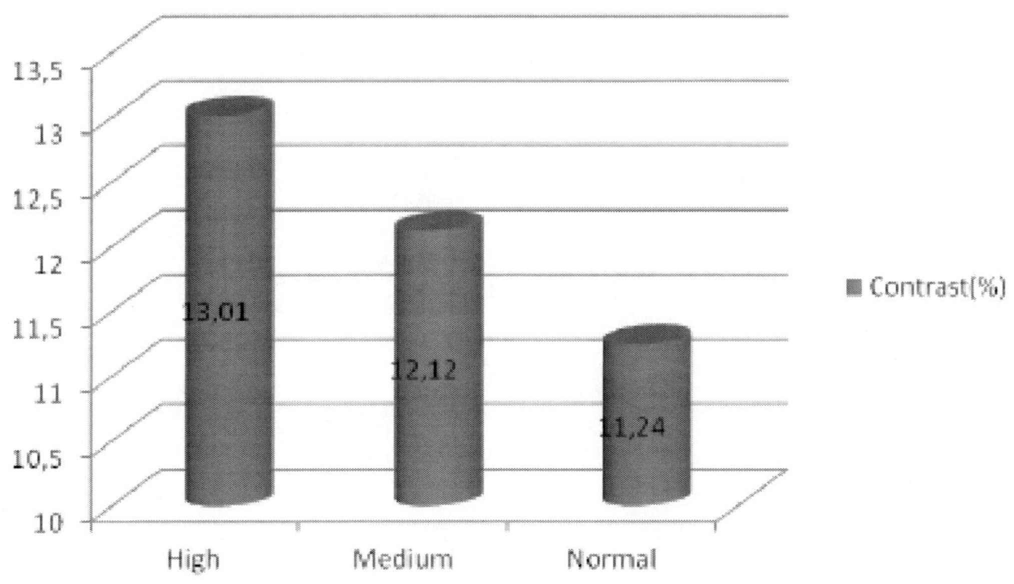

Figure 9. Contrast.

Smoothness: There is not a direct correlation between the smoothness parameter and the stress. High and medium have a similar values, quite large than for normal stress.

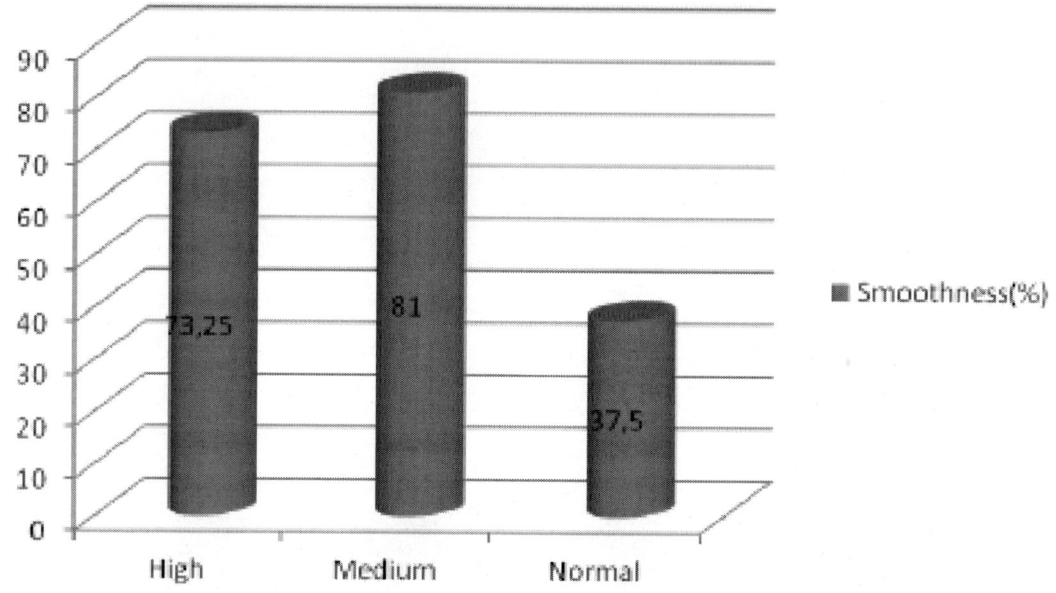

Figure 10. Smoothness.

Asymmetry: the histogram asymmetry decreases with the stress, being that focused to the right.

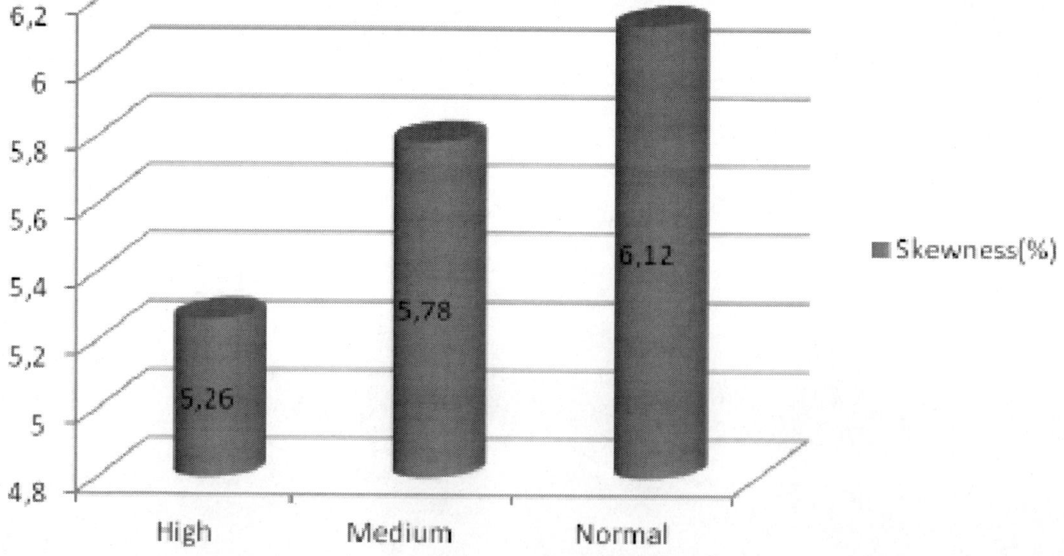

Figure 11. Asymmetry.

Homogeneity: The obtained results are logic. Lower granularity means a more cytoplasm homogeneity.

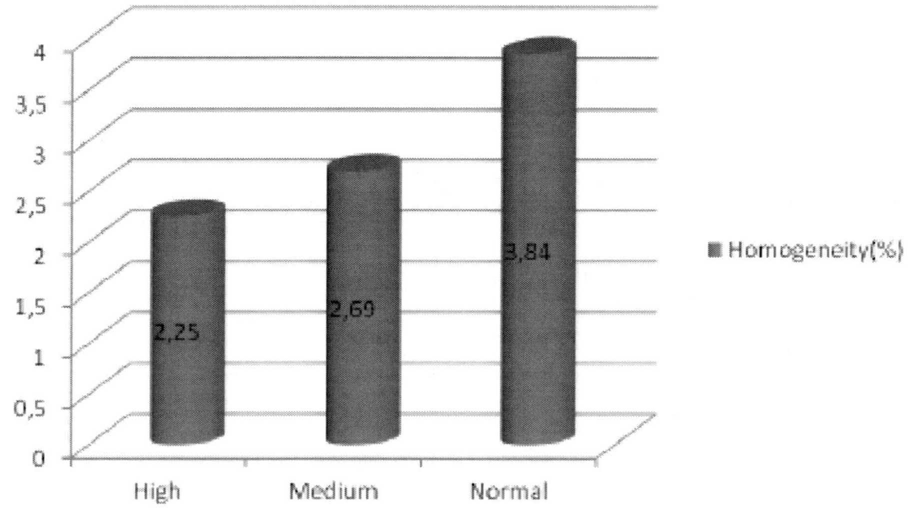

Figure 12. Homogeneity.

Entropy: This graphics shows higher granularity with desorden degree.

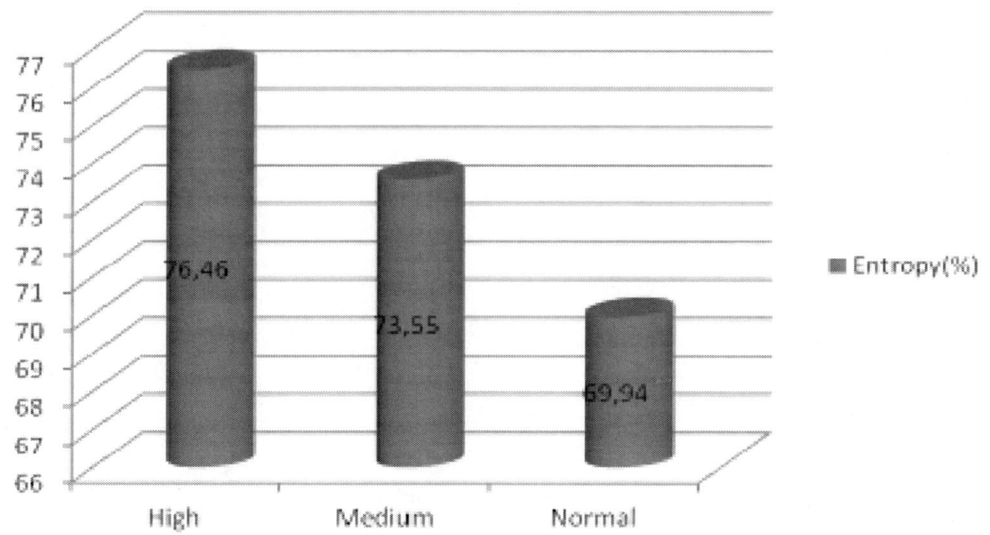

Figure 13. Entropy.

In segmentation analysis, were considered 52 images.

The test was performed over 15 oocyte images, which means 60 quarter areas, leading to 60 texture results. The results had shown that in 50 cytoplasm fragments, the result match with the expert opinion. That means the 83.3% of success. The other 10, error is always between adjacent textures (normal-medium or medium-high).

Also, the expert information it is relative to the overall oocyte status, nor by segments, so we can consider that the error in some cases are not such.

Conclusion and Discussion

This work has been conceived as a processing tool for oocyte images characterization, useful for professional biomedical experts. The main objective is to enable a new metrics to decide the oocyte quality.

The images are from microscopy, and their relative aspects are similar, so an automatic procedure for image processing has been possible. New algorithms were developed for segmentation and selection the oocyte cytoplasm.

The Sobel filter has proved to be a powerful tool to find edges (pipettes, oocyte membrane) directly without pre-processing. Segmentation algorithm has been based mainly on Hough transform, allowing fast circle detection for area cytoplasm definition. The circle search space has been limited to a subset of real possibilities, due that oocyte size is well limited. In this way, the probability of a point to belong to a given circle is increased and the search algorithm accelerates. In conclusion, the proposed method is efficient (98% correct detection) and fast.

The histogram information has been employed as the main source of data to characterize the texture (granularity) of the cytoplasm region. The case in which two images have the same or similar granularity but their histograms are quite different has been solved. This is a cases derived from different light conditions, positions of all elements, photo camera, etc. This problem requires a histogram normalized solution. Two filters have been proposed for preprocessing the cytoplasm area before to granularity characterization: the Sobel filter to enhance borders associated to high granularity, and a Gaussian filter to image smoothing. In some sense, filter texture is being associated to borders definitions (more borders, high granularity). Texture analysis has been extended to full cytoplasm area, calculating six functions for each area section (four).

In total, the 24 parameters are associated to a cytoplasm area. The intensity, contrast, asymmetry, homogeneity, smooth and entropy were defined as texture metric parameters, and classified in three main, allowing even the differentiation of different texture properties in the same cytoplasm area.

Clustering based in fuzzy methods was developed to classify the set of parameters obtained from the texture metric analysis. The fuzzy system was trained looking for three main groups of textures: normal, medium and high as was advised by the experts. Results shown a clustering efficiency of 83%, and that some parameters, as entropy, should have a biggest weight in fuzzy algorithm.

Some facts could increase the image processing complexity, in particular, the texture analysis, such as the existence of some inclusion bodies; vacuoles, liposomes. Also, future work will incorporate the polar body detection, where and many, as oocyte full description.

ACKNOWLEDGMENTS

The authors would like to thank to Mas Vida Clinical Center for delivering the oocytes photographs and biomedical advising during the specification process for of the computer tool.

REFERENCES

[1] R. Ivascu, R. Zeggari, C. Pieralli, B. Wacogne and C. Roux, Measuring the Refractive Index of Oocytes by Means of an Optical Microsystem: A Non Invasive Technique to Estimate the Evolution of Oocytes Maturity. BIODEVICES 2010 - *International Conference on Biomedical Electronics and Devices*, pp: 127-132. Valencia. Spain. Jan. (2010).

[2] T. M. A. Basile, L. Caponetti, G. Castellano, and G. Sforza, A Texture-Based Image Processing Approach for the Description of Human Oocyte Cytoplasm. *IEEE Transactions on Instrumentation and Measurements*, vol. 59, n. 10, pp: 2591-2601. Oct. (2010).

[3] Yúfera, E. Gallego and J. Molina, ImagCell: A Computer Tool for Cell Culture Image Processing Applications in Bio-Impedance Measurements. Chapter 75, pp: 733-740, in Software Tools and Algorithms for Biological Systems. Springer book series, *Advances in Experimental Medicine and Biology*, AEMB. Vol 696. Edited by H. Arabnia and Quoc-Nan Tran. Springer. 2011.

[4] Yúfera and E. Gallego, Automatic Generation of Analog Hardware Description Language (AHDL) Code from Cell-Culture Images. *IEEE International Conference on Image Processing Theory, Tools and Applications*, IPTA 2010. pp: 535-538 Paris (France), Jul. 2010.

[5] J. Aragón, Determinación del estado de maduración de ovocitos mediante el análisis de imágenes. *Computer Engineering Degree. Escuela Técnica Superior de Ingeniería Informática*. Jun. 2011.

[6] Más Vida Medical Center. http://www.masvidareproduccion.com.

[7] OpenCv Structural Analysis Reference. http://www710.univlyon1.fr/ ~bouakaz/ OpenCV-0.9.5/docs/ref/OpenCVRef_StructAnalysis.htm.

[8] OpenCv Reference Manual. http://www.seas.upenn.edu/~bensapp/ opencvdocs/ref /opencvref_cv.htm.

[9] M. Levine. Vision in Man and Machine. New York. McGraw- Hill, 1985.

[10] José L. Díez, José L. Navarro and Antonio Sala, Algoritmos de clustering en la identificación de modelos borrosos. XXII Jornadas de Automática. Barcelona, Spain. 2001.

[11] G. Jaime Correa Henao, Algoritmo de Agrupamiento Fuzzy C-Means. Universidad Nacional de Colombia. Octubre 2003.

[12] Msdn Library: http://msdn.microsoft.com/es-es/library.

In: Image Processing
Editor: Vítor Hugo Carvalho
ISBN 978-1-62081-844-2

Chapter 4

MATCHING OF INFRARED AND VISUAL IMAGES USING THE FOURIER-MELLIN TRANSFORM

J. R. Martínez-de Dios* and A. Ollero
Robotics, Vision and Control Group,
University of Seville, Spain

ABSTRACT

This chapter describes a frequency domain technique for matching infrared and visual images. Matching of images in different spectral bands is a difficult problem since the objects can appear very differently in both images.

Classical spatial domain methods have difficulties in this problem due to the lack of common features between both images. Instead, the proposed technique uses a frequency domain matching method that relies on the common structure between the images. The method uses Fourier-Mellin transforms and Symmetric Phase-Only Matched Filtering to detect rotation, scaling and translation between images. This chapter presents the main principles of the method, gives implementation details and analyses its performance.

INTRODUCTION

The fusion of images of the same object using cameras operating in different spectral bands allows a wide range of complementarities that facilitate the development of high-performance perception systems. In the last decade advances in imaging technologies have boosted the combined use of infrared and visual cameras in a growing number of applications including border patrolling [1], person detection [2], infrastructure and building inspection [3], forest fire detection [4] and monitoring [5], safety and security and search and rescue, among others.

* E-mail address: jdedios@cartuja.us.es

Image registration is the process of overlaying two or more images of the same scene taken at different times, from different viewpoints, and/or by different sensors. It geometrically aligns two images using one of them as the reference. Image registration is an important step in image processing tasks in which the information is gained from the combination of various data sources like in image fusion and change detection.

The problem of matching images from two different cameras can be formulated from diverse perspectives. In a basic scheme both cameras have a fixed arrangement, as in a stereo system. They cannot be moved or orientated independently and their optical parameters are static. In these schemes static image matching should only be computed once in the system calibration stage and the matching parameters are valid until the camera arrangement is modified.

In other cases each camera can be moved and orientated freely and their optical parameters can be modified independently of the rest of the cameras. Thus, image matching should be applied to every pair of images. If the location, orientation and optical parameters of each camera are known, image matching can be carried out using geometrical considerations. This approach is used in many multi-robot systems, where the location and orientation of the cameras onboard the robots are measured with accuracy using differential GPS receivers and Inertial Measurement Units.

In this chapter we focus on a general image matching problem in which there is no knowledge on the location or orientation of the cameras nor on its optical parameters. Thus, matching cannot rely on any sensors' measurements apart from the images themselves. A good number of image matching methods for this problem have been reported in the literature. However, the great majority implicitly assume that the images are in the same spectral band. When dealing with cameras in different spectral bands, image matching complicates since the same object can be seen very differently in different bands.

This chapter presents a frequency domain technique for matching images in different spectral bands. The method is based on the Fourier-Mellin transforms (FMT) and Symmetric Phase Only Matched Filtering (SPOMF), which rely on the global structure of the image instead of on features in the spatial domain. The proposed method can correct translation, rotation and scaling between images, which is sufficient for a good number of applications. The method was implemented efficiently for real-time execution with low computing resources. The method allows fusing images in order to achieve a *virtual camera*, which images cover a wide spectral range that includes infrared and visual bands.

This chapter is structured as follows. Section 2 introduces the problem of matching images in different spectral bands. Section 3 presents the principles of image matching using Fourier-Mellin transform and Symmetric Phase Only Matched Filtering. Section 4 shows examples that illustrate the operation of the proposed method. Section 5 analyses the performance of the proposed method and presents some practical considerations to increase its robustness, accuracy and efficiency. Finally, Section 6 is devoted to the conclusions.

MATCHING IMAGES FROM INFRARED AND VISUAL CAMERAS

The observation of an object or a scene using different electromagnetic bands enables to obtain rich information with high potentialities in a wide range of applications. Infrared cameras measure the infrared radiation intensity field of a scene. Infrared cameras can "see" in pitch black conditions and through smoke. They can also transform radiation measurements in temperature estimations using black body physics and generate thermograms with the temperature of the objects in the scene [6]. In the last decades infrared camera technology has experienced a very significant evolution. Now it is possible to find commercial off-the-shelf -COTS- infrared cameras that weight less than 150 gr, consume less than 1,5 W and require virtually no maintenance since they have no cooling system. These advances have originated the growing use of infrared cameras a wide range of problems.

Fusion of images in different spectral bands allows certain perception properties that cannot be achieved using any of the images individually. For instance, the fusion of images in the near-infrared and far-infrared spectral bands allows to see through fog [7], while fog is opaque to any of these bands individually [8]. Fusion also allows perceiving certain features that cannot be observed in none of the images. By combining infrared and visual images it is possible to perceive properties of materials. Integrated infrared-visual camera systems have been used in pharmaceutical sectors for several years.

In other cases, each, the infrared and the visual images, provide a partial perception of the object of interest and their fusion achieves the global perception. For instance, in automatic forest fire measurement, visual images can be used to measure flames geometry if smoke does not occlude the images. Infrared cameras can 'see' through smoke but cannot observe the flames since they are highly transparent to infrared cameras because flames radiation is significantly lower than that of the fire base [9]. The combination of visual and infrared images allows extracting complete measurements of the fire base and flames [5].

In many multi-sensor systems infrared images are used to provide measurements that can also be obtained by other sensors. Infrared cameras often provide measurements with low uncertainty, which improve the robustness and accuracy of the overall estimation. For instance, the forest-fire detection false alarm reduction system described in [4] uses infrared and visual cameras, among others, to confirm or discard the fire alarm. The overall decision system integrates measurements from several sensors. The measurements from infrared images have significantly higher confidence than those from the visual images.

In many cases visual images are used as a support for the perception achieved by the infrared images. For instance, in building inspection application the defects detected on the infrared images are identified on the visual images.

The aforementioned problems require matching between infrared and visual images. This chapter proposes a method for matching infrared and visual images using only the information contained in the images. Thus, the images from both cameras should have some overlapping. In the aforementioned conditions image matching is not an easy problem since the objects can appear very differently in images in different spectral bands. For instance, Figure 1 shows two images, one visual and one infrared, of the same scene. Although the main structure of both images is similar, many regions (marked in Figure 1 with dashed rectangles) are different.

Apart from the differences inherent to the nature of the measurements, infrared and visual images also have differences due to technological reasons. Infrared cameras' detectors are highly affected by several types of noise including thermal noise, shot noise and flicker noise, [10]. In fact, many cameras use cooling systems -often cryogenic- to ensure that the detector operates at very low and constant temperature. Infrared cameras with no cooling system are affected by higher levels of noise. Also, the sensitivity of infrared detectors is lower than that of standard CMOS and CCD detectors commonly used in visual cameras. This lack of sensitivity often originates low-contrasted images.

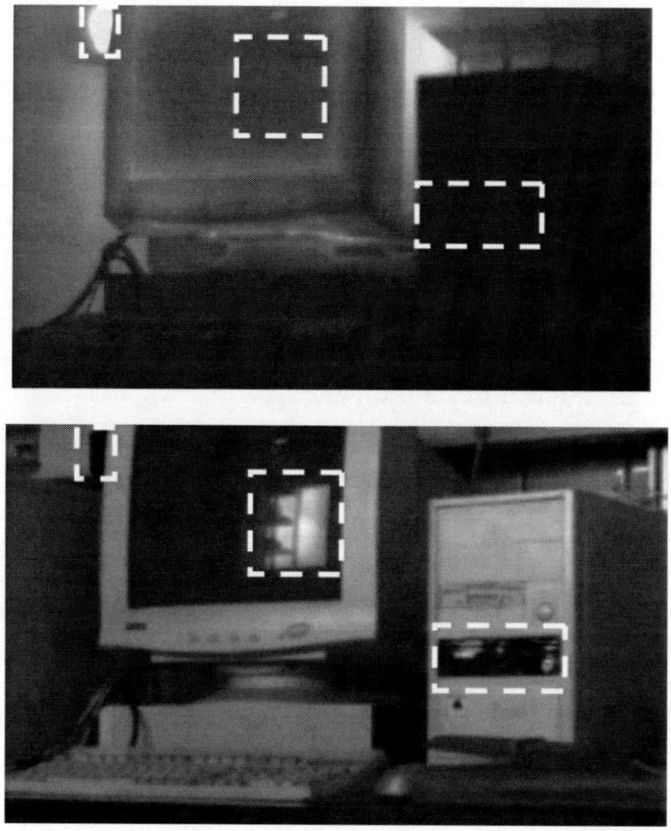

Figure 1. Two images of the same scene in different spectral bands: Left) taken with a *FLIR ThermaCAM P-20* infrared camera; Right) taken with an *ImagingSource DFK 21BF04* visual camera.

The great majority of the reported image matching techniques can be classified in spatial domain and frequency domain methods. A detailed review can be found in [11].

Spatial methods are based on matching local features identified in both images. These methods rely on detecting in both images local features corresponding to the same object. In case of detecting a sufficient number and well-distributed features, it is possible to use them for fitting an image distortion model. The homography matrix is often chosen since it allows describing the transformations originated by changes in the location and orientation of the cameras when the imaged scene can be approximated by a plane [12]. These local features are typically selected as corners [13], high-contrast points or local patterns with invariant properties, see e.g. [14]. The main difficulty of these methods in our problem is the lack of common local features in images in different spectral bands.

Frequency domain methods exploit the properties of the transform domain. Normalized cross-correlation, see e.g. [15], has been a common approach to match translated images: the location of the main peak of the cross-correlation corresponds to the relative translation between the images. The Fourier transform can be used to compute the cross-correlation between the two images, saving computational burden. In these matching methods noise and clutter in the images result in broad peaks, which hamper its localization without uncertainties. Some alternatives, such as the Symmetric Phase-Only Matched Filtering (SPOMF) produce significantly sharper peaks and are more robust to noise, partial occlusions, and other defects [16]. Also, methods based on the Fourier transform can only match translated images. The Fourier-Mellin transform (FMT) extends the method to also determine rotation and scaling by converting the images to log-polar coordinates [17].

The method described in this Chapter uses the Fourier-Mellin transform with the Symmetric Phase-Only Matched Filtering to match images in different spectral bands. The method relies on the global structure of the image and not on local features, which avoids the aforementioned difficulties of feature-based techniques. It is capable of matching translated, rotated and scaled images, which is sufficient for many applications.

IMAGE MATCHING USING THE FMT AND SPOMF

This section presents the principle of image matching using the Fourier-Mellin transform and Symmetric Phase-Only Matched Filtering.

Symmetric Phase-Only Matched Filtering

Matched filtering is one of the most extended frequency domain techniques for matching translated images. One of the main limitations of classical matched filters is that the output is affected by the energy of the image. Translation between images only influences the spectral phase of the signal. The Symmetric Phase-Only Matched Filtering (SPOMF) has been proposed as an alternative to determine translations among images with no influence of the magnitude.

Assume that $im_1(x,y)$ is replica of $im_2(x,y)$ translated (x_0,y_0) in a noisy scene, $im_1(x,y)=im_2(x-x_0,y-y_0)+n(x,y)$, where $n(x,y)$ represents a white zero mean random noise independent of $im_2(x,y)$. The SPOMF between $im_1(x,y)$ and $im_2(x,y)$ is as follows:

$$Q_{SPOMF}(u,v) = \exp\left[j\varphi_1(u,v) - j\varphi_2(u,v)\right] \qquad (1)$$

where $\varphi_1(u,v)$ and $\varphi_2(u,v)$ are the spectral phases of $im_1(x,y)$ and $im_2(x,y)$. In the absence of noise the inverse Fourier transform of $Q_{SPOMF}(u,v)$ is a Dirac delta located at (x_0,y_0), the translation between $im_1(x,y)$ and $im_2(x,y)$. SPOMF produces very sharp peaks making the detection and location of the maximum easier and more tolerant to noise, which is a significant advantage when dealing with images with high level of noise such as infrared images.

Image Matching Using the Fourier-Mellin Transform

Assume that $im_1(x,y)$ and $im_2(x,y)$ are two images of the same scene. α, σ, x_0 and y_0 are respectively the relative rotation angle, scale factor and translations between them:

$$im_1(x,y) = im_2\left(\sigma(x\cos\alpha + y\sin\alpha) - x_0,\ \sigma(-x\sin\alpha + y\cos\alpha) - y_0\right) \tag{2}$$

The matching method consists of two steps. The first one detects and corrects the rotation and scaling between $im_1(x,y)$ and $im_2(x,y)$. The corrected version of $im_1(x,y)$ is denoted $im^R{}_1(x,y)$. The second step detects and corrects the translation between $im^R{}_1(x,y)$ and $im_2(x,y)$. The translation-corrected version of $im^R{}_1(x,y)$ is denoted $im^M{}_1(x,y)$.

Rotation and Scaling Correction

From (2), the Fourier transform of $im_1(x,y)$, $IM_1(u,v)=F\{im_1(x,y)\}$, can be expressed by the following expression:

$$IM_1(u,v) = \sigma^{-2}\left|IM_2\left(\sigma^{-1}(u\cos\alpha + v\sin\alpha),\ \sigma^{-1}(-u\sin\alpha + v\cos\alpha)\right)\right|\exp\left[-j\varphi_1(u,v)\right] \tag{3}$$

where $IM_2(u,v)=F\{im_2(x,y)\}$ and $\varphi_1(u,v)$ is the phase of $IM_1(u,v)$. From (3), it is easy to notice that $|IM_1(u,v)|$ is affected by rotation and scaling but is invariant to translation:

$$\left|IM_1(u,v)\right| = \sigma^{-2}\left|IM_2\left(\sigma^{-1}(u\cos\alpha + v\sin\alpha),\ \sigma^{-1}(-u\sin\alpha + v\cos\alpha)\right)\right| \tag{4}$$

Rotation and scaling can be decoupled by converting $|IM_1(u,v)|$ and $|IM_2(u,v)|$ to polar coordinates. Let $im^P{}_1(\theta,\rho)$ and $im^P{}_2(\theta,\rho)$ be $|IM_1(u,v)|$ and $|IM_2(u,v)|$ in polar co-ordinates. Hence, from (4), $im^P{}_1(\theta,\rho)$ can be expressed as:

$$im^P{}_1(\theta,\rho) = \sigma^{-2}\, im^P{}_2(\theta - \alpha, \rho/\sigma) \tag{5}$$

In (5) the rotation has been transformed in a translation in the θ axis. Scaling can also be transformed in a translation by applying a logarithmic scale to the ρ axis, $\lambda=\log(\rho)$. In log-polar coordinates (θ,λ), (5) can be expressed as:

$$im^{lp}{}_1(\theta,\lambda) = \sigma^{-2}\, im^{lp}{}_2(\theta - \alpha, \lambda - \log(\sigma)) \tag{6}$$

where $im^{lp}{}_1(\theta,\lambda)$ and $im^{lp}{}_2(\theta,\lambda)$ are the logarithmic versions of $im^P{}_1(\theta,\rho)$ and $im^P{}_2(\theta,\rho)$, respectively. Thus, in (6) both, rotation and scaling, have been transformed to translations. Let $IM^{lp}{}_1(\upsilon,\omega)$ and $IM^{lp}{}_2(\upsilon,\omega)$ be respectively the Fourier transforms of $im^{lp}{}_1(\theta,\lambda)$ and $im^{lp}{}_2(\theta,\lambda)$. Using shift properties of the Fourier transform, (6) can be rewritten as:

$$\left|IM^{lp}{}_1(\upsilon,\omega)\right|\exp\left\{-j\varphi^{lp}{}_1(\upsilon,\omega)\right\} = \left|IM^{lp}{}_2(\upsilon,\omega)\right|\exp\left[-j\varphi^{lp}{}_1(\upsilon,\omega) - 2\pi\left(\upsilon\log(\sigma) + \omega\alpha\right)\right] \tag{7}$$

where $\varphi^{lp}{}_1(\upsilon,\omega)$ and $\varphi^{lp}{}_2(\upsilon,\omega)$ are the phases of $IM^{lp}{}_1(\upsilon,\omega)$ and $IM^{lp}{}_2(\upsilon,\omega)$, respectively.

From (7), it is simple to notice that the rotation and the scaling appear as shifts between the phases $\varphi^{lp}{}_1(\upsilon,\omega)$ and $\varphi^{lp}{}_2(\upsilon,\omega)$. The phase shift is:

$$\delta = \varphi^{lp}{}_1(\upsilon,\omega) - \varphi^{lp}{}_2(\upsilon,\omega) = 2\pi(\upsilon\log(\sigma) + \omega\alpha) \tag{8}$$

Thus, the SPOMF is as follows:

$$q_r(\theta,\lambda) = F^{-1}\{\exp[-j\delta]\} \tag{9}$$

The location of the peak of $q_r(\theta,\lambda)$, $(\theta_{max},\lambda_{max})$, represents the rotation angle $\theta_{max}=\alpha$ and the scaling factor $\lambda_{max}=\log(\sigma)$ between $im_1(x,y)$ and $im_2(x,y)$. The corrected image, $im^R{}_1(x,y)$, is obtained by rotating $im_1(x,y)$ an angle θ_{max} and scaling the resulting image by factor $\exp(\lambda_{max})$. Bilinear or bicubic interpolation is applied for image resampling.

Translation Correction

The second step detects and corrects the translational offsets between $im^R{}_1(x,y)$ and $im_2(x,y)$.

Once the rotation and scaling have been corrected, $im^R{}_2(x,y)$ and $im_1(x,y)$ are related only by translations. Then, the SPOMF can be used to determine the translational offset between them:

$$Q_t(u,v) = \exp[-j(\varphi^R{}_1(u,v) - \varphi_2(u,v))] \tag{10}$$

where $\varphi^R{}_1(u,v)$ and $\varphi_2(u,v)$ are respectively the phases of $IM^R{}_1(u,v)$ and $IM_2(u,v)$, the Fourier transforms of $im^R{}_1(x,y)$ and $im_2(x,y)$, respectively. The translations between $im^R{}_1(x,y)$ and $im_2(x,y)$ can be obtained by computing:

$$q_t(x,y) = F^{-1}\{Q_t(u,v)\} \tag{11}$$

The peak of $q_t(x,y)$ is located at $x=x_{max}$ and $y=y_{max}$. Thus, the translations between $im^R{}_1(x,y)$ and $im_2(x,y)$ are given by $x_0=x_{max}$ and $y_0=y_{max}$. The matched image, $im^M{}_1(x,y)$, is determined by shifting $im^R{}_1(x,y)$ by x_0 and y_0.

The Infrared-Visual Matching Method

The proposed technique is based on the FMT-SPOMF method but adapted for operating with images in different spectral bands and to support high levels of noise. This section illustrates its operation. The high differences between the images require also adopting a number of practical considerations in order to increase its robustness and accuracy. They will be analyzed in the next section.

The first step is to select the central regions of the images. These central regions are the input of the proposed method. Their size is selected to be power to 2 in order to facilitate efficient implementation of FFT algorithms. In this example, the size of the central region is

256x256. Figure 2 shows the selected central regions of one infrared and one visual image of the same scene related through relative rotation, scaling and translations. In this example, the infrared image will be corrected and matched with respect to the visual image, considered as reference.

Figure 2. Two images of the same scene: Left) taken with a *FLIR ThermaCAM P-20* infrared camera; Right) grey-level image taken with an *ImagingSource DFK 21BF04* visual camera.

Image Uniformization

The following step is to increase the level of similarity between the infrared and visual images. The edges of the objects in the scene are more similar in both images than their lower spatial frequency components. The low frequency components refer to the intensity levels with which the objects are seen in the visible and infrared spectral bands, which can be significantly different. On the contrary, the high frequency components correspond to object edges. The contour of an object even with low difference in their intensity level can be detected with standard gradient operators.

The proposed method applies Sobel edge detection to both images in order to intensify the contribution of the high frequency components and to cancel the contribution of the low frequency components. Prior to the Sobel edge detector, a median filtering is applied in order to smooth the noise and clutter in the images.

The output of the Sobel detector -the magnitude considering the contributions of the vertical and horizontal masks- is normalized to the image intensity range [0-255] and discretized: the resulting images contain the edges of the visual and infrared images. The intensities of the edges depend on the grey levels in the original images. Thus, the same object contour can have different edge values in the visual and the infrared edge images. To increase the similarity of the edge images, they are both submitted to a histogram equalization process.

Figure 3 shows the resulting images. Their contrast level is not high. It is not possible to obtain a uniform intensity distribution after applying the histogram equalization.

Nevertheless, after this stage the differences in the intensity levels in both images have been greatly reduced and the main edges and global structure of the scene have been enhanced in both images. Figure 3 right contains significant level of clutter originated by noise in the visual camera signal. The method is robust to this local disturbance.

Using the previous notation the results of the uniformization stage are $im_1(x,y)$ and $im_2(x,y)$. The next stage is to apply the rotation and scaling correction step.

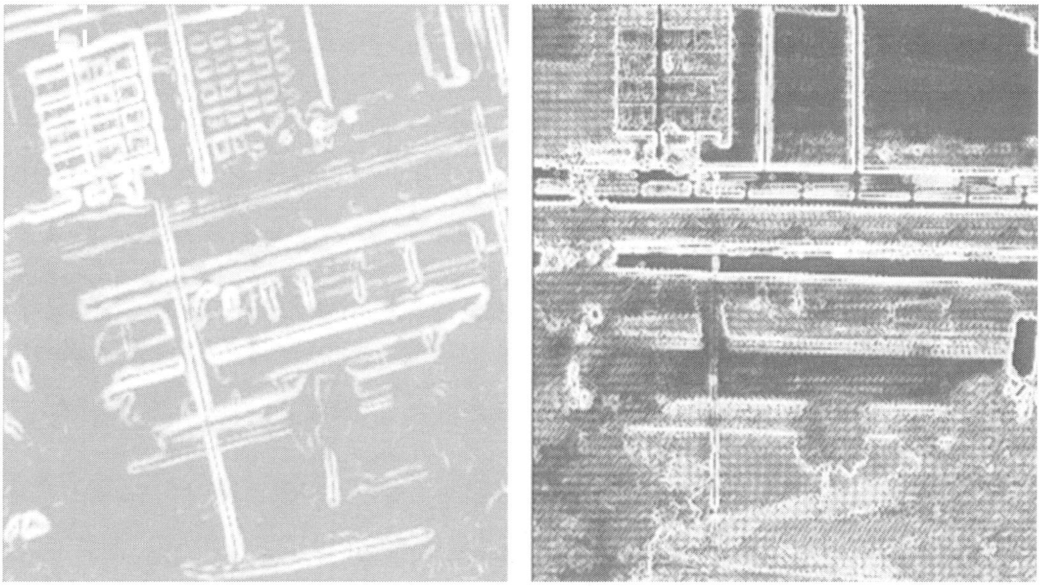

Figure 3. Resulting infrared (left) and visual (right) images after the image uniformization stage.

Rotation and Scaling Correction

The first step is to compute the Fourier transforms of $im_1(x,y)$ and $im_2(x,y)$: $IM_1(u,v)$ and $IM_2(u,v)$, respectively. A median filter is applied to smooth $|IM_1(u,v)|$ and $|IM_2(u,v)|$. Figure 4 shows the resulting $|IM_1(u,v)|$ and $|IM_2(u,v)|$. A 3D view of $|IM_1(u,v)|$ is in Figure 4left. It is simple to see that a rotation between images results in a rotation between $|IM_1(u,v)|$ and $|IM_2(u,v)|$ as predicted by (4). The conversion to polar co-ordinates transforms this rotation into a translation. Then, $|IM_1(u,v)|$ and $|IM_2(u,v)|$ are converted to polar-log co-ordinates. The computation of the Fourier transform can introduce significant spurious effects, which can deteriorate the determination of the scaling and rotation. The Hanning window is a cosine shaped positive function with values close to zero at the limits of its support region. Applying the Hanning window before computing the Fourier transform cancels high-magnitude spurious peaks that greatly disturb the matching process. In the proposed method the conversion to polar-log co-ordinates includes the Hanning window. Figure 5 shows 3D (left) and 2D (right) representations of $im^{lp}{}_1(\theta,\lambda)$ (top) and $im^{lp}{}_2(\theta,\lambda)$ (bottom). It is possible to notice a horizontal shift between them, which corresponds to the rotation angle between $im_1(x,y)$ and $im_2(x,y)$.

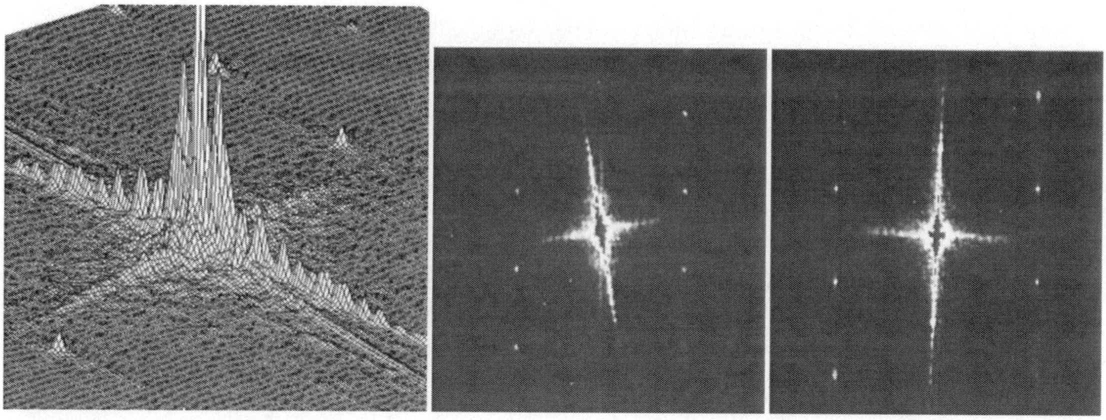

Figure 4. Resulting $|IM_1(u,v)|$ and $|IM_2(u,v)|$: Left) 3D view of $|IM_1(u,v)|$; Center) and Right) 2D views of $|IM_1(u,v)|$ and $|IM_2(u,v)|$.

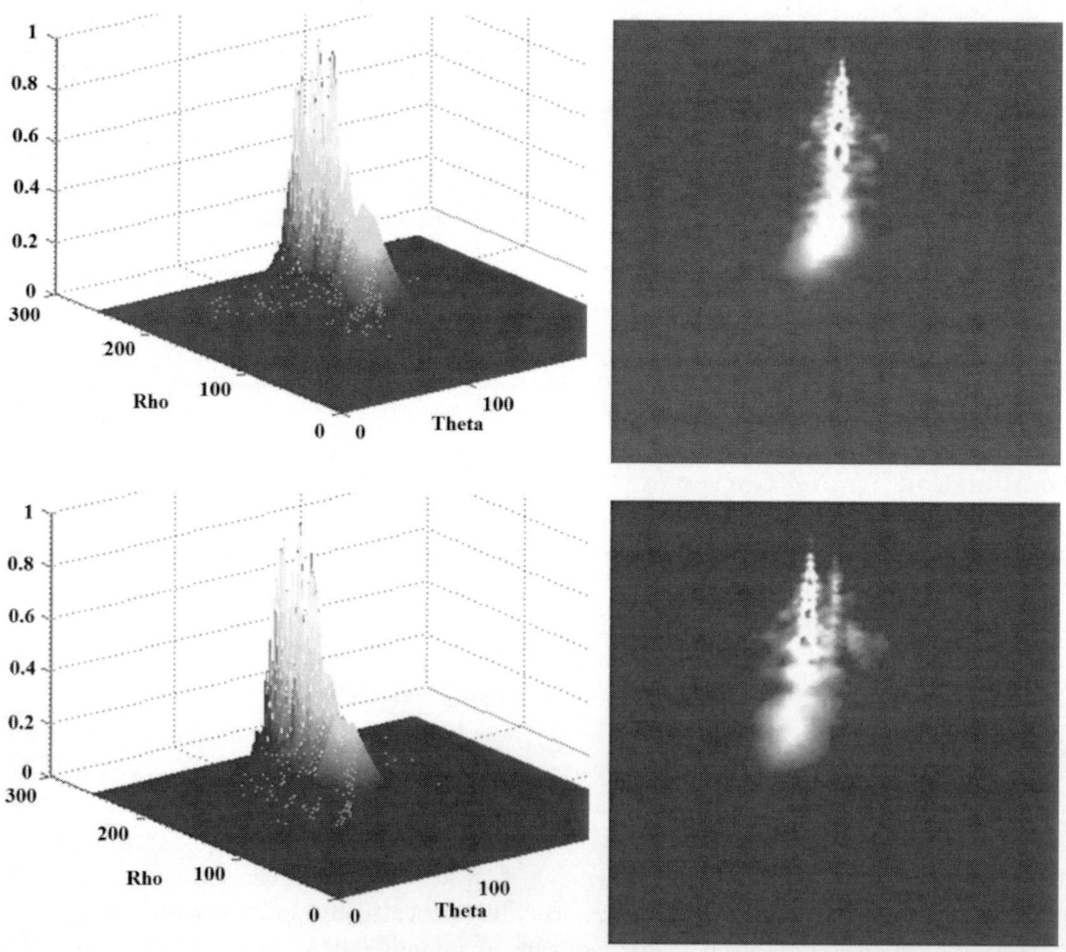

Figure 5. 3D (left) and 2D (right) views log-polar converted images $im^{lp}_1(\theta,\rho)$ (top) and $im^{lp}_2(\theta,\rho)$ (bottom).

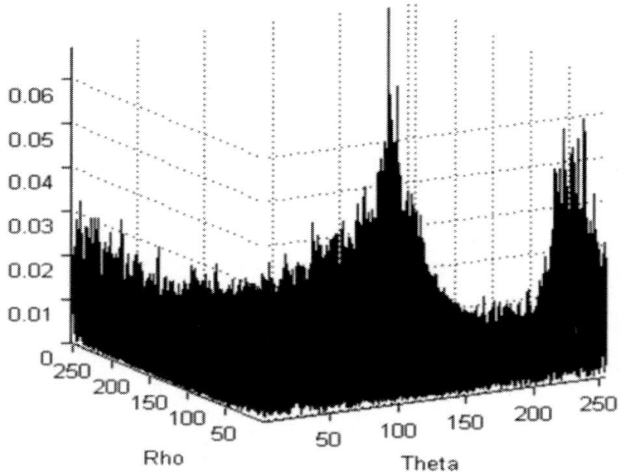

Figure 6. Left) Resulting $q_r(\theta,\lambda)$ from the SPOMF. Right) $im^M{}_1(u,v)$ matched infrared image after correcting scaling and rotation.

The next step is to apply the SPOMF to compute the shift between $im^{lp}{}_1(\theta,\lambda)$ and $im^{lp}{}_2(\theta,\lambda)$. Thus, expressions (8-9) are computed. Figure 6left shows the resulting $q_r(\theta,\lambda)$. The location of the maximum value determines the rotation angle and scaling factor. The location of the maximum corresponds to α=14.27° and σ=1.1. Figure 6right shows the infrared image after correction of scaling and rotation $im^R{}_1(x,y)$. In this example the second highest peak in $q_r(\theta,\lambda)$ is located very near the maximum peak and has a magnitude 11% lower than the maximum peak.

Translation Correction

Once the image rotation and scaling have been determined, this step computed the translations between $im^R{}_1(x,y)$ and $im_2(x,y)$. The high difference $im^R{}_1(x,y)$ and $im_2(x,y)$ require individual methods for determining the translational offsets in each axis, x and y.

The uniformization step for axis x involves the Sobel mask for vertical edges while the uniformization for axis y involves the Sobel mask for horizontal axis. The rest of the steps remain unchanged. Enhancing individually the similarities in x or y axes improves robustness to noise when applying the proposed method.

Figure 7 shows the resulting images after the uniformization step for axis x (top) and y (bottom) applied to the original infrared (left) and visual (right) images. The similarity between them has been enhanced.

Then, two SPOMF are applied, one for each axis. Figure 8 shows the result of the SPOMF for each axis. The maximum peaks are very sharp, which facilitates the determination of the translational offsets and validates the strategy of considering each axis individually. The translational offsets computed are x_0=9 and y_0=10. Figure 9 left shows the infrared image after translation correction $im^M{}_1(u,v)$.

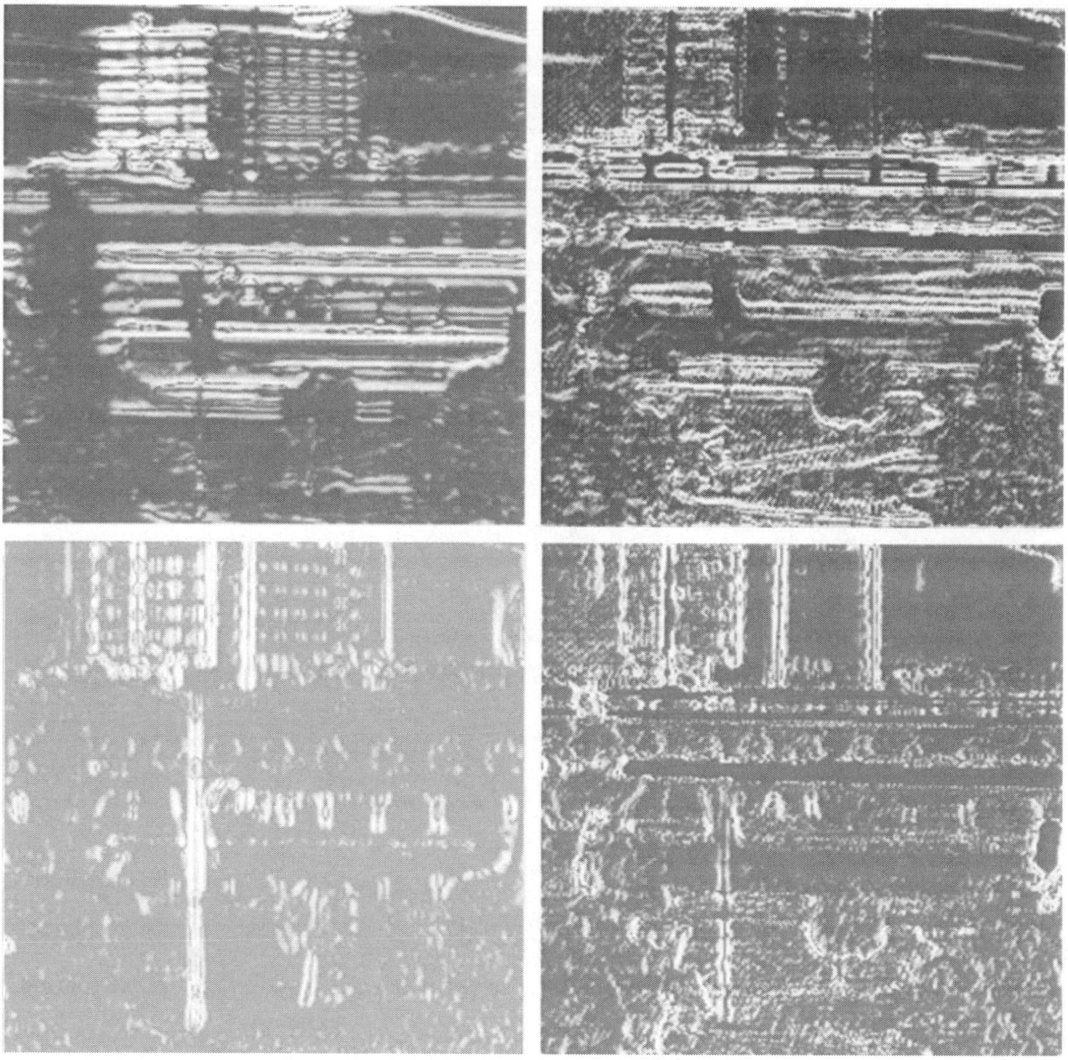

Figure 7. Resulting images after the uniformization step for axis x (top) and y (bottom) applied to the original infrared (left) and visual (right) images.

Once the images have been corrected it is necessary to fuse them in suitable way. This measurement level fusion allows developing a *virtual camera* which images cover infrared and visual spectral ranges.

In some cases it is interesting is to highlight or cancel in the fused image the objects of interest identified in the infrared images [18]. Visual images are displayed as grey levels and the intensities in the infrared images higher than a certain threshold are added to the Red colour field of the visual image. This approach allows highlighting the hot objects in the fused image. Another approach is to combine all the pixels from both images, being the infrared intensities considered only in the Red colour field. Figure 9right shows the resulting infrared-visual fused image in this example. The matching error is less than one pixel. In other schemes it can also be interesting the images in an unique grey-level image.

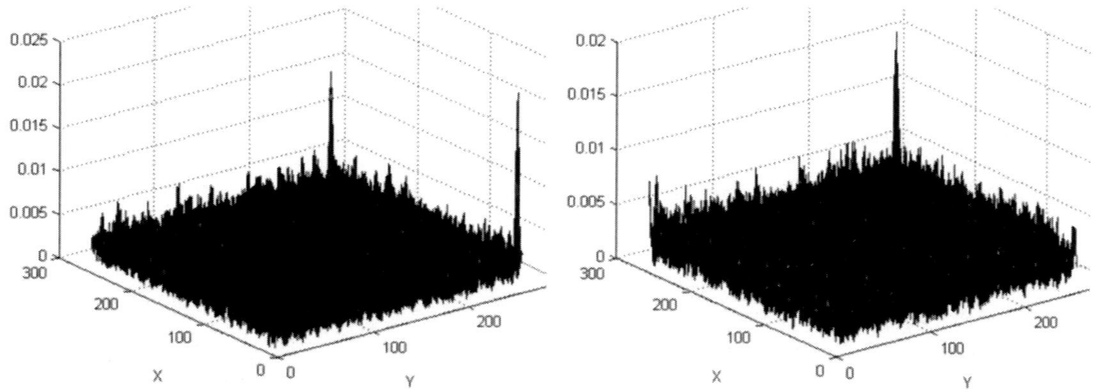

Figure 8. Resulting $q_t(x,y)$ for axes x (left) and y (right).

Figure 9. Left) $im^M{}_1(u,v)$, corrected infrared image. Right) Resulting overlapped infrared-visual image.

IMPLEMENTATION

Practical Aspects

This subsection presents additional considerations to improve the robustness, accuracy and efficiency of the proposed method.

Noise Correction

Difference between both images and image noise originate a notable level of clutter in the method. Several modifications have been included to cope with them.

Smoothing filters are used at different steps of the algorithm. For instance, the first step in the uniformization step is a median filtering to cancel the noise before applying the Sobel detector. A median filter is used before detecting the maximum peaks of $q_r(\theta,\lambda)$ and $q_t(x,y)$. Another filter is applied to smooth $|IM_1(u,v)|$ and $|IM_2(u,v)|$ in the rotation correction step. In the rotation step the low frequency components in $|IM_1(u,v)|$ and $|IM_2(u,v)|$ disturb the identification of the rotation angle after applying the log-polar conversion. To prevent errors the square central part of $|IM_1(u,v)|$ and $|IM_2(u,v)|$ are cancelled. Figure 10 shows $|IM_1(u,v)|$ and $|IM_2(u,v)|$ from the previous example, after cancellation of the low frequency components. The rotation between images can be clearly noticed.

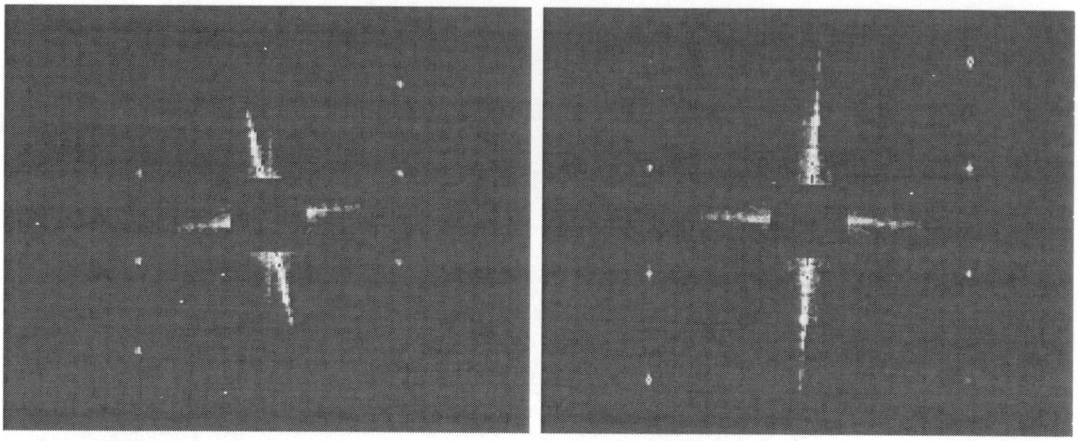

Figure 10. $|IM_1(u,v)|$ and $|IM_2(u,v)|$ in Figure 4 after cancellation of the low frequency components.

Determination of Peak Location in SPOMF

The accuracy in the computation of α, σ, x_0 and y_0 are limited by the resolution in $q_r(\theta,\lambda)$ and $q_t(x,y)$. A sub-pixel estimation method is used to determine the position of the peak. In absence of noise the SPOMF yields a Dirac delta. Noise broadens the peak.

The modification adopted detects the maximum of $q_r(\theta,\lambda)$ and establishes a neighborhood around it. The centroid in the neighborhood is considered as the location of the peak with sub-pixel resolution, involving an increase in accuracy.

This approach also increases the robustness against secondary peaks that usually take place in the proximity of the main peak.

Figure 11. Visual (left) and infrared (right) images used for the performance evaluation.

Computational Aspects

Significant efforts have been put in the reduction of the computer burden of the proposed method in order to allow its real-time operation without the need of special hardware. The 2D FFTs have been computed using the Cooley-Tukey algorithm [19] due to its balance between efficiency and simplicity. The size of the matrices was selected to be power of two. Winograd algorithm [20] is faster than the Cooley-Tuckey but it has more complexity in the data indexing involved in the FFT. To reduce the computer burden of the Fourier transforms the symmetry properties of 2D FFTs of real data are exploited. If $A(x,y)$ is a real its 2D FFT, $A(u,v)$, satisfies: $Re(A(u,v))= Re(A(-u,-v))$ and $Im(A(u,v))=-Im(A(-u,-v))$. Also, the twiddle factors of the Cooley-Tukey algorithm, which depend only on the size of the FFT vectors, are computed only once at the initialization of the system. Both measures represent a saving of 65% of the computer burden required for the computation of FFT and inverse FFT. The resolution and accuracy in the computation of α, σ, x_0 and y_0 is highly dependent on the size of the images and matrices involved. Assume that the size of the central part of $Im_1(x,y)$ and $Im_2(x,y)$ used as input to the FMT-SPOMF is MxM and that the size of $s_{pl}(\theta,\lambda)$ and $r_p(\theta,\lambda)$ is NxN. Two different modes have been defined and implemented to balance between matching accuracy and computer burden. When $M=N=128$ the method takes an average of 10 ms to match and correct one image on a Pentium IV 3.2 GHz. When $M=N=256$ the method takes an average of 36 ms.

Performance Evaluation

This subsection analyses the performance of the proposed method. Figure 11 shows two matched images of the same scene.

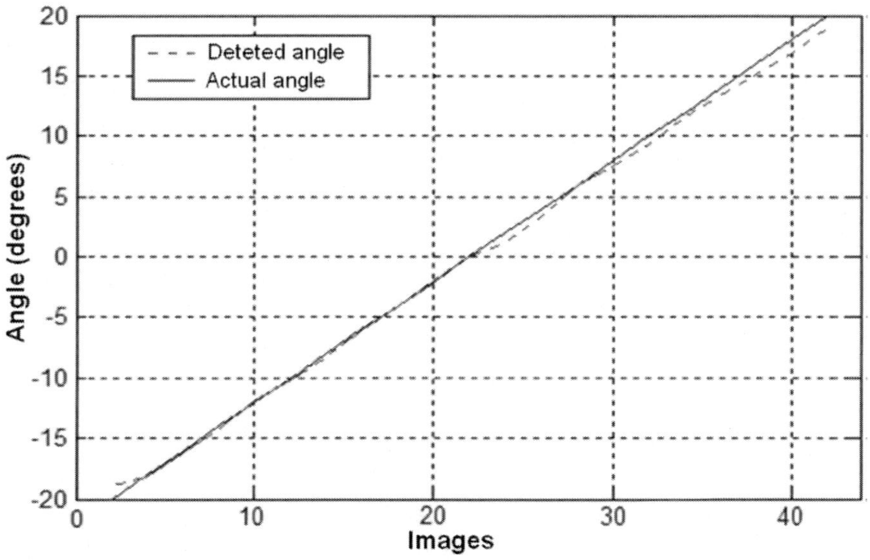

Figure 12. Performance in rotation detection: angles detected by the proposed method (dashed line) versus the actual relative rotation angle (full line).

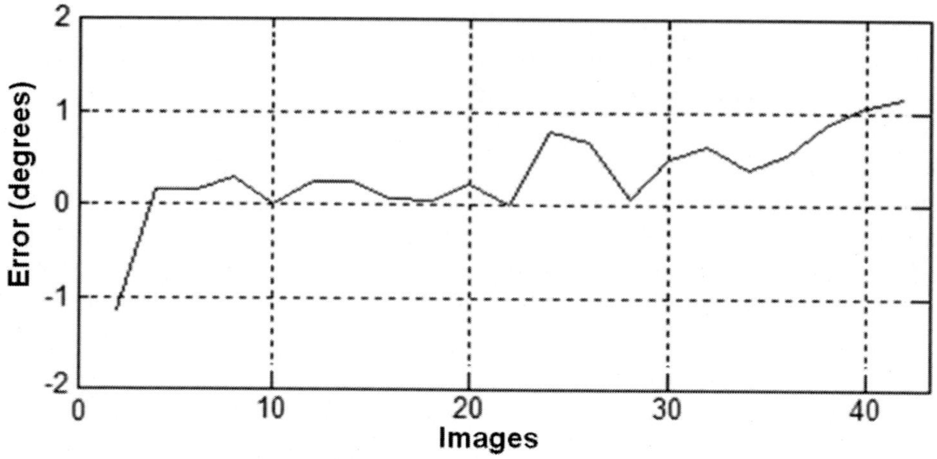

Figure 13. Rotation angle error: the maximum error is 1.2º.

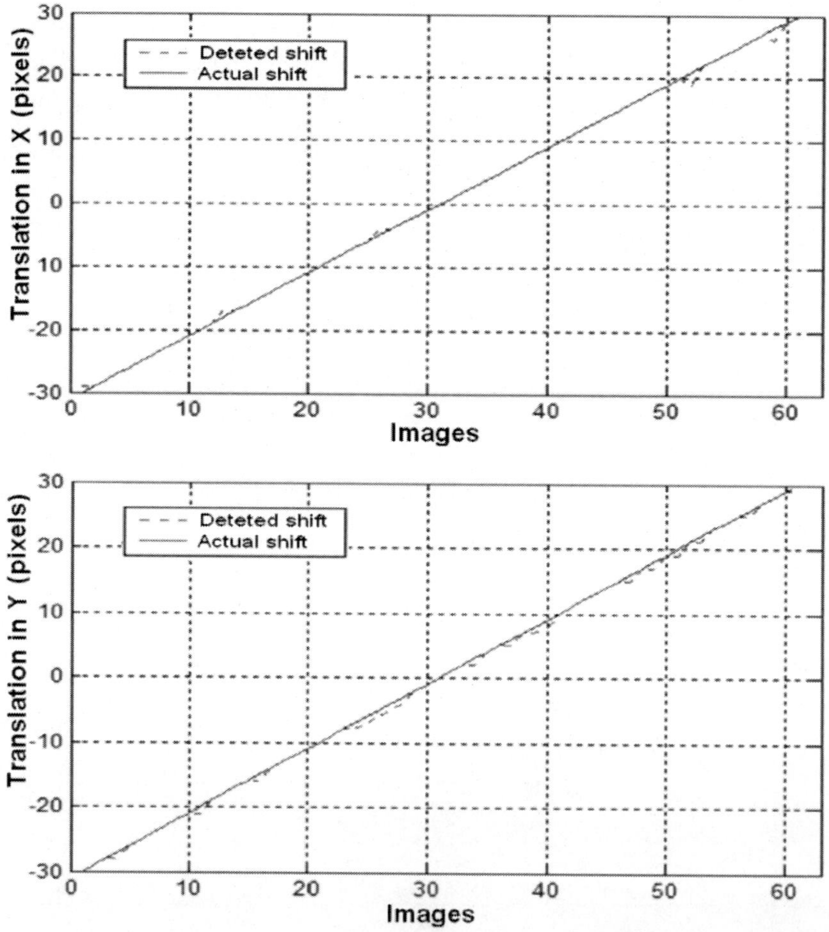

Figure 14. Performance in translations detection in the abscissa (top) and ordinate (bottom) axes. Translations detected by the algorithm are represented by the dashed line and the actual translations, by the full line.

In this study we simulate relative scaling, rotation and translation distortions between the images by modifying the infrared images and keeping the visual image unaltered. Three tests are carried out to analyze individually the performance of the detection and correction of rotation, translation and scaling. This analysis was repeated with other images confirming the conclusions found.

Rotation Detection

In this test the infrared image is distorted with rotations angles α in the range between -20° and 20°.

Figure 12 shows the rotation angles detected by the algorithm (dashed line) versus the rotation angle currently used in the test (full line). The rotation angle error can be observed in Figure 13. The maximum error is 1.2°.

Translation Detection

In this test the infrared image is distorted with a set of translations between -30 and 30 pixels in axes x and y. The rotation between the images was not modified.

Figure 14 shows the results of the analysis in axes x (top) and y (bottom). The dashed line represents the resulting translations detected and, the full line, the actual translations. In most of the cases, the error is lower than one pixel. Only in some scarce images the error is of two pixels.

Scaling Detection

First, the visual image is distorted with a set of scale factors in the range between 0.5 and 3 while the infrared image, considered as reference, is kept unaltered.

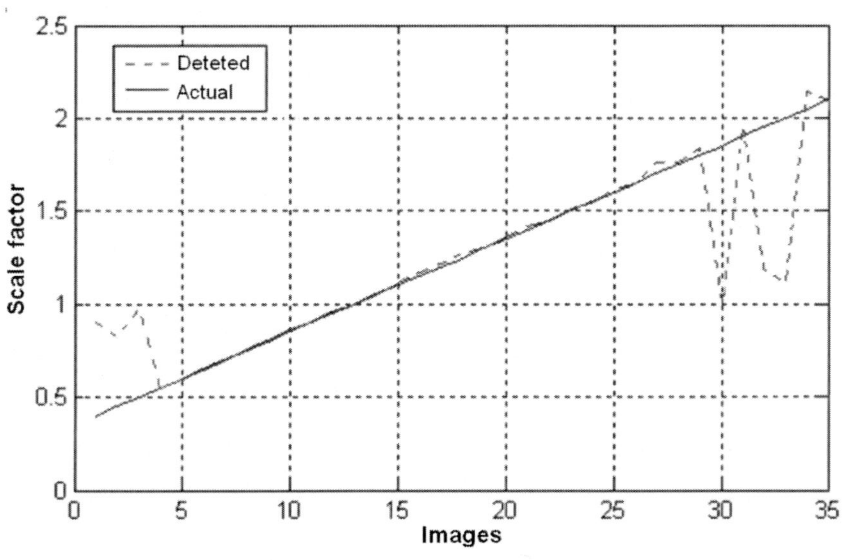

Figure 15. Performance in detecting scale factors using the infrared image as reference. Detected scale factors are represented by the dashed line and the actual values, by the full line.

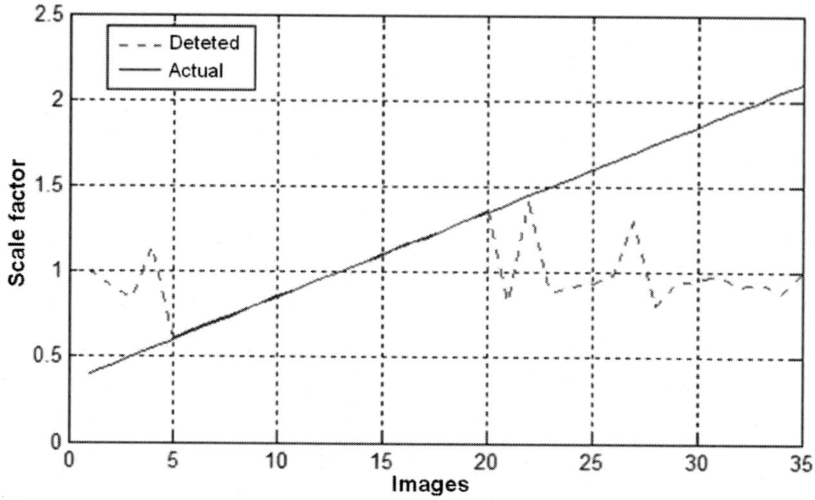

Figure 16. Performance in detecting scale factors using the visual image as reference. Detected scale factors are represented by the dashed line and the actual values, by the full line.

Figure 15 shows the scale factors resulting from the method (dashed line) versus the actual values (full line). It can be noticed that the detection is correct if the scale factor is between 0.5 and 1.8. Out of this range, the method does not perform correctly. Thus, method is useful to detect and correct scale factors close to the unity, what is suitable in applications where fine scale matching is required, for instance if the images have similar, but not exactly the same, scale.

In the next experiment, the scale factors are introduced in the infrared images and the visual image is considered as reference. Figure 16 shows the results. The algorithm performs correctly between 0.7 and 1.3, which puts is evidence that the selection of the reference image influences in the performance of the method. Although the straightforward application of the FMT-SPOMF method is independent of which image is reference, the practical considerations added to improve its performance, perform better in case of using infrared images as reference.

CONCLUSION

This chapter presents a technique for matching images of the same scene taken with infrared and visual cameras. Although a high number of matching methods have been reported, the great majority assume images in the same spectral band. The methods for matching images in different bands are very scarce. Classical matching methods fail due to the lack of common features in images.

The proposed method relies on the global structure of the images using a frequency domain analysis based on the Fourier-Mellin transform and the Symmetric Phase Only Matched Filtering. The Fourier-Mellin transform allows determining rotation and scaling between images. The Symmetric Phase Only Matched Filtering enhances the performance of image matching in presence of noise. The proposed method can correct translation, rotation and scaling between images, which is sufficient for a high number of applications.

To increase the similarity between both images, the method includes as its first step an image uniformization stage, which enhances the high frequency components and cancels the low frequency components. The similarity of the edges in both images is significantly higher than that of the low spatial frequency components.

The chapter briefly presents the principles of the FMT-SPOMF method and also includes several practical aspects to improve its robustness and accuracy.

The evaluation of the method shows good performance in detecting translations and rotations. The behavior is correct in the case of scale factors in the range between 0.7 and 1.3 but it degrades out of that range. The extension of this operation range and the use of the proposed method with images in other spectral bands such as ultraviolet are object of current research.

REFERENCES

[1] S.J. Krotosky, and M.M. Trivedi, Person Surveillance Using Visual and Infrared Imagery. *IEEE Transactions on Circuits and Systems for Video Technology*, 18, no. 8, pp. 1096-1105, (2008).

[2] T. T. Zin, H. Takahashi, T. Toriu, and H. Hama. Fusion of Infrared and Visible Images for Robust Person Detection, *Image Fusion*, Osamu Ukimura (Ed.), InTech, (2011).

[3] F. Caballero, L. Merino, J. Ferruz, A. Ollero, A. A visual odometer without 3D reconstruction for aerial vehicles. Applications to building inspection, In *Proc. IEEE International Conference on Robotics and Automation ICRA 2005*, pp. 4673-4678, (2005).

[4] B.C. Arrue, A. Ollero, J. R. Martinez-de Dios, An intelligent system for false alarm reduction in infrared detection of forest fires, *IEEE Intelligent Systems*, 15, pp. 64-73, (2000).

[5] J.R. Martinez-de Dios, B.C. Arrue, A. Ollero, L. Merino, and F. Gómez-Rodríguez, Computer vision techniques for forest fire perception. *Image and Vision Computing*, 26, pp. 550-562, (2008).

[6] R.D. Hudson. Infrared System Engineering. *John Wiley and Sons*, (1969).

[7] "Infrared system helps pilots and drivers see in fog and at night", *Physorg*, 3 may, (2006). http://www.physorg.com/news65866577.html.

[8] J. Williams, "Infrared transmission and path radiance through dust and fog", Final Report Army Research Lab., Army Research Lab., Aberdeen Proving Ground, MD, (1993).

[9] E. Den Breejen, M. Roos, K. Schutte, J. De Vries, and H. Winkel. "Infrared Measurements of Energy Release and Flame Temperatures of Forest Fires". In *Proceedings of 3rd International Conference on Forest Fire Research*, Luso, Portugal, 16–20 November 1998; pp. 2003-2012, (1998).

[10] X.P.V. Maldague. Theory and Practice of Infrared Technology for Nondestructive Testing. *John Wiley and Sons*, (2001).

[11] B. Zitová, and J. Flusser, Image registration methods: a survey. *Image and Vision Computing*, 21, pp. 977-1000, (2003).

[12] R. Hartley, and A. Zisserman, *Multiple View Geometry in Computer Vision*. Cambridge University Press, Cambridge, UK, (2004).

[13] C. Tomasi, C. *Shape and motion from image streams: A factorization method*. PhD Thesis Carnegie Mellon University, (1991).

[14] H. Bay, A. Ess, T. Tuytelaars, and L. Van Gool. SURF: Speeded Up Robust Features. *Computer Vision and Image Understanding* (*CVIU*), 110, no. 3, pp. 346-359, (2008).

[15] J. Segeman, Fourier cross correlation and invariant transformations for an optimal recognition of functions deformed by affine groups, *J. Opt. Soc. Am.*, 9, no. 6, pp. 895-902, (1992).

[16] O.K. Ersoy, and M. Zeng, (1989). Nonlinear matched filtering, *J. Opt. Soc. Am. A*. 6, pp. 636-648, (1989).

[17] Q.-S. Chen, M. Defrise, and F. Deconinck. Symmetric phase-only matched filtering of Fourier-Mellin transforms for image registration and recognition. *IEEE Transactions on Pattern Analysis and Machine Intelligence*, 16, no. 12, pp. 1156-1168, (1994).

[18] J. Heo, S. Kong, B. Abidi, and M. Abidi, "Fusion of Visual and Thermal Signatures with Eyeglass Removal for Robust Face Recognition", In Proc. *IEEE Workshop on Object Tracking and Classification Beyond the Visible Spectrum* , pp. 94-99, (2004).

[19] J.W. Cooley and J.W. Tukey, An algorithm for the machine calculation of complex Fourier series, *Math. Comput*. 19, pp. 297-301, (1965).

[20] S. Winograd, On computing the discrete Fourier transform. *Math.. Computation* 32, pp. 175-199, (1978).

In: Image Processing
Editor: Vítor Hugo Carvalho
ISBN 978-1-62081-844-2

Chapter 5

COMPARISON OF FOUR FRACTAL DIMENSIONS AND TWO LACUNARITIES TO ASSESS THE TRABECULAR BONE ARCHITECTURE OF PROXIMAL FEMUR

José Ríos-Díaz*
Research Group "Preventive Ultrasonography and Morpho-Densitometry".
Physical Therapy Department. Health Sciences Faculty. San Antonio Catholic University of Murcia (UCAM), Murcia, Spain

ABSTRACT

Fractal analysis is framed within a wide set of procedures for image analysis which seeks to quantify the complexity of the structure under study. Fractal dimension (FD) indicates how much fill the plane (in the 2D images) or the space (in 3D images) the structure of interest. Another related parameter is the lacunarity, which can be interpreted in terms of heterogeneity or porosity of the analyzed structure. In the case of the trabecular bone, fractal dimension, and not so much the lacunarity, has become part of the routine parameter set when studying bone architecture. However, not always describes adequately the method of its calculation or image processing carried out previously.

In this chapter, it will be studied the differences between the values of different fractal dimensions and lacunarity obtained on nine ROIs on the X-Ray images of proximal femur.

It was designed an observational, transversal study on 100 conventional anteroposterior X-Ray from human femurs. It were selected nine ROIs (3 on the femoral head, 3 on the femoral neck and 3 on the intertrochanteric region) with the application ROI Manager plugging for ImageJ 1.43r. The previous processing of ROIs was made with an unsharp mask equivalent to adding a highpass filtered image and thus sharpens the image. Then we performed a subtract background based on the 'rolling ball' algorithm. Finally, we applied an autothreshold to obtain binary images. Fractal and lacunarity analysis was performed with FracLac 2.5d plug-in. We calculated three fractal

* E-mail address: jrios@pdi.ucam.edu

dimensions with box-counting method: 1) Fractal dimension (FDbx), 2) smoothed (biggest) fractal dimension (SBFD), and 3) smoothed (smaller) fractal dimension (SSFD). One lacunarity (LACbx) was obtained with box-counting method. In addition, we got one lacunarity (LACsl) and one fractal dimension (FDsl) with sliding-box method. The statistical analysis was performed with a repeated measures mixed-model factorial ANOVA. The effect size with $\eta 2$ (eta square) estimator and multiple comparisons was made with Bonferroni's correction (95% CI).

FDbx showed significant differences along nine ROIs ($F=37.57$; $p \leq 0.001$) with a moderate-high effect size ($\eta 2$ = 0,281). SBFD was different on all ROIs ($F= 64.86$; $p \leq 0.001$) with a high effect size ($\eta 2$ = 0,403) and SSFD showed significant differences but lower effect size ($F= 38.23$; $p \leq 0.001$; $\eta 2$ = 0,285). Finally, FDsl presented a high effect size and significant differences on all ROIs ($F= 70.366$; $p \leq 0.001$; $\eta 2$ = 0,423). Both lacunarities exhibited significant differences along all ROIs but LACsl showed a high effect size ($F= 68.13$; $p \leq 0.001$; $\eta 2$ = 0,415) whereas LACbx presented a moderate effect size ($F= 18.63$; $p \leq 0.001$; $\eta 2$ = 0,163). The sliding-box method showed better results than box-counting method to discriminate different ROIs that had different trabecular architectures. The calculation method of FD and LAC is critical so we must be careful in the description of the method and the comparison of different DF or LAC obtained by different methods.

INTRODUCTION

The Fractal Theory

The fractal analysis (FA) falls within a wide range of mathematical techniques related to pattern recognition in the biomedical field has applications such as aid in the diagnosis from X-ray images, computed tomography, ultrasonograms electrocardiograms or electro-encephalograms [1-7]. The term fractal was coined by the mathematician Mandelbrot in 1975 [8, 9] from the Latin word fractus that means fragmented or irregular. He was referring to a series of mathematical objects that have a geometry that could not be explained by classical Euclidean geometry (triangles, squares, cubes or spheres). The Medical Subject Headings (MeSH) of PubMed/Medline defines fractal as "Patterns (real or mathematical) which look similar at different scales, for example the network of airways in the lung which shows similar branching patterns at progressively higher magnifications.

Natural fractals are self-similar across a finite range of scales while mathematical fractals are the same across an infinite range. Many natural, including biological, structures are fractal (or fractal-like).

Fractals are related to "chaos" in that chaotic processes can produce fractal structures in nature, and appropriate representations of chaotic processes usually reveal self-similarity over time" [10]. The topological dimension (TD) is the one that most of the Euclidean forms with which we are familiar. Thus, a point has a TD = 0, a line has TD = 1, a plane hast TD =2, and for a three-dimensional form, TD = 3.

However, a dimension greater than its topological dimension (a fractional number) characterizes fractal shapes. This fractional dimension corresponds to the most characteristic property of fractal forms: self-similarity, which combined with scaling constant, measures the degree of irregularity in each case [11].

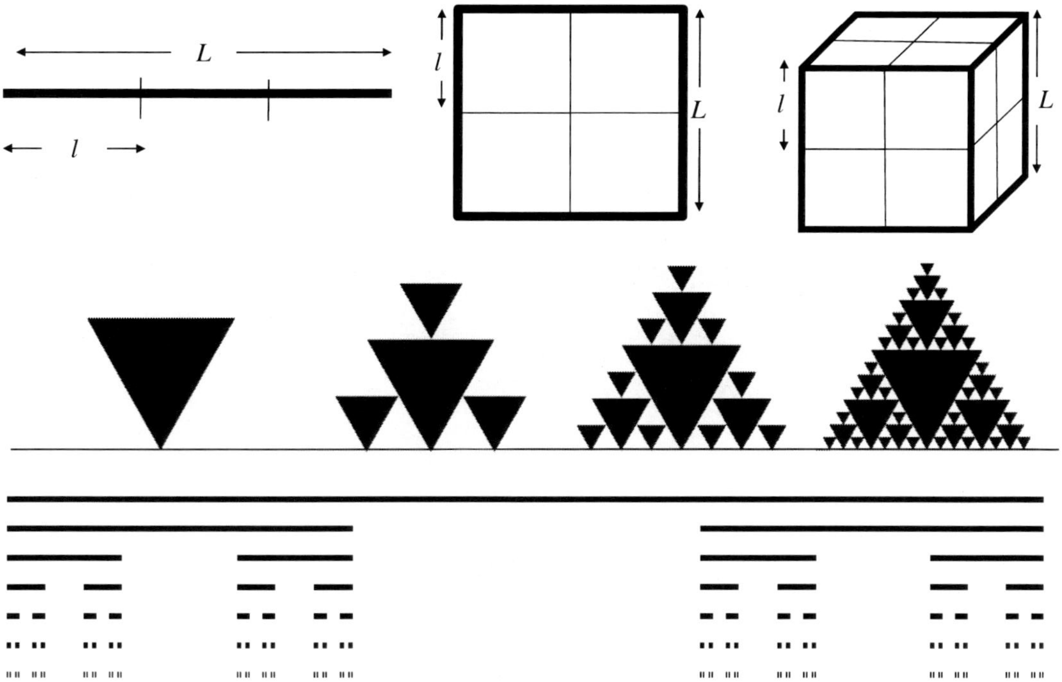

Figure 1. *Euclidean and fractal dimensions of geometric objects.* At the top shows the dimensions of a line, a square and a cube. In the middle row and bottom are two fractal sets of those considered "monsters" at the beginning of last century. Center: Sierpinski's Triangle (four iterations) formed from an equilateral triangle divided into four parts, whose sides are half the original, the result is four new equilateral triangles which eliminates central, resulting in a DF = log (3) / log (2) = 1.584 (between the size of a line and a plane). Bottom: Cantor's Dust (five iterations), is constructed from a line that in which each iteration is divided into three parts and remove the central. The theoretical fractal dimension is DF = log (2) / log (3) = 0.6309 which lies between the dimension of a point and a line.

For Falconer (1990) the definition of "fractal" should be approached in a similar way as biologists address the definition of "life." There is no single and good definition for the life but a series of features that most life forms share with exceptions for each of these characteristics. In the case of fractals, their peculiarities can be summarized in three of the characteristics that define them: a feature-length measured by fractal dimension, self-similarity and complexity [12].

Perhaps an example better understand (figure 1). Suppose we have a line of length L = 1 m, and divide it into three equal pieces of length l = 1/3 m. In this case, the number of partitions that are generated (N) is obtained by determining how many times does a portion (l) of the total (L).

$$l = \frac{L}{3} \Rightarrow N = \frac{L}{l} = \left(\frac{L}{l}\right)^1 = 3 \qquad (1)$$

If we repeat the process with a square of side L = 1 m and divide it into smaller squares of side l = 1/2, then the area is l2 = 1/4 m2, and the number of partitions is:

$$l = \frac{L}{2} \Rightarrow N = \frac{L^2}{l^2} = \left(\frac{L}{l}\right)^2 = 4$$

(2)

Finally, if we extend the reasoning to a cube, we have that:

$$l = \frac{L}{2} \Rightarrow N = \frac{L^3}{l^3} = \left(\frac{L}{l}\right)^3 = 8$$

(3)

In summary, the number of sections (N) is determined by the following expression:

$$N = \left(\frac{L}{l}\right)^{D_F}$$

(4)

where DF is the fractal dimension of the object, which is neither more nor less than a way of quantifying the shape of any object. We will have that DF is:

$$D_F = \frac{\log(N)}{\log(L/l)}$$

(5)

The Box-Counting Method

We have seen how easy to calculate its size with certain types of fractals. Nevertheless, this method is complexity and not useful to quantify the fractal dimension of a natural curve as a coast, the profile of a mountain, the outline of a cloud or trabecular bone.

The Box-counting method is relatively simple. The basic procedure is systematically lay a series of grids of decreasing caliber (the boxes) over an image and record data (the counting) for each successive caliber (Figure 2).

Counting is usually a matter of counting how many of the boxes in each grid had any part of the important detail in the image in them. In the image shown here, the important detail is the black pixels, which are on the "unimportant" white background.

If the process is repeated successively, we will have two sets of data: the box size (ε) and the number of boxes (N) occupied for each box size (figure 3). When these data are transferred to a bi-logarithmic plot is obtained a straight line whose slope is the object [9, 13-16].

Have a set S and let N (ε) the number of cells with size ε needed to cover the set S, then the dimension of S is:

$$D_F = \lim_{\varepsilon \to 0} \left(\frac{\log(N(\varepsilon))}{\log(1/\varepsilon)} \right)$$

(6)

This algorithm is the one that usually comes bundled with software packages for image analysis and we have used in this chapter [19-23]. Although the method has certain limitations as applied to images of a finite representation defined by a set of discrete elements (image pixels), is one of the most used.

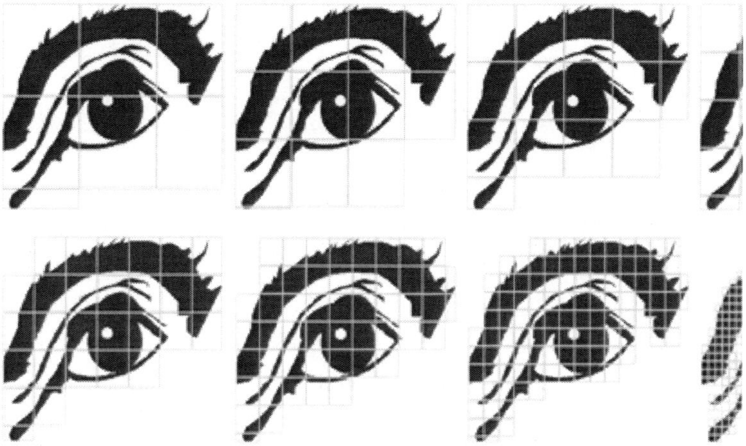

Figure 2. Box-counting method. The box-counting method involves the successive superposition of a grid with a determined cell size. At each step, the algorithm records the number of cells that are "occupied" by the object. There are represented only eight cell sizes.

size	count
2	7600
3	3595
4	2119
6	1045
8	632
12	317
16	190
32	57
64	16

D=1.7648

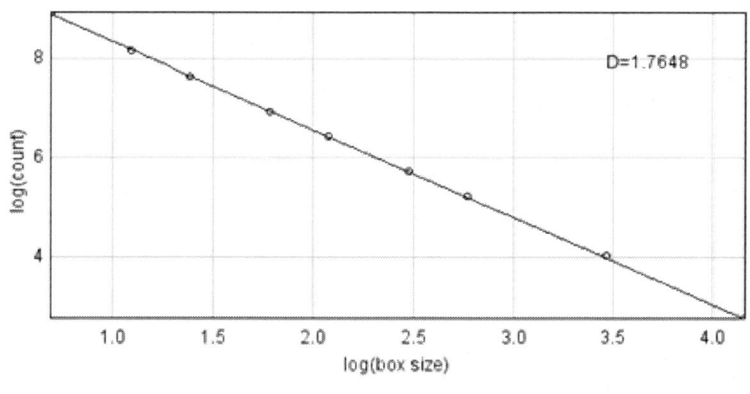

Figure 3. Fractal dimension log-log plot. The method consists of successive overlapping a grill with a given cell size. In the size column shows the cell-size in pixels and column-count the number of cells occupied by an element of the image. The fractal dimension is the slope of the line. Fractal Box-counting algorithm [17] for ImageJ v1.43r [18].

The Sliding-Box Method

Another limitation of the fractal dimension calculated from the box-counting method is that sometimes does not discriminate between clearly different structures (figure 4) that show the same fractal dimension [9, 24-26].

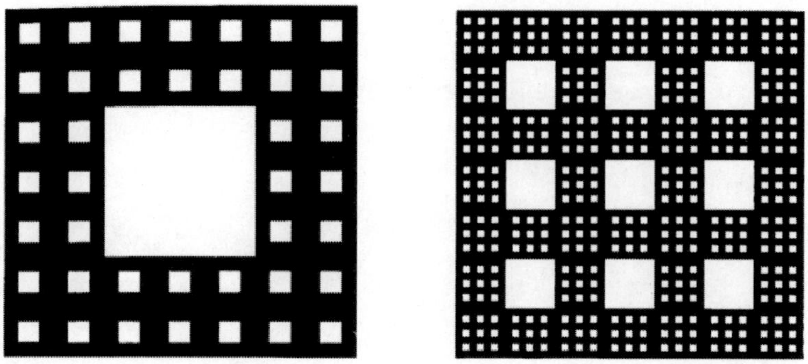

Figure 4. Fractal dimension and lacunarity. This figure shows two different forms of a Sierpinski's carpet. The fractal dimension is similar in both figures (DF ≈ 1.88), but the lacunarity or porosity (λ) is different: λ = 1.31 for the figure on the left, and λ = 1.11 for the right one. FracLac Algorithm for Image J [21-23].

This has given rise to some variants of the box-counting method not only provided information on "how" fill the plane's structure but also "as" it does. One of these methods, also used in this chapter is the sliding-box method, allowing us to obtain information on the degree of lacunarity or porosity [23, 27-30]. The word "lacunarity" literally refers to a gap or pool as derived from the word for "lake", but in morphological analysis it has been variously defined as gappiness, visual texture, inhomogeneity, translational and rotational invariance, etc [22, 31].

The lacunarity estimates the deviation of a geometrical structure of the translational invariance, or in other words, represents the size distribution of gaps, holes or gaps that appear in the image. So that the greater is the lacunarity, the image becomes heterogeneous in the sense that not to present a uniform pattern in the sizes of their gaps [32-35].

The algorithm for obtain lacunarity does not differ much from the box-counting method: the lacunarity is calculated using the pixel distribution. To find the pixel distribution, the number of pixels in each ε-sized box in a grid that was placed on an image is counted during standard box counting. Then, lacunarity or λ for each grid of caliber ε is calculated from the standard deviation (σ), and mean (μ), for pixels per box. That is, there is a λ value for each ε in each series of grid sizes in each grid orientation (g), in a set of grid orientations (7).

$$\lambda_{\varepsilon,g} = CV^2_{\varepsilon,g} = \left(\frac{\sigma_{\varepsilon,g}}{\mu_{\varepsilon,g}}\right)^2 \quad (7)$$

where σ is the standard deviation and μ the average size of pixels for a given ε and orientation g.

If the calculations were made using different cell sizes, we obtain an average value for the lacunarity:

$$\Lambda_g = \overline{\lambda} \quad (8)$$

Figure 5. Sliding-box method. The grid cell size ε slides horizontally and vertically over the figure and recorded the number of pixels of interest are contained in each cell position. The lacunarity is the coefficient of variation squared and represents the heterogeneity of the image.

Therefore, the fractal dimension obtained by box-counting method, and the lacunarity, by the sliding-box method, are two different but complementary features of the structure analyzed, the first one characterized the degree "irregularity", the second one the "heterogeneity" of the analyzed shape.

The Image Binarization Problem

Generally, for the fractal and lacunarity analysis, it is necessary work over binary images, i.e., a set of black and white pixels. Consequently, the problem is the selection of appropriate method for thresholding in order to obtain a new image in which areas or objects of interest (foreground) are distinguished from others (background). Filtering and image segmentation is one of the most interesting areas in the field of image processing, so experts have created hundreds of filters, many of them for very specific problems [36-39]. Indeed, the way we conceive this segmentation (Figure 6) will be decisive for the outcome because there is no universal segmentation technique applicable to all situations and no segmentation technique is perfect [40-46].

Finding the appropriate segmentation method becomes a test of trial and error since they depend largely on the histogram gray level distribution [20, 48-50].

As the spongy bone in the proximal femur has a complex and heterogeneous trabecular disposition, it can be study with fractal and lacunarity analysis.

In this chapter, it will be studied the differences between the values of different fractal dimensions and lacunarity obtained on nine regions of interest on the X-Ray images of proximal femur.

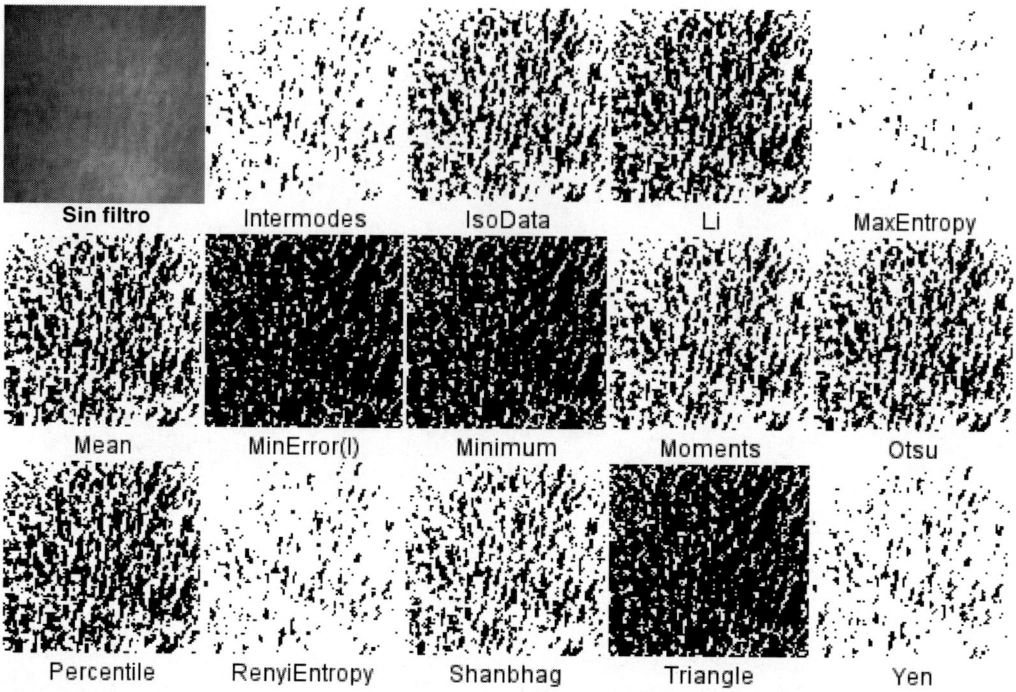

Figure 6. Segmentation methods for binarization. The result of segmentation of an image can be very different depending on the filter used. This image shows a sequence for the same X-Ray image of a femoral cancellous bone after application of some of the best-known methods. Auto Threshold algorithm v.1.10 for ImageJ [47].

MATERIAL AND METHODS

Sample

We performed an observational, transversal and descriptive study with 100 X-Ray of human proximal femur. A selection was made non-randomized from a collection of 273 femoral specimens of an adult Mediterranean population (collected in the Anatomy Laboratory of Health Sciences Faculty. Catholic University of San Antonio, Murcia-Spain). The study was approved by the Institutional Ethics Committee.

X-Ray Image Acquisition

Conventional radiographs were taken in anteroposterior projection with 150 kV and focal point size of 0.6/1.0 and 40/80 kW (Siemens Siregraph CF, Multipuls Generator Polydoros SX 65, Munich, Germany, 2000).

The radiographs were performed individually for each specimen was placed in physiological position, with appropriate references for reproducible imaging method. All of them were obtained with a 63 kV, 1.84 mAs and exposure of 6.8 s and 105 cm distance between the focus and the plane of the femur was placed.

The X-Ray dispositive was equipped with Siemens Compact Fluorospot software and the images were stored in DICOM format with an image size of 1024 x 1024 10-bit. Subsequently exported to Tagged Image File Format (TIFF *) without compression.

Image Processing

The image data were analyzed using the ImageJ v1.44 (Wayne Rasband, National Institutes of Health, USA; 2010) [18] software to determined with FracLac algorithm by Karperien [21-23].

A digital graphics tablet was also available (Wacom® tablet Wacom Co., Ltd. 2007, USA) to trace regions of interest (ROI).

Nine ROIs (100x100 px at 8 bits, 72 px/inch resolution) were selected in the proximal femur with ROI Manager algorithm for Image J as shown in Figure 7.

Areas of interest were selected based on references by various authors so that the principal trabecular trajectories were observed [51-55]: Three on femoral head, three on femoral neck and three on intertrochanteric region.

Unsharp Mask filter was applied to all ROI to improve the focus and eliminate blurring transition between background and foreground (in this case the trabeculae). This filtering removes a blurred copy of the original image using a Gaussian type blur and it is equivalent to a high-pass filter followed by focus mask [56, 57].

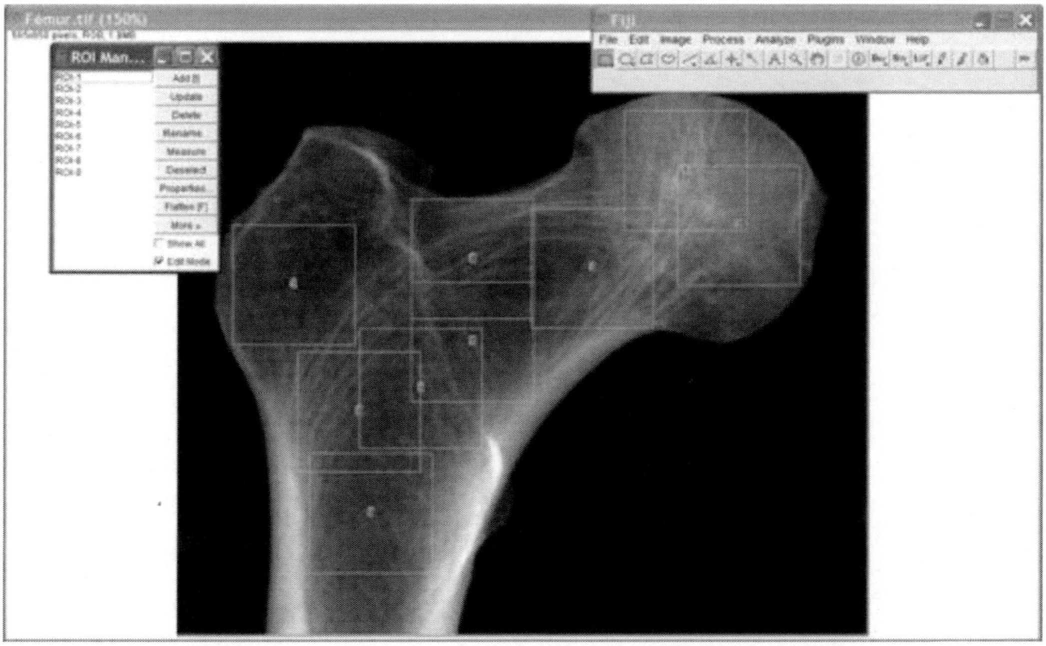

Figure 7. Areas of interest localization. ROI Manager can store different areas of analysis in relation to some specific coordinates that are reproducible from one image to another and minimal adjustments by the analyst. The areas of analysis had dimensions of 100 x 100 px (8 bits, 72 px/inch resolution). The ROI were exported and labeled for further processing.

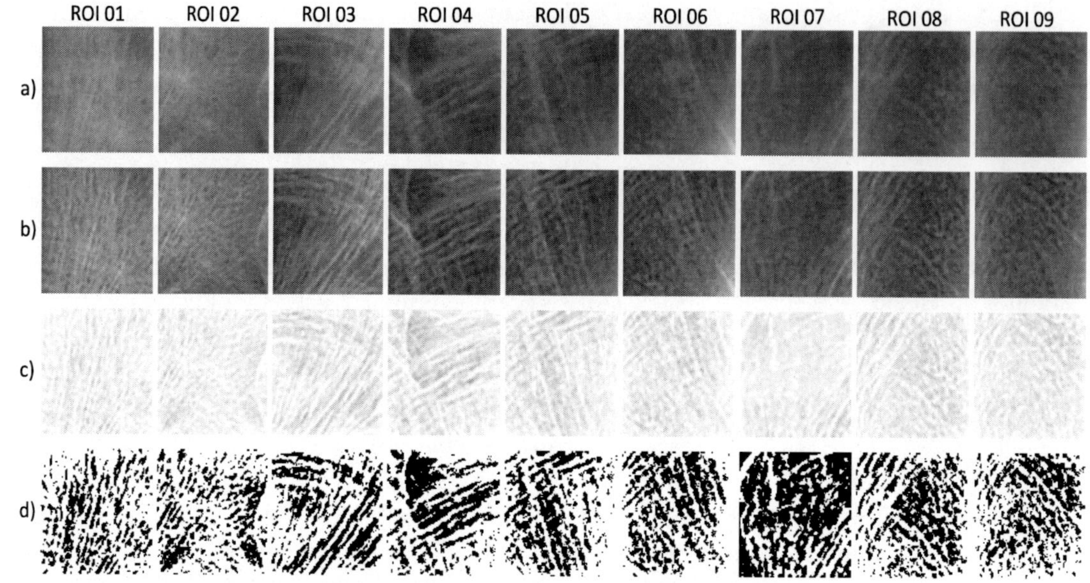

Figure 8. Image processing of nine ROIs. Example of image processing in a particular specimen. (a) Original image. (b) After applying the Unsharp Mask filter. (c) After adding over (b) a background subtraction (Rolling Ball). (d) Binarization of the images shown in (c).

Then, it was applied a background subtraction filter with Rolling Ball algorithm described by Sternberg [48, 49, 58, 59]. Finally, images were binarized [47]. The processing is shown in Figure 8.

FracLac Analysis

FracLac v 2.5d is an application developed in Java by Karperien and Troy (2007) for ImageJ [21-23]. This application uses variables based on fractal geometry and it is possible to obtain the fractal dimension and the lacunarity by different methods (figure 9).

For the box-counting method, it was perform a multiple analysis with 20 randomized grid positions. Thus, the software provides an average value. Although the computation time increases, the result is more efficient because it minimizes the influence by the grid localization.

In addition, the cell size (ε) increased linearly at a fixed interval between a minimum and maximum value, also set. The minimum size was set to two pixels, while the maximum value was set at 45% the size of the ROI, so for each analysis, the algorithm applied 44 different cell sizes in increments of two pixels.

The line regression may be presents constant segments, which means that there is no variation.

This gives us a non-realistic fractal dimension. So to solve this problem, we can estimate smoothed data calculated from data transformed for periods of no change in the regression data: 1) In smoothed fractal dimension (biggest), a filter that s shrinks the series calculated after delete the series by starting at the smallest box size and keeping only counts greater than the successor going from smallest to largest size. 2) In smoothed fractal dimension (smallest), a filter that shrinks the series by starting at the largest size and keeping only counts smaller than the successor, which assumes that increases in count with increases in size should be ignored and that the smallest possible box for a given count holds density most efficiently.

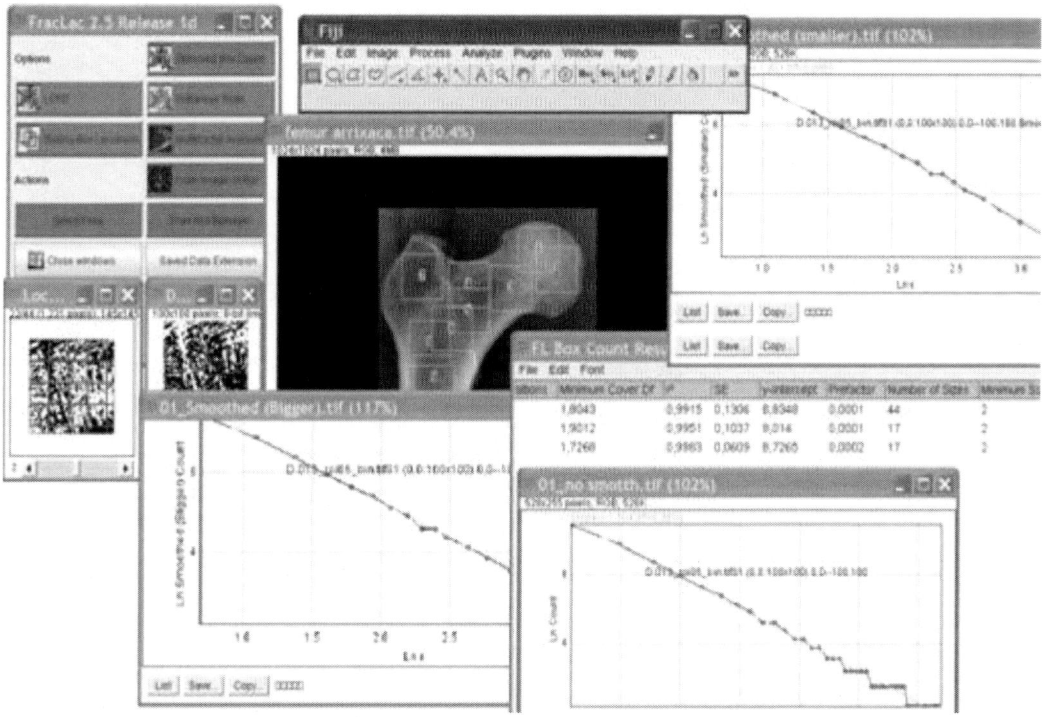

Figure 9. Startup interface and example of fractal and lacunarity analysis with FracLac. FracLac allows standard fractal analysis by box-counting or lacunarity analysis by sliding-box method. The picture shows some of the windows resulting in a basic analysis.

Thus, we calculated three fractal dimensions by box-counting method: 1) standard fractal dimension (FDbx), 2) smoothed (biggest) fractal dimension (SBFD), and 3) smoothed (smaller) fractal dimension (SSFD).

As it were applied different grid locations, it is also possible to calculate a special lacunarity that we will name lacunarity box-counting (LACbx).

For the sliding-box method, it was set the same parameters than in box-counting method, and the grid running 2 px, both vertically and horizontally.

It is possible obtain two variables: a special fractal dimension (FDsl) and a lacunarity (LACsl).

Statistical Analysis

Statistical analysis was performed with software (SPSS, version 16.0; SPSS, Chicago, Illinois). Continuous variables were expressed as means, standard deviation (SD) and standards error of the mean (SEM).

The FracLac parameters along nine ROIs were compared by using a multivariate analysis of variance (MANOVA) for repeated measures with Bonferroni correction.

Eta squared (η2) was calculated for each contrast that represent the partial effect size and it is interpreted as the fraction of variability attributable to differences intra-groups. A p value <0.05 was considered indicative of a statistically significant difference.

RESULTS

Fractal Dimensions

Table 1 shows all data for the four fractal dimensions and in Figure 10 are represented error-bars.

The FDbx was statistically different in nine ROIs (F_8=37.44; p≤0.001; η2=27.4%). Three ROIs of femoral head were greater than in other regions. This indicates a greater complexity in the trabecular lattice (Figure 11). The minimum complexity recorded in the Ward triangle (in the lower part of the femoral neck).

The partial effect size (η2) was very high, which means that the variable is able to detect most of the variability within groups.

Respect to SBFD, it presented differences between nine ROIs (F_8=65.60; p≤0.001; η2=39,9%). As we can see in Table 1 mean values were smaller than FDbx mean values and the differences intragroups were more evident. The partial effect size was even greater than in FDbx.

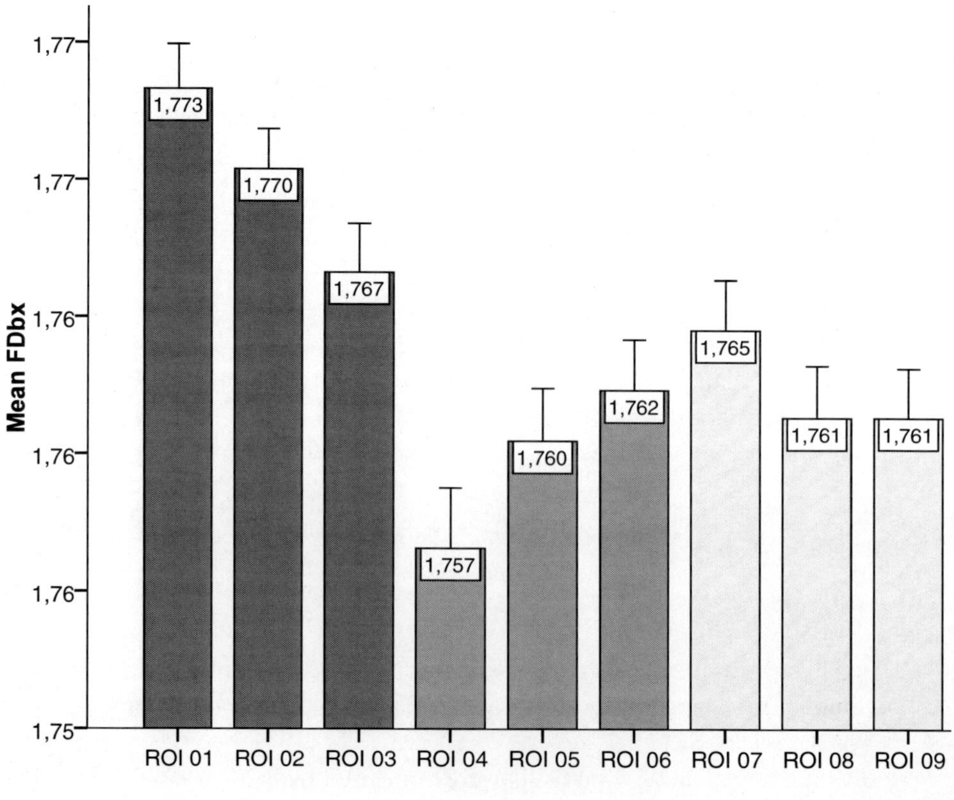

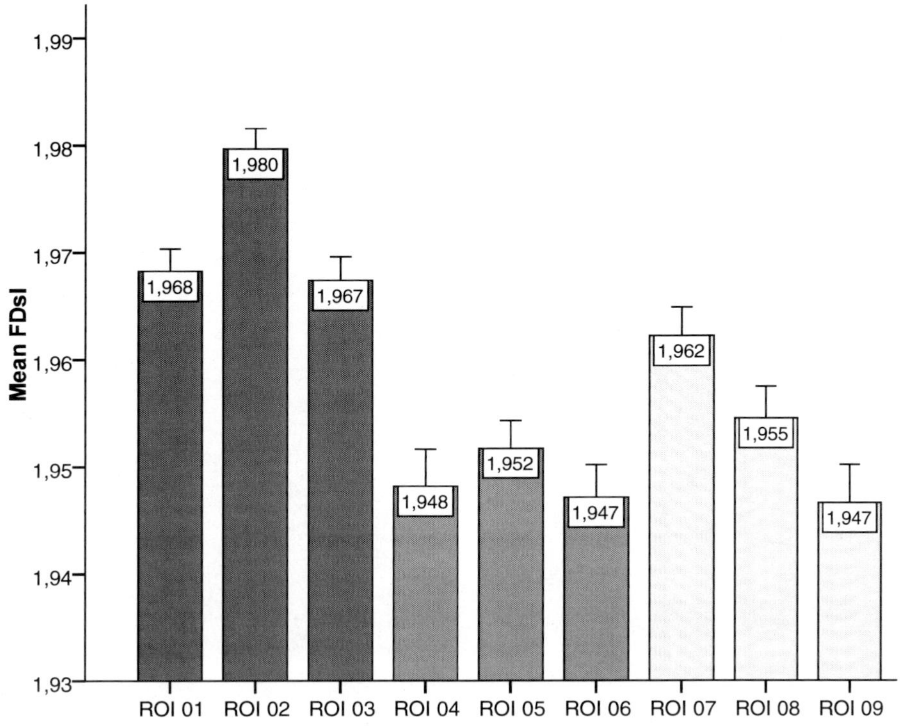

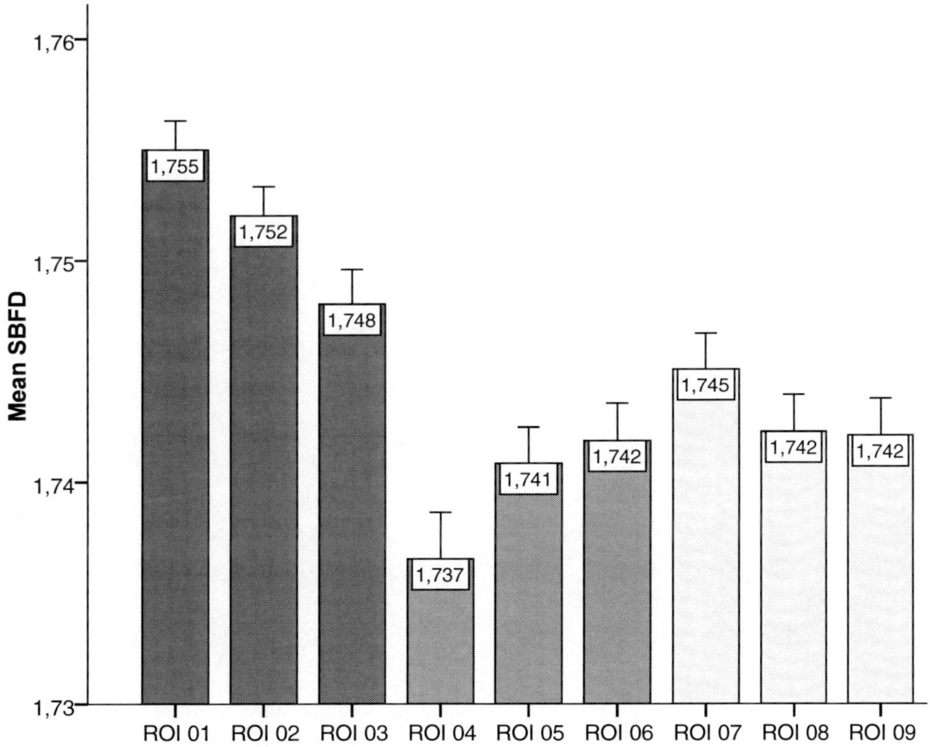

Figure 10. (Continued).

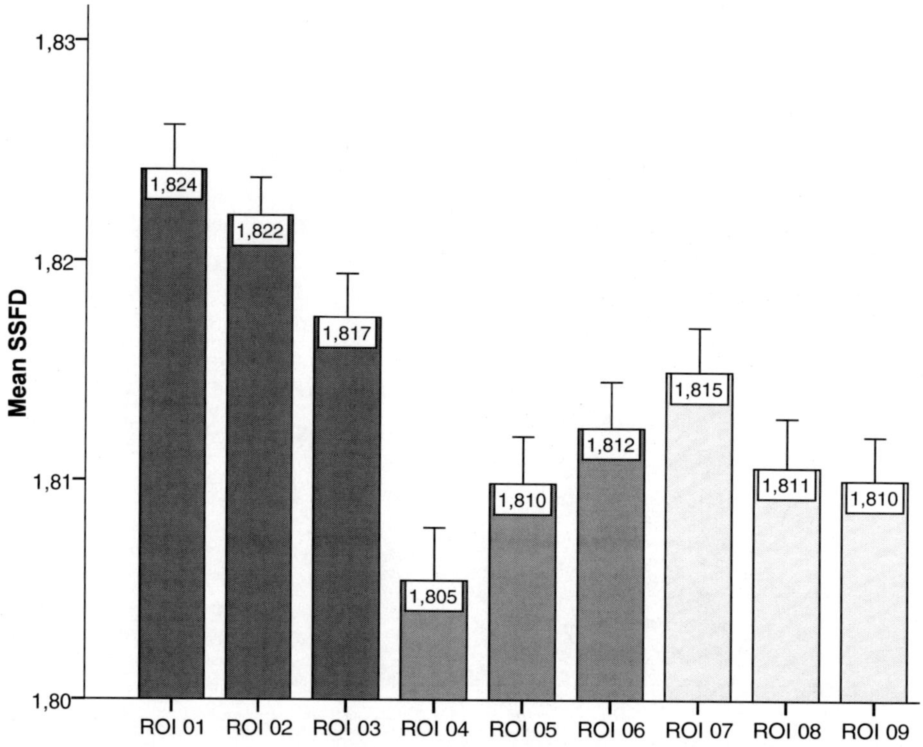

Figure 10. Error-bar charts for fractal dimensions. Error-bars represent mean and confidence interval at 95%. FDbx: Fractal dimension Box-counting. FDsl: Fractal dimension Sliding-box. SBFD: Fractal dimension with biggest smooth. SSFD: Fractal dimension with smaller smooth. Head ROIs in dark gray. neck ROIs in medium gray. intertrochanteric ROIs in light gray.

Similarly, SSFD was statistically different between groups ($F8=38,19$; $p\leq0.001$; $\eta2=28,4\%$).

The mean values in all ROI were higher than in the other two FD. Again, the maximum fractal dimension corresponded to femoral head ROIs and minimum FD with femoral neck ROIs.

Finally, FDsl showed great variability between groups ($F8=77.69$; $p\leq0.001$; $\eta2=44.0\%$).

The partial effect size was excellent and this means that the fractal dimension calculated by sliding-box method is the best option to discriminate between nine ROIs (Figure 10).

In summary, the fractality was generally high for all regions (> 1.7 taking into account the possible values range from 1, the dimension of a line and 2, the dimension of a plane). In broad terms, FD values of the femoral head ROIS were considerably higher than in other regions, while the FD recorded in the Ward triangle (in the lower part of the femoral neck) is the one with lower fractal dimensions.

As expected, the dimensions smoothed (BSDF and SSDF) offer different dimension values although the patterns of differences between regions are more or less stable.

Hence, this allows us to suggest that the method from which to compute the fractal dimension is crucial in the ability to discriminate between regions, and that perhaps, the FD obtained by either method are characterizing different fractal properties.

Table 1. Descriptives for Fractal Dimensions

	ROI	Maximum	Minimum	Mean	SD	SEM
	Fractal Dimension (Box-counting)					
Head	1	1.799	1.753	1.773	0.0083	0.0008
	2	1.787	1.748	1.770	0.0074	0.0007
	3	1.788	1.743	1.767	0.0089	0.0009
Neck	4	1.779	1.730	1.757	0.0111	0.0011
	5	1.783	1.742	1.760	0.0097	0.0010
	6	1.796	1.746	1.762	0.0094	0.0009
Intertrochanter	7	1.786	1.740	1.765	0.0092	0.0009
	8	1.782	1.741	1.761	0.0095	0.0010
	9	1.779	1.734	1.761	0.0091	0.0009
	Fractal Dimension (Smooth Biggest)					
Head	1	1.770	1.735	1.755	0.0067	0.0007
	2	1.765	1.730	1.752	0.0066	0.0007
	3	1.768	1.723	1.748	0.0078	0.0008
Neck	4	1.757	1.710	1.737	0.0106	0.0011
	5	1.760	1.724	1.741	0.0082	0.0008
	6	1.779	1.726	1.742	0.0085	0.0008
Intertrochanter	7	1.766	1.724	1.745	0.0081	0.0008
	8	1.761	1.720	1.742	0.0084	0.0008
	9	1.758	1.718	1.742	0.0083	0.0008
	Fractal Dimension (Smooth Smaller)					
Head	1	1.855	1.800	1.824	0.0102	0.0010
	2	1.851	1.798	1.822	0.0086	0.0009
	3	1.841	1.788	1.817	0.0100	0.0010
Neck	4	1.829	1.777	1.805	0.0122	0.0012
	5	1.835	1.788	1.810	0.0109	0.0011
	6	1.844	1.787	1.812	0.0106	0.0011
Intertrochanter	7	1.836	1.787	1.815	0.0103	0.0010
	8	1.841	1.786	1.811	0.0114	0.0011
	9	1.838	1.782	1.810	0.0101	0.0010
	Fractal Dimension (Sliding-box)					
Head	1	1.989	1.929	1.968	0.0105	0.0010
	2	1.997	1.941	1.980	0.0096	0.0010
	3	1.989	1.941	1.967	0.0111	0.0011
Neck	4	1.989	1.902	1.948	0.0176	0.0018
	5	1.992	1.903	1.952	0.0132	0.0013
	6	2.004	1.910	1.947	0.0153	0.0015
Intertrochanter	7	1.992	1.915	1.962	0.0135	0.0014
	8	1.991	1.912	1.955	0.0150	0.0015
	9	1.988	1.905	1.947	0.0178	0.0018

SD: standard deviation. SEM: standard error of mean. ROI: region of interest.

Lacunarities

Table 2 shows all data for the two lacunarities and in Figure 11 are represented error-bars.

Lacunarity can be interpreted as the heterogeneity of the interest object. In this chapter was calculated two different lacunarities: Box-counting lacunarity and Sliding-box lacunarity.

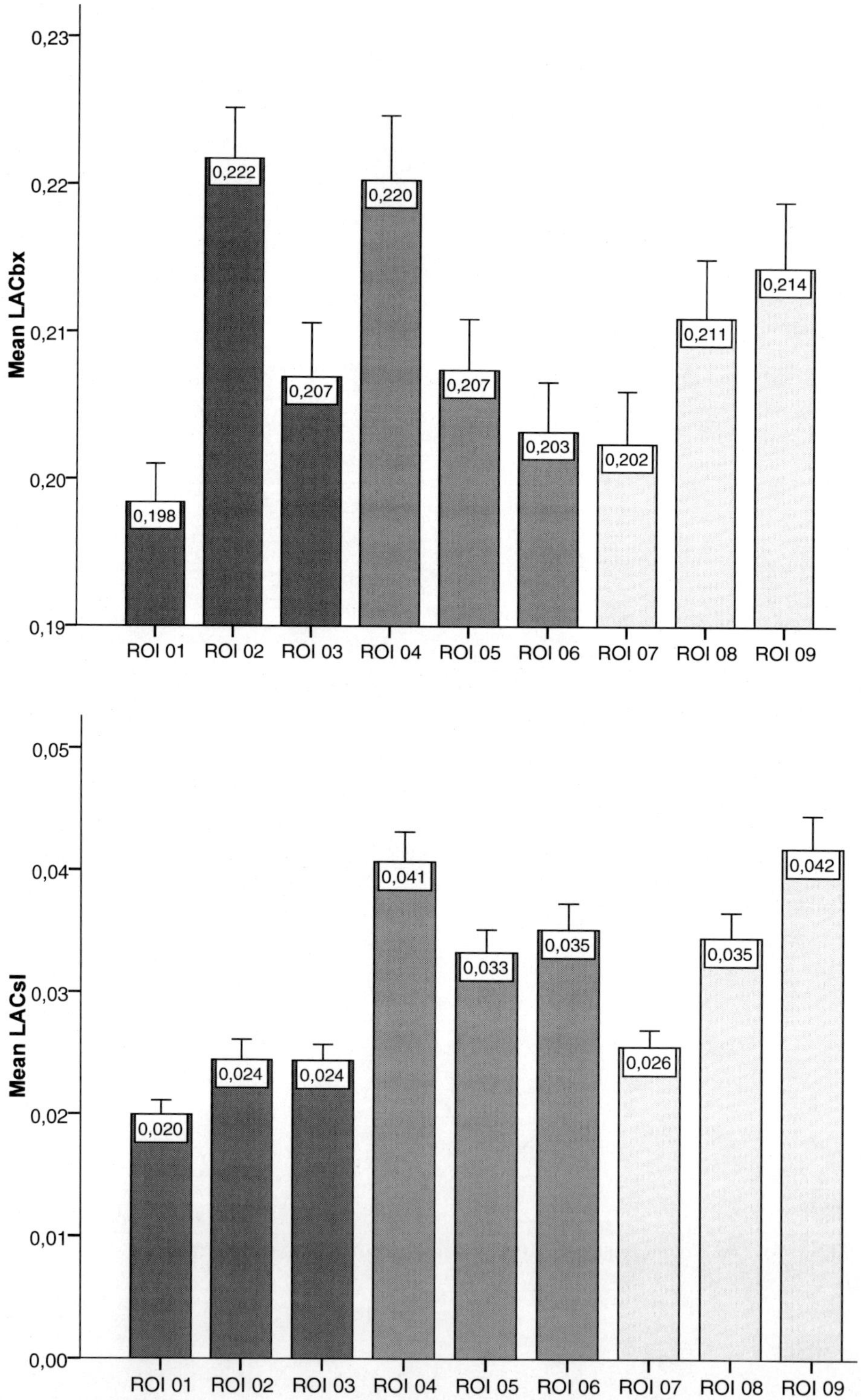

Figure 11. Error-bar charts for lacunarities. Error-bars represent mean and confidence interval at 95%. LACbx: Lacunarity Box-counting. LACsl: Lacunarity Sliding-box Head ROIs in dark gray. neck ROIs in medium gray. intertrochanteric ROIs in light gray.

Table 2. Descriptives for Lacunarities

	ROI	Maximum	Minimum	Mean	SD	SEM
	Lacunarity (Box-counting)					
Head	01	0.232	0.166	0.198	0.0131	0.0013
	02	0.275	0.192	0.222	0.0173	0.0017
	03	0.280	0.173	0.207	0.0184	0.0018
Neck	04	0.282	0.180	0.220	0.0222	0.0022
	05	0.272	0.175	0.207	0.0174	0.0017
	06	0.263	0.172	0.203	0.0169	0.0017
Intertrochanter	07	0.272	0.165	0.202	0.0181	0.0018
	08	0.282	0.177	0.211	0.0202	0.0020
	09	0.280	0.164	0.214	0.0225	0.0022
	Lacunarity (Sliding-box)					
Head	01	0.048	0.009	0.020	0.0059	0.0006
	02	0.051	0.013	0.024	0.0082	0.0008
	03	0.042	0.014	0.024	0.0067	0.0007
Neck	04	0.085	0.020	0.041	0.0123	0.0012
	05	0.064	0.015	0.033	0.0095	0.0009
	06	0.065	0.002	0.035	0.0107	0.0011
Intertrochanter	07	0.051	0.015	0.026	0.0069	0.0007
	08	0.065	0.016	0.035	0.0105	0.0010
	09	0.087	0.019	0.042	0.0138	0.0014

SD: standard deviation. SEM: standard error of mean. ROI: region of interest.

The LACbx was statistically different in nine ROIs ($F8=19,19$; $p \leq 0.001$; $\eta2=16.2\%$) and the LACsl also was different between ROIs ($F8=71,43$; $p \leq 0.001$; $\eta2=42.0\%$). LACsl discriminated more effectively the nine ROIs than LACbx (Figure 11).

In general, it seems that areas with greater trabecular cross correspond with increased (ROI 2 and ROI 4).

Average patterns vary between ROIs depending on the method used to calculate the lacunarity; therefore, the behavior of the parameters in the different regions is strongly related to the method used.

CONCLUSION AND DISCUSSION

About Image Processing

Since the calculation of the parameters FracLac be done on binary images, the regions of analysis should be subjected to a pre-processing and subsequent segmentation. In the image analysis field this is one of the perennial problems faced by researchers: Separate structures for which no interest with minimum loss of information [40-46].

Almost all the authors who have worked with fractal analysis in biomedical imaging warn about the precautions to be taken regarding the acquisition of the radiographs, which involve both the dosimetry and the type of film used-in the process X-ray scanning in filters and pre-processing [48, 49, 60-66].

A proposal for improvement and future research in this line could be an essay about a battery processing and filter and check with which produces better discriminant functions between different areas, n a similar way as Cendre et al. [68].

About FracLac Analysis

In this chapter, FDsl and SBFD provided the best discrimination between ROIs. In this regard, Cross et al. [69], Chung et al. [70], Buczkowski et al. [71], Parkinson et al.[72], noted that the fractal dimension calculated using the box-counting method could lead to incorrect estimates because constant intervals that could present certain cell sizes. Cortet et al. [73] report that the cell counting method is one of the most widely used by theoretical and computational simplicity but not the one who gives the best results.

It seems that the fractal dimension (extended to the four DF) registered on the regions located on the femoral head (ROI 01 and 02) and one of the main regions of trabeculae intersecting (ROI 03), are the areas in which higher fractal dimensions were recorded. On the other hand, central femoral neck (ROI 04) usually presented lower fractal dimensions.

Lin et al. [53] found that the FD of the areas under compression (head and sub-trochanteric trabeculae) were those that showed better correlations with biomechanical parameters of resistance. Similarly, the values obtained in the Ward's triangle region offered little prediction of the mechanical characteristics and justified by the large variability that can make this radiolucent area in terms of age-related subject.

These results are consistent with those found by Andresen et al. [74] on CT images of vertebral cancellous bone. The FD was statistically different in four patient groups (normal, osteopenia, osteoporosis without fractures and severe osteoporosis with fractures), with a decrease in the FD along the four groups linked to the loss of structural complexity.

It may therefore be said that the trabecular bone of the proximal femur has a high fractality, consistent with the fact that the trabecular bone is an organized structure that occupies so much space available with a minimum requirement of material.

The lacunarity by the sliding-box method (LACsl) was significantly better than that calculated by the box-counting method (LACbx) and were generally low, which shows a low invariance or, if preferred, high homogeneity in the trabecular distribution [75].

Although the patterns of lacunarity were different depending on the algorithm used (Figure 11), seems that the lower values correspond to the ROIs 01 to 03 and the highest values in ROIs 04 and 09.

As for the few differences shown in fractal dimension values and lacunarity between some ROI may be due, as noted by et al. [76], the fact that the radiographic projection there is a trabecular overlap and that the pattern will be reflected in the 2D image is that which prevails in three dimensional space, with the obvious loss of information.

Although, as we have seen, the fractal dimension it has been used extensively to characterize the complexity of the trabecular bone did not occur with the lacunarity. We found few studies that link this parameter to the study of trabecular bone.

Dougherty [77] compared the fractal dimension and the lacunarity of high and low resolution CT images and concluded that both parameters could evaluate the structural characteristics of trabecular bone in a clinical situation but obviously with less precision. Dougherty and Henebry [78] published a technical paper in which they evaluated the potential usefulness of the lacunarity (and FD) in the study of bone texture. These same authors, in another later work [79] conducted a pilot study on vertebral bone CT images and concluded that it could be useful in discriminating osteoporotic bone.

Recently, Majumder and Mazumdar [80] suggest and argue that the lacunarity provides information about the porosity of the structure, and could be useful in assessing the cancellous bone and, they add, that this possibility has not been investigated.

It is still surprising that this has not happened. From a mathematical view, the interpretation is equally complex as the fractal dimension, and from a practical view, the calculation is easy, at least as the fractal dimension.

In this chapter, the sliding-box method showed better results than box-counting method to discriminate different ROIs that had different trabecular architectures. The calculation method of FD and LAC is critical so we must be careful in the description of the method and the comparison of different DF or LAC obtained by different methods.

References

[1] Sutton R and Hall EL, Texture measures for automatic classification of pulmonary disease. *IEEE Trans. Comput.* 1972;C-21:667-76.

[2] Antognetti PF. Dellepiane S. Serpico SB and Vernazza G, Applicazione di tecniche frattali per la discrminazione di immagini radiografiche. *Radiol. Med.* (Torino). 1989;77(5):535-9.

[3] Caldwell CB. Stapleton SJ. Holdsworth DW. Jong RA. Weiser WJ. Cooke G and al, Characterisation of mammographic parenchymal pattern by fractal dimension. *Phys. Med. Biol.* 1990;35(2):235-47.

[4] Tuceryan M and Jain AK, Texture analysis. En: Chen CH. Pau LF. Wang PSP. editores. The handbook of pattern recognition and computer vision. 2nd editon. Singapore: World Scientific Publishing; 1998. p.207-48.

[5] Materka A. Cichy P and Tuliszkiewicz J, Texture analysis of X-ray images for detection of changes in bone mass and structure. In: Pietikäinen MK. editor. Texture analysis in Machine Vision. Series in Machine Perception and Artificial Intelligence (volume 40). University of Oulu: Oulu (Finland); 2000. p.189-95.

[6] Cheng HD. Shi XJ. Min R. Cai XP and Du HN, Automated detection of masses in mammograms. En: Chen CH. Wang PSP. editores. Handbook of pattern recognition and complexity visión. 3th ed. Singapore: World Scientific Publishing; 2005.p.303-23.

[7] Theodoridis S and Koutroumbas K, Pattern recognition. 3th ed. San Diego: Academic Press; 2006.

[8] Mandelbrot BB, Los objetos fractales. 4th ed. Barcelona: Tusquets Editores; 1996.

[9] Mandelbrot BB, La geometría fractal de la naturaleza. 2nd ed. Barcelona: Tusquets Editores; 2003.

[10] MeSH Browser [Internet]. Bethesda (MD): National Library of Medicine (US); 2009-Fractals [cited 2011 Oct 30]; [about 1 p.]. Available from: http://www.ncbi.nlm.nih.gov/mesh?term=fractal.

[11] Jelinek HE. Jones CL. Warfel MD. Lucas C. Depardieu C and Aurel G, Understanding fractal analysis? The case of fractal linguistics. *Complexus*. 2006;3:66-73.

[12] Falconer K, Fractal geometry: mathematical foundations and applications. Chichester (England): John Wiley and Sons Ltd.; 1990.

[13] Mandelbrot BB, How long is the coast of Britain? Statistical self-Similarity and fractional dimension. *Science*. 1967; 156(3775):636-8.

[14] Frame M, A web-based fractal geometry course for non-science students. In: Barnsley MF. Saupe D. Vrscay ER. editors. Fractals in multimedia. Springer Verglag Inc.: New York; 2002.p.233-58.

[15] Sornette D, Critical phenomena in natural sciences. Chaos. fractals. selforganization and disorder: Concepts and tools. 2nd ed. Berlin: Springer-Verlag; 2006.

[16] Frame M. Mandelbrot B and Neger N, Fractal geometry [Homepage] Mathematics Department. Yale University. [cited 2011 Sept 25]. Available from: http://classes.yale.edu/fractals/index.html.

[17] Smith TG Jr. Lange GD and Marks WB, Fractal methods and results in cellular morphology: dimensions. lacunarity and multifractals. *J. Neurosci. Methods.* 1996;69(2):123-36.

[18] Rasband W, ImageJ v1.43r. U.S. National Institutes of Health. Bethesda. Maryland. USA. 1997-2011. Available from: http://rsb.info.nih.gov/ij/.

[19] Gonzalez RC and Woods RE, Digital image processing. 2nd ed. New Jersey: Prentice Hall; 2002.

[20] Russ JC, The image processing handbook. 4th ed. Boca Raton (Florida): CRC Press LLC; 2002.

[21] Karperien A and Roy TR, Fractal dimensión and lacunarity (FracLac v2.5d) for ImageJ [cited 2011 Oct 30]. Available from: http://rsb.info.nih.gov/ij/plugins/fraclac/fraclac.html.

[22] Karperien A, FracLac for ImageJ: morphologic image analysis tools. Online User's Guide for FracLac. V. 2.5 June 2007 [cited 2011 Oct 30]. Available from: http://rsbweb.nih.gov/ij/plugins/fraclac/FLHelp/ Introduction.htm.

[23] Karperien A, FracLac for ImageJ: Using FracLac V 2.0 for ImageJ. [cited 2011 Oct 30]; [38 p.]. Available from: http://rsb.info.nih.gov/ ij/plugins/fraclac/fraclac-manual.pdf.

[24] Plotnick RE. Gardner RH and O'Neill RV, Lacunarity indices as measures of landscape texture. *Lands Ecol*. 1993;8(3):201-11.

[25] Plotnick RE. Gardner RH and Hargrove WW, Prestegaard K. Perlmutter M. Lacunarity analysis: a general technique for the analysis of spatial patterns. *Phys. Rev. E.* 1996;53(5):5461-68.

[26] Sun W. Su G. Gong P and Liang S, Fractal analysis of remotely sensed images: a review of methods and applications. *Int. J. Rem. Sens.* 2006;27(22):4963-90.

[27] Dong P, Test of a new lacunarity estimation method for image texture analysis. *Int. J. Remote Sensing*. 2000;21(17):3369-73.

[28] Nekka F and Li J, Characterization of fractal structures through a Hausdorf measure based method. In: Novak MM. editor. Thinking in patters: fractals and related phenomena in nature. Singapore: World Scientific Publishing; 2004. p.213-20.

[29] Wu Y. Wang N and Ruchey K, An analysis of spatial complexity of ridge and slough patterns in the Everglades ecosystem. *Ecol Complex*. 2006;3:183-92.
[30] Feagin RA. Wu XB and Feagin T, Edge effects in lacunarity analysis. *Ecol. Model.* 2007;201:262-8.
[31] De Melo RHC. Veira EA and Conci A, Characterizing the lacunarity of object and image sets and its use as a technique of textural patterns. In: Blanc-Talon J. Philips W. Popescu D. Scheunders P. editors. Advanced Concepts for Intelligent Vision Systems Lecture Notes in Computer Science. Volume 4179. Berlin: Springer Verlag; 2006b.p.208-19.
[32] Butson CR and King DJ, Lacunarity analysis to determine optimum extents for sample-based spatial information extraction from high-resolution forest imaginery. *In J. Remote Sens*. 2006;27(1):105-20.
[33] Chmiela J. Słota D and Szala J, Analysis of emptiness (lacunarity) as a measure of the degree of space filling and of the internal structure of a set. *Mater Char*. 2006;56(4-5):421-8.
[34] Myint SW and Lam, A study of lacunarity-based texture analysis approaches to improve urban image classification. *Comput. Environ. Urban Syst.* 2005;29:501-23.
[35] Myint SW. Mesev V and Lam N, Urban textural analysis from remote sensor data: Lacunarity measurements based on the differencial box counting method. *Geogr. Anal.* 2006;38:371-90.
[36] Glasbey CA and Horgan GW, Image analysis for the biological sciences. Chichester: John Wiley and Sons. Inc.; 1995.
[37] Qiu P, Image processing and jump regression analysis. New Jersey: John Wiley and Sons. Inc.; 2005.
[38] Kim C, Segmenting a low-depth-of-field image using morphological filters and region merging. *IEEE Trans. Image Process*. 2005;14(10):1503-11.
[39] Wong WCK and Chung ACS, Bayesian image segmentation using local iso-intensity structural orientation. *IEEE Trans. Image Process.* 2005;14(10):1512-23.
[40] Schulze MA, Biomedical image processing with morphology-based nonlinear filters [Dissertation]. Austin. Texas (USA): Faculty of the Graduate School of the University of Texas; 1994.
[41] Seul M. O'Gorman L and Sammon MJ, Practical algorithms for image analysis: description. examples. and code. New York: Cambridge University Press; 2000.
[42] Jähne B, Digital image processing. 5th ed. Berlin: Springer; 2002.
[43] Zou JJ, A fast skeletonization method. En: Sun C. Talbot H. Ourselin S. Adriaansen T. editors. Proceedings VIIth Digital Image Computing: Applications and Methods (DICTA). Sidney. 10-12 Dec 2003. Sidney (Australia): The University of Queensland; 2003. p.283-8.
[44] Gonzalez RC and Woods RE, Eddins SL. Digital image processing using Matlab. New Jersey: Pearson Prentice-Hall; 2004.
[45] Pratt WK, Digital image processing. 4th ed. New Jersey: John Wiley and Son; 2007.
[46] Young IT. Gerbrands JJ and van Vliet LJ, Image processing fundamentals. Quantitative Imaging Group. Department of Imaging Science and Technology. Faculty of Applied Sciences. Delft University of Technology; Netherlands. 2009. [Updated 2009 Agt 2011; cited 2011 Oct 2011]. Available from: http://www.ph.tn.tudelft.nl/Courses/ FIP/ noframes/fip.html.

[47] Landini G, Auto Threshold v1.108 for ImageJ (2011 May 25). [Updated 2011 May 26; cited 2011 Oct 2011]. Available from: http://pacific.mpi-cbg.de/wiki/index.php/Auto_Threshold.

[48] Ríos-Díaz J. Martínez-Payá JJ. Palomino MA and del-Baño-Aledo ME, Influencia de cinco procesamientos de imagen diferentes en el valor de la dimensión fractal del hueso trabecular de la cabeza femoral. *Rev. Esp. Enferm Metab. Óseas.* 2006;15(6):119-32.

[49] Ríos-Díaz J. Martínez-Payá JJ. Palomino MA. Martínez LM. Calvo MC. del-Baño-Aledo ME. and al, Influencia del procesamiento de la imagen en el análisis fractal del hueso trabecular en radiografía convencional de calcáneo. In: Esparza F. Fernández T. Martínez JL. Guillén P. editors. Prevención de las lesiones deportivas. Murcia: Quaderna Editorial; 2006. p.127-36.

[50] Hermes TH. Miene A and Kreyenhop P, On textures: a sketch of a textural-based image segmentation approach. Computer Graphics and Knowlegde Visualization. 2008: 8 pages. [Updated 2008. cited 2009 Sept 14; 8 p.]. Available from: http://v3d2.tu-bs.de/V3D2/pubs.collection/Avanta/hermes00a.pdf.

[51] Singh M. Riggs L. Beabout JW and Joesey J Femoral trabecular-pattern index for evaluation of spinal osteoporosis. *Ann. Intern. Med.* 1972;77:63-7.

[52] Smyth PP. Adams JE. Whitehouse RW and Taylor CJ, Application of computer texture analysis to the Singh Index. *Br. J. Radiol.* 1997;70:242-7.

[53] Lin JC. Grampp S. Link T. Kothari M. Newitt DC. Felsenberg D. and al, Fractal analysis of proximal femur radiographs: correlation with biomechanical properties and bone mineral density. *Osteoporos Int.* 1999;9:516-24.

[54] Issever AS. Vieth V. Lotter A. Meier N. Laib A. Newitt D. and al, Local differences in the trabecular bone structure of the proximal femur depicted with high-spatial-resolution MR imaging and multisection CT. *Acad. Radiol.* 2002;9(12):1395-406.

[55] Gregory JS. Stewart A. Undrill PE. Redi DM and Aspden RM, Bone shape. structure. and density as determinant of osteoporotic fracture. *Investig Radiol.* 2005;40(9):591-7.

[56] Ferreira TA and Rasband W, The ImageJ user guide. Version 1.43. [Updated 2010 Abr; cited 2011 Oct 12] [189 p.]. Available from: http://rsbweb.nih.gov/ij/docs/user-guide.pdf.

[57] Ríos-Díaz J. Caeiro-Rey JR. Martínez-Payá JJ. Dapía-Robleda S and del-Baño-Aledo ME, Relationship between the morpho-structural variables fractal dimension. entropy lacunar and trabecular bone of the proximal femur. *Rev. Esp. Enferm Metab. Óseas.* 2009;18(1):2-8.

[58] Young IT. Gerbrands JJ and van Vliet LJ, Image processing fundamentals. Quantitative Imaging Group. Department of Imaging Science and Technology. Faculty of Applied Sciences. Delft University of Technology; Netherlands. 2009. [Update 2009 Aug 18. cited 25 Oct 20119] Available from: http://www.ph.tn.tudelft.nl/Courses/FIP/noframes/fip.html.

[59] Sternberg SR. Biomedical image processing. *IEEE Computer.* 1983; 16(1): 22-34.

[60] Ruttimann UE and Ship JA, The use of fractal geometry to quantitate bone structure from radiographs. *J. Dental Res.* 1990; 69:287A1431.

[61] Majumdar S, Link TM, Millard J, Lin JC, Augat P, Newitt D, and al, In vivo assessment of trabecular bon estructure using fractal analysis of distal radius radiographs. *Med. Phys.* 2000;27(11):2594-9.

[62] Benhamou CL, Lespessailles, Jacquet G, Harba R, Jennane R, Loussot T, and al, Fractal organization of trabecular bones images on calcaneus radiographs. *J. Bone Miner Res.* 1994; 9(12):1909-18.

[63] Buckland-Wright JC, Lynch JA, Rymer J and Fogelman I, Fractal signature analysis of macroradiographs measures trabecular organization in lumbar vertebrae of postmenopausal women. *Calcif. Tissue Int.* 1994;54:106-12.

[64] Caligiuri P, Giger ML and Favus M, Multifractal radiographic analysis of osteoporosis. *Med. Phys.* 1994;21(4):503-8.

[65] Haidekker MA, Andresen R, Evertsz CJG, Banzer D and Peitgen HO, Issues of threshold selection when determining the fractal dimensión in HRCT slices of lumbar vertebrae. *Br. J. Radiol.* 2000;73:69-72.

[66] Tabor Z, Analysis of the influence of image resolution on the discriminating power of trabecular bone architectural parameters. *Bone.* 2004;34:170-9.

[67] Chappard C, Pascaretti-Grizon F, Gallois Y, Mercier P, Baslé MF and Audran M, Medullar fat influences texture analysis of trabecular microarchitecture on X-ray radiographs. *Eur. J. Radiol.* 2006;58:404-10.

[68] Cendre E, Kaftandjian V, Peis G, Jourling M, Mitton D and Babot D, An investigacion of segmentation methods and texture analysisi applied to tomographic imagen of human vertebral cancellous bone. *J. Microsc.* 2000;197(3):305-16.

[69] Cross SS, Rogers S, Silcocks PB and Cotton DW, Trabecular bone does not have a fractal structure on light microscopic examination. *J. Pathol.* 1993; 170 (3):311-3.

[70] Chung HW, Chu, Underweiser M and Wehrli FW, On the fractal nature of trabecular structure. *Med. Phys.* 1994;21(10):1535-40.

[71] Buczkowski S, Kyriacos S, Nekka F and Cartilier L, The modified box-counting method: analysis of some characteristic parameters. *Patt. Recog.* 1998;31:411-8.

[72] Parkinson IH and Fazzalari NL, Methological principles for fractal analysis of trabecular bone. *J. Microsc.* 2000;198:134-42.

[73] Cortet B, Boutry N, Dubois P, Bourel P, Cotten A and Marchandise X, In vivo comparison between computed tomography and magnetic resonance image analysis of the distal radius in the assessment of osteoporosis. *J. Clin. Densitom.* 2000;3(1):15-26.

[74] Andresen R, Haidekker MA, Radmer S and Banzer D, CT determination of bone mineral density and structural investigations on the axial skeleton for estimating the osteoporosis-related fracture risk by means of a risk score. *Br. J. Radiol.* 1999;72:569-78.

[75] Myint SW, Mesev V and Lam N, Urban textural analysis from remote sensor data: Lacunarity measurements base don the differencial box counting method. *Geogr. Anal.* 2006;38:371-90.

[76] Steines D, Liew SW, Arnaud C, Vargas-Voracek R, Nazarian A, Müller R, and al, Radiographic trabecular 2D and 3D parameters of proximal femoral bone cores correlate with each other and with yield stress. *Osteoporos Int.* 2009;20(11):1929-38.

[77] Dougherty G, A comparison of the texture of computed tomography and projection radiography images of vertebral trabecular bone using fractal signature and lacunarity. *Med. Eng. Phys.* 2001;23:313-21.

[78] Dougherty G and Henebry GM, Fractal signature and lacunarity in the measurement of the texture of trabecular bone in clinical CT images. *Med. Eng. Phys.* 2001;23:369-80.

[79] Dougherty G and Henebry GM, Lacunarity analysis of spatial pattern in CT images of vertebral trabecular bone for assesing osteoporosis. *Med. Eng. Phys.* 2002;24:129-38.

[80] Majumder SR and Mazumdar S, Mechanical breakdown of trabecular bone: dependence on microstructure. *Physica A*. 2007;377:559-64.

In: Image Processing
Editor: Vítor Hugo Carvalho
ISBN 978-1-62081-844-2

Chapter 6

IMAGE PROCESSING FOR THE ENHANCEMENT OF SATELLITE IMAGERY

*Amelia Carolina Sparavigna**
Dipartimento di Fisica, Politecnico di Torino,
Torino, Italy

ABSTRACT

The aim of this chapter is a discussion of some image processing methods for increasing the potentialities of the satellite imagery provided by free Internet services, such as Google Maps for instance, to the detection and survey of ancient remains, human modified landforms or landscape patterns. In particular, quite interesting results can be achieved by means of some tools freely available, developed originally for astrophysical researches. Of course, the same processing methods can be applied to images obtained by means of aerial or other remote sensing surveys. We will see that the use of the freely available satellite images is particularly suitable for the study of the remains of ancient landscapes. This archaeological survey is an important and challenging issue, because there are continuously increasing worries and difficulties for the preservation of these ancient structures from the assault of urbanization and modern agricultural methods.

INTRODUCTION

The identification and subsequent studies of the sites of our past is the main task of archaeology. In fact, several other sciences are involved in investigating the heritage of our past activities, such as in their preservation. As a well-known example of the interdisciplinary of contemporary archaeology, let us remember the radiocarbon dating, a method based on the naturally occurring radioisotope Carbon-14, developed in the physics laboratories and used to evaluate the age of carbon-bearing materials. Besides physics and chemistry, other sciences are necessary for a correct identification, protection and management of sites: among them we

* E-mail address: amelia.sparavigna@polito.it.

have geology, photogrammetry, remote sensing and information technology. Moreover, logistics can be involved to have profits from tourism for now and future generations. This is an important and challenging issue too, because several archaeological sites need for preservation from the assaults of urbanization and aggressive agricultural systems, and a profit could help in this task.

The use of remote sensing in archaeology is based on images obtained by means of aerial or satellite surveys. Depending on the sensors which constitute the equipment of airplanes or satellites, we can have different information on the surface and uppermost layers of the ground. An interesting opportunity is given by the freely available satellite imageries that we find on the World Wide Web: for several areas we have a high enough resolution, rendering these maps suitable for archaeological investigation. These images can be further enhanced and analysed by some methods of image processing. In this chapter, we will discuss in particular the use of some processing approaches, based on tools which are freely available, primarily developed for astrophysical researches. We will see that these methods are increasing the potentialities of satellite imagery, in the detection of ancient remains, human modified landforms or landscape patterns. After a review of some recent references on the application of remote sensing in archaeology and a discussion on the considered image processing methods, some case studies will be proposed. We will discuss in particular the use of satellite imagery for detecting and mapping large-scale features, ancient agricultural patterns and irrigation networks.

ARCHAEOLOGY AND REMOTE SENSING

As discussed in [1], it is during the last two decades that the development of new remote sensing techniques and facilities of the Information and Communication Technologies (ICTs) produced their strong application in support of the cultural heritage studies. The reference is listing the possible techniques, available for the remote sensing. These are the use of aerial multispectral and hyper-spectral imagery, the use of active airborne data of the Light Detection and Ranging (LIDAR) and Synthetic Aperture Radar (SAR), and the detection and spatial reconstruction of sub-surface remains by using Ground-Penetrating Radar (GPR), and magnetic and electrical tomography. Actually, the remote sensing is often integrated by means of ICTs with image processing, 3D visualization and virtual reconstruction of landscape and sites in the Geographic Information Systems (GIS). Therefore, a GIS is a system developed to collect and manipulate all types of geographically referenced data [2, 3]. Besides being a system that stores and displays geographic information, a GIS application allows users to create interactive queries and edit data [3].

For what concerns the aerial photos, their use for surveying and documentation is well known [4]. Usually, a large quantity of photos is used to obtain, after the processing with digital photogrammetric methods, the desired outputs as maps or 3D models. It is necessary to note that one of the most important applications of the aerial survey is in the detection of buried archaeological remains. Under the proper conditions, when viewed from above, these remains are best identified. In [4], the researchers evaluated the possibilities that the high resolution satellite imagery offers in the field of archaeological research. In particular, they worked on the identification of buried remains, using the satellite images of Quickbird 2, with a spatial resolution of 0.70 m, that cover an extended area of the archaeological site of Philippoi in Greece. Applying a statistical evaluation on the fusion of panchromatic and multispectral images, to facilitate the detection of some revealing traces, the authors compared the results from the satellite survey with the results coming out from previous researches. They found that the spatial ground resolution of satellite images allows the identification of a large range of archaeological features. Let us remember that Quickbird 2 is the USAF designation of QuickBird, a high-resolution commercial constellation of satellites, owned by DigitalGlobe. The satellites collect panchromatic imagery at a resolution of 0.7 m and multispectral imagery at a lower resolution, 2.5 m approximately [5]. The imagery can be used in GIS packages for analysis or for mapping applications, such as Google Earth and Google Maps.

In fact, it was GeoEye, the commercial satellite imagery company based in Virginia [6], which launched the first sub-meter commercial IKONOS satellite. It is an Earth observation satellite, offering multispectral and panchromatic imagery. As soon as the IKONOS imagery became available, it was integrated in GIS applications, such as in an archaeological survey of Tuscany [7]. A detailed evaluation of the use of IKONOS imagery was performed in Ref.8, where the authors presented an extensive study on the use of IKONOS in detecting some sub-canopy Maya settlements. Their investigations led to the conclusion that, sometimes, IKONOS imagery could be highly effective in detecting and predicting Maya settlement. But, changing the environmental conditions, the results are less satisfactory or absent.

Figure 1. Google Maps is an example of a popular GIS. The image shows the map corresponding to the archaeological site of Stonehenge. The service gives on the satellite maps labels and icons of Wikipedia, associating information to the geographical coordinates. Dragging the icon of Street View on the map, several dots and lines appear on it; each dot corresponds to a picture and the line to a panoramic view. It is interesting to compare these pictures and movies of the landscape to the aerial view.

Figure 2. Two panels show an example of image processing, made by means of a freely downloadable tool, the GNU Image Manipulation Program, GIMP. The upper panel shows the original satellite image from Google Maps of the Stonehenge site. We can adjust its brightness and contrast. The lower panel shows the output image. After the processing, we can clearly see in the framed areas some burial places.

Images from DigitalGlobe, GeoEye and others constitute the imagery of the Google Maps. This Web service is an example of a popular GIS. Let us consider for instance, the archaeological site of Stonehenge. The service provides on the satellite maps labels and icons of Wikipedia. To the geographical coordinates we have then associated information. Moreover, dragging the icon of Street View on the map, several dots and lines appear coloured in blue on it; each dot corresponds to a picture and the line to a panoramic view (Figure 1). It is then possible to check by means of pictures and movies how the landscape is seen from the ground and compare it with the aerial view. It is immediately clear that the satellite imagery is fundamental to have a precise location of the archaeological remains.

In fact, the images can be further enhanced using the image processing. A freely downloadable tool for processing is the GNU Image Manipulation Program, GIMP [9]. Using it, we can act on an image balancing its brightness and contrast. Let us consider the Stonehenge site again. Figure 2 shows the original image in its upper part. The lower panel is instead the image that we can see after adjusting brightness and contrast. After the processing, we can see in the framed areas several burial places. GIMP has other tools suitable to improve the images: they can be applied on the original images that we can obtain from an aerial survey, or to the images pre-processed with other methods, not implemented by GIMP, such as methods based on wavelets filtering and fractional gradient.

USING WAVELETS

Wavelets can be used to reduce the noise and extract the features of textures displayed in the image, because on wavelets, some transforms are based that allow an effective separation of signal and noise and a multi-scale analysis. Numerous research works have discussed the image processing by means of wavelets, concluding that it is a very efficient method. This is due to the fact that the wavelet transforms have great design flexibility, offering a processing of the signal tuned to its intrinsic properties.

One of the most important features of wavelet transforms is their multi-resolution representation. According to [10], some physiological analogies suggest that wavelet transforms are similar to the visual perception. This gives the possibility of investigating a particular problem choosing various ranges of spatial frequencies, allowing a "coarse to fine" procedure. Implementing such a procedure, all the textures exhibited by the image can be enhanced. [10] has a very good and concise discussion of the theoretical background of wavelets. Let us just remember that the use of wavelets is one of the solutions to the fundamental problem in signal processing, that of finding a representation of the data, able to simplify the procedure of their analysis.

Several methods of analysis are based on the use of transformations, which decompose the signal on a set of basis functions. These methods, besides being a topic of theoretical studies, are an always interesting subject of applied works. The most popular transformation is the Fourier transform that dominated for a long time the linear processing of signals. The associated basis functions are the complex sinusoidal waves. A signal, defined in a temporal or in a spatial domain has a Fourier transform, which is defined in the frequency domain. A suitable masking of frequencies or an adjustment of frequency coefficients gives, after anti-transformation, another temporal or spatial signal with enhanced some specific features. Instead of using sinusoidal function, in the wavelet transformations, we use some wave-like oscillations, having amplitudes that start out at zero, increase, and then decrease back to zero, as in a brief oscillation.

To illustrate how the wavelet analysis is able to change the input image into images more suitable for archaeological investigation, with details at different scales, let us use an image processing program having a wavelet tool. This program is Iris, freely downloadable, originally developed for astronomical images [11]. It has a wavelet dialog box that can be opened from the processing menu [12]. After uploading the image we can adjust it, enhancing certain wavelet components. As an example, let us consider the image of the archaeological area of Saqqara, Egypt, as shown by the Google imagery (Figure 3). Using the Iris dialog box, let us increase 4.3x the finest, 7.8x the fine, 4.3x the medium, and 4.3x the largest scales, but the large scale and remain we let unaltered. The resultant image is shown in the same figure, with the snapshot of the settings of dialog box used for filtering. Note how the image is clearly showing the ancient structures of this desert area.

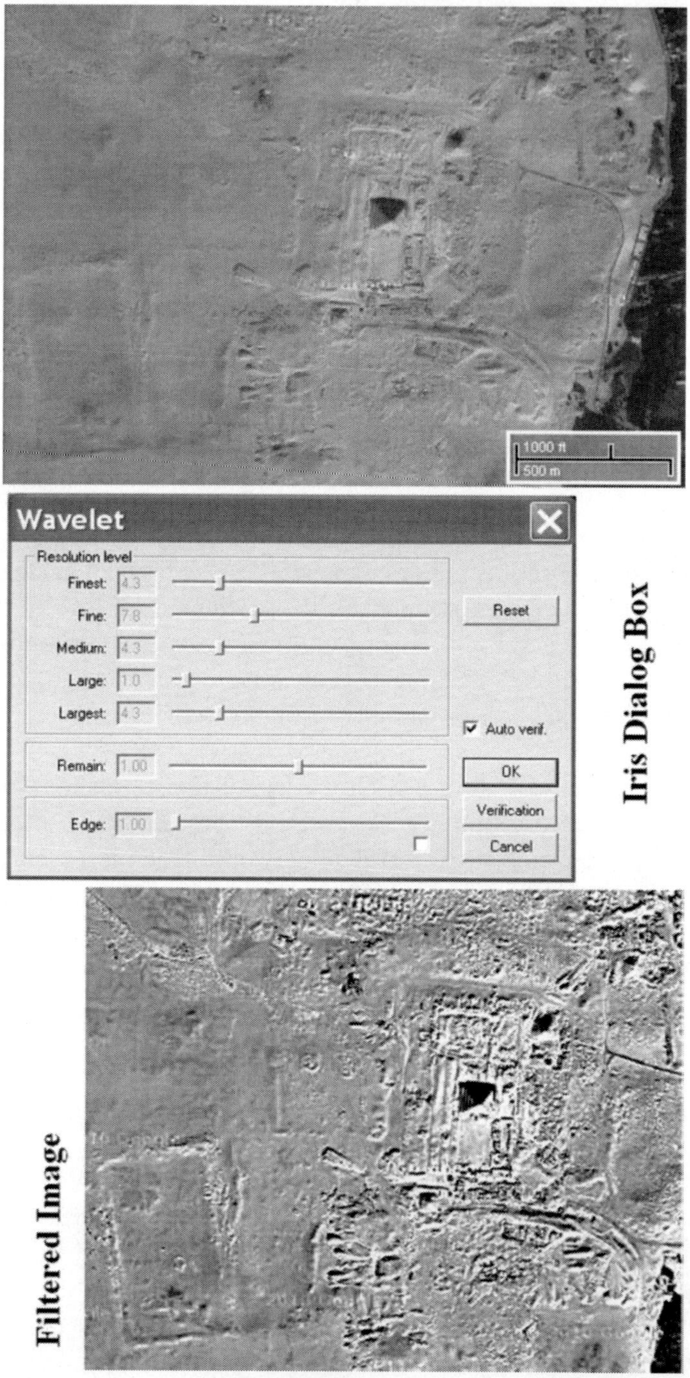

Figure 3. Using the Wavelet dialog box of Iris, we can adjust an image, enhancing certain wavelet components. In the upper panel, we can see a part of the archaeological area of Saqqara as shown by the Google imagery. Setting the parameters of the dialog box as in the middle panel, we have a filtered image as in the lowest panel. Note that the final image is clearly showing the ancient structures of this desert area.

As we can see, the dialog box has five scales. Note that we can change all the five settings, and also the residual image which is added to have the final output. The individual components of the wavelet transform can be extracted by using the console command WAVELET [12]. To the author's knowledge, the use of the wavelet filter of Iris software on satellite imagery has been proposed for the first time in [13] and [14]. In these papers, I used the Iris wavelet tool, combined with another image processing tool based on the fractional calculus.

USING FRACTIONAL GRADIENT

Fractional calculus is generalizing derivative and integration of a function to non-integer orders. As discussed by many researchers, a name as "generalized calculus" would be better than "fractional", which is actually used, to describe this calculus. We are familiar with the definition and use of first and second order derivatives, but not so used to the derivatives with a fractional order, in spite of the fact that their study is rather old. Leibnitz already discussed the fractional derivatives in the eighteenth century and other famous names of the past contributed to the development of fractional calculus in the field of pure mathematics [15-18]. Compared to these pure studies, the first application of the fractional calculus to image processing is quite recent indeed [19, 20].

Allowing integration and derivation of any real order, the fractional calculus can be considered a branch of mathematical analysis, which deals with integral-differential equations. For this reason, the calculus of fractional order derivatives is not as straightforward as the calculus of integer order derivatives. Since image processing is usually working on quantized and discrete data, we can use a discrete implementation of the fractional order derivation. Let us remember that two-dimensional image maps are arrays of pixels, each pixel having three colour tones. The recorded image is then a discrete signal, because it is discrete the position of each pixel in the map. Moreover, the signal is quantized, since the colour tones are ranging from 0 to 255. To have partial derivatives suitable for calculations on the image maps, let us define the discrete fractional differentiation as proposed in [21, 22]. Defining a fractional gradient, we can have a processing tool suitable for edge enhancement and detection [23].

In [24], a free tool was proposed for the analysis of astronomical images, named AstroFracTool, able to evaluate the fractional gradient of an image map (in JPG and BMP formats). The dialog box of AstroFracTool allows choosing the fractional order and a coefficient to adjust the visibility of the output image. Let us consider again Saqqara as view by Google Maps. The result that we obtain using AstroFracTool is shown in Figure 4. We see that the tool is marking the edges of the structures. To have a better visualization, the output image from this tool can be adjusted by means of the GIMP tools. Let us consider that for the edge detection, several methods already exist and are proposed by the Edge tool in GIMP. The advantage of the use of fractional gradients is that the fractional order gives an enhancement of edges in the original image, without destroying it. The original map remains partially visible in the output map. A pre-processing with AstroFracTool gives also to the final image an embossment effect.

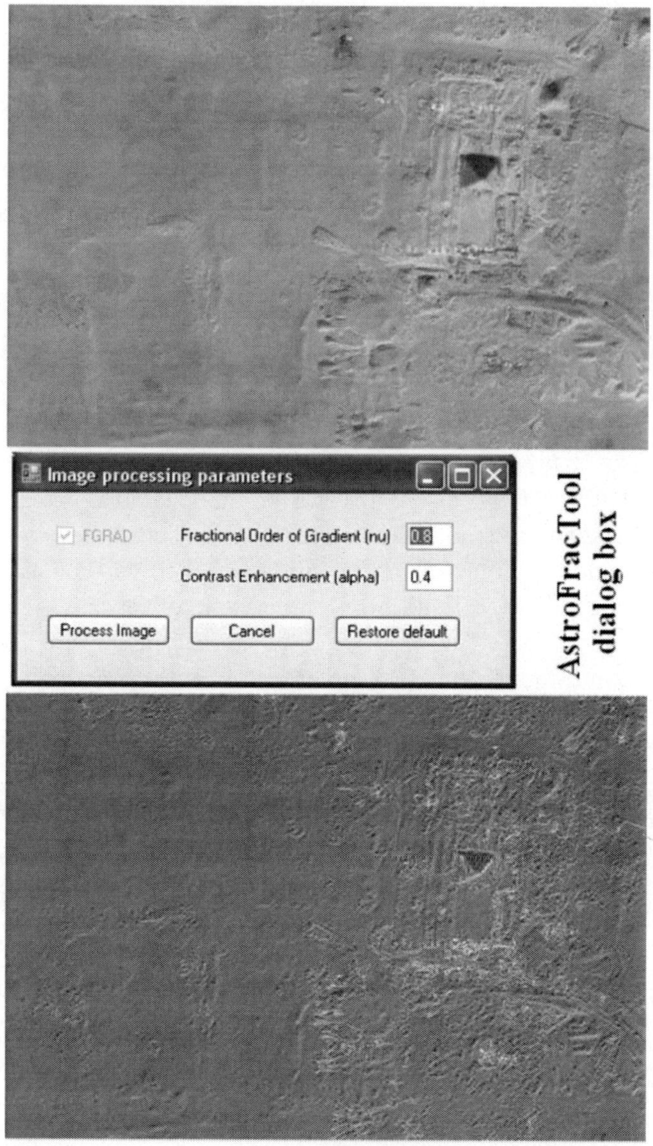

Figure 4. AstroFracTool is an image processing tool able to evaluate the fractional gradient of JPG or BMP images. A dialog box allows choosing the fractional order and a coefficient to adjust the visibility of the output image. The result of the fractional processing is shown in the lowest panel. The tool is marking the edges of the structures. To have a better visualization, this output image can be adjusted using GIMP.

MERGING TECHNIQUES IN SOME CASE STUDIES

As previously told, the result obtained applying an image processing tool can be improved using another tool. For instance, we can apply the brightness-contrast tool of GIMP to the image obtained from a processing with AstroFracTool. The final result appears as in Figure 5.c. A color inversion produces the image 5.d, where the embossment effect of the edges is more visible. To appreciate the difference between an image and the image that we have after an edge enhancement, we can compare 5.c with 5.b. Figure 5.b is obtained with a simple adjustment of brightness and contrast of original 5.a.

There is another interesting possibility in the processing of images: GIMP has a tool able to combine several images. Using this tool, each image becomes a layer that can be superimposed to the other layers in a given percentage. In this manner, we can have an output image using several layers, created from a pre-processing with AstroFracTool, Iris or GIMP itself. I used this approach based on the merging of two or three layers in several papers, devoted to discuss the satellite survey of some archaeological areas in Egypt [25-27]. An interesting case study could be the mapping of Amarna: I have collected some differently processed images in a Web site [28]. The site is showing that the use of image processing can be helpful in preparing a total survey of this area.

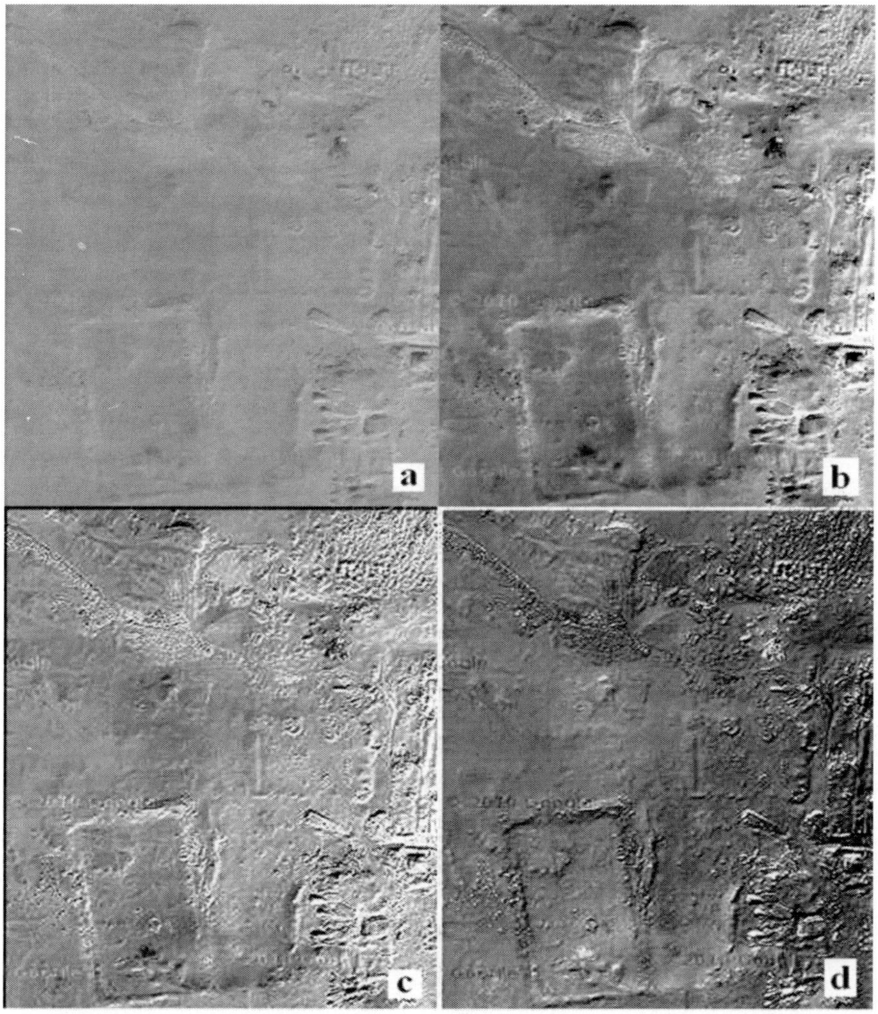

Figure 5. Panel (a) is giving the original image of a part of the Saqqara archaeological site as shown by Google Maps. Panel (b) is the image obtained adjusting its brightness and contrast with GIMP. Panel (c) is proposing the output of AstroFracTool, after adjusting brightness and contrast with GIMP. Panel (d) is the same as (c) after a color inversion, where we can see the embossment effect.

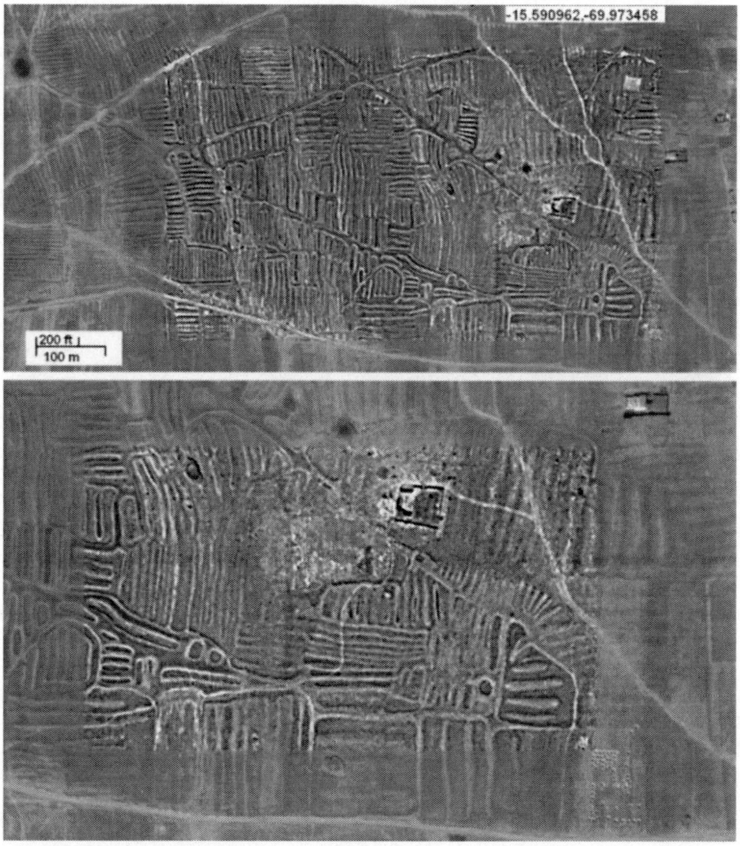

Figure 6. Any landform composed of fine-grained materials evolves in wide and flat relieves, due to the down-slope transport of its materials over time. The earthworks of the raised fields are subjected to the same destiny of being widened and flattened as a consequence of the natural degradation processes. But these ancient structures can be clearly seen in satellite imagery as a texture superimposed to the background landform. To have a better view of this texture, a processing of the images is necessary when the landform is strongly degraded or is under the modern cultivations. The figure shows an example of waru-waru creating a geoglyph. The central part of the two panels has been enhanced with a merging of wavelets and fractional gradient. The surrounding part is left as it appears in the original Google Maps.

Other references [29, 30] discussed the use of image processing for some archaeological investigations that can be only performed using the satellite imagery. These are the surveys of large-scale features, such as ancient agricultural patterns and irrigation networks. In fact, satellite imagery was fundamental in discovering the huge geoglyphs of the deforested sections of the Amazon Basin, in the eastern Acre State, Brazil. These geoglyphs are earthworks that appear as squared or round structures, often connected by lines (see [29], and references therein). Another wonderful landscape, created by an ancient network of earthworks, can be observed using the Google satellite imagery near the Titicaca Lake. We see the slopes of hills criss-crossed with terrace walls and the surfaces of the plains covered with raised fields, indicating that this was once a highly productive agricultural place for the south central Andes. Some of the landforms are rather remarkable, because they are creating zoomorphic shapes, where ponds are representing the eyes [30]. The network of earthworks is the remains of an extensive ancient agricultural system built and used by the Andean people many centuries ago. People created the system of raised fields (also known as "waru-waru" or "camellones"), which were large elevated planting platforms, with the corresponding drainage canals. This system improved the soil and the temperature and moisture conditions for crops. The ponds and canals between the raised fields acted as sources of moisture during the periods of drought. Moreover, water in the deep canals might have been used to cultivate aquatic plants and fish, as well as attract lake birds [31]. The remains of prehistoric raised fields are the evidence of impressive engineering abilities of people who lived in pre-Columbian times.

Any landform composed of fine-grained materials evolves in wide and flat relieves, due to the down-slope transport of its materials over time. The earthworks of the raised fields are subjected to the same destiny, to be widened and flattened as a consequence of the natural degradation processes [32, 33]. The evolution of ancient earthworks indicates that a variety of initial earthwork forms can result in a sinusoidal profile apparent on the current landscape [34]. Therefore, these ancient structures can be clearly displayed by satellite imagery as a texture superimposed to the background landform. The raised fields of Titicaca have different forms and size, generally being 4-10 m wide, from 10 to 100 m long, and 1 m tall. In spite of erosion, the network of earthworks is clearly visible from the space. A processing of the images, performed as we have previously discussed, is necessary when the landform is strongly degraded or is under the modern cultivations. An example of waru-waru is shown in Figure 6. The central part of the two panels has been enhanced with a merging of wavelets and fractional gradient. The surrounding part, which seems blurred, is as it appears in the original Google Maps.

Another interesting research in the area near the Titicaca Lake is the mapping of the agricultural system of qochas. In Quechua, the term "qocha" refers to a lake, pool or pond of natural or artificial origin. These ponds appear at the vertices of a network of canals, as depressions, natural or dug by men on the ground surface, that can be flooded. This agricultural system can be found in several areas on the Andean highlands of Peru and Bolivia. Qochas are very numerous and dense in the department of Puno, Peru, where they were discovered and documented [35]. A project on anthropological studies of the Pennsylvania State University, the AnthSpace Analytical Cartography Lab, is monitoring the qochas in Peru by means of satellites [36]. As in the case of the raised fields, the qochas can be seen in the Google Maps imagery, and the details of these structures enhanced by image processing.

CONCLUSION

Besides the identification and monitoring of qochas, we could study the lines of the Nazca desert and its system of puquios, which are irrigation canals [37]. Or we could map and monitor the Andenes, terraces built by the pre-Hispanic cultures on the slopes of mountains for agricultural purposes. For all these large networks of ancient human activity that modified the natural landscape, the only successful instruments are satellites. This kind of archaeological survey is important because these ancient structures are fragile and needs to be preserved from the assault of modern agricultural methods. The same is true for the archaeological sites of the ancient Egypt.

In the chapter we have proposed the use of image processing methods based on wavelets and fractional calculus, to improve the details of freely available satellite images. Of course, the use of these images, combined with image processing, is just at the beginning and several other examples and case studies can be proposed in the future.

REFERENCES

[1] R. Lasaponara and N. Masini, *Advances on remote sensing for archaeology and cultural heritage management, preface of the Proceedings of the 1st International EARSeL Workshop CNR,* 30, Sept. 2008 (Rome, Italy).

[2] P. Bolstad, *GIS Fundamentals: A First Text on Geographic Information Systems,* Eider Press, White Bear Lake (2005).

[3] K.-T. Chang, *Introduction to Geographic Information Systems,* McGraw Hill, Boston (2006).

[4] O. Georgoula, D. Kaimaris, M. Tsakiri and P. Patias, *From the aerial photo to high resolution satellite image: tools for the archaeological research, in the Proceedings of the XXth ISPRS Congress,* 12, Jul. 2004 (Istanbul, Turkey).

[5] http://www.digitalglobe.com/index.php/85/QuickBird.

[6] http://www.geoeye.com/CorpSite/.

[7] S. Campana, Ikonos-2 multispectral satellite imagery to the study of archaeological landscapes: an integrated multi-sensor approach in combination with "traditional" methods, CAA 2002 The Digital Heritage of Archaeology, Computer Applications and Quantitative Methods in Archaeology, in the *Proceedings of the XXXth Conference,* 2, April 2002 (Heraklion, Crete) pp219-225.

[8] T. G. Garrison, S. D. Houston, C. Golden, T. Inomata, Z. Nelson and J. Munson, *Journal of Archaeological Science,* 35, 2770 (2008).

[9] http://www.gimp.org/.

[10] Y. Jin, E. Angelini and A. Laine, Wavelets in medical image processing: de-noising, segmentation, and registration, in the Handbook of Biomedical Image Analysis, *Topics in Biomedical Engineering,* International Book Series, Springer, Berlin, 2005.

[11] http://www.astrosurf.com/buil/us/iris/iris.htm.

[12] http://www.astrosurf.com/buil/iris/tutorial11/doc28_us.htm.

[13] A. C. Sparavigna, *Enhancing the Google imagery using a wavelet filter,* 2010, arXiv:1009.1590, at http://arxiv.org/abs/1009.1590.

[14] A. C. Sparavigna, *Crater-like landform in Bayuda Desert* (a processing of satellite images), 2010, arXiv:1008.0500, at http://arxiv.org/abs/1008. 0500

[15] M. Kleinz and T. J. Osler, *The College Mathematics Journal,* 31, 82 (2000).

[16] P. L. Butzer and U. Westphal, An introduction to fractional calculus, in Applications of Fractional Calculus in Physics, R. Hilfer Editor, *World Scientific,* Singapore, 2000, pp1-85.

[17] A. A. Kilbas, H. M. Srivastava and J. J. Trujiilo, *Theory and applications of fractional differential equations,* Elsevier, Amsterdam, 2006.

[18] D. Cafagna, *IEEE Industrial Electronic Magazine,* Summer 2007, pp35-40.

[19] M. D.Ortigueira and J. A. Tenreiro Machado, *Signal processing,* 83, 2285 (2003).

[20] F. Falzon and G. Giraudon, *Fractals,* 2, 387 (1994).

[21] Jia Huading and Pu Yifei, Fractional calculus method for enhancing digital image of bank slip, in *the Proceedings of the 2008 Congress on Image and Signal Processing,* CISP'2008, May 2008, (Sanya, Hainan, China), 3, pp326-330.

[22] Y. Pu, W. X. Wang, J. L. Zhou, Y. Y. Wand and H. D. Jia, Sci. China Ser. F-Inf. Sci., 51, 1319 (2008).

[23] A. C. Sparavigna, *Fractional differentiation based image processing,* 2009, arXiv:0910.2381, at http://arxiv.org/abs/0910.2381.

[24] R. Marazzato and A. C. Sparavigna, *Astronomical image processing based on fractional calculus: the AstroFracTool*, 2009, arXiv:0910.4637, at http://arxiv.org/abs/0910.4637.

[25] A. C. Sparavigna, *The satellite archaeological survey of Egypt,* Archaeogate, June 6, 2011.

[26] A. C. Sparavigna, *The cradle of Egyptian pyramids in satellite images,* Archaeogate, June 14, 2011.

[27] A. C. Sparavigna, *Abusir: from Pliny the Elder to Google Maps,* Archaeogate, June 28, 2011.

[28] Amarna (satellite imagery), at https://sites.google.com/site/ amarnasatellit eimagery/.

[29] A. C. Sparavigna, Lines under the forest, Archaeogate, May 31, 2011.

[30] A. C. Sparavigna, *The geoglyphs of Titicaca, Archaeogate,* October 13, 2010.

[31] C. L. Erickson, *Expedition,* 30, 8 (1988).

[32] A. C. Londoño, *Geomorphology,* 99, 13 (2008).

[33] M. A. O'Neal, M. E. O'Mansky and J. A. MacGregor, *Geoarchaeology,* 20, 739 (2005).

[34] A. C. Sparavigna, Qochas on Andean highlands, *Archaeogate,* May 5, 2011.

[35] *Qocha inventory, Remote sensing inventory and spatial analysis of Qochas, Northern Lake Titicaca Basin,* Peru, Pennsylvania State University, at http://www.personal.psu.edu/ nmc15/blogs/anthspace/ research/qocha-inventory.html.

[36] K. J. Schreiber and J. Lancho Rojas, *Latin American Antiquity,* 6, 229 (1995).

In: Image Processing
Editor: Vítor Hugo Carvalho
ISBN 978-1-62081-844-2

Chapter 7

IMAGE PROCESSING IN THE ANALYSIS OF NEURONAL DENDRITIC BRANCHING PATTERNS: DOES STRUCTURE FOLLOW FUNCTION ACROSS DIFFERENT SPECIES?

***Herbert F. Jelinek*[1], *Nebojša T. Milošević*[2], *Dušan Ristanović*[2] *and David Cornforth*[3,1]**

[1]Center for Research in Complex Systems, School of Community Health, Charles Sturt University, Australia
[2]Department of Biophysics, School of Medicine, University of Belgrade, Serbia
[3]School of Design, Communication and IT, University of Newcastle, Australia

ABSTRACT

Structure and function are closely related in biology. This chapter describes the analysis of alpha retinal ganglion cells that are seen as preserving their function across species, to determine whether structure follows function, that is, whether similar structures can be observed. Two-dimensional images of the alpha retinal ganglion cells of three orders of mammals are investigated in order to determine the consistency of the dendritic branching pattern across eleven mammalian species. Using the linear two-dimensional Sholl method, we present a mathematical model, which includes the critical and maximal values of the number of intersections, and the abscissae of the inflection points of the branching points and terminal tips, with respect to the radius. Differences among these parameters for the eleven mammalian species were statistically significant. We therefore propose a hypothesis that the morphology of the alpha retinal ganglion cells are not conserved in mammals, coming from different habitats and having a wide variety of behaviors, despite similar function.

* E-mail address: D.Cornforth@adfa.edu.au.

Introduction

Basic neurobiology states that the function of a nerve cell is largely dependent on its structure. In order to understand how a neuron integrates its synaptic inputs to generate an appropriate response, a complete knowledge of the cell's morphology and geometry is required [1]. Many quantitative parameters have been used to characterize the morphology of nerve cells. The simple models that have been used for cellular shape, such as spheres, ellipsoids and polyhedrons, and their corresponding two-dimensional profiles, are useful for many purposes, but certainly fall short in dealing with a cell's inherent structural complexity [1]. The dendritic branching patterns of neurons are commonly used as an anatomical feature. However dendritic branching, which reflects a neuron's function, has frequently been avoided as a morphological feature. Therefore, a topological description that calls attention to the form and complexity of the dendritic tree is a useful addition to the repertoire of standard metric characteristics, such as dendritic diameter, dendritic length and dendritic field area [2].

In order to analyze how the number of neuronal branches vary with the distance from the cell body, Sholl used a series of concentric spherical shells as reference coordinates and presented histograms showing the distributions of the numbers of dendritic branches as a function of distance from the cell body for stellate and pyramidal cells [3]. Following Sholl's methodology many high-quality morphometric neuronal studies have been presented [4-10]. Others pointed to shortcomings in the Sholl method [2, 8, 11-15]).

The linear Sholl method is a modification of Sholl's analysis for a two-dimensional structure and determines the relationship between the number of dendritic intersections found within the concentric and regularly spaced circles as a function of the circle radii. But the question arises whether the number of dendritic intersections with a circle is an elementary count or consists of some basic components. In this study, we propose a mathematical model, which incorporates a supposition that the number of dendritic intersections with a circle of a given radius can be resolved into two components: the number of branching points with the circle and the number of terminal tips within the concentric shell, being the space between two circles of increasing radii. Strictly speaking, the number of intersections can be obtained if the number of terminal tips within the circle is subtracted from the sum of the number of primary dendrites and branching points within the previous (smaller) concentric shell. To our knowledge, only [16] specified the number of branching points and terminal tips per concentric shell, while [17] analyzed and used a similar model in a two-dimensional case. Applying our model on two-dimensional images of the alpha retinal ganglion cells (RGCs) from three orders of mammals, we investigate the dendritic pattern across species belonging to the same mammalian order and between species belonging to either the 'domestic' or 'wild' group to emphasize habitat.

Materials and Methods

Materials

The alpha RGCs from the retinae of eleven species belonging to three orders of mammals were used for this study (Table 1). For laboratory animals (guinea pig, rat, cat and dog) the eyes were taken, usually at the end of other experiments, after an overdose of barbiturate or chloral hydrate. Ox and pig eyes were obtained at the slaughterhouse, while chinchilla eyes from fur farms. Other eyes came from zoos when the animals died of age or disease [18]. The two-dimensional neuronal images were obtained using the histological procedure as described in [18, 19]. In brief, each animal eye was enucleated and the dendritic tree morphology of the RGCs were visualized using intracellulary injected Lucifer Yellow. Since RGC morphology is known to change with eccentricity in some species, all cells were sampled from approximately the same range of eccentricity. Table 1 summarizes the data used in this study, with the third column showing the number of cells available for each species. Previous studies have shown that the alpha cells throughout various species are monostratified with a clear distinction in dendritic morphology between inner and outer subpopulation [20, 18, 21]. To avoid this, only cells which belonged to the same subpopulation (the inner alpha RGCs) were included in the analysis.

All cells were drawn using camera lucida projection, as seen in a wholemount preparation. The camera lucida drawings of one hundred and twenty nine alpha RGCs (Fig. 1) were scanned into the computer using a scanner at 600 dpi. All transformations were carried out using the public domain Image J software, developed at the US National Institute of Health. For the further analysis of the dendritic branching pattern, axons and spines (if they were present) were removed digitally from the drawings.

Table 1. Mammalian species examined for alpha RGCs morphology

Order	Species	Cell count	Eccentricity (mm)
Rodentia	Chinchilla	7	2.9 – 5.9
	Guinea pig	11	3.0 – 6.6
	Rat	17	3.4 – 6.2
Carnivora	Ferret	10	2.8 – 7.0
	Cat	18	3.8 – 8.1
	Dog	11	3.5 – 7.0
Artiodactyla	Guanaco	6	4.0 – 8.0
	Reindeer	11	4.1 – 11.0
	Niglau antilope	10	3.8 – 9.0
	Ox	11	4.0 – 10.0
	Pig	17	3.5 – 7.0

Mathematical Model of Neuronal Branching Pattern

Formulation of the mathematical model, which describes the dendritic branching pattern of the neuron, is based on a graphical model of a hypothetical neuron shown in Figure 2. Such a model of a neuron satisfies three assumptions: (1) each branch is represented as a straight-line segment which radiates away from the "cell body" or dendritic parent segment and cuts a superimposed circle at a specific radius only once, (2) each segment of the dendritic tree can only branch dichotomously and (3) the dendritic terminations dominate in a region more radially distant from the region in which the branching occurs. Using the spans between the circles in arbitrary units, the neuron was overlaid by a series of equidistantly arranged concentric circles centred at the "cell body". The number of intersections of dendrites with these circles, as well as the numbers of branching points and terminal tips of dendritic branches between adjacent circles (a concentric shell) were counted.

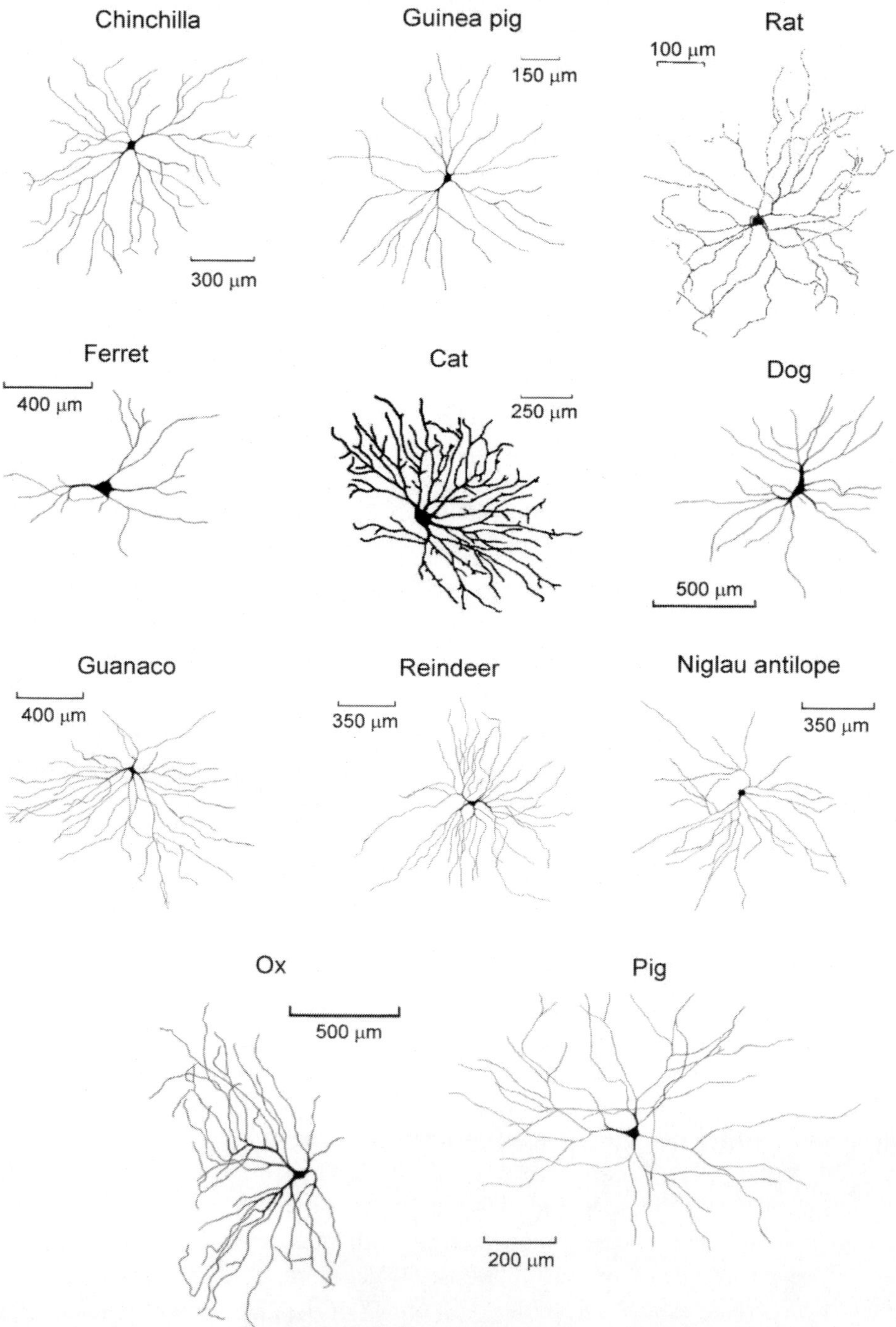

Figure 1. Representative drawings of the alpha RGCs in eleven species. Scale bar is also shown.

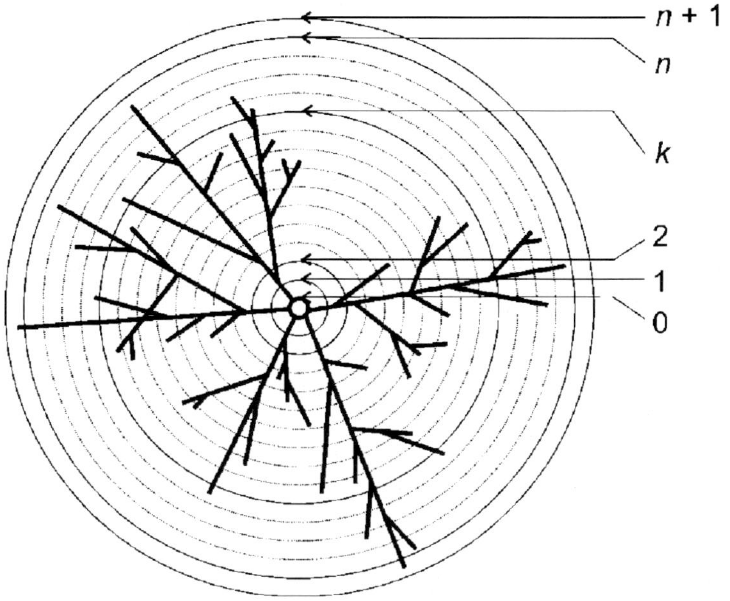

Figure 2. Graphical model of a hypothetical neuron in two dimension: a network of concentric equidistant circles is superimposed over the drawing, starting with circle 0 (the "cell body") and finishing with circle *n + 1*.

If the first circle (circle 0 in Figure 2) symbolizes the cell body of a neuron and N_0 is the number of primary dendrites, then the number of intersections of the dendrites with the second circle (circle 1 in Figure 2) is given by equation

$$N_1 = N_0 + N_{B0} - N_{T0}, \tag{1}$$

where N_{B0} is the number of branching points and N_{T0} is the number of terminal tips in the region bounded by circles 0 and 1. Similarly, the number of dendrites intersecting the third circle (circle 2 in Figure 2) is given by

$$N_2 = N_1 + N_{B1} - N_{T1} = N_0 + (N_{B0} + N_{B1}) - (N_{T0} + N_{T1}). \tag{2}$$

Therefore the number of dendrites intersecting any circle (for, instance, circle k in Figure 2) can be obtained by the equation

$$N_k = N_{k-1} + N_{Bk-1} - N_{Tk-1} = N_0 + \sum_{i=0}^{k} (N_{Bi} - N_{Ti}). \tag{3}$$

For the most peripheral circle (circle $n+1$ in Figure 2), Eq. (3) gives the solution $N_{n+1} = 0$, indicating that no dendritic branches cut the last circle. Therefore, Eq. (3) represents the mathematical model of a neuronal dendritic branching pattern, showing the relationship between the number of intersections of dendritic segments with a concentric circle, and the difference between the total number of branching points and terminal tips, encompassed by this circle.

Parameters of Dendritic Arborisation Emerging from the Model

The function which adequately fits the example neuron of Figure 2 can be obtained by fitting a polynomial regression using the number of intersections *(N)* as a function of the radius *r*. This function is shown in Figure 3. For our data a polynomial of degree 5 provides an optimal plot with a high correlation coefficient *R* [2]. Such a polynomial allows the calculation of two important parameters: (1) the critical radius (r_c) and (2) the maximum value (N_m) of the number of intersections with the circle of radius r_c. In order to calculate the maximum of the function *N(r)*, it is necessary to find the first derivative of *N(r)* with respect to *r* from the equation $N'(r) = 0$, find the solutions for *r* and select the critical value for which the function has a maximum.

Correspondingly, the numbers of branch points N_B and terminal tips N_T versus the circle radius *r* for the model in Figure 2 are shown in Figure 4A and B, respectively. A polynomial of the same degree (as it was used for the number of intersections *N*) is fitted to these data and the correlation coefficient, as well as the values of the two parameters (r_c, and N_m) are calculated. In both cases, the data points scatter around the curve resulting in a low correlation coefficient, as compared to the plot in Figure 3. This problem can be successfully avoided if the cumulative frequencies are taken, since it is known that any symmetrical distribution can be represented as an S-shaped cumulative frequency distribution. Such transformation improves the analysis of the distributions shown in Figure 4. The cumulative frequency distribution of N_B and N_T obtained from the example data of Figure 2 are shown in Figure 5.

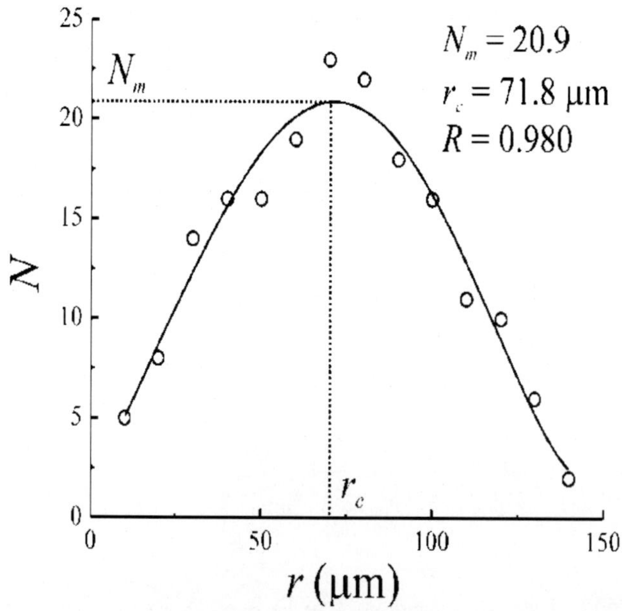

Figure 3. Number of intersections (*N*) of dendrites with circles versus the radius of the circles (*r*). The graph is obtained by fitting the polynomial of degree 5 to data points measured on the drawing in Fig. 2. *R* is the coefficient of correlation, r_c is the critical value and N_m is the maximum value of the function *N(r)*.

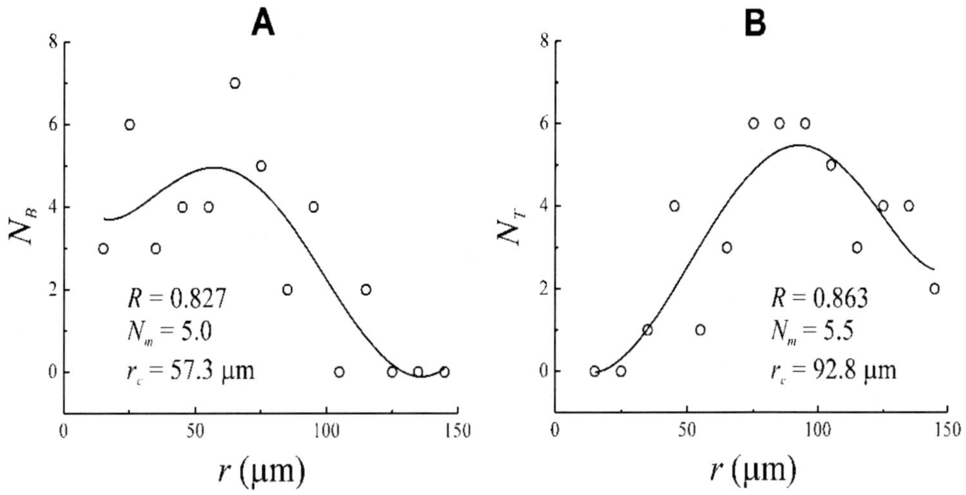

Figure 4. The number of branching points (N_B) and number of terminal tips (N_T) versus the radius of the circles (r), using the intervals between the pairs of adjacent circles of 10μm.

It has been shown previously that the best function that fits data in Figure. 5A and B is the Boltzmann logistic transcendental function [2]. When this function is fitted to the cumulative frequencies N_B and N_T (Figures 5A and B, full lines), the correlation coefficients increase in comparison to the corresponding values in Figure 4. The most important parameter that emerges from Boltzmann function is the abscissa of the inflection point rip. The first derivate of the Boltzmann function (i.e. the density function *Dr(CN)*) is found and shown in Figure 5 (dashed lines). The value of r (i.e. the critical value rc) where the function *Dr(CN)* has a maximum indicates the position (and value) of the inflection points rip. Finally, the cumulative frequency distributions of N_B and N_T result in two new parameters: the critical radius of branching points $(r_c)_B$ and critical radius of terminal tips $(r_c)_T$.

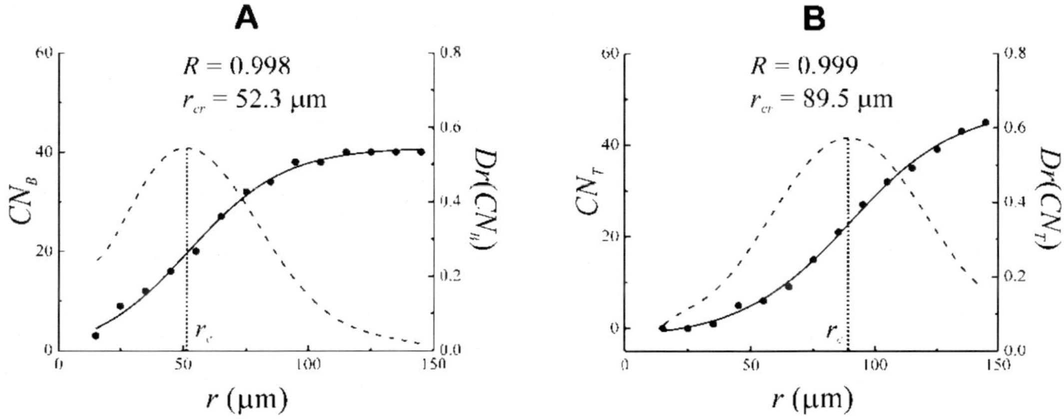

Figure 5. Cumulative frequency data distributions (black circles) of the number of branching points (A) and that of terminal tips (B), taken from Figs. 4A and B, respectively. Data are fitted with Boltzmann's function (full lines). Density functions (*Dr(CN)*) for cumulative number of branching points and terminal tips are represented with dashed lines. The critical radius of branching points and terminal tips is designated by r_c.

RESULTS

Figure 6 shows the relative frequency polygons of four parameters calculated for eleven the species, which belong to three orders of mammals included in this research: the rodentia, carnivora and artiodactyla. As can be seen from Figure 6, all distributions were normal, either bell-shaped or skewed. Therefore, the central tendency and dispersion measure of our four parameters (N_m, r_c, $(r_c)_B$ and $(r_c)_T$) for each of the eleven species can be expressed by the mean and standard error while further statistical analyses were performed by appropriate parametric statistics.

Dendritic Branching between Species of the Same Mammalian Order

The values of the four parameters, which quantify the dendritic branching pattern of the alpha RGCs in the eleven species, are summarized in Table 2. In order to explore whether there were significant differences in the mean N_m, r_c, $(r_c)_B$ and$(r_c)_T$ among species that belong to the same mammalian order, a one-way ANOVA was used. To assess how many pairs of means N_m, r_c, $(r_c)_B$ and $(r_c)_T$ were significantly different, a Schéffe post hoc test was applied. The results of these calculations are summarized in Table 3.

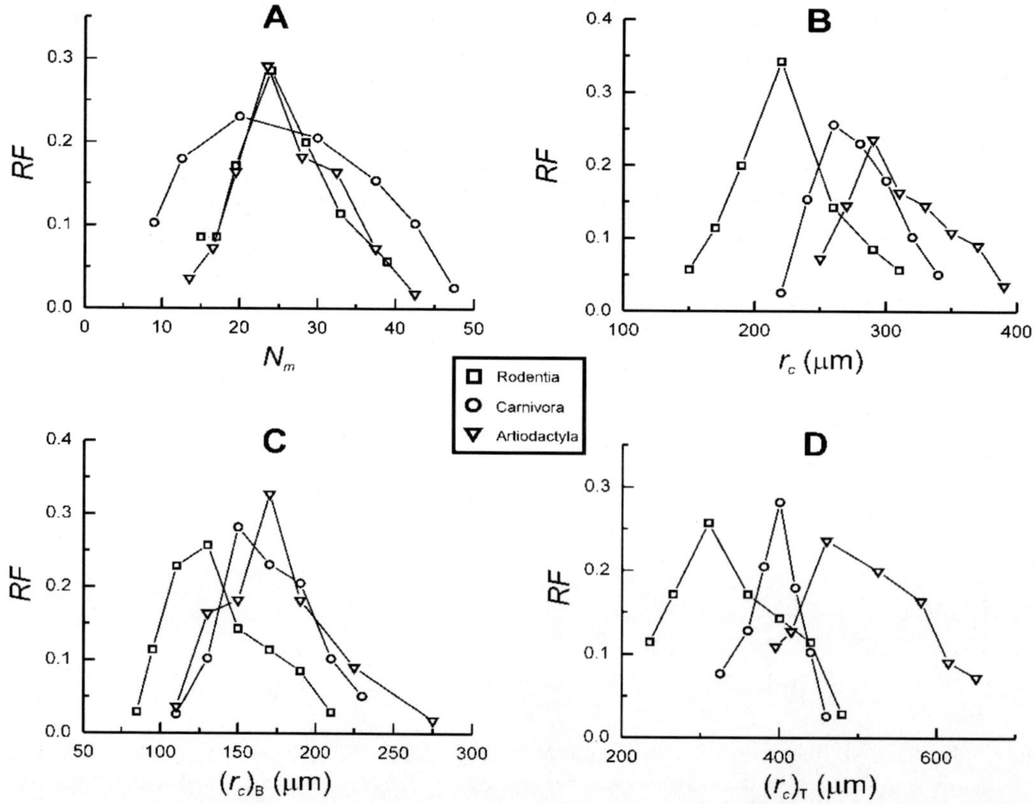

Figure 6. Relative frequency polygons of the maximal number of intersections (A), critical radius of intersections (B), critical radius of branching points (C) and critical radius of terminal tips (D) of alpha RGCs in three orders of mammals.

As for the alpha RGCs of rodentia, the rat cells differed significantly from both chinchilla and guinea pig for all parameters (Table 3). Between chinchilla and guinea pig, a significant difference was also found in the mean r_c ($p < 0.01$) and $(r_c)_B$ ($p < 0.001$).

The alpha cells of the three carnivora species also showed differences in dendritic morphology, with the cat and dog cells being significantly different for the mean N_m, r_c and $(r_c)_B$, whereas ferret cells differed from those of the cat and dog in the mean N_m only (Table 3).

The statistical analysis of the alpha cells of five species, which belonged to the artiodactyla confirmed differences in their dendritic branching pattern. A significant difference in means of all parameters was found between guanaco and reindeer only. Six pairs of species (niglau antilope-guanaco, niglau antilope-reindeer, niglau antilope-ox, guanaco-pig, reindeer-pig and ox-pig) differed significantly in three of four parameters (Table 3). On the other hand, a significant difference between means for only one parameter was found in three pairs: niglau antilope-pig ($(r_c)_T$), guanaco-ox ($(r_c)_B$) and reindeer-ox (N_m).

Table 2. The values of the maximal number of intersections N_m, critical radius of intersections r_c, critical radius of branching points $(r_c)_B$ and critical radius of terminal tips $(r_c)_T$ for the alpha RGCs of eleven species, which belonged to three orders of mammals. Each value is shown as the mean ± standard error

Order	Species	N_m	r_c (μm)	$(r_c)_B$ (μm)	$(r_c)_T$ (μm)
Rodentia	Chinchilla	18.7 ± 0.9	278 ± 12	178 ± 8	404 ± 18
	Guinea pig	21.6 ± 1.5	227 ± 9	106 ± 5	383 ± 11
	Rat	29.3 ± 1.3	195 ± 7	139 ± 7	273 ± 8
Carnivora	Ferret	11.6 ± 1.1	266 ± 11	163 ± 10	387 ± 6
	Cat	36.7 ± 1.3	288 ± 7	186 ± 7	389 ± 10
	Dog	19.5 ± 1.2	264 ± 5	153 ± 5	404 ± 7
Artiodactyla	Niglau ant.	22.6 ± 1.3	284 ± 10	145 ± 7	452 ± 9
	Guanaco	24.5 ± 1.7	323 ± 6	253 ± 4	612 ± 12
	Reindeer	32.8 ± 1.8	351 ± 8	162 ± 6	563 ± 10
	Ox	22.9 ± 1.8	340 ± 9	174 ± 6	582 ± 12
	Pig	25.0 ± 1.5	280 ± 5	159 ± 5	417 ± 5

Dendritic Branching for Wild and Domestic Group

As the next step in our investigation, we divided the eleven species into two groups: domestic and wild animals as a possible indicator of habitat influence. Six species (chinchilla, guinea pig, cat, dog, ox and pig) were included in the group of domestic animals, while five species (rat, ferret, guanaco, niglau antilope and reindeer) were classified as wild animals. The mean N_m and their standard error for the two groups are illustrated in Figure 7, whereas the mean r_c, $(r_c)_B$ and $(r_c)_T$ are shown in Figure 8. In each case, the top of the shaded bar represents the mean.

Table 3. Distributions of N_m, r_c, $(r_c)_B$ and $(r_c)_T$ over pairs of samples tested for significance

Order	Pairs	N_m	r_c (μm)	$(r_c)_B$ (μm)	$(r_c)_T$ (μm)
Rodentia	Chinchilla-Guinea pig	/	**	***	/
	Chinchilla-Rat	***	***	**	***
	Guinea pig-Rat	***	**	**	***
Carnivora	Ferret-Cat	***	/	/	/
	Ferret-Dog	***	/	/	/
	Cat-Dog	***	*	**	/
Artiodactyla	Niglau ant.-Guanaco	/	*	***	***
	Niglau ant.-Reindeer	***	***	/	***
	Niglau ant.-Ox	/	***	**	***
	Niglau ant.-Pig	/	/	/	**
	Guanaco-Reindeer	*	*	***	**
	Guanaco-Ox	/	/	***	/
	Guanaco-Pig	/	***	***	***
	Reindeer-Ox	***	/	/	/
	Reindeer-Pig	**	***	/	***
	Ox-Pig	/	***	*	***

* means p <0.05, ** means p < 0.01, *** means p < 0.001 and / indicates no significance.

Within the group of domestic animals, only the cat has significantly different mean N_m (Figure 7A). The mean N_m of the pig differed from the mean of three species: the cat, chinchilla and ox. As for the mean r_c, $(r_c)_B$ and $(r_c)_T$, the ox differed from all other species (Figure 8A). No statistically significant difference in the mean $(r_c)_B$ between pairs ox-chinchilla and ox-cat was found. A similar result was obtained for the guinea pig: the means of r_c and $(r_c)_B$ differed significantly than these means of four species belonged to two orders of the mammals. On the other hand, a significant difference in the mean $(r_c)_T$ was found between the guinea pig and two species of artiodactyla only. Additional significant difference was found among following pairs: dog-pig (r_c), chinchilla-dog ($(r_c)_B$), chinchilla-pig ($(r_c)_B$) and cat-pig ($(r_c)_B$ and $(r_c)_T$).

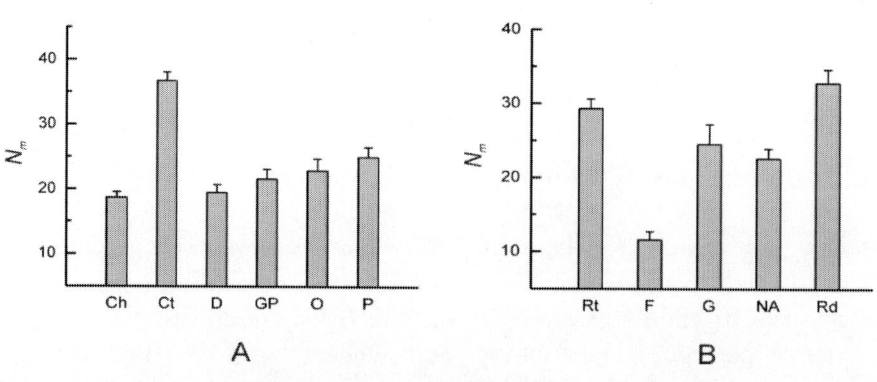

Figure 7. Mean number of intersections (N_m) of the alpha RGCs in domestic (A) and wild (B) species. Abbreviated species names are (left to right) Chinchilla, Cat, Dog, Guinea Pig, Ox and Pig (A), and Rat, Ferret, Guanaco, Niglau Antilope and Reindeer (B).

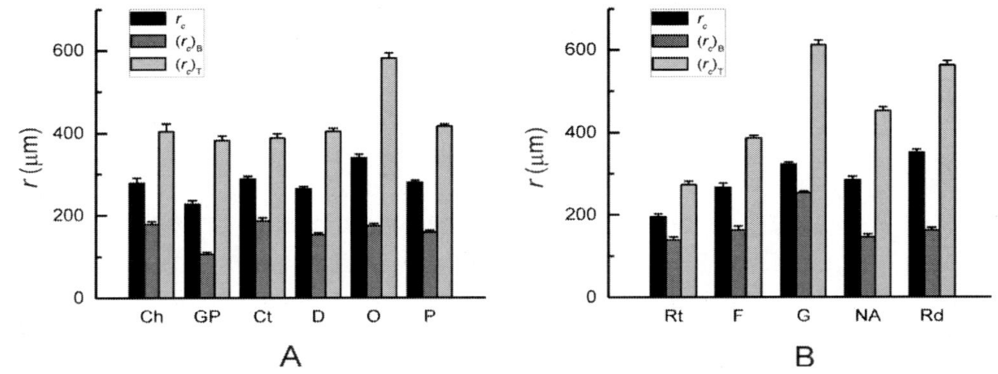

Figure 8. Mean critical radius of intersections (r_c), critical radius of branching points ($(r_c)_B$) and critical radius of terminal tips ($(r_c)_T$) of the alpha RGCs in domestic (A) and wild (B) species. Abbreviated species names are (left to right) Chinchilla, Guinea Pig, Cat, Dog, Ox and Pig (A), and Rat, Ferret, Guanaco, Niglau Antilope and Reindeer (B).

When the means N_m, r_c, $(r_c)_B$ and $(r_c)_T$ of five species of wild animals were analyzed, the mean N_m of the ferret was statistically different to the mean of all other species (Figure 7B). Besides these pairs, a significant difference was found between three more pairs: rat-niglau antilope, guanaco-reindeer and niglau antilope-reindeer. As for the mean r_c, the rat, guanaco and reindeer differed significantly from all other species (Fig. 8B). Additional significant differences in mean r_c was found between the guanaco and niglau antilope. The mean $(r_c)_B$ of the guanaco was significantly different from all other species, while the mean $(r_c)_B$ of the rat differed significantly from the ferret and reindeer. Finally, the means $(r_c)_T$ differed significantly between all possible pairs of species.

Conclusion and Discussion

Quantitative Analysis of Dendritic Arborisation

Even though the original Sholl method [3] or its several modifications, such as the 2D Sholl method [16], linear, semi-log and log-log Sholl technique [22] is commonly used for quantifying some specific branching properties of the dendritic tree, other analysis has suitably quantified dendritic arborisation. In these, dendritic branching and/or terminations were included in the analysis, along with other measures. A detailed analysis of dendritic tree structure has been published, where several parameters for the quantification of neuronal shapes have been reviewed [13]. The variation in the number of dendritic intersections has been shown to be due only to branching events and terminations [17], but that study did not analyze these events as a possible tool in neuronal description. Retinal ganglion cells of cat have been analyzed using a number of shape features, among them the number of dendritic terminations [14]. That study showed that this feature can successfully quantify some aspects of dendritic complexity. Several studies have proposed a 'dendogram' as a suitable method for illustration of dendritic branching pattern and the arrangement of branchings and terminations in the dendritic field [6, 10, 23].

In this study, we present a mathematical model, which incorporates a supposition that the number of dendritic intersections with a circle of a given radius can be resolved into two components: the number of branching points and the number of terminal tips within the circle. Strictly speaking, the number of intersections can be obtained if the number of terminal tips within the circle is subtracted from the sum of the number of primary dendrites and branching points within the circle. Such approach give rise to four morphometric parameters: the critical (r_c) and maximal (N_m) values of the number of intersections, and the critical values of branching points ($(r_c)_B$) and terminal tips ($(r_c)_T$), with respect to the radius. We have shown previously that these parameters can be considered as an additional tool for morphological classification schemes of vertebrate RGCs [2]. Now we are showing its utility to offer some additional knowledge for better understanding the neuro-architectonics of dendritic patterns.

The mathematical model has been formulated on the basis of a graphical model of a hypothetical neuron, shown in Figure 2, which satisfies three assumptions (1), (2) and (3). One can easily see that the first assumption of a dendrite as a straight line segment could not be completely fulfilled when images of real neurons are analyzed, since in these cases the left side of (3) is not equal to its right side (for instance, see rat cell in Figure 1). Does this mean that our model cannot be applied on images of real neurons? To explain this, we have to bear in mind that neuronal structure is among the most complex of all cellular morphologies [7]. Dendritic trees of neurons usually exhibit enormously diverse forms: sometimes dendrites are twisted and wavy, or even extend back towards the soma cutting the same circle several times. Thus, the count of dendritic intersections with concentric circles cannot be equal to that predicted by the right side of (3) (usually, it will be larger). However a previous study has applied this model to images of several RGC types [2] and has shown that the left side of (3) was statistically equal to its right side in all cases. So for the first assumption, our model stands even for real neurons.

The second assumption of dichotomous branching has been adopted from numerous observations of neuronal branching structure. The dichotomous branching of neurons (including RGCs) is a natural starting point for the development of a classification model based on dendritic branching complexity [24, 25]. The branch points from which more than two dendritic segments arise can occur in neuronal branching patterns, but with a very low frequency [26, 27]. Therefore this assumption is reasonable.

The third assumption, of terminations occurring at larger radius than the corresponding branch point, describes reality even better than the previous two. There is much convincing evidence for this assumption. For instance, [14] showed that the density of the dendritic tips is most pronounced at greater distances from the cell body, whereas [28] showed that the terminal segments in nearly all types of neurons measured have a manifold larger length than the branching (intermediate) segments. Therefore the three assumptions made are reasonable and unlikely to detract from an accurate analysis of these structures.

The Alpha Retinal Ganglion Cell (RGC)

Since the earliest histological studies of vertebrate retinae, it has been recognized that RGCs come in different shapes and sizes [21]. After Cajal's analytical paper, many others were to follow describing the morphological diversity of ganglion cells in various species

[29]. A specific morphological type of ganglion cell, the alpha cell, was first defined in the cat retina by [20]. It commonly has the largest somata of all ganglion cells, large caliber axons and large, circular-to-oval dendritic fields with radial, relatively densely branched dendrites that rarely overlap [18]. It has between three and six thick primary dendrites, which regularly and successively branch towards the periphery of the dendritic field. The dendritic tree is monostratified in both the inner and outer lamina of the inner plexiform layer. The pattern of branching of the dendrites is characteristic and the dendritic field size increases monotonically from smaller in the central area to larger in the periphery. Between the branch points, dendrites are rather straight and neighboring branches seldom overlap [20]. Up to now, these cells are among the most extensively studied of the ganglion cells.

As for their functional significance, the alpha cells have been identified as the same type as the brisk-transient Y cells described in physiology [30, 31, 32] with large, concentrically organized receptive fields, a nonlinear phasic ON- or OFF-center response to stationary flicker light stimuli, and good responsiveness to moving stimuli [33]. They are not color-coded and their axons have a high conduction velocity [31]. The receptive-field centers of individual alpha cells match the position, shape, and size of their dendritic fields, allowing for the additional spread of the bipolar and amacrine cells that form their input [34]. The dendritic stratification level in the inner plexiform layer (IPL) defines the cell's center response as being ON (inner sublamina) or OFF (outer sublamina) [31].

The Alpha Cells in Mammals

After the alpha RGCs were first defined in the cat retina, this cell type has been found in a wide range of mammalian retinae, including several orders of placental and marsupial mammals [31, 18, 21, 35]. Moreover, from the qualitative and quantitative descriptions of the alpha cells, given in these studies, it is evident that this cell type may well be a basic feature of all placental mammalian retinae. Previous investigations have drawn the conclusion that the morphology of the alpha cells and many features of both single cells and of the cell population, are conserved across species with different habitats and life-styles. This suggests that the alpha cells are a consistent obligatory ganglion cell type in every mammalian retina and probably subserve some fundamental tasks in visual performance [21].

From the qualitative investigations of the alpha RGCs throughout various species, the alpha cell mosaics, the coverage of the retina by alpha cells, the shape of both soma and dendritic field, the density of branched dendrites, the cell stratification and axonal projections were described in detail [31, 21]. In later quantitative studies both soma and dendritic field diameter, the inner to outer ratio, both central and peripheral alpha cell density and the alpha cell coverage factor have been reported. On the other hand, we have not being able to find any quantitative study which analyzes the dendritic branching of the alpha RGCs throughout various mammalian species.

This study investigated the dendritic branching pattern of the alpha RGCs across eleven species belonging to the three orders of mammals. Applying our model on two dimensional images of these cells, we evaluated four properties of the alpha RGCs morphology: the maximal density of the dendritic tree, distance (from the soma) of that density, distance of the maximal dendritic branching and distance of the maximal dendritic terminations. Moreover, in each species, the cell morphology was evaluated from six to eighteen characteristic images of the alpha RGCs, with the same stratification and similar distance from the optic disk (i.e. the eccentricity). With such selection, we have avoided any possible errors in our analysis, caused by the differences in the dendritic branching complexity and the dendritic field size as is the case when the alpha cells with diverse stratification and various eccentricities are compared.

When the alpha RGC morphology between species within the same order was analyzed, results have shown that these cells have different dendritic branching patterns: each species differed significantly to others in at least one of four properties (Table 2). As for the difference in the alpha RGC morphology between mammalian orders, we have avoided such analysis since we have not enough data (i.e. species) in each of the three mammalian orders. On the other hand, starting from the hypothesis that different lifestyle and habitats might be correlated with different densities and distributions of retinal ganglion cells as well as with the size and optics of the eye [36], we divided the species into two groups: the wild and the domestic animals, and investigated whether there are common or different morphological properties among the species belonging to the same group or to one or the other group. Our analysis has shown that these cells have different dendritic branching, either among species within the same group or among domestic and wild group (Table 2 and Figures 7 and 8). Finally, our results support previous hypothesis regarding to the alpha RGC morphology in various species [37] – the difference in the dendritic branching pattern of these cells could be caused by possibly slightly different visual information processing in terms of electrotonic properties of the neurons that reflect the ecological diversity/similarity or degree of evolutionary divergence.

ACKNOWLEDGMENT

We wish to thank Leo Peichl for providing the slides of the retinae and Colin Payne for technical assistance.

REFERENCES

[1] Fernández E and Jelinek HF, Use of fractal theory in neuroscience: methods, advantages, and potential problems. *Methods* 24: 309–321, (2001).

[2] Ristanović D, Milošević NT and Štulić V, Application of modified Sholl analysis to neuronal dendritic arborisation of the cat spinal cord. *J Neurosci Meth* 158: 212-218, 2006.

[3] Sholl DA, Dendritic organization of the neurons in the visual and motor cortices of the cat. *J Anat* 87: 387-406, 1953.

[4] Scheibel ME and Scheibel AB, Terminal axonal patterns in cat spinal cord. II. The dorsal horn. *Brain Res* 9: 32-58, 1968.

[5] Schoenen J, The dendritic organization of the human spinal cord: the dorsal horn. *Neuroscience* 7: 2057-2087, 1982.

[6] Lowndes M, Stanford D and Stewart MG, A system for the reconstruction and analysis of dendritic field. *J Neurosci Meth* 31: 235-245, 1990.

[7] Neale EA, Bowers LM and Smith-Jr TG, Early dendrite development in spinal cord cell cultures: a quantyitative study. *J Neurosci Res* 34: 54-66, 1993.

[8] Caserta F, Eldred WD, Fernández E, Hausman RE, Stanford LR, Bulderev SV, Schwarzer S and Stanley HE, Determination of fractal dimension of physiologically characterized neurons in two and three dimensions. *J Neurosci Meth* 56: 133-144, (1995).

[9] Elston GN, Tweedale R and Rosa MG, Cellular heterogeneity in cerebral cortex: a study of the morphology of pyramidal neurones in visual areas of the marmoset monkey. *J Comp Neurol* 415: 33-51, (1999).

[10] Duan H, Wearne SL, Rocher AB, Macedo A, Morrison JH and Hof PR, Age-related dendritic and spine changes in corticocortically projecting neurons in macaque monkeys. *Cereb Cortex* 13: 950-996, (2003).

[11] ten Hoopen M and Reuver HA, Growth patterns of neuronal dendrites - an attempted probabilistic description. *Kybernetik* 8: 234-239, 1971.

[12] Uylings HBM, Pelt J, Verwer RVH and McConnell P, Statistical analysis of neuronal population; In Copowasky JJ (ed) Computer techniques in neuroanatomy, New York, Plenum, pp. 241-264, 1989.

[13] Uylings HBM and van Pelt J, Measures for quantifying dendritic arborisation. *Network Comput Neural Syst* 13: 397-414, 2002.

[14] Jelinek HF, Cesar-Jr RM, Leandro JJG and Spence I, Automated morphometric analysis of the cat retinal alpha/Y, beta/X and delta ganglion cells using wavelet statistical moment and clustering algorithms. *J Integr Neurosci* 3: 415-432, 2004.

[15] Jelinek HF, Elston GN and Zietsch B, Fractal analysis: pitfalls and revelations in neuroscience; In Losa GA, Merlini D, Nonnenmacher F, Weibel ER (eds): *Fractals in Biology and Medicine IV,* Basel-Boston-Berlin: Birkhäuser, pp. 85-94, 2005.

[16] Eayrs JT, The cerebral cortex of normal and hypothyroid rats. *Acta Anat Basel* 25: 160-185, (1955).

[17] Gutierrez H and Davies AM, A fast and accurate procedure for deriving the Sholl profile in quantitative studies of neuronal morphology. *J Neurosci Meth* 163: 24-30, 2007.

[18] Peichl L and Ott H Boycott BB, Alpha ganglion cells in mammalian retinae. *Proc Royal Soc* B 231: 169-197, 1987.

[19] Peichl L, Alpha and delta ganglion cells in the rat retina. *J Comp Neurol* 286: 120-139, 1989.

[20] Boycott BB and Wässle H, The morphological types of ganglion cells of the domestic cat's retina. *J Physiol Lond* 240: 397-419, (1974).

[21] Peichl L, Alpha ganglion cells in mammalian retinae: common properties, species differences, and some comments on other ganglion cells. *Vis Neurosci* 7: 155-169, 1991.

[22] Milošević NT and Ristanović D, The Sholl analysis of neuronal cell images: Semi-log or log-log method? *J Theor Biol* 245: 130-140, 2007.

[23] Jarvinen MK and Powley TL, Dorsal motor nucleus of the vagus neurons: a multivariate taxonomy. *J Comp Neurol* 403: 359-377, 1999.

[24] Bassingthwaighte JB Liebovitch LS and West B.J, *Fractal physiology* New York-Oxford: Oxford University Press, (1994).

[25] Mandelbrot BB, *The fractal geometry of nature,* 20th ed. New York: WN Freemen and Co, 2004.

[26] Verwer RWH and van Pelt J, Analysis of binary trees when occasional multifurcations can be considered as aggregates of bifurcations. *Bull Math Biol* 52: 629-641, 1990.

[27] van Pelt J, Effect of pruning on dendritic tree topology. *J Theor Biol* 186: 17-31, 1997.

[28] Uylings HBM, Ruiz-Marcos A and van Pelt J, The metric analysis of three-dimensional dendritic tree patterns: a methodological review. *J Neurosci Meth* 18: 127-151, 1986.

[29] Ramon y Cajal S, *Histologie du Systeme Nerveux de l'Homme et des Vertebres.* Paris: Maloine, 1911.

[30] Cleland BG, Levick WR Wässle H, Physiological identification of a morphological class of cat retinal ganglion cells. *J Physiol* 248: 151-171, (1975).

[31] Peichl L Wässle H, Morphological identification of ON and OFF-center brisk-transient (Y) cells in the cat retina. *Proc Royal Soc B* 212: 139-156, 1981.

[32] Fukuda Y, Hsiao CF and Watanabe M Ito H, Morphological correlates of physiologically identified Y, X, and W cells in cat retina. *J Neurophysiol* 52: 999-1013, (1984).

[33] Stone J and Fukuda Y, Properties of cat retinal ganglion cells: a comparison of W cells with X and Y cells. *J Neurophysiol* 37: 722-748, 1974.

[34] Peichl L Wässle H, The structural correlate of the receptive- field center of alpha ganglion cells in the cat retina. *J Physiol* 341: 309-324, 1983.

[35] Peichl L, Morphological types of ganglion cells in the dog and wolf retina. *J Comp Neurol* 324: 590-602, 1992.

[36] Hughes A, The topography of vision in mammals of contrasting life-style: comparative optics and retinal organization; In Crescitelli R. (ed): Handbook of Sensory Physiology; vol. VII/S. *The Visual System of Vertebrates,* Berlin: Springer Verlag, pp. 697-756, 1977.

[37] van Pelt J Schierwagen A, Electrotonic properties of passive dendritic trees- effect of dendritic topology, In van Pelt J, Corner MA, Uylings HBM, Lopes da Silva FH, (eds): *Progress in brain research,* 102, BV, Elsevier Science, pp. 127-149, 1994.

In: Image Processing
Editor: Vítor Hugo Carvalho

ISBN 978-1-62081-844-2

Chapter 8

COLOR MODELS AND ILLUMINATION CHANGES

Duarte Duque*
Polytechnic Institute of Cávado and Ave, Portugal

ABSTRACT

Color model representation allows characterizing in a quantitative manner, any defined color spectrum of visible light, i.e. with a wavelength between 400nm and 700nm. To accomplish that, each model, or color space, is associated with a function that allows mapping the spectral power distribution of the visible electromagnetic radiation, in a space defined by a set of discrete values that quantify the color components composing the model. Some color spaces are sensitive to changes in lighting conditions. Others assure the preservation of certain chromatic features, remaining immune to these changes. Therefore, it becomes necessary to identify the strengths and weaknesses of each model in order to justify the adoption of color spaces in image processing and analysis techniques.

This chapter will address the topic of digital imaging, main standards and formats. Next we will set the mathematical model of the image acquisition sensor response, which enables assessment of the various color spaces, with the aim of determining their invariance to illumination changes.

INTRODUCTION

In the digital processing of the image, whether it is the analysis of a single frame or a video sequence made up of a large number of frames, the processing target is the image and data contained therein. The information on the intensity and color of each pixel of the image is encoded by a given color model. A model or color space provides a formal method of representation of the colors. By adopting a three-dimensional coordinate system, that represents values of three orthogonal components of a color space, you can represent any color of the visible spectrum (with wavelengths between 400nm and 700nm), also allowing the use of analytical techniques on this color space.

* E-mail address: dduque@ipca.pt.

In order to carry out, in a coherent way, a comparative analysis of models or color spaces, it is necessary to define a rating system for the description of images, as well as its structure. Thus, within the scope of this chapter, I is defined as the digital image obtained in a given time. A digital image is a representation, in two dimensions, on a finite set of elements that take discrete values, arranged in a matrix of M by N elements. These elements, which store the value of the luminous intensity of the image in that coordinate, are known as pixels. On this basis, the intensity of a pixel in the x and y coordinates of the I image is defined by I(x,y), where $0 \leq x \leq M$, $0 \leq y \leq N$ and I(x,y) takes values of a default range.

In the case of a color image, each pixel is defined by the set of several color components. Thus, for example, an image represented in a fictional ABC color space is defined by I={IA(x,y), IB(x,y), IC(x,y)}, where IA(x,y), IB(x,y) and IC(x,y) respectively represent the value of A, B and C components intensity, for the pixel defined by the coordinates (x,y), of the digital image acquired in a given point-in-time.

A simple model of color representation, based on the way the human eye acquires it [1], is the RGB color space. In this color model, defined by the RGB cube, the origin represents black (IR(x,y)=0, IG(x,y)=0, IB(x,y)=0), while the opposite corner describes the white (IR(x,y)=255, IG(x,y)=255, IB(x,y)=255). The diagonal axis running through the origin to the white is an achromatic area, which defines a gray scale. The magnitudes of the three components on that diagonal take the same value, i.e., IR(x,y)=IG (x,y)=IB(x,y). Besides the inherent geometric simplicity, the RGB color space has the added benefit of requiring little processing to obtain it. This is because many sensors of video cameras acquire and display the image in this color model. Despite the intrinsic benefits, the RGB color space demonstrates some limitations. In particular, the model does not display a uniform behavior in terms of color perception, since a change in unit value in the RGB cube is not reflected equally in all three components of the model.

The weaknesses of this model achieve greater relevance, when applied, for instance, in object segmentation techniques, where there is a need to compare the similarity of colors between points of an image and a reference object. In real environments, often occurs the variation of illumination conditions. It appears that the change of light intensity incident upon the surface of an object causes a translation in RGB space, of the coordinates that define the color, which manifests itself in a diverse manner in the three components of the model. It is common not to get a correspondence between points of a same surface when changing lighting conditions. According to von Kries [3], the trichromatic responses measured on a surface under different lighting conditions are spaced from simple scaling factors. Therefore, the RGB color space, whereas (IR(x,y), IG(x,y), IB(x,y)) and (I’R(x,y), I’G(x,y), I’B(x,y)) represent the color responses to the point of a surface under two lighting conditions then, according to von Kries rule, we have:

$$\begin{bmatrix} I_R(x,y) \\ I_G(x,y) \\ I_B(x,y) \end{bmatrix} = \begin{bmatrix} \alpha & 0 & 0 \\ 0 & \beta & 0 \\ 0 & 0 & \gamma \end{bmatrix} \cdot \begin{bmatrix} I'_R(x,y) \\ I'_G(x,y) \\ I'_B(x,y) \end{bmatrix} \tag{1}$$

This definition is particularly useful in cases where light variation is not proportional in the three primary components. Such situations would be due to, for example, the application of an optical filter that would cause an increase or decrease of a certain color component. However, in outdoor environments such events do not occur often, considering that a source of light radiates proportionally the three color components. Thus, von Kries rule can be simplified by applying a scale factor (φ), common to all components on the variation of light intensity, where:

$$\begin{bmatrix} I_R(\mathrm{x},\mathrm{y}) \\ I_G(\mathrm{x},\mathrm{y}) \\ I_B(\mathrm{x},\mathrm{y}) \end{bmatrix} = \varphi \cdot \begin{bmatrix} I'_R(\mathrm{x},\mathrm{y}) \\ I'_G(\mathrm{x},\mathrm{y}) \\ I'_B(\mathrm{x},\mathrm{y}) \end{bmatrix} \tag{2}$$

Consequently, based on the rule of von Kries, an invariant model of color representation should allow the storage of information regardless of the color of the lighting level applied to a surface, i.e. should eliminate the scale component related to the lighting changing conditions (φ). This process is called cancelation of the factor φ. Von Kries proposal is however simplistic. In an image acquired by a video camera, the color set at each point is a function of several factors, namely: sensor characteristics, incident lighting composition on the object and reflective properties of the surface. Thus, there is the need for the definition of a more comprehensive model that covers all the conditions that influencing color perception.

Dichromatic Reflection Model

The dichromatic reflection model was introduced in 1985 [2] as a way to characterize the reflected light on non-homogeneous objects, such as polymers, fabrics or rocks, which exhibit two distinct types of reflections: diffuse and specular. The specular reflection consists in the radiation component incident on the object surface that is reflected at a given angle. According to the law of reflection, the reflection angle has a value equal to the angle that the incident ray makes with the normal one to the point of the object surface where the radiation falls. This type of reflection varies with the refractive coefficient of the object material, since some radiation may be absorbed by the object. On the other hand, the diffuse reflection is a function of the object radiation absorption, by setting the component of radiation that penetrates the sample, suffering dispersion before it returns to the surface and being subsequently reflected in several directions.

The spectral power distribution (SPD) of the specular reflection is identical to the light that illuminates the object. In diffuse reflection it represents the color that characterizes it. In perfect reflective surfaces we only verify the existence of specular reflection, while an ideal diffuse surface, also known as Lambert surface, behaves as a perfect light diffuser. However, in nature, the materials exhibit the two reflective components, comprising a greater or lesser diffusion degree or specular reflection. In practice, the specular reflection is not perfect and the reflected light can be seen by the observer in regions close to the direction of the reflected light beam. This phenomenon causes the formation of brightness on the object surface which intensity varies with the observer position. Considering the two types of reflection, the dichromatic reflection model describes the light reflected on a non-homogeneous object as a linear combination of the components of specular and diffuse reflection. Therefore, the sensor response to the radiation emitted at a point on a non-homogeneous object, which image is acquired via digital video camera, and over which a uniform illumination can be described by Lukac and Plataniotis [4]:

$$I(x,y) = w_d(n,s)\cdot\int_{\Omega} c_d(\lambda)\cdot e(\lambda)\cdot q(\lambda)\cdot d\lambda + w_s(n,s,v)\cdot\int_{\Omega} c_s(\lambda)\cdot e(\lambda)\cdot q(\lambda)\cdot d\lambda \tag{3}$$

where I(x,y)={IR(x,y), IG(x,y), IB(x,y)} vector defines the color of a point in the image, in RGB format, based on the coordinates (x,y) for the visible light spectrum (Ω=[400nm,700nm]). The SPD of the light falling on the object is expressed by e(λ), being independent of spatial location since it is assumed the existence of a uniform illumination. The variables wd(n,s) and ws(n,s,v) are important factors for the diffuse and spectral reflections. Both factors are a function of the normal to the surface of the object (n), and the illumination direction (s). The valuable factor of the reflection spectrum also depends on the direction of the observer (v).

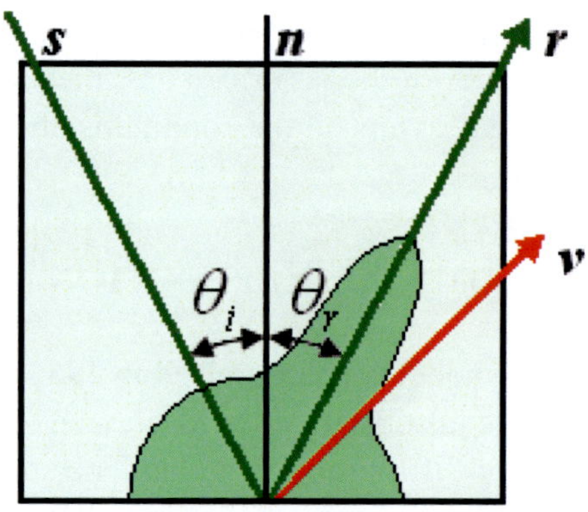

Figure 1. Radiation on a surface.

In Figure 1, the angle of incidence of radiation on a surface is defined by θi, while θr specifies the angle of reflection, being θi=θr. The variation of the intensity of radiation emitted for each angle of the incidence plane of incidence is defined by a semicircular part, which concerns the diffuse reflection, and a specular component that forms a peak in the region close to the specular reflection vector (r).

The diffuse reflection coefficient is represented by cd(λ), while the specular reflection coefficient is defined by cs(λ). The sensor's sensitivity to red, green and blue color components are defined by the vector q(λ)=(qR(λ), qG(λ), qB(λ)). Neglecting the gain and noise in the sensor image acquisition, assuming that the light reflected on the surface of the object is roughly the same SPD of the light source, and this source radiating the same energy density at all wavelengths of the spectrum visible light (white light), then we have: e(λ)=E and cs(λ)=Cs, i.e. are constant in the visible light spectrum, and that:

$$\int_{\Omega} q_R(\lambda) = \int_{\Omega} q_G(\lambda) = \int_{\Omega} q_B(\lambda) = q \tag{4}$$

By adopting these conditions, the equation that defines the value measured by the image acquisition sensor can be rewritten in the following way:

$$I(x,y) = w_d(n,s) \cdot E \cdot \int_{\Omega} c_d(\lambda) \cdot q(\lambda) \cdot d\lambda + w_s(n,s,v) \cdot C_s \cdot E \cdot q \tag{5}$$

This dichromatic reflection model is a useful tool to describe the reflected light on a point of an object surface as a result of merging two different reflections. Through this model it is possible to analyze the color spaces with respect to the invariant features to various conditions, e.g. the angle of view direction and geometry of the object, the variation of the illumination intensity and presence of brightness.

INVARIANT COLOR SPACES

In digital image processing there is often a need for invariant features to enable, for instance, identifying a particular image of an object from an image type, or finding regions of divergent points of the pattern specified by a reference image (motion detection). Such processes require, among other operations, the computation of a similarity measure, point to point, in the color space set.

Due to the inability to control the environment observed, it is frequent experimenting different lighting conditions and viewing angle variations. Such variability produce dramatic changes, if it is used a color space sensitive to changes in the RGB model, even if the target objects remain still and preserve their morphology. For example, consider the following scenario, in which we intend to detect motion in a sequence of images acquired in an outdoor environment, using the RGB color space. For this purpose, the procedure is initially to acquire a reference image, which should only contain objects related to the background.

After obtaining this reference image, the process continues with video sequence processing. Thus, for each image sequence is calculated, for each point, a measure of similarity with the corresponding point of the reference image. If, during the acquisition of the sequence, it is detected a lighting conditions fluctuation, for example through the obstruction of sunlight by the passage of a cloud, it would probably detect regions of considerable movement, even if all the objects remain motionless. In response to these limitations, it is necessary to use color models, invariant to illumination conditions (shadows and brightness), which also have invariance characteristics with respect to viewing angle and geometry of the objects. Thus, an invariant color model must be able to reduce to minimum possible irrelevant information, while it retains as much amount of discriminatory features as possible.

Invariability to Illumination Intensity

It is possible to analytically assess the invariability of a color space in relation to the illumination intensity (in which shadows are included), by applying the dichromatic reflection model. To this end, we consider the sensor response to light reflected at a point of a Lambert surface illuminated by a white light source (light source that radiates the same energy density at all wavelengths of visible light spectrum). According to (5), and taking into account the conditions above, the reflection of non-homogeneous materials on white light is described in [4]:

$$\begin{bmatrix} I_R(\mathrm{x},\mathrm{y}) \\ I_G(\mathrm{x},\mathrm{y}) \\ I_B(\mathrm{x},\mathrm{y}) \end{bmatrix} = w_d(\mathrm{n},\mathrm{s}) \cdot E \cdot \int_{\Omega} c_d(\lambda) \cdot \begin{bmatrix} q_R(\lambda) \\ q_G(\lambda) \\ q_B(\lambda) \end{bmatrix} \cdot d\lambda \tag{6}$$

In order to obtain a more compact formulation, it is considered that:

$$\begin{bmatrix} K_R \\ K_G \\ K_B \end{bmatrix} = \int_{\Omega} c_d(\lambda) \cdot \begin{bmatrix} q_R(\lambda) \\ q_G(\lambda) \\ q_B(\lambda) \end{bmatrix} \cdot d\lambda \tag{7}$$

Thus, the equation (6) can be rewritten by:

$$\begin{bmatrix} I_R(\mathrm{x},\mathrm{y}) \\ I_G(\mathrm{x},\mathrm{y}) \\ I_B(\mathrm{x},\mathrm{y}) \end{bmatrix} = w_d(\mathrm{n},\mathrm{s}) \cdot E \cdot \begin{bmatrix} K_R \\ K_G \\ K_B \end{bmatrix} \tag{8}$$

The sensor response is then conditioned by the geometric factor of the diffuse reflection, by the SPD of the incident light on the object and by the sensor sensitivity to the light spectrum that characterizes this object (KR,G,B). A color space invariant to light intensity changes should only be a function of the elements KR, KG e KB, canceling the remaining factors.

Invariability to Brightness

The sensor response to the light reflected on a point of an object, on which focuses a white light, and whose surface has a strong specular component, is fully defined by the equation (5). To obtain a more compact formulation, it is considered that:

$$S = w_s(\mathrm{n},\mathrm{s},\mathrm{v}) \cdot C_s \cdot q \tag{9}$$

Through the application of the expressions defined in (7) and (9), (5) can be rewritten by:

$$\begin{bmatrix} I_R(\mathrm{x},\mathrm{y}) \\ I_G(\mathrm{x},\mathrm{y}) \\ I_B(\mathrm{x},\mathrm{y}) \end{bmatrix} = E \cdot \left(w_d(\mathrm{n},\mathrm{s}) \cdot \begin{bmatrix} K_R \\ K_G \\ K_B \end{bmatrix} + S \right) \tag{10}$$

Thus, we can see that the sensor response is the function of the SPD light product that falls on the object, by the sum of the specular component (expressed by S) with the geometric factor of the diffuse reflection enhanced by the sensitivity of the sensor to the specific light spectrum of the object. In a similar way to the one presented in the definition of invariability to illumination intensity, so that the brightness invariance occur, it is necessary that the color space do the cancellation of all factors except the sensitivity of the sensor to the light spectrum, which is proper of the matter the object is made of.

One must however reiterate that the color models in which we verify this type of invariability to brightness may however be sensitive to brightness generated by the lighting conditions in which the object is hit with radiation composed only by the visible light spectrum, i.e., colored lighting. The study of the illumination color invariability, although feasible, is not considered in this chapter, although in certain scenarios (e.g. nightclubs and concert halls) such lighting conditions are verified regularly.

rgb Color Space

The rgb color space, also known as standard rgb, results of a normalization process of the rgb color space. This process consists of the quantification of the importance of each color component, in relation to the sum of the three primary components (red, green and blue). Thus, the occurrence of a change in brightness, which will equally affect all three components of RGB color space, will not affect the rgb space. By applying the transformations specified by (11), we can then get a rgb color space, from the RGB space.

$$\begin{bmatrix} I_r(\mathrm{x},\mathrm{y}) \\ I_g(\mathrm{x},\mathrm{y}) \\ I_b(\mathrm{x},\mathrm{y}) \end{bmatrix} = \frac{255}{I_R(\mathrm{x},\mathrm{y}) + I_G(\mathrm{x},\mathrm{y}) + I_B(\mathrm{x},\mathrm{y})} \cdot \begin{bmatrix} I_R(\mathrm{x},\mathrm{y}) \\ I_G(\mathrm{x},\mathrm{y}) \\ I_B(\mathrm{x},\mathrm{y}) \end{bmatrix} \tag{11}$$

Each component of the new color space takes values between predefined ranges (e.g., [0, 255] in 8 bits resolution images). A null value in one of the components of the rgb space indicates that this component does not contribute to the color, while the maximum value (255 = 8 bits) indicates the single component as in the definition of color.

An example of the color image splitting, in the three components that make up the rgb space, is shown in Figure 2. In this example, the images that show the contribution of each color component (Ir, Ig e Ib) are presented in a gray scale in which white indicates the maximum value and black the minimum value allowed by the scale.

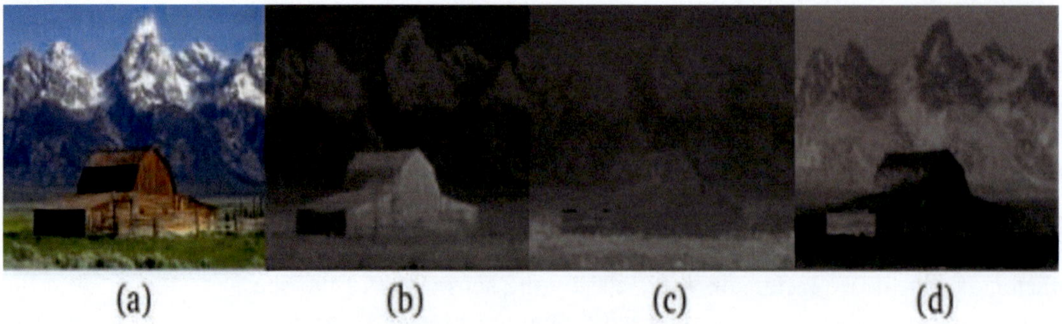

Figure 2. (a) Original image; (b) r component; (c) g component and (c) b component.

By applying the dichromatic reflection model it is possible to analytically assess the invariability of a color space concerning the light intensity and brightness. The invariability properties of the rgb color space to changes in brightness are shown here, assuming a Lambert surface enlightened by a white light source (light source that radiates the same energy density at all wavelengths of visible light spectrum). The study of the sensitivity to the intensity of illumination is accomplished by replacing the RGB color components in (11), by the equivalent values defined by (8). Thus, we have that:

$$\begin{bmatrix} I_r(\mathrm{x},\mathrm{y}) \\ I_g(\mathrm{x},\mathrm{y}) \\ I_b(\mathrm{x},\mathrm{y}) \end{bmatrix} = \frac{255}{K_R + K_G + K_B} \cdot \begin{bmatrix} K_R \\ K_G \\ K_B \end{bmatrix} \tag{12}$$

According to the results obtained in (12), it appears therefore that the rgb color space is not sensitive to the direction and intensity of illumination, depending only on the sensitivity of the sensor to the light spectrum that characterizes the object. The response of the color space to brightness is obtained by the sensor response to a surface with a strong specular component and on which it hits a white light. Thus, replacing the RGB components of the (11), by the equivalent expressions defined in (10), we conclude that the rgb color space is influenced by the specular reflection coefficient, being sensitive to the presence of brightness on the surface of an object, as shown in (13):

$$\begin{bmatrix} I_r(\mathrm{x},\mathrm{y}) \\ I_g(\mathrm{x},\mathrm{y}) \\ I_b(\mathrm{x},\mathrm{y}) \end{bmatrix} = \frac{255}{(K_R + K_G + K_B) + 3 \cdot \frac{S}{w_d(\mathrm{n},\mathrm{s})}} \cdot \begin{bmatrix} K_R + \frac{S}{w_d(\mathrm{n},\mathrm{s})} \\ K_G + \frac{S}{w_d(\mathrm{n},\mathrm{s})} \\ K_B + \frac{S}{w_d(\mathrm{n},\mathrm{s})} \end{bmatrix} \tag{13}$$

$c_1c_2c_3$ Color Space

Another way of representing color, to which invariable properties are given to certain lighting conditions, the space is c1c2c3 [5]. This color model is obtained by a transformation of RGB space, determined by the following operations:

$$
\begin{aligned}
c_1(\mathrm{x},\mathrm{y}) &= \arctan\left(\frac{I_R(\mathrm{x},\mathrm{y})}{\max(I_G(\mathrm{x},\mathrm{y}),I_B(\mathrm{x},\mathrm{y}))}\right)\cdot\frac{255}{90}\\
c_2(\mathrm{x},\mathrm{y}) &= \arctan\left(\frac{I_G(\mathrm{x},\mathrm{y})}{\max(I_R(\mathrm{x},\mathrm{y}),I_B(\mathrm{x},\mathrm{y}))}\right)\cdot\frac{255}{90}\\
c_3(\mathrm{x},\mathrm{y}) &= \arctan\left(\frac{I_B(\mathrm{x},\mathrm{y})}{\max(I_R(\mathrm{x},\mathrm{y}),I_G(\mathrm{x},\mathrm{y}))}\right)\cdot\frac{255}{90}
\end{aligned}
\tag{14}
$$

In which c1, c2 and c3 take values contained in the interval [0, 255] to represent a discrete numerical value of 8 bits, the interval [0°, 90°[. In the Figure 3 it is shown the decomposition of a color image on 24-bit RGB format, on three components of the color space invariable c1c2c3. The images of the components of this color space are presented in a gray scale.

The analysis of the sensitivity of the color space c1c2c3 to variations in light intensity is performed by replacing, in the operations defined in (14), the color components IR, IG, and IB of the RGB space, by their counterparts defined in (8). The results of this analysis are presented in (15).

$$
\begin{aligned}
c_1(\mathrm{x},\mathrm{y}) &= \arctan\left(\frac{K_R}{\max(K_G,K_B)}\right)\cdot\frac{255}{90}\\
c_2(\mathrm{x},\mathrm{y}) &= \arctan\left(\frac{K_G}{\max(K_R,K_B)}\right)\cdot\frac{255}{90}\\
c_3(\mathrm{x},\mathrm{y}) &= \arctan\left(\frac{K_B}{\max(K_R,K_G)}\right)\cdot\frac{255}{90}
\end{aligned}
\tag{15}
$$

As shown, the components c1, c2 and c3 are solely due to the sensor sensitivity, i.e., KR, KG e KB. The remaining factors were canceled. Therefore, the condition of invariability of this color space to the light intensity is validated. Similarly to the analysis in the rgb color space, the response of the space c1c2c3 to brightness is obtained by studying the sensor behavior to the radiation received from a surface, with a strong specular component, illuminated by a white light source. On this basis, the RGB color components of equations (14) are replaced by the equivalent expressions presented in (10).

$$c_1(x,y) = \arctan\left(\frac{K_R + \frac{S}{w_d(n,s)}}{\max(K_G, K_B) + \frac{S}{w_d(n,s)}}\right) \cdot \frac{255}{90}$$

$$c_2(x,y) = \arctan\left(\frac{K_G + \frac{S}{w_d(n,s)}}{\max(K_R, K_B) + \frac{S}{w_d(n,s)}}\right) \cdot \frac{255}{90} \qquad (16)$$

$$c_3(x,y) = \arctan\left(\frac{K_B + \frac{S}{w_d(n,s)}}{\max(K_R, K_G) + \frac{S}{w_d(n,s)}}\right) \cdot \frac{255}{90}$$

By the analysis of the expressions developed in (16), it is observed that the color space c1c2c3 not only depends on the sensitivity of the sensor to the light spectrum, characteristic of the subject matter of which is composed, but also of the specular component of the incident light. It is concluded that the space c1c2c3 is not invariable to brightness generated by white light sources.

(a) (b) (c) (d)

Figure 3. (a) Original image; (b) c_1 component; (c) c_2 component and (c) c_3 component.

$l_1l_2l_3$ Color Space

The color space was developed by Gevers and Smeulders [5] l1l2l3 in order to determine the direction of the triangular color plane in RGB space. Its acquisition, from the RGB color space is specified in (17).

$$\begin{bmatrix} l_1(x,y) \\ l_2(x,y) \\ l_3(x,y) \end{bmatrix} = \frac{255}{(I_R(x,y)-I_G(x,y))^2 + (I_R(x,y)-I_B(x,y))^2 + (I_G(x,y)-I_B(x,y))^2} \cdot \begin{bmatrix} (I_R(x,y)-I_G(x,y))^2 \\ (I_R(x,y)-I_B(x,y))^2 \\ (I_G(x,y)-I_B(x,y))^2 \end{bmatrix} \qquad (17)$$

The components of the color space l1l2l3, take values between [0, 255]. The decomposition of a color image, in the three components that define the color space l1l2l3 is illustrated in Figure 4.

The invariability of the color space l1l2l3 to the illumination intensity is obtained by replacing components of the IR, IG, e IB in (17), by their equivalents defined by (8), from which results:

(a) (b) (c) (d)

Figure 4. (a) Original image; (b) l_1 component; (c) l_2 component and (c) l_3 component.

$$\begin{bmatrix} l_1(\mathrm{x},\mathrm{y}) \\ l_2(\mathrm{x},\mathrm{y}) \\ l_3(\mathrm{x},\mathrm{y}) \end{bmatrix} = \frac{255}{(K_R - K_G)^2 + (K_R - K_B)^2 + (K_G - K_B)^2} \cdot \begin{bmatrix} (K_R - K_G)^2 \\ (K_R - K_B)^2 \\ (K_G - K_B)^2 \end{bmatrix} \qquad (18)$$

The results obtained in (18) show that the color space l1l2l3 is not susceptible to disturbances generated by the variation of intensity of illumination, since it depends solely on the sensor's sensitivity to the three components of the spectrum (red, green and blue).

The study of the brightness influence in the color space l1l2l3 is done by replacing the RGB color components of (17), by the equivalent expressions in (10). With this operation, it is possible to see that the response of the sensor surface with a strong specular component, with a white light source, is described by:

$$\begin{bmatrix} l_1(\mathrm{x},\mathrm{y}) \\ l_2(\mathrm{x},\mathrm{y}) \\ l_3(\mathrm{x},\mathrm{y}) \end{bmatrix} = \frac{255}{(K_R - K_G)^2 + (K_R - K_B)^2 + (K_G - K_B)^2} \cdot \begin{bmatrix} (K_R - K_G)^2 \\ (K_R - K_B)^2 \\ (K_G - K_B)^2 \end{bmatrix} \qquad (19)$$

Based on the results obtained in (19), we can conclude that the color space l1l2l3 is also invariable to brightness. The specular element is cancelled, only remaining the sensor's sensitivity function (KR, KG e KB).

HSV Color Space

The HSV color space is a transformation of the RGB space that allows the color description in a more natural way for humans. The HSV acronym derives from Hue, Saturation, and Value.

In the HSV color space, the hue consists of an angular measure of basic component of the color definition. This ranges from red (for a value of 0 degrees), through yellow (60 degrees), green (120 degrees), cyan (180 degrees), blue (240 degrees) and magenta (300 degrees). The component of saturation describes the intensity of color. For minimum values of saturation, it is obtained a discoloration of the dominant color specified by the hue. As the saturation value increases, so the staining level of the hue component increases too. Finally, the component value allows quantifying the dominant color amplitude. Considering MAX=max(IR(x,y), IG(x,y), IB(x,y)), and MIN=min(IR(x,y), IG(x,y), IB(x,y)) than, obtaining the HSV model from a RGB space is done through the following operations:

$$I_H(\mathrm{x},\mathrm{y})=\begin{cases} undefined \\ \quad , \ if \quad MAX=MIN \\ 60\cdot\dfrac{I_G(\mathrm{x},\mathrm{y})-I_B(\mathrm{x},\mathrm{y})}{MAX-MIN} \\ \quad , \ if \quad MAX=I_R(\mathrm{x},\mathrm{y}) \ \wedge \ I_G(\mathrm{x},\mathrm{y})\geq I_B(\mathrm{x},\mathrm{y}) \\ 60\cdot\dfrac{I_G(\mathrm{x},\mathrm{y})-I_B(\mathrm{x},\mathrm{y})}{MAX-MIN}+360 \\ \quad , \ if \quad MAX=I_R(\mathrm{x},\mathrm{y}) \ \wedge \ I_G(\mathrm{x},\mathrm{y})< I_B(\mathrm{x},\mathrm{y}) \\ 60\cdot\dfrac{I_B(\mathrm{x},\mathrm{y})-I_R(\mathrm{x},\mathrm{y})}{MAX-MIN}+120 \\ \quad , \ if \quad MAX=I_G(\mathrm{x},\mathrm{y}) \\ 60\cdot\dfrac{I_R(\mathrm{x},\mathrm{y})-I_G(\mathrm{x},\mathrm{y})}{MAX-MIN}+240 \\ \quad , \ if \quad MAX=I_B(\mathrm{x},\mathrm{y}) \end{cases} \tag{20}$$

$$I_S(\mathrm{x},\mathrm{y})=\begin{cases} 0 \ , \ if \quad MAX=0 \\ \left(1-\dfrac{MIN}{MAX}\right)\cdot 255 \ , \ otherwise \end{cases} \tag{21}$$

$$I_V(\mathrm{x},\mathrm{y})=MAX \tag{22}$$

An example of the decomposition of the HSV space in the hue (H), saturation (S) and value (V) is shown in Figure 5. By observing the picture, one can see that in the hue component are defined the dominant colors, while saturation indicates the level of staining, and the value identifies its intensity.

The analysis of invariance to changes in illumination of the HSV color space is similar to that made in other color models. So, the replacement of components IR, IG, and IB is made, in equations (20), (21) and (22), by their equivalents defined in (8).

It can be seen that the components IH and IS have properties of invariability to changes in brightness. However, the component IV does not have this property, being sensitive to lighting conditions. The behavior of the HSV color space, respecting the presence of brightness, is made by replacing the color components IR, IG, e IB of the equations (20), (21) and (22), defined by the equivalent expressions in (10). By the analysis of the results obtained in (26), (27) and (28), it can be seen that only the component IH presents the brightness invariability. The remaining components (IS e IV) are sensitive to the presence of spectral reflection on a surface.

$$I_H(\mathrm{x},\mathrm{y}) = \begin{cases} undefined \\ \quad , \; if \quad MAX = MIN \\ 60 \cdot \dfrac{K_G - K_B}{\max(K_R, K_G, K_B) - \min(K_R, K_G, K_B)} \\ \quad , \; if \quad MAX = I_R(\mathrm{x},\mathrm{y}) \;\wedge\; I_G(\mathrm{x},\mathrm{y}) \geq I_B(\mathrm{x},\mathrm{y}) \\ 60 \cdot \dfrac{K_G - K_B}{\max(K_R, K_G, K_B) - \min(K_R, K_G, K_B)} + 360 \\ \quad , \; if \quad MAX = I_R(\mathrm{x}) \;\wedge\; I_G(\mathrm{x}) < I_B(\mathrm{x}) \\ 60 \cdot \dfrac{K_B - K_R}{\max(K_R, K_G, K_B) - \min(K_R, K_G, K_B)} + 120 \\ \quad , \; if \quad MAX = I_G(\mathrm{x}) \\ 60 \cdot \dfrac{K_R - K_G}{\max(K_R, K_G, K_B) - \min(K_R, K_G, K_B)} + 240 \\ \quad , \; if \quad MAX = I_B(\mathrm{x}) \end{cases} \tag{23}$$

$$I_S(\mathrm{x},\mathrm{y}) = \left(1 - \frac{\min(K_R, K_G, K_B)}{\max(K_R, K_G, K_B)}\right) \cdot 255 \tag{24}$$

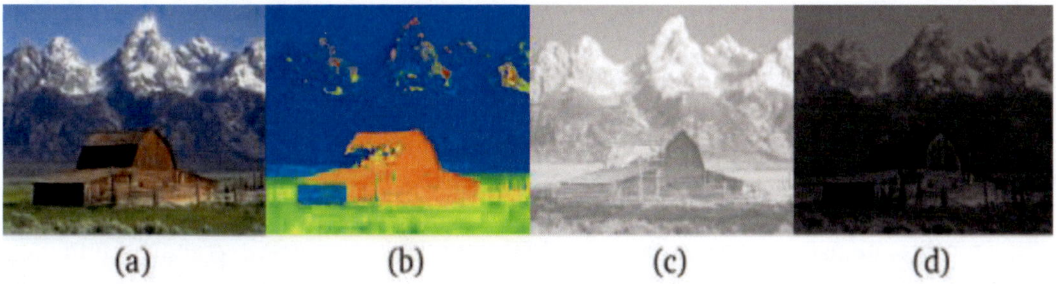

Figure 5. (a) Original image; (b) *H* component; (c) *S* component and (c) *V* component.

$$I_V(\mathrm{x},\mathrm{y}) = w_d(\mathrm{n},\mathrm{s}) \cdot E \cdot \max(K_R, K_G, K_B) \tag{25}$$

$$I_H(\mathrm{x},\mathrm{y})=\begin{cases} undefined \\ \quad , \; if \quad MAX = MIN \\ 60\cdot\dfrac{K_G-K_B}{\max(K_R,K_G,K_B)-\min(K_R,K_G,K_B)} \\ \quad , \; if \quad MAX = I_R(\mathrm{x},\mathrm{y}) \;\wedge\; I_G(\mathrm{x},\mathrm{y}) \geq I_B(\mathrm{x},\mathrm{y}) \\ 60\cdot\dfrac{K_G-K_B}{\max(K_R,K_G,K_B)-\min(K_R,K_G,K_B)}+360 \\ \quad , \; if \quad MAX = I_R(\mathrm{x},\mathrm{y}) \;\wedge\; I_G(\mathrm{x},\mathrm{y}) < I_B(\mathrm{x},\mathrm{y}) \\ 60\cdot\dfrac{K_B-K_R}{\max(K_R,K_G,K_B)-\min(K_R,K_G,K_B)}+120 \\ \quad , \; if \quad MAX = I_G(\mathrm{x},\mathrm{y}) \\ 60\cdot\dfrac{K_R-K_G}{\max(K_R,K_G,K_B)-\min(K_R,K_G,K_B)}+240 \\ \quad , \; if \quad MAX = I_B(\mathrm{x},\mathrm{y}) \end{cases} \tag{26}$$

$$I_S(\mathrm{x},\mathrm{y})=\left(1-\frac{\min(K_R,K_G,K_B)+\dfrac{S}{w_d(\mathrm{n},\mathrm{s})}}{\max(K_R,K_G,K_B)+\dfrac{S}{w_d(\mathrm{n},\mathrm{s})}}\right)\cdot 255 \tag{27}$$

$$I_V(\mathrm{x},\mathrm{y})=E\cdot\left(w_d(\mathrm{n},\mathrm{s})\cdot\max(K_R,K_G,K_B)+S\right) \tag{28}$$

Conclusion

The color models addressed here have features that both seem like advantages or disadvantages according to the nature of each processing problem and image analysis. It is therefore critical the study of the color spaces in response to three conditions: viewing angle and geometry of the object; lighting intensity and brightness.

The RGB color space is seen as the basis from which all other color spaces derive. The RGB model is sensitive to variations of viewing angle and geometry of objects, to lighting intensity fluctuations and to the formation of brightness on the surface. Although it might be assumed that these factors are important limitations on certain image processing tasks, it is possible to take advantage of these features in, for example, motion segmentation processes. The extreme sensitivity of the RGB color space to lighting conditions allows the segmentation of movement that minimizes false negatives, however generating a high number of false positives (for instance, from shadows and brightness).

In the presence of white light, the rgb color space proved to be invariant to the viewing angle, to the geometry of the object and to changes in light intensity (e.g. shadows). Through the normalization process we obtain a model which color information becomes immune to changes in lighting intensity. Nevertheless, this model is affected by brightness and also presents high instability at low lighting intensities. As a result of its invariance, the rgb color space does not allow running the detection of regions affected by brightness, despising also some useful information for motion segmentation tasks.

The color space c1c2c3 ensures invariance to the viewing angle, to the geometry of the object and the lighting intensity variations. The detection of shadows in this color space is likely to be performed by using only a single image, i.e. without the need of a reference image. However, this is only possible through the application of contour detectors (e.g. Sobel, Prewitt or Canny) on the components gradient fields of space c1c2c3 and RGB space, thereby distinguishing the contours of the regions affected by shadows, since they do not have contours in the invariant color space. Though it is effective, such an operation entails large computational resources, which can be prohibitive for applications with real-time requirements. Examples of this type of solution can be found in the work developed in [6, 7].

The space c1c2c3 does not have the characteristics of invariance to brightness. However, it has advantages in what concerns the rgb color space. According to the study carried out in [8] it can be verified that the space c1c2c3 ensures greater stability than the rgb, which exhibits some instability in regions near the vertex of origin of the RGB cube.

The only color model, among those examined, which has invariability in all the considered factors is the color space l1l2l3. Not being affected by variations of viewing angle, of the geometry of the object, of fluctuations in lighting intensity and brightness, it would be expected that this would be the ideal choice for motion detection tasks. This is because ideally the results would be found free of errors originated by changes in lighting conditions. However, in [9], it was demonstrated that this color space is more sensitive to RGB values fluctuations caused by camera noise than the remaining areas. The same study points to the existence of problems for low saturation values, i.e., IR=IG=IB.

Finally, the HSV space has distinct characteristics from the other color spaces addressed here, since its components exhibit different behaviors concerning the different lighting conditions examined. Thus, the hue component, responsible for setting the color, reveals invariable to the angle of viewing, to the geometry of the object, to variations in lighting intensity and to the presence of brightness. Saturation, in turn, reveals sensitivity to the brightness reflected on the surfaces of the objects, while the value component is affected by all the conditions, i.e. viewing angle, geometry of the object, variability of the lighting intensity and brightness. Despite the characteristics of invariability of the hue component, it displays instability in regions near the axis that defines the gray scale (low saturation values) [9]. This problem also affects the saturation component. The hue component also has the inconvenience of a reduced capacity for discrimination, which can cause major limitations in motion segmentation techniques.

REFERENCES

[37] J. E. Dowling, *The Retina: An Approachable Part of the Brain,* Belknap Press, (2002).

[38] S. A. Shafer, "Using color to separate reflection components", *Color Research and Applications,* vol. 10. 1985, pp210-218.

[39] V. Kries, Chromatic Adaptation, *Festschrift der Albrecht-Ludwigs-Universitt,* pp145-148, (1902).

[40] R. Lukac and K. N. Plataniotis, *Color image processing: methods and applications,* CRC Press. 2007, pp205.

[41] T. Gevers and A. W. M. Smeulders, Color based object recognition, *Pattern Recognition,* vol. 32, n. 3. 1999, pp453-464.

[42] E. Salvador, A. Cavallaro and T. Ebrahimi, Shadow identification and classification using invariant color models, *Proceedings of the International Conference on Acoustics,* Speech, and Signal Processing, vol. 3. 2001, pp1545-1548.

[43] E. Salvador and T. Ebrahimi, Cast shadow recognition in color images" *Proceedings of the 11th European Signal Processing Conference,* vol. 3. 2002, pp555-558.

[44] A. Trias, Shadow Detection In *Videos Acquired By Stationary And Moving Cameras,* Master Thesis, University of Maryland, (2005).

[45] E. Salvador, Shadow Segmentation And Tracking In Real-World Conditions, Thèse n° 3076, *École Polytechnique Fédérale de Lausanne,* Lausanne, (2004).

In: Image Processing
Editor: Vítor Hugo Carvalho
ISBN 978-1-62081-844-2

Chapter 9

A REGION-BASED ALGORITHM FOR AUTOMATIC BONE SEGMENTATION IN VOLUMETRIC CT

Pedro L. Rodrigues[1,*], António H. J. Moreira[1], Jaime C. Fonseca[2], A. C. Pinho[3], Nuno F. Rodrigues[4,5] and João L. Vilaça[1,4]

[1]Life and Health Sciences Research Institute (ICVS), School of Health Sciences, University of Minho, Braga, Portugal and ICVS/3B's - PT Government Associate Laboratory, Braga/Guimarães, Portugal

[2]Industrial Electronics Department, University of Minho, Guimarães, Portugal

[3]Mechanical Department, University of Minho, Guimarães, Portugal

[4]DIGARC – Polytechnic Institute of Cávado and Ave, Barcelos, Portugal

[5]DI-CCTC - University of Minho, Braga, Portugal

ABSTRACT

In Computed Tomography (CT), bone segmentation is considered an important step to extract bone parameters, which are frequently useful for computer-aided diagnosis, surgery and treatment of many diseases such as osteoporosis. Consequently, the development of accurate and reliable segmentation techniques is essential, since it often provides a great impact on quantitative image analysis and diagnosis outcome.

This chapter presents an automated multistep approach for bone segmentation in volumetric CT datasets. It starts with a three-dimensional (3D) watershed operation on an image gradient magnitude. The outcome of the watershed algorithm is an over-partioning image of many 3D regions that can be merged, yielding a meaningful image partitioning. In order to reduce the number of regions, a merging procedure was performed that merges neighbouring regions presenting a mean intensity distribution difference of ±15%. Finally, once all bones have been distinguished in high contrast, the final 3D bone segmentation was achieved by selecting all regions with bone fragments, using the information retrieved by a threshold mask. The bones contours were accurately defined

* E-mail address: pedro.rodrigues17@gmail.com.

according to the watershed regions outlines instead of considering the thresholding segmentation result.

This new method was tested to segment the rib cage on 185 CT images, acquired at the São João Hospital of Porto (Portugal) and evaluated using the dice similarity coefficient as a statistical validation metric, leading to a coefficient mean score of 0.89. This could represent a step forward towards accurate and automatic quantitative analysis in clinical environments and decreasing time-consumption, user dependence and subjectivity.

INTRODUCTION

Segmentation of bone tissue from images acquired with medical imaging modalities is an important component in many applications, such as bone densitometry, neurosurgical practice or bone-subtraction for assisted surgery. The rapid development and distribution of three-dimensional (3D) medical imaging technologies must be accompanied by advanced 3D analysis methods. Image acquisitions modalities used in radiology such as magnetic resonance imaging (MRI) or computed tomography (CT) are increasingly capable of generating high-resolution volumetric data sets. Commonly, these technologies produces images with a very wide dynamic range, where linear intensity window setting techniques must be used to provide adequate contrast and detail within specific imaged tissues such as bones, soft-tissues and lung detail.

The extraction of bone structures from the surrounding soft tissue is one of the most critical procedures to achieve 3D skeleton visualization. Such procedures have been simplified with the increase of CT high-resolution volumetric generation, and the definition of planar regions of interest to reduce the amount of processing data.

The bone segmentation can be manual or automatic. Manual segmentation is time-consuming, user-dependent, error-prone, subjective, and requires expert knowledge to yield accurate and robust results. In contrast, semi-automatic/automatic methods have the potential to provide fast, robust, user-independent and accurate segmentation. Semi-automatic /automatic approaches are required in today's challenging clinical environment.

The main difficulties in bone segmentation include ambiguity between the bone outline and the surrounding tissue or anatomic organ, irregular shape and size, different anatomic locations and patient conditions, presence of neighboring structures/organs with the same density/values, non-uniformity of bone tissue (ranging from dense cortical bone to textured spongy bone), small inter-bone spaces and the inherent blurring of CT imaging. Due to these multiple difficulties, new methods represent a nontrivial task and sometimes seem to be inadequate.

According to the literature [1] fully automated methods rely upon manual post processing, since the performance of image processing algorithms is often sensitive to noise and image contrast. Some pre-processing is usually necessary to achieve more efficiency in detecting weak edges and suppress others caused by noise. A variety of editing tools were developed [1] to correct or improve results of initial automatic segmentation procedures: hole-filling, point-bridging, and surface-dragging.

Semi-automatic approaches have also been proposed for different actors. The most conventional techniques are based on thresholding algorithms by manually or automatically selecting a Hounsfield Unit (HU). The major drawbacks of these algorithms reside on the global thresholding procedure, which does not consider local gray value variations within bone structure, and adaptive thresholding occasionally results in the merging of small gaps between bones [2-5]. The performance of this methods are highly dependent on image quality acquired from the medical imaging modalities and material density, single thresholds tend to fail in providing correct segmentations in more complex scenarios. Consequently, too large segmentation occurs if the threshold is too low to define the boundary line, too far away from the real bone boundary. On the other hand, a bone structure becomes too small for higher thresholds, because the boundary line cuts away some of the bone.

Therefore, intensity based algorithms have advantages, such as the speed in the case of global thresholding, and disadvantages, like the need for post-processing like edge linking, depending on the CT volumetric data sets quality.

Consequently, better segmentation results are achieved by combining thresholding methods with other image processing algorithms [6]. A highly automated 3D based method for bone segmentation in volumetric CT datasets, was developed in [7]. They use a multistep approach starting with region-growing and local adaptive thresholds, followed by procedures to correct bone boundary discontinuities. Zhou et al. [8] developed a computer-aided diagnosis scheme for automatically segment skin, soft tissue and bone structures from high-resolution torso CT images. This method was based on gray-level threshold to separate the regions of interest from the background. The skeleton was segmented by a region growing process using an optimal threshold value. A ray casting algorithm presented in [9] overcome threshold drawbacks, by using a gray value gradient, which is also not affected by gray value variations with low frequencies.

Other segmentation methods described in the literature use the combination of region-based, edge-based and deformable algorithms to improve segmentation procedures. In [2], the authors use a method based on region growing from initialized seeds, where growth is modulated by a skeletally-mediated competition between neighbouring regions. This method combines the advantages of deformable models with region growing and region competition. Hahn presents an interactive watershed transform to separate bone from white matter in an MRI. The use of watersheds to segment objects of interest in images often produce more stable results as well as continuous segmentation boundaries, independently of image contrast or noise level [10, 11].

Most of these methods have some limitations, as they are relatively slow, not very accurate and highly computationally-intensive particularly for large images. Moreover, the segmentation of image regions is still one of the major bottlenecks, especially for 3D image analysis, as most segmentation approaches are 2D based. The segmentation of 3D structures from 2D results are error prone, most often require intensive user interactions and neglect the three-dimensional character of the structures to be segmented.

In this work, a fully 3D automated method is proposed, based on a watershed operation that is applied to the image gradient magnitude. The result of the watershed operation, an image with several primitive regions, was input to a merging procedure that selectively merges similar regions and maintains the relevant bone boundaries. The final bone segmen--tation was achieved by automatic select the merged regions with the information retrieved by a threshold mask. The implemented strategy is independent of image specific parameters and can also be applied in images from different imaging modalities allowing it to be used by clinical experts.

This chapter is organized as follows: the next sub-chapter describes all algorithms used to segment the bone structures; then it is presented and discussed some simulation and statistical results followed by the main conclusions.

METHODS

Since the segmentation of images into meaningful regions has been an important area in medical image analysis, the implemented strategy is based on (1) image partitioning into small primitive regions, (2) region merging and (3) the selection of merged regions using information provided by a threshold mask.

To verify the suitability of the proposed method, tests were run on CT images acquired at São João Hospital of Porto (Portugal), according to the ethical review board of the University of Minho. The tests were conducted on 185 CT data sets from different patients. Each CT slice size has 512 x 512 pixels, with a slice thickness of 5 mm. The pixel resolution ranged from 0.46 to 0.84 mm (for both vertical and horizontal directions). An overview of the different stages of the method is given in Figure 1.

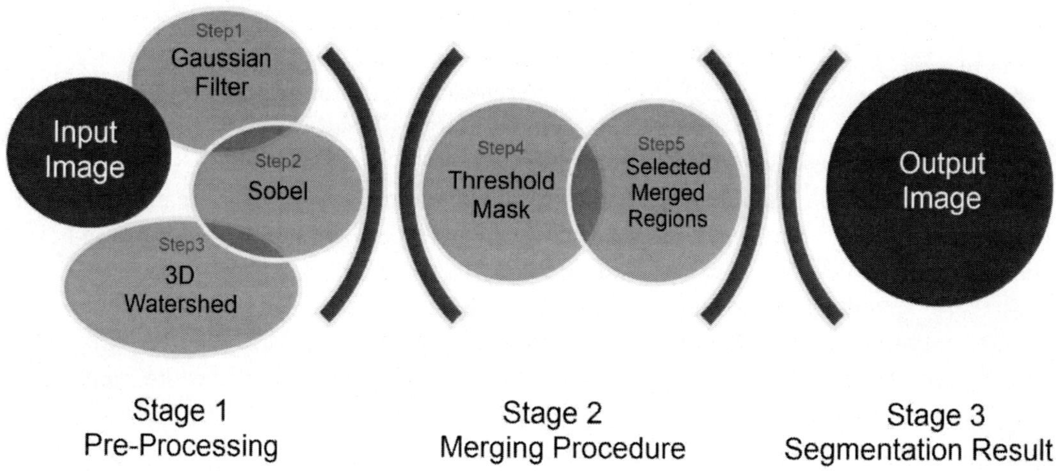

Figure 1. Block diagram giving an overview of the different bone segmentation steps.

PRE-PROCESSING

The aim of this stage was to calculate an image partitioning within several primitive 3D regions.

Due to the stochastic processes during the image creation, noise is always present. Therefore the meaningful information of an image object can be lost if the noise level is too high compared with the object intensity. To this extent, the noise corrupting the image was initially reduced using a Gaussian filter (Figure 1, Stage 1, Step 1).

The Gaussian filter was implemented as in [21] to reduce the image noise. Considering $f(x,y)$ a two-dimensional function, the Gaussian filter is a 2D low-pass transformation which performance depends on the standard deviation of the filter. In this work, the standard deviation was experimentally calculated with a final value of 1.8 pixels, allowing an output image with a right equilibrium between smoothing and edge details.

Then, the gradient of the smoothed image is calculated using the Sobel operator. This operator is used in image processing, particularly within edge detection algorithms. Technically, it works as a similarity measure, computing an approximation of the gradient ∇f of the image intensity function f. Mathematically, the gradient ∇f is at each image voxel a 3D vector with the components given by the derivatives in all directions (Figure 1, Stage 1, Step 2) [12, 13].

The magnitude outcome of the Sobel operator was input to a 3D watershed algorithm to segment the bone regions (Figure 1, Stage 1, Step 3). Briefly, the watershed operation assigns different labels to whole pixels that are separated by an image edge. Although many techniques have been suggested for edge detection, which performances are very sensitive to noise and image contrast. The use of watersheds often produce more stable segmentation results as well as continuous segmentation boundaries, independently of image contrast or noise level [14-16].

The probability that a single region will suitably associate to each object of interest is small. Knowing this limitation, a good design goal was to create several small primitive regions and try to semantically link them into a hierarchy. An optimal number of regions are essential to achieve a good segmentation.

Thus, pixels that are separated by an image edge, which correspond to a gradient magnitude ridge, will be assigned a different label. In order to create the segmentation primitives correctly, the following restrictions are all considered:

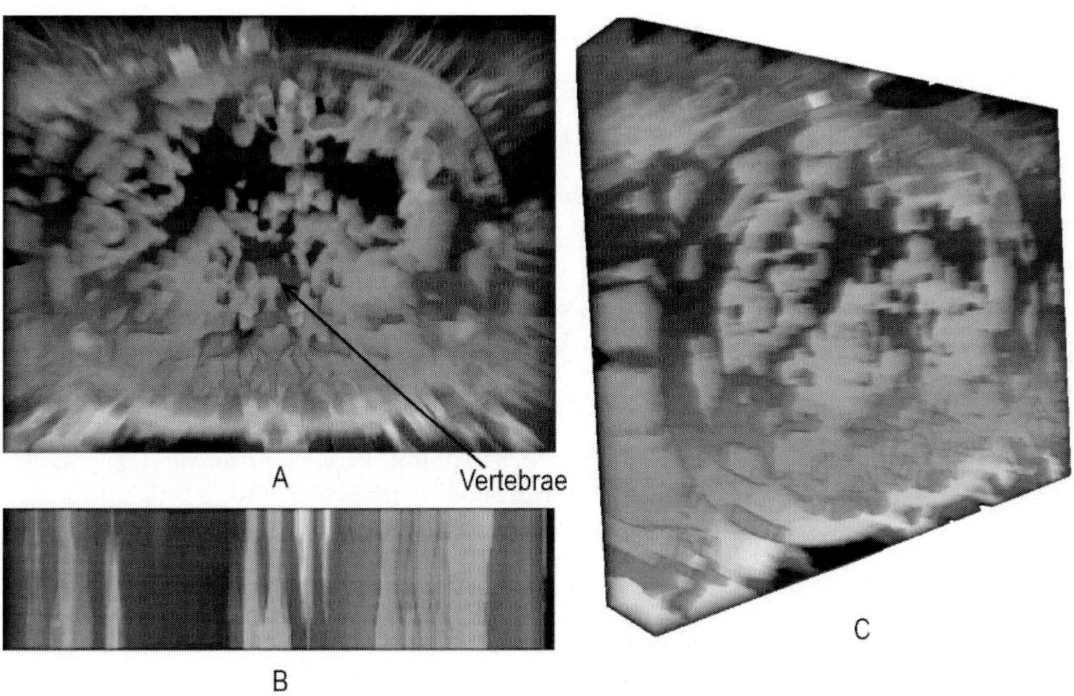

Figure 2. 3D watershed operation result: the colour map illustrates the region extension along X, Y and Z directions.

1. After creating the primitive regions, every pixel must be in a region;
2. $R_i \cap R_j = \emptyset$ for all i and j, $i \neq j$, indicating that the regions must be disjoint;
3. $P(R_i) = \text{TRUE}$ for $i = 1,2,\ldots,n$, which means that properties in a segmented region must be satisfied by the pixels;
4. $P(R_i \cup R_j) = \text{FALSE}$ for $i \neq j$, indicates that regions R_i and R_j are different in the sense of predicate $P(R_i)$;
5. A pixel p, which is a boundary pixel, belongs to the region $R_{(p)}$ if there is at least one pixel q in the 4-connected in 2D (or 6-connected in 3D) neighbourhood of p that does not belong to $R_{(p)}$. This pixel q is a boundary pixel of its region $R_{(q)}$ and the common pixel boundary of p and q is a boundary line element (in 2D, or surface element in 3D) of $R_{(p)}$ and $R_{(q)}$;
6. The boundary between two regions is the union of all their common boundary elements.

Considering these restrictions, in this work watershed regions were labeled by a starting point and following the flow line, whose direction was the gradient of intensity to a local minimum: for each pixel p in the image, it was created a gradient path between p and q, where q is the pixel on the 27-neighborhood of p with the smallest gradient magnitude. Each time that there is no pixel q in p' neighbourhood with smaller gradient magnitude, the pixel q is marked as a local minimum of the gradient magnitude and assigned a distinct label. The process continues until all image volume is processed (Figure 2).

In the end, the whole image is segmented into primitive regions and the quality of the watershed segmentation results will depend on:

1. The number of pixels of the same object that are within one region;
2. The ratio of image edges that correspond to regions edges.

MERGING PROCEDURE

As shown in (Figure 2), the output of the watershed algorithm is an oversegmented image, containing a set of non-overlapping regions. Although oversegmentation increases the probability for a region boundary to correspond to boundaries of important objects, it can also create many insignificant boundaries.

This section describes how the 3D bone structures were automatically determined. Briefly, this procedure consisted on the identification of regions edges and its connections with similar intensity, ignoring all other regions with wide mean intensity variations. It assumes that:

- All pixels within the same region are homogeneous;
- Regions within bone regions have homogeneous intensity variations;
- Regions within bone regions are considerably different from other outside neighbouring regions;

- R_i with $i=1,2,3,...,n$ is a connected region, which means that a region must be connected to their neighbourhood region in some predefined sense;

Since all pixels within the same region are homogeneous and considerably different from other neighbouring regions, there are neighbouring regions belonging to the bone structures that could be merged, yielding to a meaningful image partitioning.

After establishing the image segmentation through the application of the watershed algorithm, this merging procedure performs feature identification in each region, by identifying the centroid, mean intensity distribution, minimum and maximum values, region edges, and edges region neighbours.

Each time two neighbourhood regions present a mean intensity distribution difference of ±15%, these two regions are merged and the edge between them is removed. Different merged results from the input image (Figure 3 A) can be obtained when different percentage similarities are used - Figure 3 B.

The bone segmentation was finally achieved by selecting all regions with bone fragments, using the information retrieved by a threshold mask (Figure 3 - C and Figure 1 - step3). This level was calculated through a basic threshold algorithm, using a value higher than the one that was needed to precisely identify the bone outlines (0.9/1 threshold level). All regions that possessed white pixels on their interior, corresponding to bone regions, were chosen as final result (Figure 3 D).

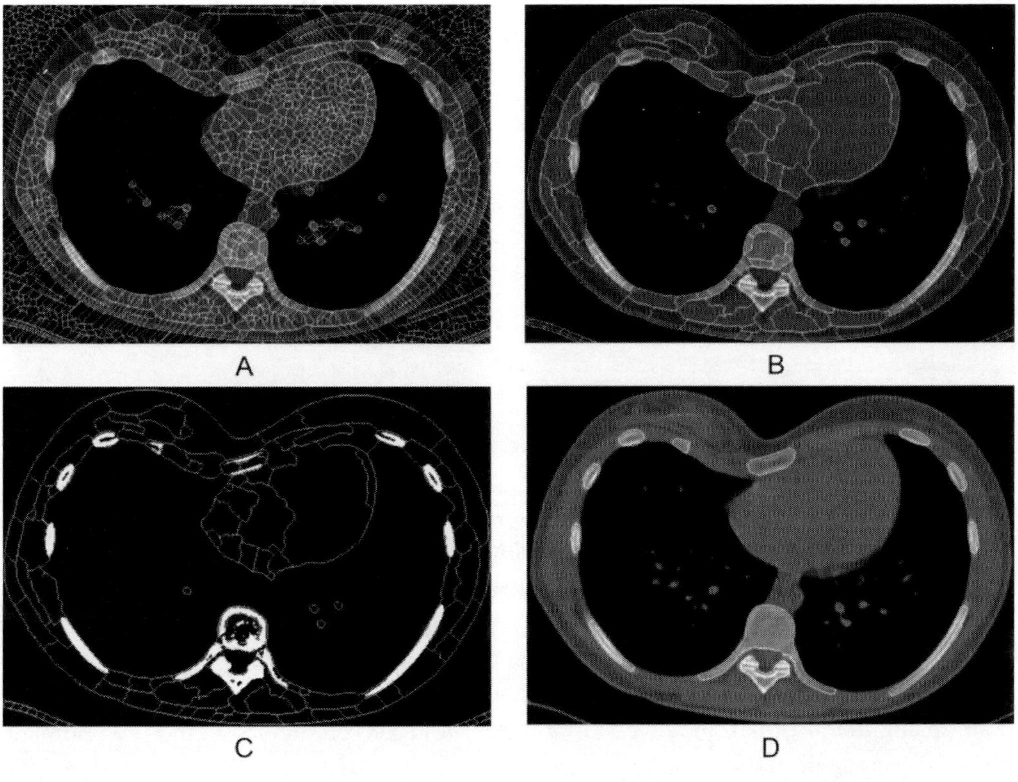

Figure 3. Representation of the bone segmentation procedure outline: A) watershed operation result in a 2D image; B) merging procedure (15% of difference between regions); C) Threshold masks to automatically select all the regions belonging to the bone regions; D) final segmentation result.

The bone outline was defined by only taking into account the information of the region contours after the merging process; thus, the segmentation result was not influenced by the threshold value that determines the bone outline thickness.

3D reconstructions of two patients are shown in Figure 4. The colour map illustrates the differences between the regions produced by the watershed algorithm and the binary image used for the regions selection after fusion.

These differences were computed using a Ray-Triangle intersection method, which was used to compute the minimal distance between two triangle meshes: the bone structure constructed using the threshold mask (Ts) and the bone structure acquired using the proposed method (Tp).

For each triangle facet of the Tp(i) (with i = 0, 1, 2,... N, with N being the total number of triangles on the bone structure), a ray R(i) was defined with the Y direction (Figure 4 (c)), starting at a point Pi(i) within Tp(i) and ending at a Pf(i) (point above bone structure from the threshold mask). Then, its intersection with Ts(j) (with j = 0, 1,2,... Nt, with Nt being the total number of mesh triangles) was checked.

Based on these distances, the bone structure facets from the watershed algorithm were colored according to the color-map defined on the color bar in Figure 4.

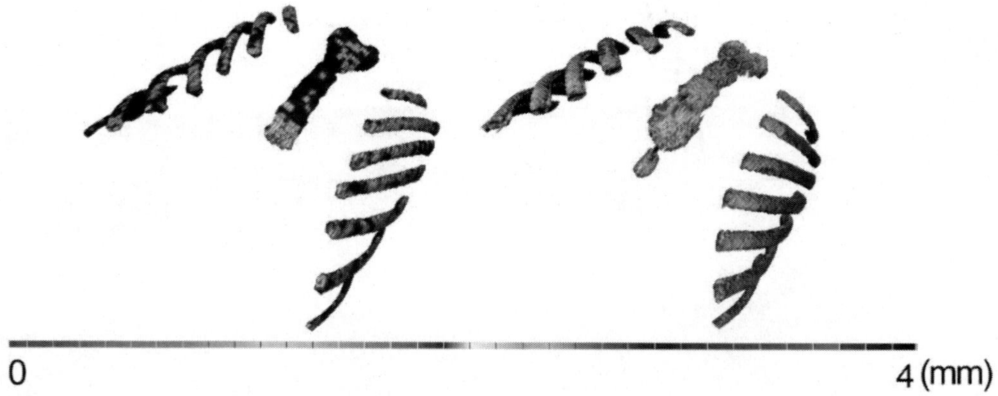

Figure 4. 3D reconstructions of the anterior chest bones of two patients.

RESULTS

A proper estimation of bone volume and structure are useful for several applications such as computer-aided diagnosis, surgery and treatment response evaluation. Due to the limited number of images available for each patient, clinical planning and quantitative monitoring of disease evolution requires fast segmentation methods with high reproducibility. Thus, this chapter introduces a segmentation methodology to automatic segment bone regions.

The segmentation procedure was reduced by selecting merged regions of a watershed operation using the information retrieved by a threshold mask. Therefore, the total number of decisions to segment bone structures was drastically reduced, increasing segmentation efficiency and robustness and decreasing time-consumption, user dependence, and subjecttivity. The observer variability also decreased since all regions were computed automatically without any user intervention.

The merging procedure was used to selectively merge watershed regions based on their image mean intensity distribution. However, a proper segmentation can only be accomplished with an optimal number of regions since such a sequence of merges does not guarantee the construction of an optimal image partitioning. False merges depends both on size of the regions to be merged and on the noise present in the image.

A small number of regions with larger granularity (higher merging percentage difference) can be used for fast and rough segmentations of big bones; while a higher number of regions with smaller granularity (small merging percentage difference) should be used to segment smaller bones. Although the segmentation procedure is automatic, the user can always erase and produce detailed segmentation by manually selecting regions of interest. Figure 5 shows results of different merging procedures according to different merging percentage differences.

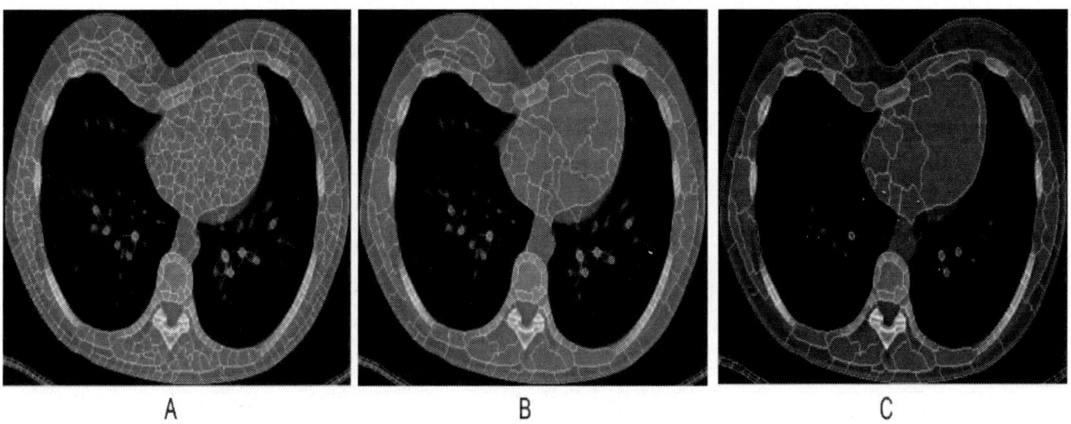

Figure 5. Merging procedure results with different merging percentage differences: A -5%, B – 10% and C – 5%.

The number of watershed regions was also dependent on the standard deviation of the Gaussian filter value. High standard deviation values may destroy some image details and object boundaries, which cannot be recovered at the merging stage. This is justified from the fact that when the standard deviation value is high, the noise reduction algorithm may over-smooth part of the image intensity discontinuities, resulting in low magnitudes.

Therefore, the segmentation procedure could be interpreted as an optimization problem of some parameters (standard deviation Gaussian filter value, percentage value to merge watershed regions and the threshold values mask) in order to reduce unsatisfactory results as "undermerged" or "overmerged" segmented results.

The quality and performance of the segmentation quality of this work was evaluated using the Dice Similarity Coefficient (DSC) metric. It measures the spatial overlap between two segmentation results: automated segmentation result (A) and manual segmentation (B). As indicated by Zijdenbos [17] a good overlap occurs when DCS > 0.7. For each segmentation (A, B) the DSC was determined showing a mean value of 89% (range from 73% to 96%) with a standard deviation equal to 4.9%. A total of 185 CT data sets were used in this study, comprising patients with different pathologies and different image intensities.

Although DSC is quite simple to interpret, there are several limitations in using DCS as an overlap measures since it is not robust in terms of size of the target. For small tumors others metrics might be considered like ROC analysis, odds ratio or distance measures.

Conclusion

An automatic algorithm was presented for bone segmentation in CT images. The segmentation was reduced by selecting all merged regions belonging to the bone structure using the information retrieved by a threshold mask. This procedure showed high sensitivity detecting bone boundaries located near other anatomical structures, identifying weak edges, robustness against image noise, and being able to segment hyperdense and hypodense bones with different size and shape.

Best results were achieved when an optimal number of regions were created depending on the percentage value to merge watershed regions and the standard deviation Gaussian filter value.

The proposed segmentation technique was implemented for 2D and 3D cases, producing successful results in the 2D performance and execution. Further work is needed in the 3D merging procedure and also in the evaluation of the method by clinical experts. Hereupon, new research paths based on this work have to be investigated. For example, this algorithm should be tested and validated in other bone structures besides the rib cage in order to increase and validate the algorithm suitability.

Acknowledgment

The authors acknowledge to Foundation for Science and Technology (FCT) - Portugal for the fellowships with the references: SFRH/BD/74276/2010; SFRH/BD/68270/2010; and, SFRH/BPD/46851/2008. This work was also supported by FCT R&D project PTDC/SAU-BEB/103368/2008.

References

[1] Y. Kang and al., Interactive 3D editing tools for image segmentation. *Medical Image Analysis,* vol. 8, pp. 35-46, 2004.

[2] T. B. Sebastian and al., Segmentation of carpal bones from CT images using skeletally coupled deformable models. *Medical Image Analysis,* vol. 7, pp. 21-45, 2003.

[3] M. N. Coleman and M. W. Colbert, Technical note: CT thresholding protocols for taking measurements on three-dimensional models. *Am J Phys Anthropol,* vol. 133, pp. 723-5, May 2007.

[4] R. J. Fajardo and al., Nonhuman anthropoid primate femoral neck trabecular architecture and its relationship to locomotor mode. *Anatomical Record-Advances in Integrative Anatomy and Evolutionary Biology,* vol. 290, pp. 422-436, Apr 2007.

[5] T. N. Hangartner, Thresholding technique for accurate analysis of density and geometry in QCT, pQCT and microCT images. *J Musculoskelet Neuronal Interact,* vol. 7, pp. 9-16, Jan-Mar 2007.

[6] L. I. Wang and al., Validation of bone segmentation and improved 3-D registration using contour coherency in CT data. *Ieee Transactions on Medical Imaging,* vol. 25, pp. 324-334, Mar 2006.

[7] Y. Kang and al., A *new accurate and precise 3-D segmentation method for skeletal structures in volumetric CT data* vol. 22. New York, NY, ETATS-UNIS: Institute of Electrical and Electronics Engineers, 2003.

[8] X. R. Zhou and al., *Automated segmentations of skin, soft-tissue, and skeleton from torso CT images.* Medical Imaging 2004: Image Processing, Pts 1-3, vol. 5370, pp. 1634-1639 , 2158, 2004.

[9] H. Scherf and R. Tilgner, A new high-resolution computed tomography (CT) segmentation method for trabecular bone architectural analysis. *American Journal of Physical Anthropology,* vol. 140, pp. 39-51, 2009.

[10] L. Vincent and P. Soille, Watersheds in digital spaces: an efficient algorithm based on immersion simulations. *IEEE Transactions on Pattern Analysis and Machine Intelligence,* vol. 13, pp. 583-598, 1997.

[11] H. K. Hahn, *Morphological Volumetry: Theory, Concepts, and Application to Quantitative Medical Imaging*. PhD thesis, University of Bremen, 2005.

[12] R. O. Duda and P. E. Hart, Eds., *Pattern Classification and Scene Analysis.* New York, 1973, p.^pp. Pages.

[13] I. N. Bankman, Segmentation. in *Handbook of Medical Image Processing and Analysis* (Second Edition), N. B. Isaac and PhD, Eds., ed Burlington: Academic Press, 2009, pp. 71-257.

[14] Z. Peter and al., A constrained region growing approach based on watershed for the segmentation of low contrast structures in bone micro-CT image. *Pattern Recognition,* vol. 41, pp. 2358-2368, 2008.

[15] C. R. Jung and J. Scharcanski, Robust watershed segmentation using wavelets. *Image and Vision Computing,* vol. 23, pp. 661-669, 2005.

[16] F. C. Flores and R. d. A. Lotufo,Watershed from propagated markers: An interactive method to morphological object segmentation in image sequences. *Image and Vision Computing,* vol. 28, pp. 1491-1514, 2010.

[17] A. P. Zijdenbos, and al., Morphometric analysis of white matter lesions in MR images: method and validation. *Medical Imaging, IEEE Transactions* on, vol. 13, pp. 716-724, 1994.

In: Image Processing
Editor: Vítor Hugo Carvalho
ISBN 978-1-62081-844-2

Chapter 10

PROVED IMAGE SEGMENTATION

M. V. Kharinov*
St. Petersburg Institute for Informatics and Automation of Russian Academy of Sciences, St. Petersburg, Russia

ABSTRACT

In this chapter we address the problem of automatic object detection in a digital image of arbitrary content. Object detection is treated as a non-formalized interpretation of image segmentation and related to the solution of the so-called segmentation problem. Statement of the problem of segmentation is reduced to exact definition of the segmented image. To formalize the segmentation we use a proven model of Mumford-Shah, which enables to distinguish the segmented image from the images simply divided into pieces in some or another way. A segmented image is defined for each segment number as an optimal piecewise constant approximation which minimally differs from the image by the standard deviation. It is established that the series of optimal approximations is not hierarchical. Then an iterative segment merging employed in Mumford–Shah model to obtain the optimal approximations of an image turns out insufficient. To overcome this challenge in addition to segment merging the operation of segment correction by means of reclassification of pixels is introduced. For pixel reclassification a formulae analogous to known expression for the criterion of segment merging are derived. A comparative analysis of the segmented images by the standard deviation is carried out. The improvement of optimization results is demonstrated and the computations are discussed.

INTRODUCTION

The concept of segmentation is often described as ill-posed. That is true if segmentation is defined as a process of image partitioning into some meaningful segments corresponded to visible objects or their parts. More precise statement of the segmentation problem is reduced to definition of «adaptively segmented» or simply «segmented» image as certain partitioning of an image into proper segments. The one of known correct definitions of segmented image

* E-mail address: khar@iias.spb.su, mvkhar@gmail.com.

consists in specifying a certain functional, which attains the minimal value for the segmented image compared with the values of this functional for arbitrarily partitioning of an image into segments. At that the definition of segmented image does not appeal nor to a visual perception nor to a priori prescribed image segmentation technique. So for image of any content it appears possible to obtain the minimal values of the numerical functional and calculate the proper segmented representations. We start to solve the mentioned task in terms of optimal piecewise constant image approximations which are used in the Mumford–Shah model [1–7].

According to the Mumford–Shah model, a functional to be minimized usually depends on standard deviation of approximation from an image and the total length of the boundaries between image segments. Accounting for segment boundaries was introduced to describe a non-trivial minimum of the functional for a certain number of segments. Though it simplifies the analytical solution for optimization problem but forces the use of an extra control parameter [1–3]. In special case of ignoring of segment borders the optimization reduces to minimizing the standard deviation of approximation from an image [5]. In this case the optimal approximation turns out trivial and coincides with the partition of an image into separate pixels, or segments of identical pixels corresponded to zero value of the functional. However, for meaningful statement of the problem avoiding any functional complications it seems perfect to minimize the functional for each possible segment number that guarantees the existence of solutions and simplifies the interpretation of the functional. The requirement of minimizing of functional for each segment number is a generalization of the problem statement that is commonly used. But it should be noted that the consideration of a sequence of optimal approximations instead of single approximation maintains the logic of practical computations as the selection of the desired image approximation from a set of calculated ones is often provided within a supplementary «stopping condition» [3–7] that treated in addition to initial minimization requirement. Nevertheless, for more effective utilization of the model it is useful to clarify and carefully experimentally verify the concept of optimal approximation avoiding an overestimation of the results of computer calculations.

MUMFORD–SHAH MODEL

The original approach to the problem of image segmentation as a problem of optimization was founded by D. Mumford and J. Shah in former century in [1, 2] followed by a number of subsequent key studies [3–7] that are implemented into practice of image processing e.g. in program package «ENVI» (Environment for Visualizing Images, http://www.ittvis.com/portals/0/pdfs/envi/Feature_Extraction_Module.pdf). These studies base on the formalization of segmentation problem as the minimization of the functional presented as:

$$SE + \lambda L = \min, \tag{1}$$

where SE (abbreviated «square error») is the sum of squared deviations of intensities from intensity mean values calculated within the segments; L is the total length of the boundaries between the segments and λ is a parameter which may depend on the number of segments according to version [3] and also on the image itself according to the version FLSA (Full λ– Scheduled Algorithm) [4, 6, 7].

In accordance with Mumford–Shah model the segmentation task is solved using the algorithms of iterative segment merging. In the version [3] of Mumford–Shah model the merging criterion is expressed as:

$$\Delta SE_{merge} - \lambda \cdot l_{1,2} = \min, \tag{2}$$

where $\Delta SE_{merge} \equiv SE_{1\cup 2} - SE_1 - SE_2$ is the value of nonadditivity of SE, estimated for segments 1, 2 and their union $1 \cup 2$ as the sum of squared deviations of intensities within the segment from intensity mean value and $l_{1,2}$ is the length of the common boundary between the segments 1 and 2.

The formula (2) simply describes the increment of the functional value for current iteration of segment merging. To avoid the control parameters in [4] the estimation of λ as the minimal value that formally equates to zero the expression (2) was suggested detrimentally to the source idea of minimizing of functional (1). Thus the criterion for segment merging according to FLSA version is expressed as ΔSE_{merge} divided by the length $l_{1,2}$:

$$\frac{\Delta SE_{merge}}{l_{1,2}} = \min. \tag{3}$$

Though the dependence of the lambda from an image violates the clear interpretation of functional, which is divided into two terms, just this version of the Mumford–Shah model is preferably implemented to the practice of image processing due to exclusion of control parameter. Perhaps that is why in mentioned papers there is a shortage of the experimental data that would clearly indicate the obtained values of minimized functional.

To compare the different methods we accept the standard deviation $StdDev$ of the image from piecewise constant approximation as a unified criterion of approximation optimality.

KEY IDEAS

Insufficiency of Segment Merging

Let us illustrate the notion of optimal approximation by the example of the digital image of the four pixels, comparing the image and its approximation by the standard deviation $StdDev$ of approximation from the image (Figure 1).

Leftmost matrix in Figure 1 is an image example. Intensity values of pixels are written in the cells. Other matrices describe the partitions of the image that are converted to piecewise constant approximations by filling the segments with averaged intensity values. The values of $StdDev$ are written under the matrices.

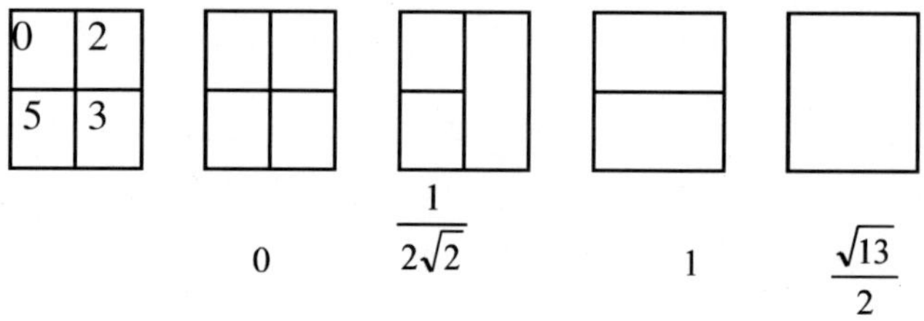

Figure 1. Image partitions inducing optimal approximations.

The piecewise constant image approximation is called optimal if in comparison with any other approximation constituted of the same number of segments less differs from the image by the value of the standard deviation $StdDev$, calculated as the square root of the additive square error SE divided by the number of pixels N_0:

$$StdDev = \sqrt{SE/N_0} \ . \tag{4}$$

Image partition that induces the optimal approximation we also call optimal.

By direct exhaustive search one can check up that Figure 1 demonstrates just optimal partitions. Comparing in Figure 1 the partitions of the image into two and three segments, it is easy to notice that segments from different partitions are not nested within each other but overlap one another. Therefore, it is impossible to obtain the sequence of optimal approximations of an image into $n = 1, 2, 3, \ldots N_0$ segments by iterative segment merging.

For images of several pixels the exhaustive search can be performed manually. But even for the image of 10×10 pixels, computing resources are not enough to generate and analyze all possible approximations.

To improve an image approximation according the standard deviation it is useful to combine the merging of segments with their correction.

Segmentation Criteria

The simplest criterion for merging of adjacent segments 1 and 2 according to version [5] of Mumford–Shah model is presented as:

$$\Delta SE_{merge} \equiv \frac{n_1 n_2}{n_1 + n_2} \cdot (\Delta I)^2 = \min \,, \tag{5}$$

where ΔI is the difference of intensities averaged within the segments; n_1 and n_2 are the segment squares (pixel numbers).

Similarly to (2) the formula (5) describes the increment of SE at the current iteration of segment merging and provides the strict minimization of $StdDev$ for merging of first pair of pixels. For subsequent iterations, we introduce the operation of segment correction.

The correction is iteratively performed by the reclassification of pixels, and consists in exclusion of the given pixels from the list of pixels of the segment 1 and inclusion these pixels into the list of pixels of the segment 2.

For generality let us consider the reclassification of k pixels of the same intensity value I. Then the increment $\Delta SE_{correct}$ caused by the reclassification of pixels is obtained by subtracting from the ΔSE_{merge} of a non-negative value of δSE:

$$\Delta SE_{correct} = \Delta SE_{merge} - \delta SE. \tag{6}$$

The value of $\delta SE \geq 0$ is expressed as:

$$\delta SE = \frac{n_1 n_2}{n_1 + n_2}\left[\frac{I - I_1}{\alpha} + (I_2 - I)\cdot\alpha\right]^2, \tag{7}$$

where I_1, I_2 are the mean intensity values for the segments 1 and 2, respectively, and the positive α is defined as $\alpha \equiv \sqrt{\dfrac{n_2(n_1 - k)}{n_1(n_2 + k)}} < 1$.

Obviously the reclassification of pixels results in a decrease of the standard deviation $StdDev$ under the condition of the negative value $\Delta SE_{correct} < 0$:

$$\Delta SE_{merge} < \delta SE, \tag{8}$$

calculated in accordance with (5)–(7).

By elementary transformations the condition (8) of the standard deviation decreasing is reduced to:

$$J\cdot\mathrm{sign}(I_1 - I_2) < \frac{|I_1 - I_2|}{2}\cdot\beta \quad \vee \quad J\cdot\mathrm{sign}(I_1 - I_2) > \frac{|I_1 - I_2|}{2}\cdot\frac{1}{\beta}, \tag{9}$$

where $J \equiv I - \dfrac{I_1 + I_2}{2}$ is the deviation of intensity I from the half-sum of I_1 and I_2; the function sign posses the values -1, 0, 1 for negative, zero and positive argument, respectively and the positive β is defined as $\beta \equiv \dfrac{1-\alpha}{1+\alpha} < 1$.

The last expression states that if the intensity of the given pixels out of a certain range, then the reclassification of these pixels from the segment 1 into the segment 2 is accompanied with the standard deviation decrease. It is characteristic that mean pixel intensity I_1 of the donor segment 1 belongs to a specified range. Therefore, if the intensity of pixels coincides with the average intensity of the donor segment, their reclassification always results in standard deviation increase.

As a negation of (9) we obtain the criterion of stable segmentation:

$$\frac{|I_1 - I_2|}{2} \cdot \beta \le J \cdot \operatorname{sign}(I_1 - I_2) \le \frac{|I_1 - I_2|}{2} \cdot \frac{1}{\beta}. \tag{10}$$

If the stability criterion (10) is true for each set of identical pixels from the segment 1, and holds for any pair of adjacent segments 1 and 2, then segment correction does not decrease the value of $StdDev$, so that the image approximation and corresponding partition into segments are stable.

Merge–and–Correct Segmentation Method

Nearly Optimal Approximation

It should be noted that the computational problem of the optimal approximating has no an exact solution so far, even for individual images of actual dimensions and the case of several connected segments. However for reliable discussion of the properties of optimal approximations it seems necessary to obtain the examples of nearly optimal approximations.

Basing on the equivalent conditions (8)–(10) we have developed a pilot version of algorithm for correcting of segments, which provides the converting of any image approximation into an optimized approximation of an image with the same number of segments, but a lower or at least the same standard deviation. In the case of two segments with our version of algorithm for correction of segments we have obtained the nearly optimal image approximation which stays invariant under correcting and is restored after introducing of small distortions (Figure 2).

Figure 2 by the example of the standard Lenna image demonstrates the nearly optimal approximation. This approximation called a nearly optimal as it is characterized by a minimum value of the standard deviation $StdDev$ compared with other piecewise constant approximations that obtained in available algorithms using both interactive and automatic modes. The appropriate value of *StdDev* is written under the approximation.

In Figure 2 either segment of nearly optimal approximation covers several objects connected to each other with connective lines and other ties of one pixel wide. Connectivity in this case means that to recolor the approximation it is enough to click once on the dark and bright pixels in "Flood Fill" mode of any image editor. To notice the mutual connectivity of the dark or light objects, one should pay attention to the partially dark and partially light frame around the perimeter of the image approximation.

31.603

Figure 2. Nearly optimal piecewise constant image approximation with two segments. The original image is shown on the left and its approximation is shown on the right.

30.646

Figure 3. Global image approximation with two gradations accordingly Otsu method.

To estimate the attainable limit of the standard deviation, we used the Otsu method [8] consisting in automatic computing of the intensity threshold value which minimizes the standard deviation of an image from its global approximation with two gradations (Figure3).

In Figure 3 the result of standard Lenna image approximation with two gradations calculated by averaging of the intensities, separated by a threshold value is shown. The appropriate value of the standard deviation $StdDev$ is written under the approximation.

The result of the threshold transformation visually is very similar to a nearly optimal approximation (Figure 2). But it contains 351 segments and for this segment number is far from an optimal that can be easily detected using segment correcting. Nevertheless, assuming that the approximation according to Otsu can be converted into nearly optimal approximation by adding the connective elements, we accept the corresponding value of standard deviation $StdDev = 30.646$ as the estimation of attainable minimum of $StdDev$ for the particular standard Lenna image. So we suppose that the attained value of the standard deviation $StdDev = 31.603$ is small enough to nearly optimal approximation possesses the features of the optimal approximations. Most likely, the latter merely presents a slightly larger number of objects.

To clarify the features of optimal approximations it is useful to compare the nearly optimal approximation Figure 2 with the approximations, obtained in the Mumford–Shah model by means of segment merging (Figure 4).

Figure 4 shows the examples of approximations of the standard Lenna image with two segments obtained in original versions of the Mumford-Shah model. The appropriate values of the standard deviation $StdDev$ are written under the approximations.

Contrary to the nearly optimal approximation Figure 2 in the approximations obtained by means of segment merging, a number of objects are lost due to missing of connective elements. Moreover in this case the results of the iterative segmentation of an image into several segments depend on the variable intensity of image pixels, the initial partition of the image into indivisible super-pixels, and even from rounding errors. Therefore the reliable minimization of the standard deviation is useful for robust object detection regardless of the segment number. It is noteworthy that, the nearly optimal approximation of the image prompts a very simple model of optimal approximation, which presents the objects in the image as mutually connected regions. At that the connective elements of one pixel wide visibly describe the proximity of objects to each other, which should be calculated adaptively to each individual image in accordance with known Descriptive approach [9].

In this section we have considered the correction of segments in the special case of the image partitioning into two connected segments. In general case to divide the image into different number of segments a procedure of segment correcting is combined with the segment merging as described in the next section of this chapter.

Standard Deviation Analysis

The case of different segment number is described by the graphs of the standard deviation, depending on the number of segments (Figure 5).

50.454

49.170

Figure 4. Approximations of the standard Lenna image with two segments according to different versions of the Mumford–Shah model.

In Figure 5 the dependencies of standard deviation $StdDev$ on the segment number in the range from 1 to 1000 are presented for standard Lenna image.

The bold dot in Figure 5 marks the nearly optimal image approximation with two segments demonstrated above in Figure 2. The horizontal dash-dotted line below the bold dot indicates the lower limit of $StdDev$ for attainable optimal approximation.

A pair of upper gray curves in Figure 5 is obtained for the heuristic segment merging that is resulted in destruction of the image content in the case of several segments.

To discriminate the selection of segmentation algorithms we have derived the simple threshold estimation offering the maximum admitted value of standard deviation $StdDev$ for segment number N or vice versa limiting N for given $StdDev$:

$$N \leq N_0^{1-\frac{StdDev}{StdDev(1)}}, \tag{11}$$

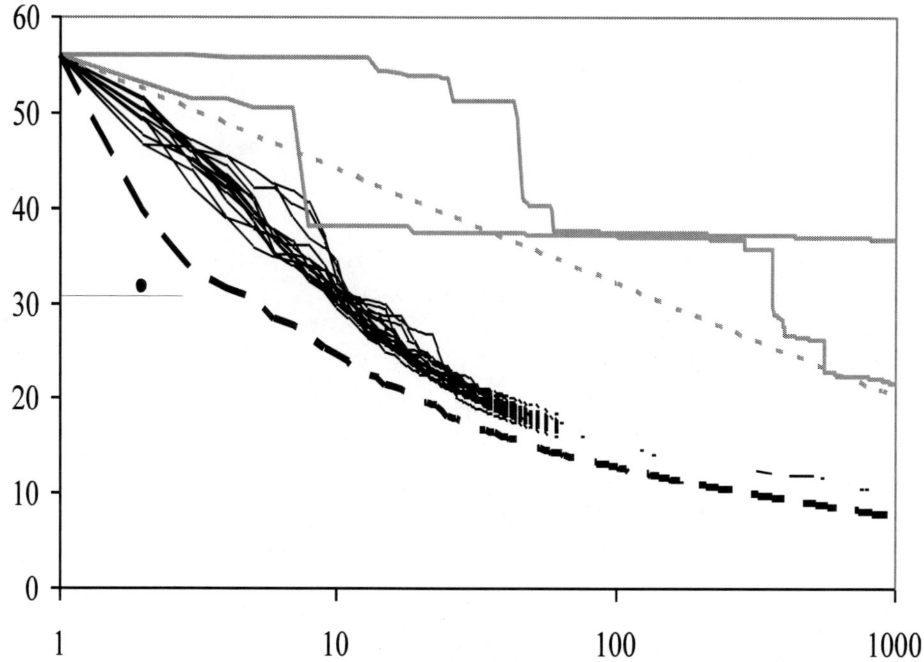

Figure 5. The dependencies of $StdDev$ on segment number.

where N_0 is the number of elementary segments and $StdDev(1)$ is the standard deviation of pixel values from their arithmetic average within the whole image in the case of $N=1$.

In accordance with the proposed estimation (11) the curves in Figure 5 must lie below the downward dotted line and for small values of the segment number at least hyperbolic decrease of standard deviation $StdDev$ with an increase of the segment number is expected.

The twenty black interlaced curves filling some strip, show the dependencies of $StdDev$ on the segment number for different versions of Mumford–Shah model. These weakly decreasing curves describe the hierarchies of nested partitions obtained by iterative merging of adjacent segments according to FLSA version of Mumford-Shah model (3), simplest criterion (5) according to [5] and a number of experimentally chosen another functions of segment features. To generate the appropriate piecewise constant image approximations the variation of initial image partitioning into super-pixels and normalization of intensities to invariant values with respect to certain image transformations [10] were also used.

Dashed curve corresponds to a non–hierarchical sequence of partitions with overlapping of segments from different partitions. This curve describes the piecewise constant image approximations automatically obtained by iterative merging of adjacent segments according to merging criterion (5) in turn with automatic correction of the segments based on (8)-(10). To strengthen the reduction of the standard deviation the Monte–Carlo method is used. In this method, for each segment number dozens of thousands approximations were calculated. Then the selection of soundness segmentation results according to the monotony condition:

$$N_1 \leq N_2 \quad \Rightarrow \quad StdDev(N_1) \geq StdDev(N_2), \tag{12}$$

was performed, where N_1, N_2 are the numbers of segments in partitions.

As for the effect of segment correcting, which is used in addition to their merging, it is not a surprise that the improvement of approximations by the standard deviation is accompanied by improvement of visual perception. In this case the anomalous behavior of the standard deviation with the increasing of segment number usually indicates the disappearance of the objects (Figure6).

99 segments, *StdDev*=16.465

99 segments, *StdDev*=12.674

101 segments, *StdDev*=15.911

Figure 6. The improvement of visual quality of the image approximation.

Figure 6 by example of standard Lenna image demonstrates the approximations consisting of about equal number of segments. The left image is obtained by segment merging. The pair of other images is obtained by alternating of segment merging and correcting. The values of segment number and standard deviation $StdDev$ are written under the approximations.

The above pair approximationst in Figure 6, characterized by a smaller value of standard deviation look more similar to the original than the left approximation, characterized by a larger value of standard deviation. The last approximation in Figure 6 shows, that the loss of those or other objects implies some increase in standard deviation value but may improve the visual quality of some remaining objects.

MERGING TECHNIQUE

Although the correction of the segments along with their merging improves the segmentation results, but at the same time exacerbates the problem of the iterative computation, storage, and transformation of a sequence of image partitions. This problem is typical for hierarchical image partitioning in the Mumford-Shah model and is usually overcome by laborious programming of the algorithmic optimization [6, 7]. The latter results in program complication and hinders further development and generalization of computer realization. It is not excluded that in the tasks of so-called adaptive hierarchical segmentation we have some advantages since our solutions were worked out for old-fashioned computers about twenty years ago [11]. So, on modern computers, we can to study and generalize the Mumford-Shah model in terms of some special data structure [11, 12] avoiding a routine programming. However, it should be noted that the data structure only supports accelerating of the image processing in a limited volume of computer memory, but does not change the obvious sense of segment merging which should be discussed before the implementation details of the algorithms.

Fast Pairwise Segment Merging

The interpretation of merging criterion according (3), (5) and others expressions, as the criterion for global minimization over all pairs of adjacent segments enables to obtain mostly binary hierarchy due to the pair-wise merging of the segments one by one. In this case the resulted hierarchy is constituted of a maximal number of nested segments that strengthens adaptability of approximations to the image content. However, in this case, to obtain a binary hierarchy of segments the same or at least comparable number of iterations, as a number of pixels in the image is needed.

In order to avoid a labor-consuming optimization of multiple processing iterations, we use a synchronous segment merging over the whole image, as in version SLBM (Synchronous locally best merging) of the Mumford-Shah model [6]. Contrary to the classical algorithm of segment merging basing on the global minimum search in our realization of locally best merging [12] the minimization is performed for each segment by analyzing its proximity to neighbors (Figure 7).

As it is shown in Figure 7, for each segment one or several proximal adjacent segments characterized by minimal value of merging criterion are found at first. Then the merging of mutually proximal segments is performed

If the criterion of segment merging is invariant under the replacement of segments on each other as in (3), (5), then an iterative merging of segments finishes only when they all are merged into one segment covering the whole image.

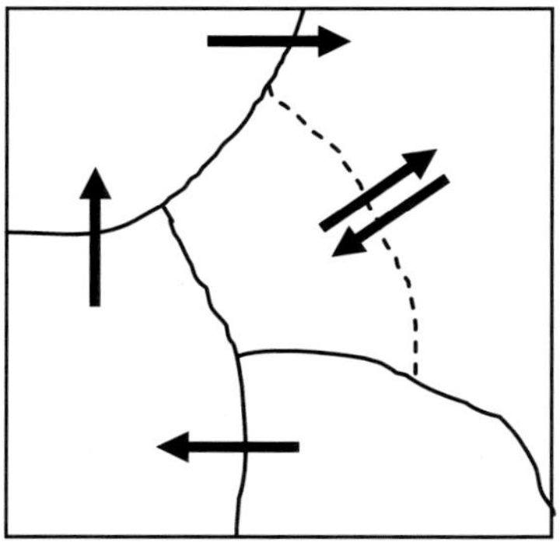

Figure 7. Merging of mutually proximal segments.

The pair-wise merging is supported by requiring of mutual proximity of the segments that can be merged. Owing to synchronous segment merging over the whole image the iteration number and also the processing time are reduced in thousand times, without any efforts to optimize the computations. At that the relevant speed for generation of hierarchical multi-segmentation attains a values from half million till one million pixels per second.

However it should be noted that by means of synchronous segment merging we obtain the raw hierarchy of segments with their casual repetitions in the sequence of image partitions. In this case the quality of approximations may be disturbed as it is rightly noted in [6]. In the frameworks of our Hierarchy-to-Hierarchy transforms, this obstacle turns out surmountable by redistributing of segments with required repetitions in the image partitions.

Hierarchy-to-Hierarchy Transforms

Although the notions related to hierarchical segmentation are quite obvious, but for algorithmic implementation they require some clarification of terminology.

A hierarchical segmentation is treated as a sequence of nested image partitions into segments. In contrast to the hierarchy of segments in the hierarchy of partitions the image segments are treated with their repetitions. Numerated image partition called level is visually presented as piecewise constant approximation consisting of segments filled with intensities averaged within each segment.

A hierarchy of image partitions or approximations is named compact if it doesn't contain repeated composite (divisible) segments on different levels [12]. So in compact hierarchy the repetitions of elementary segments grouping on more detailed levels are only admitted.

Let C be an isotone transform of an arbitrary hierarchy into compact hierarchy, which is carried out without distortion of hierarchical order of the segments and reduced to substitution of repetitive segments in upper hierarchy levels containing smaller number of segments by the segments from nearest lower levels containing more segments.

If several first upper hierarchy levels under consideration contain only divisible segments and each divisible parent segment on each level splits into minimal number of two nested ones then the compact hierarchy of partitions turns binary for considered levels and constituted by the image partitions into $1, 2, 4, ...$ segments.

Let divisible segments are ordered according to positive values of some none-negative parameter $p \geq 0$ and elementary segments are corresponded to minimal value of that parameter. The parameter p is taken to be the sum of squared deviations of intensities from their arithmetic average within the segment, the drop of the standard deviation caused by segment splitting, the segment square or otherwise in a variety of different ways.

Hierarchy of image partitions or approximations is named expanded if its initial partition contains the single segment covering the whole image and each next partition is produced by splitting on current level the segments corresponded to maximal value of considered parameter.

If p for the union of segments 1 and 2 is not less than the value of each, so that p satisfies the monotony condition:

$$p(1 \cup 2) \geq p(1), p(2), \tag{12}$$

then in expanded hierarchy the maximum of p computed for level weakly decreases while segment number increases.

If compact hierarchy appears binary and the values of parameter p are different for different segments, then expanded hierarchy consists of image partitions into sequential number of $1, 2, 3, ...$ segments. In this case it is called a sequential hierarchy of nested partitions.

Let E be the transform of an arbitrary hierarchy into expanded hierarchy which is isotone transform likewise C transform. For certain choice of parameter p the transforms C and E satisfy the same commutative relations:

$$\begin{aligned} C^2 &= C, \quad E^2 = E, \\ CE &= C, \quad EC = E, \end{aligned} \tag{13}$$

i. e. each considered hierarchy transform is idempotent and the result of one transform does not depend on preliminary performing of the other transform.

It's remarkable that commutative properties of C and E transforms of hierarchies of image partitions reproduce the properties of image transformations describing the steganographic message embedding [13]. Thus, between the opposite processes of video data embedding and retrieval an algebraic analogy is established. This analogy is conditioned by the similarity of the ordering algorithms, which are applied to different sets, namely sets of pixels in the steganography, and sets of segmented images in the area of the automatic object detection.

To empower the tools of object approximation with image segments the transform F producing the segment filtration is provided in addition to transforms C and E. The transform F is reduced to selection of some segments from different hierarchy levels and constituting a new hierarchy levels with selected and complementary segments. Implying repetitive execution of segment filtration the transform F may be treated as idempotent:

$$F^2 = F, \tag{14}$$

similarly to C and E transforms.

Unlike C and E transforms which does not modify the initial image partition the transform F generally induces an enlargement of elementary segments of equal pixels adaptively to selected segments.

To illustrate the results of the hierarchical segmentation, we use a sample from the Berkeley Segmentation Dataset and Benchmarks [14] (Figure 8).

Figure 8 shows the original image. Figure 9 demonstrates the results of its different hierarchical partitioning into nested segments.

In Figure 9 the horizontally arranged image approximations show the hierarchical levels. In each series the first level, which contains a single segment, is omitted. The upper series of approximations shows the levels of the parent hierarchy of the partitions. The second, third and the fourth horizontal series show the results of converting of the parent hierarchy by E, C and FC transforms, respectively.

The number of segments for each level is indicated in the columns of the table.

In the table the designation «source» is used to specify the parent hierarchy, and the other hierarchies are designated by the transforms, which were used to obtain them from the parent hierarchy. The first column specifies the consecutive numbers of the levels. The last row shows the total number of levels in the corresponding hierarchy of approximations.

The parent hierarchy of partitions, which is shown as the upper series in Figure 9, contains 55 levels, as indicated in the second column of the table. It is this hierarchy that is described above as a raw hierarchy with casual repetitions of segments in the sequence of image partitions obtained by means of synchronous segment merging under the condition of square error minimizing for the union of segments.

The second series in Figure 9 and the third column of the table describe the expanded hierarchy of partitions obtained from the parent raw hierarchy by means of E transform with the parameter p, which is taken to be the drop of the standard deviation caused by the splitting of the segment. The expanded hierarchy contains 43762 levels. The segment number mostly incrementally increases by one, so that in the table the column of consecutive numbers coincides with the column of segment numbers and only four values are missed in the range of segment numbers from 1 to 1000, i.e. in this case the expanded hierarchy turns out to be almost sequential.

Figure 8. The image sample from Berkeley Segmentation Dataset and Benchmarks.

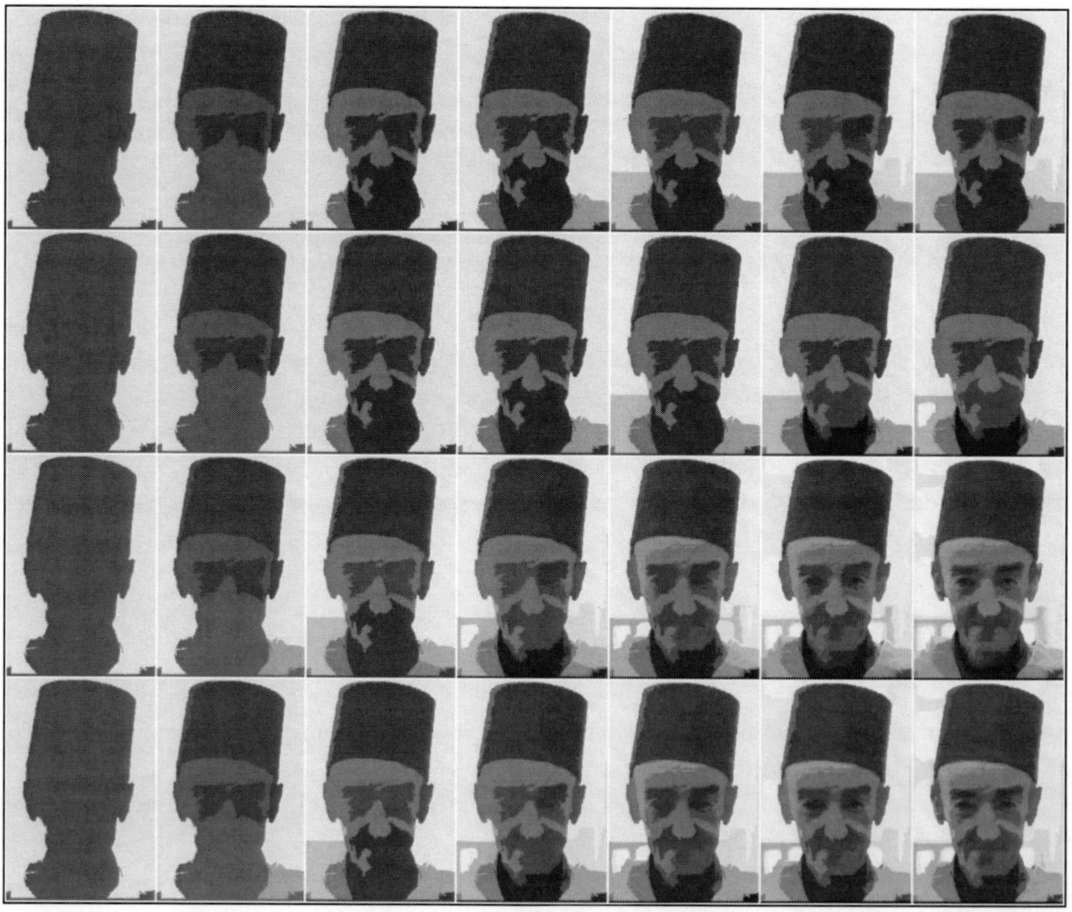

Figure 9. The hierarchical sequences of the image approximations.

Table 1. The numbers of segments

Level number	Source	E	C	FC
1	1	1	1	1
2	2	2	2	2
3	3	3	4	4
4	4	4	8	7
5	5	5	16	12
6	8	6	32	21
7	10	7	64	35
8	12	8	128	63
Total	55	43762	33	32

The compact hierarchy of partitions, which is shown as the third series in Figure 9 and described by the fourth column of the table, contains 33 levels. It is obtained by the transform C of the parent hierarchy and turns out binary up to the level that contains 512 segments.

The lower series of approximations in Figure 9, as well as the rightmost column of the table, show the filtered compact hierarchy of the 32 approximations, which are obtained by FC transform of the parent hierarchy. In this case, the transform F consists in a selection of the segments that are local extrema according to average intensity. In the levels with a sufficiently large consecutive number the approximately twice reducing of the number of segments is provided without noticeable distortion of image content.

In the tasks with special requirements for processing speed it is permissible to use the raw hierarchy of partitions with unordered repetitions of segments in the consecutive levels.

The expanded hierarchy, obtained by E transform, is regarding as a base for optimizing of image approximations according to standard deviation. The other advantage of E transform consists in that it supports the approximation of the image with given number of segments and permits to pre-equalize the images in segment number for subsequent comparison. We experimentally noticed that a comparison turns out more effective if the images to be compared are pre-equalized in segment number. In this case the lower standard deviation value indicates the greater visual similarity. It should be noted that to increase the processing speed the generation of the expanded hierarchy for a specified range of prescribed values of segment number or parameter p is available.

The compact hierarchy, obtained by C transform, distinguishes primarily in that it reveals the mostly binary hierarchy of segments. In image recognition tasks the compact hierarchy of partitions is suitable for analysis of individual features of separate segments skipping their repetitions in different levels.

In nontrivial combinations with C and E the transform F, producing a filtered hierarchy of image approximations, seems needful for effective application of hierarchical segmentation not only for image analysis and comparison but also for detection and recognition of hierarchically structured objects.

Data Structure

The generation, storage, and also conversions of the hierarchy of digital image approximations are supported by our data structure of so-called Dynamic Trees. Although the data structure of Dynamic Trees was developed long ago [11, 12], but it is still interesting for the implementation.

The structure of Dynamic Trees is an alternative to the 4-connected lattice, which is used in the popular segmentation method of Graph Cuts [15]. To laconically describe the segment we use instead of a lattice the formal tree uniting the pixels. In this case, the connectivity of pixels in the segments persists as long as it is not affected by the operations with the segments.

The idea of Dynamic Trees is quite simple and consists in that in terms of our data structure each segment is represented as a tree of pixels, and segment merging is described with merging of trees. At that an initial pixel we regard as an elementary segment associated with an elementary tree, containing a single root node. To merge the trees the root nodes are linked with each other by means of the arc. To restore the trees at some processing stage an appropriate value of some index is assigned to each arc.

In the C programming language the merging of trees is presented as follows:

```
BOOL TreeMerging
(int index, int * Arcs, int * Indices, int a, int b)
{int ii, iii;
  for(ii = Arcs[a]; ii != Arcs[ii]; ii = Arcs[ii]);
  for(iii = Arcs[b]; iii != Arcs[iii]; iii = Arcs[iii]);
  if(ii < iii){Arcs[iii] = ii ; Indices[iii] = index;          ,
                return TRUE ;
             }
  else if(ii > iii){Arcs[ii] = iii ; Indices[ii] = index;
                    return TRUE ;
                 }
 return FALSE ;
}
```

where $TreeMerging$ is the Boolean function for merging of trees, specified by the nodes a and b, which return $FALSE$ if a and b turn out the nodes of the same tree; $index$ is the consecutive number of the processing stage or simply is the clock parameter; $Arcs$ and $Indices$ are the line-wise ordered matrix of arcs and corresponding matrix of indices; ii and iii are the variables, calculated as root nodes for given nodes a and b; $Arcs$ is initiated as $Arcs[i] \equiv i$, while $Indices$ initially is zeroed $Indices[i] \equiv 0$ for each pixel coordinate i.

For the vivid imagination of our tree-structured data, we simply visualized the matrix of arcs and the matrix of indices in Figure 10.

Figure 10 shows two formal matrices that define a hierarchy of image partitions into segments like any one of the partition sequences presented in Figure 9. The matrix of arcs is shown on the left and the matrix of indices is shown on the right. These matrices are stored in a fixed volume of computer memory, regardless of the number of levels constituting a hierarchy of partitions.

Obviously, to convert a given partition into corresponding approximation the image matrix (Figure 8) is needed, besides the matrix of arcs and the matrix of indices (Figure 10). The Hierarchy-to-Hierarchy transforms Figure 9 are also represented in terms of transformations of these three matrices constituting the kernel of the data structure of Dynamic Trees.

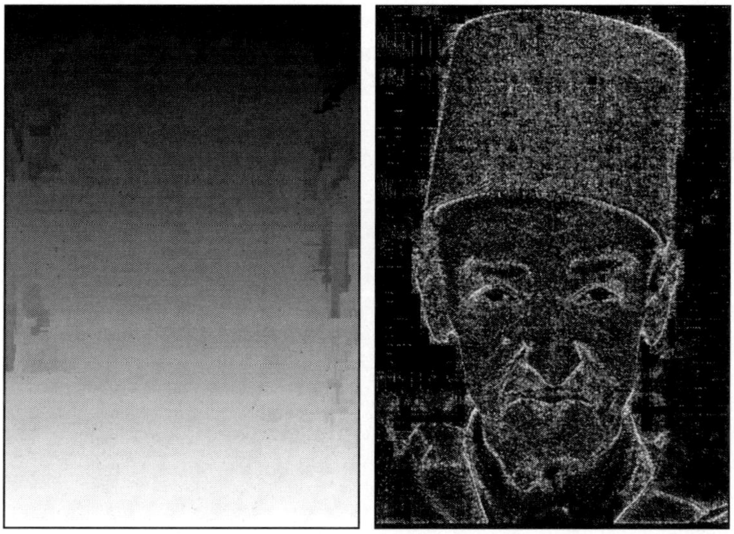

Figure 10. The matrix of arcs and the matrix of indices.

To clarify the advantages of the implementation of our data structure it may be sufficient to note that owing to some complete set of algorithms, exemplified above by merging procedure, the Dynamic Trees provide all of the capabilities of traditional trees, but without related excessive expenses of the computer resources.

CONCLUSION

In the chapter we have tried to validate that at the present level of computer processing of digital images the segmentation problem is more practical than theoretical. The problem statement, consisting in accurate definition of segmented image, is provided, at least, in the Mumford–Shah model that treats the segmented image as an optimal piecewise constant image approximation. The main limitation of the practical implementation of the Mumford-Shah model consists in that traditional methods for generating of piecewise constant approximations are restricted to utilization of iterative segment merging. Since the iterative segment merging is insufficient to obtain strictly optimal approximations, the practical results of Mumford–Shah segmentation do not quite match the desired optimal result. So the practically used piecewise constant approximations essentially depend on the segmentation algorithms and are characterized by the excessive values of standard deviation.

To improve the segmentation, which is assessed by standard deviation, we have generalized the Mumford-Shah model by introducing the correction of segments in addition to their merging. In this way, we have obtained the sample of nearly optimal approximation and suggested a model of a segmented image consisting of mutually connected regions. To prevent from the relapse of computational challenges caused by the implementation of the segment correction in accompany with resource-expensive segment merging, we have outlined the data structure of Dynamic Trees supporting the fast generation and also transformations of the hierarchies of the image partitions.

The principal scientific result presented in this chapter is expressed by the elementary formulae (8)–(10), describing either the criterion of segment correction (8), (9), either surprisingly simple stability condition (10) of the image partition relative to reclassification of pixels. Similarly to the criterion of segment merging (5), the formulae (8)–(10) for segment correction can be implemented in different ways.

Thus, we have proposed a method for segmentation of digital images by means of segment merging accompanied with segment correction according to formulae (5), (8)–(10). By means of the proposed Merge-and-Correct method we succeeded in improvement of image segmentation. However, it is remarkable that the value of $StdDev$ for interactively obtained nearly optimal approximation turns out significantly less than the corresponding value of $StdDev$, obtained by the automatic segmentation according to Merge-and-Correct method (Figure 5). So the opportunities to improve the automatic segmentation and obtain a series of nearly optimal approximations most likely have not yet been exhausted. In our opinion, for the best disclosure of (8)-(10) it may be sufficient to treat the segments in some generalized sense, namely, as interconnected sets, consisting of pixels, not necessarily connected to each other within the individual segment. This hypothesis should be experimentally verified in the nearest future, the more so as our data structure of Dynamic Trees without any modification supports the generalized segments.

ACKNOWLEDGMENTS

This work was supported by the Russian Foundation for Basic Research, grant no. 11–07–00685–a.

REFERENCES

[1] D. Mumford and J. Shah, Boundary detection by minimizing functionals, I. Proc. IEEE Comput. *Vision Patt. Recogn. Conf.*, San Francisco, 1985. pp. 22–26.

[2] D. Mumford and J. Shah, Optimal Approximations by Piecewise Smooth Functions and Associated Variational Problems. *Communications on Pure and Applied Mathematics,* Vol. XLII, No 4, 1989. pp. 577–685.

[3] G. Koepfler, C. Lopez and J.A. Morel, Multiscale Algorithm for Image Segmentation by Variational Method. *SIAM Journal on Numerical Analysis,* Vol. 31, No 1, 1994. pp. 282–299.

[4] N.J. Redding, D.J. Crisp, D.H. Tang and G.N. Newsam, An efficient algorithm for Mumford–Shah segmentation and its application to SAR imagery. *Proc. Conf. Digital Image Computing Techniques and Applications* (DICTA '99), 1999. pp. 35–41.

[5] A.S. Bugaev and A.V. Khelvas, Pilot studies and development of methods and tools for analysis and automatic recognition of media flows in global information systems. *Scientific and Technical Report*, Moscow: Moscow Institute of Physics and Technology (MIPT), Vol. 1, 2001. 140 p. (in Russian).

[6] D.J. Crisp and T.C. Tao, *Fast Region Merging Algorithms for Image Segmentation. The 5th Asian Conf. on Computer Vision* (ACCV2002), Melbourne, Australia, 23–25 January 2002. pp. 1–6.

[7] B.J. Robinson, N.J. Redding and D.J. Crisp, Implementation of a fast algorithm for segmenting SAR imagery. *Scientific and Technical Report,* Australia: Defense Science and Technology Organization, Australia, 01 January 2002. 42 p.

[8] Nobuyuki Otsu, A Threshold Selection Method from Gray-Level Histograms. *IEEE Transactions on systems,* MAN, and CYBERNETICS, Vol. SMC-9, No. 1, January 1979, pp.62-66.

[9] I.B. Gurevich and V.V. Yashina, Descriptive Approach to Image Analysis: Image Models. Pattern Recognition and Image Analysis: Advances in Mathematical *Theory and Applications,* Vol. 18, No.4, 2008, pp. 518–541.

[10] M.V. Kharinov, Invariant Representation of Information and Information Quantity in Image-Processing Tasks. *Pattern Recognition and Image Analysis*, Vol. 18. No 4, 2008, pp. 643-648.

[11] M.V. Kharinov, Data structures of learning system for automatic image recognition. PhD thesis, St. *Petersburg Institute for Informatics and Automation of Russian Academy of Sciences, 1993*, 20 p. (n Russian)

[12] M.V. Kharinov, *Storage and Adaptive Processing of Digital Image Informatio.* Ed. by R.M. Yusupov, St. Petersburg University Press, 2006. 138 p. (in Russian).

[13] M. V. Kharinov, Algebraic Description of Data Embedding Basing on Idempotent Image Transformations. *Pattern Recognition and Image Analysis: Advances in Mathematical Theory and Applications,* Vol. 19, No.3, 2009, pp. 491-496.

[14] D. Martin, C. Fowlkes, D. Tal, and J. Malik, A database of human segmented natural images and its application to evaluating segmentation algorithms and measuring ecological statistics. *Proc. 8th Int. Conf. Computer Vision (ICCV),* Vol. 2, 2001, pp. 416-423,

[15] Y. Boykov and V. Kolmogorov, An Experimental Comparison of Min-Cut/Max-Flow Algorithms for Energy Minimization in Vision. *IEEE Trans. Pattern Anal. Mach. Intell.,* Vol. 26, No.9, Sept. 2004, pp. 1124-1137.

In: Image Processing
Editor: Vítor Hugo Carvalho
ISBN 978-1-62081-844-2

Chapter 11

AUTOMATIC VISUAL SURVEILLANCE OF VEHICLES IN COMPLEX SCENARIOS

José J. González, Jesús B. Alonso, Carlos M. Travieso* and Miguel A. Ferrer

Technological Centre for Innovation in Communications,
Departments of Signals and Communications,
University of Las Palmas de Gran Canaria,
Las Palmas de Gran Canaria, Spain

ABSTRACT

The identification of moving objects with an outdoor surveillance camera is one of the most important applications in the field of computer visual applications. Surveillance cameras are usually inexpensive and easily found but require a team of operators to be constantly monitoring the recordings. Due to the large volume of information, it is almost impossible to review all the videos obtained. The goal of automated visual surveillance would reduce the workload of the operators by providing a computer system that can automatically analyze the videos. In this work, we propose a vehicle detection method for traffic flow from the analysis of videos taken by cameras situated in high places on the road, such as bridges, thus making it possible to estimate important traffic parameters. The analysis of videos is based on image processing where it is proposed a methodology for different aspect like the background subtraction in changing environment, removing shadows of the vehicle and tracking the trajectories of different vehicles throughout the time. The algorithm is able to locate and track vehicles in different settings and weather conditions. As a direct result the following information would be obtained: vehicle count, vehicle speed, vehicles travelling counter flow, stationary vehicles and those performing lane changes.

* E-mail address: ctravieso@dsc.ulpgc.es.

INTRODUCTION

Surveillance cameras are cheap and ubiquitous, but the manpower required to supervise them is expensive. Consequently the video from these cameras is usually monitored sparingly or not at all. The goal of automated visual surveillance is to reduce the burden on operators by including software in a surveillance system that can analyse behaviour automatically.

In computer vision, Background Subtraction [1] is a commonly used method to extract moving objects. Despite it all, moving object detection in complex environments is still far from being completely solved. In the context of this work, background modelling methods can be classified into two categories: Methods that employ local (pixel-wise) models of intensity and Methods that have regional models of intensity. Most background modelling approaches tend to fall into the first category of pixel-wise models.

Probabilistic methods have become a popular choice for robust modelling and removal of complex and changing backgrounds at the pixel level. In the work of Friedman and Russell [2], a Gaussian Mixture Model was used for background modelling. Subsequently, Elgammal, Duraiswami, Harwood and Davis proposed Non Parametrical Model [3], in which probability density function was estimated according to some samples using a kernel function.

Many methods like these, are computationally expensive and are not applicable to real-time applications, or require specialised hardware to operate in the real-time domain. However, methods such as Pfinder [4], W4 [5] and Beymer et al [6] are designed to extract targets in real-time. On the other hand, there exist algorithms that employ region models, or combine local and region models. This type of systems [7] are designed to be unaffected by light conditions. In Wallflower [8], a three-level processing was proposed but the spatial correlations were only used in post-processing.

In this work we propose a motion detection system in grey scale videos based on regional models of intensity [7]. The motion detection approach is improved by evaluating the similarity between little textured patches, since shadow or highlight regions present same textural characteristics in each frame and in the corresponding adaptive background model. The method is computationally low-power and produces good results, so it could be merged in wide integrated vision systems.

VIDEO PROCESSING MODULES

The proposed system follows this data flow, which consists of five major processing blocks:

1. Preprocessing.
2. Motion Detection.
3. Data Validation.
4. Tracking.
5. Understanding Information.

Figure 1. Typical camera placement.

These processing blocks are discussed in detail in the following chapters.

Preprocessing

In most computer vision systems, simple spatial low-pass filter (smoothing) are used in the early stage of processing to reduce camera noise. Smoothing can also be used to remove transient environmental noise such as rain and snow captured in outdoor camera.

On the other hand, for real-time systems, frame-size and frame-rate reduction are commonly used to reduce the data processing rate. In this work we divide preprocessing in two stages:

- Low-pass spatial filtering [9].
- Convert RGB image to grey scale [7].

Images are often corrupted by White Noise (Gaussian Noise). Linear filters, such as the mean filter, are the primary tool for smoothing digital images degraded by additive noise. A mean filter replaces each pixel value with the mean of the pixels in a window of a given size cantered on the selected pixel. This has the effect of eliminating pixel values which are unrepresentative of their surroundings. Mean filtering is usually thought of as a convolution filter. Like other convolutions it is based around a window, which represents the shape and size of the neighborhood to be sampled when calculating the mean. In this work, we propose a 3×3 square windows with coefficients s=1.

On the other hand, we propose the use of grey scale video sequences, because RGB images can be quite large. Converting these video sequences to grayscale, can reduce the size of the file to three times, and improve the characteristic of real time response.

Motion Detection

Motion Detection is a very important task for many computer vision applications. It provides a classification of the pixels into either moving objects, or stationary objects. When the camera is stationary, Background Subtraction [1] is a commonly used method to extract moving objects. The principle of this method is to build a model of the static scene (without moving objects) called background, and then to compare every frame of the sequence to this background in order to discriminate the regions of unusual motion, called foreground (the moving objects). Once these images have been compared, a threshold operation is applied in order to eliminate the regions that do not belong to any objective.

Following equation shows Background Subtraction formula:

$$T(x,y)=\begin{cases}1\Rightarrow \left|I(x,y)-B(x,y)\right|>\delta \\ 0\Rightarrow \left|I(x,y)-B(x,y)\right|<\delta\end{cases} \tag{1}$$

In this equation, I(x, y) is the current frame, B(x, y) is the background image, δ is a threshold and T(x, y) is the binary image. Binary images are images that have been quantised to two values, usually denoted 0 and 1. Typically pixels are either a 1 (foreground) or 0 (background).

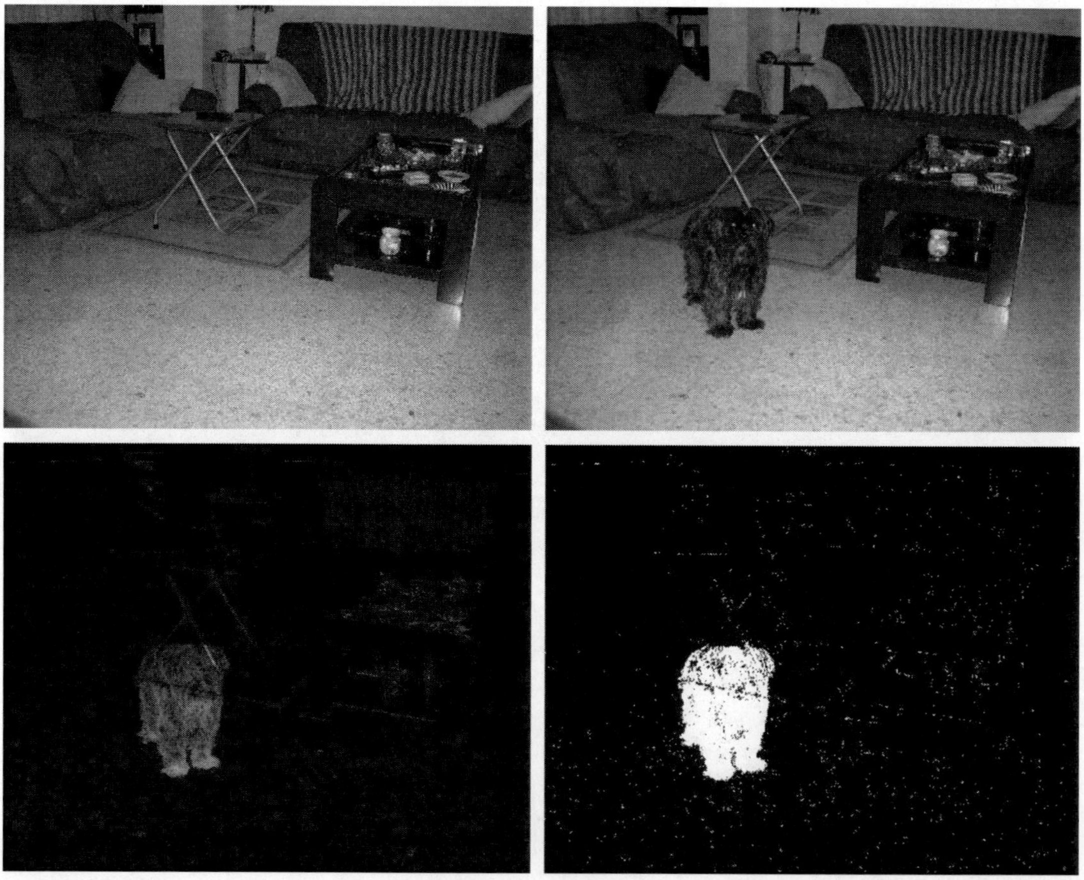

Figure 2. Background Subtraction: Top left: Background model. Top right: Current frame. Bottom left: Difference image. Bottom right: Binary image.

Background Modeling

One of the most desirable qualities of a video surveillance system is the ability to be effective at all times. A robust Background Subtraction method for outdoor scenarios requires the timely updating of a background model to cope with gradual changes in lighting, such as the changes from day to night.

Background modelling techniques are basically classified into two broad categories [10]:

- Non Recursive Techniques.
- Recursive Techniques.

Not Recursive Techniques stores a buffer of the previous K frames, and estimates the background image based on the temporal variation of each pixel within the buffer. The most commonly used non recursive techniques are Frame Differencing [10], Median Filter [11], Linear Predictive Filter [8], Non Parametrical Model [12], etc.

Recursive techniques recursively update a single background model and do not store a buffer of frames. As a result, input frames from distant past could have an effect on the current background model. Compared with non recursive techniques, recursive techniques require less storage. The most popular recursive techniques are Aproximated Median Filter [13], Kalman Filter [4], Mixture of Gaussians [2], Running Average [4], etc.

In this work, a recursive background model is updated using a Running Average, calculated according to:

$$B(x,y)_n = \alpha \cdot B(x,y)_{n-1} + (1-\alpha) \cdot I(x,y)_n \tag{2}$$

where n is the time index, I(x,y) is the current frame, B(x,y) is the background image and α is a user defined learning factor in the range [0,1]. This learning factor, is typically 0.99, with a frame rate of 15 fps.

The rate at which the models adapt is determined by this learning factor. Large values of α make the model adapt slowly, and small values of α cause rapid adaptation. When the background model adapts at a slower rate than the foreground scene, large areas of false detections often occur. If the background model adapts too fast, it will fail to identify the portion of a vehicle that has corrupted the background model.

On the other hand, it is important to initialize a first background model using a training video sequence which may include foreground objects. In such a case, a robust method is required to handle random occurrences of vehicles.

In this chapter, we propose a simple but efficient algorithm for the purpose of background model initialization. The algorithm takes as input a video sequence in which moving vehicles are present, and outputs a statistical background model describing the static parts of the scene. It consists of calculating the temporal mean value [11] of the previous N video frames as follow (N is typically 500 frames):

$$B(x,y) = \frac{1}{N}\sum_{n=1}^{N} I(x,y)_n \tag{3}$$

where n is the time index, I(x,y) is the current frame, B(x,y) is the background image and N is the total number of frames processed.

BACKGROUND SUBTRACTION

Background Subtraction is the process of separating out foreground objects from the background in a sequence of video frames. The principle of this method is to build a model of background, and then to compare every frame of the sequence to this background.

The background model above can handle gradual illumination changes but can easily be confused by rapid ones, due to varying cloud-cover overhead. It is possible though to overcome these problems by using this dynamic background together with normalized cross-correlation [7] to detect moving objects under complicated illumination conditions.

In this section we propose an efficient Background Subtraction algorithm that considers spatial texture information of a pixel, which is invariant to sudden illumination changes. The basic idea behind this spatial likelihood model is to capture texture while keeping a pixel independence assumption [7]. This method is independent of average intensity and hence moving objects can be discriminated from lighting changes.

Following equation shows cross-correlation Background Subtraction formula.

$$C(x,y) = \frac{\left[B(x,y)\cdot I(x,y)\right]\otimes h(x,y)}{\sqrt{\left[I(x,y)^2 \otimes h(x,y)\right]\cdot\left[B(x,y)^2 \otimes h(x,y)\right]}} \tag{4}$$

Where B(x,y) is the background image, I(x,y) is the current frame and h(x,y) is a 3×3 square windows with coefficients s=1. If the difference C of (4) is less than 0.99 (a threshold experimentally selected), then the examined pixel is marked as static.

The proposed algorithm is able to extract only the effective moving foreground objects despite of rapid illumination changes in the scene, because background regions present the same texture both in reference and current image.

However, these algorithms suffer from an aperture problem. Cross-correlation algorithms cannot detect the pixels belonging to untextured foreground regions. As a result, they typically enable to detect the borders of foreground objects but not their interior parts. The following chapter describes a possible solution to this problem.

Data Validation

Data Validation is the process of improving the candidate foreground mask based on information obtained from outside the background model. As a result of the Background Subtraction step, a lot of small false positives and false negatives will occur distributed across the candidate foreground mask.

To solve this problem we have to discard all foreground blobs (a group of connected pixels is commonly called a blob) which have such a small size that the object can never be a vehicle. Using morphological operations on foreground masks, the system is able to eliminate isolated foreground pixels or merges nearby disconnected regions. Finally, is very important to remove all shadows from moving candidate objects in the image, because shadow areas can be wrongly identified as another foreground object.

To summarize, the proposed validation system follow this data flow:

Figure 3. a) Current frames. b) Classical Background Subtraction. c) Cross-correlation Background Subtraction.

- Discard small size blobs (area filtering).
- Morphologic operations.
- **Shadow removing.**
- **ROI** definition.

Candidate foreground masks are often corrupted by small false positives. Only blobs, whose area exceeds a threshold ψ, are taken for further processing. The blobs, whose size falls below threshold, are considered as part of the background. In this work, a recursive threshold is updated as follow:

$$AM_n = \beta \cdot AM_{n-1} + (1-\beta) \cdot AA > 0 \quad (5)$$

$$\psi = 0.2 \cdot AM_n \quad (6)$$

The above equation is only used when there are objects in the current image. Where n is the time index, AM is the temporal mean area of foreground objects, AA is the mean area in the current frame (Total number of foreground pixels in the courrent image / Total number of objects in the courrent image), ψ is a user defined threshold (typically 20 percent of AM), and β is a user defined learning factor in the range [0,1] (typically 0.99, with a frame rate of 15 fps).

The basic idea behind this model is to discard all foreground blobs which are smaller than the adaptive threshold ψ.

Secondly, a morphological filter is performed by passing a structuring element over (we propose a 5×5 square windows). In this work, morphological filter is a very important tool used to:

- Suppressing noise (Opening).
- Merges nearby disconnected regions (Closing).
- Filling holes.

Thirdly, shadows of vehicles should be detected and eliminated by the validation block, because the shadows can cause errors and the unwanted merging of vehicles might occur, as one easily appreciates in Figure 4.

Before applying shadow suppression the previous step consists in detecting moving vehicles with self shadows. The first step starts by applying an image division operation:

$$D(x,y) = \frac{I(x,y)}{B(x,y)} \tag{7}$$

Where B(x,y) is the background image and I(x,y) is the current frame. This operation refers to those parts of frames corresponding to previously detected blobs.

The second step consist of discarding all of pixels of D(x,y) with values less than a threshold. We experimentally found this value ranging from 0 to 0.6:

$$D'(x,y) = \begin{cases} D(x,y) \rightarrow D(x,y) < 0{,}6 \\ 0 \rightarrow D(x,y) \geq 0{,}6 \end{cases} \tag{8}$$

Finally we calculate a range value in order to find uniform regions:

$$D''(x,y) = rangefilt\,(D'(x,y)) \tag{9}$$

This operation performs range filtering of the input image D' where each output pixel contains the range value (maximum value - minimum value) of the 3×3 square windows around the corresponding pixel in the input image D'. The filter is implemented as a convolution with a 3×3 square window. We then perform a thresholding operation (10), that yields the ultimate binary image G, regarding with this first stage. We experimentally found this value ranging from 0 to 0.1:

$$G(x,y) = \begin{cases} 1 \rightarrow D''(x,y) < 0.1 \\ 0 \rightarrow D''(x,y) \geq 0.1 \end{cases} \tag{10}$$

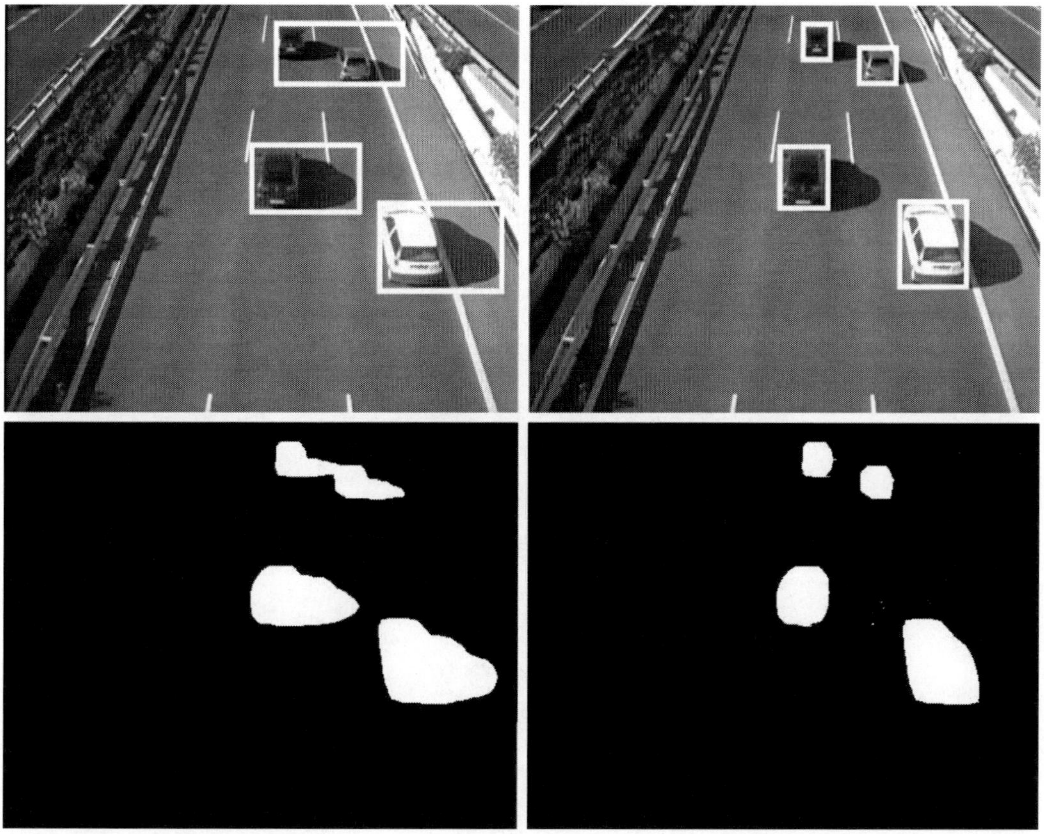

Figure 4. Shadow Detection: Top left: Vehicle detection without shadow detection. Top right: Vehicle detection with shadow detection. Bottom left: Background Subtraction without shadow detection. Bottom right: Background Subtraction with shadow detection.

Finally, the user must select a portion of the image to explore this part in detail (Figure 5). The user can draw or define a region of interest (ROI) by hand. This ROI represents the area of the road that is used in the movement for the entire sequence, and all blobs outside the ROI, like pedestrians or trees, are ignored.

Tracking

Foreground tracking is the critical task in many computer vision applications. The Tracking Module solves the evolution of the foreground blob from frame I(t-1) to frame I(t). The basic idea behind this model is to label each blob. Resulting blobs are 8-connected, and are classified according to the following two characteristic features:

- Bounding box.
- Centroid of foreground blob.

Finally, we use a tracking algorithm to connect the points into trajectories. A trajectory is geometrically a polyline represented by a collection of points called centroids that represent the centre of the foreground. The Kalman filter algorithm is the most popular tool for tracking objects in video sequences [14]. Kalman filter is able to predict the relative position of the foreground object in the next frame. Afterward, the algorithm uses the real position (measurement) to carry out the state correction.

Figure 5. Top left: Current frame. Top right: Foreground mask. Bottom left: Region of interest. Bottom right: Blobs created outside of the ROI are ignored.

Many methods like these are computationally expensive and are not applicable to real-time applications. In this work we propose a simple and fast algorithm for tracking objects in real-time applications. This algorithm calculates the distance between two centroids in the trajectory and connects all those adjacent centroids if the distance between those centroids falls below a user-defined area.

Finally, if the number of centroids in a trajectory is less than 10, it is rejected. It allows detecting only real movements, discarding false alarms due to strange or unexpected movements of the blobs like noise.

Understanding Information

In this work, Understanding Information is a very important step used to:

Figure 6. Top: Vehicle recognition. Down: Trajectory reconstruction.

- Road lane segmentation.
- *Trajectory* analysis.

Road lanes are easily detected on a grey scale background model by a top-hat transform. This filtering computes the morphological opening of the image and then subtracts the result from the original image. Top-hat is based around a window, which represents the shape and size of the neighbourhood. In this work, we propose a 10×10 square windows with coefficients s=1. Afterwards, we need to choose a threshold and convert the grey scale image into binary image. In this case, it is not difficult to choose a threshold value by selecting the valley between the two peaks of the histogram. This is essentially because in this case, the image histogram will be strongly bimodal. Finally, the road lanes are described using low order polynomial models. User must select the order of the polynomial from 0 (a straight line) to a limit of order 5.

In the other hand, trajectories analysis, provide rich spatiotemporal information about an object's motion. For example, it is possible to extract the following information.

- Vehicle count.
- Speed of vehicles.
- Wrong way vehicles detection.
- Stopped vehicles detection.
- Lane change detection.

Vehicle count: A virtual line is defined perpendicular to the road. Every time a trajectory crossing the line a counter is increased.

Speed of vehicles: Two parallel virtual lines are defined perpendicular to the road. The time using for a trajectory crossing the first line and the second line is used to calculate the speed of the vehicle. The distance between these two lines must be known to determine the real speed.

Wrong way vehicles detection: The relative position of the first and last centroids of a trajectory can provide information about motion direction.

Stopped vehicles detection: When the first and last centroids of a trajectory are very close an alarm is generated.

Lane change detection: Every time a trajectory crossing the road lane an alarm is generated.

CONCLUSION

In this work, we propose a vehicle detection method for traffic flow images from grey scale video sequence. Many computer vision systems depend on Background Subtraction in order to identify moving objects. The proposed algorithm is robust to intensity changes in the scene. A present background image is updated using a Running Average method. Then, the foreground region is extracted by Background Subtraction. Using texture information gives more accurate detection than classical Background Subtraction.

In this chapter, we evaluate a number of popular Background Subtraction algorithms. It is expected that this work results in a list of recommendations that can be used to improve these computer vision applications.

REFERENCES

[1] M. Piccardi, Background Subtraction techniques: a review. 2004 *IEEE International Conference on Systems, Man and Cybernetics,* vol. 4, pp. 3099-3104, Oct. 2004.

[2] C. Stauffer and W.E.L. Grimson, Adaptive background mixture models for real-time tracking. In *IEEE International Conference on Computer Vision and Pattern Recognition*, pp. 246-252, Jun. 1999.

[3] A. Elgammal, R. Duraiswami, D. Harwood, and L. S. Savis, Background and Foreground Modeling Using Nonparametric Kernel Density Estimation for Visual Surveillance. In *Proceedings of the IEEE,* Vol.90, No.7, pp.1151-1163, July 2002.

[4] C. Wren, A. Azarbayejani, T. Darrell, and A. entland, Pfinder: Real-Time Tracking of the Human Body. *IEEE Trans. On Pattern Analysis and Machine Intelligence,* vol. 19, no. 7, pp. 780-785, July 1997.

[5] I. Haritaoglu, D. Harwood and L.S. Davis, W4: real-time surveillance of people and their activities. *IEEE Transactions on Pattern Analysis and Machine Intelligence* 22, pp. 809{830, Aug 2000.

[6] B. Coifman, D. Beymer, P. McLauchlan and J. Malik. A realtime computer vision system for vehicle tracking and traffic surveillance. *Trasportation Research: Part C,* vol. 6, no. 4, pp. 271-288, 1998.

[7] P. Spagnolo, M. Leo, T and D'Orazio, A. Distante Robust moving object segmentation by Background Subtraction. *International Workshop on Image Analysis for Multimedia Interactive Services WIAMIS,* pp. 21-23, April 2004.

[8] K. Toyama, J. Krumm, B. Brumitt, and B. Meyers, Wallflower: Principles and practice of background maintenance. in *Proc. IEEE Int. Conf. Computer Vision,* pp. 255–261, 1999.

[9] S. Elhabian, K. El-Sayed and S. Ahmed, Moving Object Detection in Spatial Domain using Background Removal Techniques - State-of-Art. *Recent Patents on Computer Science,* vol. 1, no. 1, pp. 32-54, Jan 2008.

[10] S. Cheung and C. Kamath, Robust Techniques for Background Subtraction in Urban Traffic Video. *Video Communications and Image Processing,* Volume 5308, pp. 881–892, SPIE Electronic Imaging, San Jose, 2004.

[11] R. Cucchiara, M. Piccardi, and A. Prati, Detecting moving objects, ghosts, and shadows in video streams. *IEEE Transactions on Pattern Analysis and Machine Intelligence* 25, pp. 1337-1342, Oct 2003.

[12] A. Elgammal, D. Harwood, and L. Davis, Non-parametric model for Background Subtraction. in *Proceedings of IEEE ICCV'99 Frame-rate workshop,* Sept 1999.

[13] P. Remagnino, An integrated track and pedestrian model-based vision system. in *Proceedings of the Eighth British Machine Vision Conference,* pp. 380-389, 1997.

[14] D. Koller, J. Weber, T. Huang, and al., Towards robust automatic traffic scene analysis in real-time. in Proc. *IEEE International Conference on Computer Vision and Image Processing* (CVPR '94), pp. 126-131, October 1994.

INDEX

D

E

F

G

H

T

U

V

W

Y